Artificial Intelligence in Business and Society

Artificial Intelligence in Business and Society: Global Insights

EDITED BY

RAMESH CHANDRA DAS

Vidyasagar University, India

emerald PUBLISHING

United Kingdom – North America – Japan – India – Malaysia – China

Emerald Publishing Limited
Emerald Publishing, Floor 5, Northspring, 21-23 Wellington Street, Leeds LS1 4DL.

First edition 2026

British Library Cataloguing in Publication Data
A catalogue record for this book is available from the British Library

ISBN: 978-1-83708-023-6 (Print)
ISBN: 978-1-83708-022-9 (Online)
ISBN: 978-1-83708-024-3 (Epub)

Printed and bound by CPI Group (UK) Ltd, Croydon, CR0 4YY

INVESTOR IN PEOPLE

The book is for my parents
Late Bhabani Das and Sri Rajendranath Das

Contents

List of Abbreviations

Chapter 1

AI:	Artificial intelligence
GMM:	Generalized method of moments
GDP:	Gross domestic product
R&D:	Research and development

Chapter 2

AI:	Artificial intelligence
BCC Model:	Banker, Charnes, and Cooper Model
CCR Model:	Charnes, Cooper, and Rhodes Model
DEA:	Data envelopment analysis
DMU:	Decision-making unit
OTE:	Overall technical efficiency
PMJDY:	Pradhan Mantri Jan Dhan Yojana
PSB:	Public sector bank
PTE:	Pure technical efficiency
RBI:	Reserve Bank of India
RPA:	Robotic process automation
RTS:	Returns to scale
SE:	Scale efficiency
SME:	Small- and medium-sized enterprises

Chapter 3

ADB:	Asian Development Bank
AI:	Artificial intelligence
GDP:	Gross domestic product
GAI:	Global Artificial Intelligence Index
HDI:	Human Development Index
HLAI:	Human-like artificial intelligence
IMF:	International Monetary Fund
IT:	Information technology
IFS:	International financial statistics
OLS:	Ordinary least squares
TOT:	Terms of trade
UK:	United Kingdom

UNDP: United Nations Development Programme
US: United States

Chapter 4
AI: Artificial intelligence
GDP: Gross domestic product
ICT: Information and communication technology
IFR: International federation of robotics
ILO: International Labour Organization
IoT: Internet of things
IR3: Industrial revolution 3
IR4: Industrial revolution 4
ML: Machine learning
NEET: Not in education, employment, or training
NEP: National education policies
NEMP: National employment policies
OECD: Organisation for Economic Co-operation and Development
PLI: Production linked incentive
TVET: Technical and vocational education and training

Chapter 5
AI: Artificial intelligence
DEMATEL: Decision-making trial and evaluation laboratory
LVDC: Low voltage direct current

Chapter 6
AI: Artificial intelligence
EPO: European Patent Office
GDP: Gross domestic product
OECD: Organisation for Economic Co-operation and Development
R&D: Research and development

Chapter 7
AI: Artificial intelligence
GDP: Gross domestic product
GPT: Generative pre-training transformer
IoT: Internet of things
NLP: Natural language process
OECD: Organisation for Economic Co-operation and Development
UNESCO: United Nations Educational, Scientific and Cultural Organization

Chapter 8
AI: Artificial intelligence
CV: Contingent valuation
GDP: Gross domestic product
VIF: Variance inflationary factor

Chapter 9

AEs:	Advanced economies
AIOE:	Artificial intelligence occupational exposure
AIRI:	Artificial Intelligence Readiness Index
AISI:	AI Susceptible Index
C-AIOE:	Complementarity-adjusted artificial intelligence occupational exposure
EMDEs:	Emerging market and developing economy
ICT:	Information and communication technology
OECD:	Organisation for Economic Co-operation and Development
PCA:	Principal component analysis
PIAAC:	Programme for the international assessment of adult competencies
SML:	Suitability for machine learning
STEP:	Systematic tracking of exchanges in procurement

Chapter 10

AI:	Artificial intelligence
A&H:	The arts and the humanities
BCE:	Before the common era
CorX:	ChoReographiceXpert system
ELT:	English language teaching
ML:	Machine learning
NLP:	Natural language processing

Chapter 11

AI:	Artificial intelligence
ANN:	Artificial neural networks
ANOVA:	Analysis of variance
CAGR:	Compound annual growth rate
CRD:	Chronic respiratory disease
CVD:	Cardiovascular disease
GDP:	Gross domestic product
HER:	Electronic health record
IBM:	International business machines
MANOVA:	Multivariate analysis of variance
MRI:	Magnetic resonance imaging
NHS:	National Health Service
OECD:	Organisation for Economic Co-operation and Development
R&D:	Research and development
ROI:	Return on investment
SD:	Standard deviation
SIP:	Strategic innovation promotion program
UPS:	United parcel service
VC:	Venture capital

Chapter 12

4IR:	Fourth industrial revolution
AI:	Artificial intelligence
AIpi:	Private investment in artificial intelligence
BCSLM:	Bias-corrected-scaled Lagrange multiplier
BPLM:	Breusch–Pegan Lagrange multiplier
BRICS:	Brazil, Russia, India, China, and South Africa
CD:	Cross-sectional dependence
DOLS:	Dynamic ordinary least squares
ECM:	Error correction model
ECT:	Error correction term
ED:	Economic development
FMOLS:	Fully modified ordinary least squares
GBD:	Global burden of disease
GDP:	Gross domestic product
HEc:	Current Health Expenditure
HIV:	Human immune deficiency virus
IoT:	Internet of things
PCD:	Pesaran cross-sectional dependence
PMG/ARDL:	Pooled mean group auto-regressive distributed lag
PSLM:	Pesaran-scaled Lagrange multiplier
RSNA:	Radiological Society of North America
VAag:	Agriculture value-added
VAi:	Industry value-added
WHO:	World Health Organization

Chapter 13

AI:	Artificial intelligence
BNP:	Bangladesh Nationalist Party
PTI:	Pakistan Tehreek-e-Insaf

Chapter 14

AI:	Artificial intelligence
ICCPR:	International Covenant on Civil and Political Rights
ICESCR:	International Covenant on Economic, Social and Cultural Rights
OHCHR:	Office of the United Nations High Commissioner for Human Rights
UDHR:	Universal Declaration of Human Rights
UN:	United Nations
UNESCO:	United Nations Educational, Scientific and Cultural Organization
UNHCR:	United Nations High Commissioner for Refugees
UNO:	United Nations Organization
USSR:	Union of Soviet Socialist Republics
WHO:	World Health Organization

Chapter 15

AI: Artificial intelligence
GPS: Global positioning system
ISTAT: International Society of Transport Aircraft Trading
TFL: Transport for London

Chapter 16

AI: Artificial intelligence
ASD: Autism spectrum disorder
Fin-Tech: Financial technology
GANs: Generative adversarial networks
GDP: Gross domestic product
IoP: Internet of people
IoT: Internet of things
PEAT: Progressive and environmental and agricultural technologies
QSAR/QSPR: Quantitative structure activity and property

About the Editor

Ramesh Chandra Das, PhD, is presently Professor and Head of the Department of Economics, Vidyasagar University, India, with more than 25 years of teaching and research experience. He has published more than 100 articles in reputed journals and edited books, and more than 20 books to his credit. His research interests lie in applied macroeconomics, public economics and environmental economics.

About the Contributors

Martina De Anna earned a master's degree in Management from the University of Genoa and is currently pursuing a PhD in Economics and Quantitative Methods at the same institution. Her main research interests include transport economics and environmental economics, with a focus on the economic dynamics of sustainable mobility and the environmental impact of transport infrastructure.

Kaushiki Banerjee is presently working as Assistant Professor of Economics at Barasat Government College, and Research Scholar, Department of Economics, Jadavpur University, India. She was a UGC-NET Junior Research Fellow. Her research interests include gender, health, environment, and econometrics. She has made paper-presentation in national/international-conferences, and publications in journals/edited-volumes.

Omar Alejandro Guirette Barbosa, PhD, is an Industrial Engineer and a Research Professor in the Biotechnology Engineering Programme at the Polytechnic University of Zacatecas. He earned his PhD in Administration from the Autonomous University of Zacatecas in 2020. His areas of interest and research include management, industrial engineering, quality management systems, food safety systems, statistics, experimental design, multivariate analysis, accreditations, and certifications.

Joydev Barman teaches Indian Political Thoughts at the Political Science Department at Khejuri College (Baratala, Khejuri, Purba Medinipur). He has research experience in the fields of Indigenous studies, identity politics and social movements. Presently, he is pursuing his PhD degree in the Political Science Department of Vidyasagar University. He has already written chapters in various research books like *Women in Indian Politics* (2021) and *Human Rights: Theory and Practice* (2022) with articles in various research journals.

Rajib Bhattacharyya, PhD, is an Associate Professor in the Department of Economics, Goenka College of Commerce and Business Administration, Kolkata, India. His fields of interests are international trade, finance, Indian economic development, and women empowerment. He has edited, published, and also contributed as reviewer in many articles in reputed national and international journals/books.

Selene Castañeda Burciaga, PhD, has a bachelor's degree in Accounting, a bachelor's degree in Psychology, Industrial Management Engineering, a master's and doctorate in Education and a doctorate in Strategic Business Administration. He has worked in the education sector in the administrative and financial areas, in addition to teaching and research activities. He is a member of the Mexican National System of Researchers. His main areas of research are within the educational and administrative fields.

Suman Chakraborty, PhD, is working as an Assistant Professor and Head of the Department at the Department of Economics of Raja N. L. Khan Women's College (Autonomous), India. His research and teaching experience is more than 17 years. His main area of interest of research is the study of socio-economic issues and also the issues of financial economics. He has published more than 16 papers in different reputed journal and book chapters. His thesis is associated with the own resource mobilization (tax as well as non-tax revenue) of panchayats of West Bengal vis-à-vis other states in India.

Nilendu Chatterjee, PhD, is an Assistant Professor in the Department of Economics, Bankim Sardar College, West Bengal, India. He has research interest in resource economics, general equilibrium, and development economics. He has published a number of research articles in several international journals of economics.

Tonmoy Chatterjee, PhD, is an Assistant Professor in the Department of Economics, Bhairab Ganguly College, West Bengal, India. He has research interest in international trade theory, general equilibrium, health economics, and development economics. He has published a number of research articles in several international journals of economics.

Kenneth Chilton, PhD, is Professor of Public Administration and Policy at Tennessee State University in Nashville, TN, USA. His research focusses on corporate single-family rental investors. Primarily, he analyses ownership trends of single-family rental properties by Real Estate Investment Trusts and Private Equity investors. At present, he is analysing the relationship between single-family investors and neighbourhood-level racial transition.

Saber Ahmed Chowdhury, PhD, serves as the Associate Professor and Chairman of the Department of Peace and Conflict Studies at the University of Dhaka, Bangladesh. He earned his MPhil from the University of Bergen and his PhD from La Trobe University. His research interests include human rights, elections, peace and conflict studies, refugee issues, and democracy.

Hasan Dinçer, PhD, is Professor of Finance at Istanbul Medipol University, Istanbul, Turkey. He has more than 100 scientific articles, and some of them are indexed in Social Science Citation Index (SSCI). He is also editor of many different books published by Springer and IGI Global.

Serkan Eti works as an Associate Professor in IMU Vocational School at Istanbul Medipol University. Serkan, who graduated from Yıldız Technical University (YTU) with a bachelor's degree in Mathematics, completed his doctorate in Quantitative Methods. He received his Associate Professor in Quantitative Decision Methods in 2023, continues his studies on fuzzy logic, artificial intelligence, and statistics.

Yaşar Gökalp is a PhD in the Department of Health Management, Faculty of Health Sciences, Istanbul Medipol University. He holds a bachelor's degree in Health Management from Sivas Cumhuriyet University. He also earned his master's and doctoral degrees in Health Management. He continues his studies in the fields of health economics, health management, health policies, and energy economics.

Enrico Ivaldi, PhD, is Associate Professor of Demography and Social Statistics at the Free University of Languages and Communication IULM in Milan, Italy. He holds a PhD in Applied Economics and Quantitative Methodologies from the University of Genoa. He is a member of the Editorial Board of *Social Indicators Research* (Class A, SECS-S/05 sector), *Quality and Quantity* (Class A, SECS-S/05 sector), *Scientific Reports* (Class A, Area 13), *International Journal of Transport Economics*, *Revista de Estudios Andaluces*, *PLOS One*, *Sustainability*, the Scientific Committee of the National Nautical Observatory, the *Centro de Investigaciones en Econometría* at the University of Buenos Aires, Argentina, and the Pontifical International Marian Academy in Vatican City.

Eyasin Khan, PhD, is presently working as Associate Professor in the Department of Political Science at Vidyasagar University, India. Previously, he served as Assistant Professor at Bankura Christian College, India. He stood first class first at the UG and PG levels for which he was awarded gold medals. He has 18 books to his credit. He has also participated and presented papers in more than 70 international-, national-, and state-level seminars and conferences and published about 64 research articles in various national and international journals and edited books, besides editing a journal, *Nabyasrote*.

Napoleon Kurantin, PhD, is the Dean and a Senior Research Fellow at Ghana Armed Forces Command and Staff College – A Constitute College of the National Defence University. His teaching and research interest include research and practice methodology (advanced quantitative methods and data analytics); regional science and economic development theories; political economy and international trade; defence, military science, and economics of war; natural resource management; artificial intelligence, GIScience, and spatial econometrics.

Sagnik Maity is a Doctoral Research Scholar (UGC-JRF) in the Department of Commerce of University of Calcutta. His research mainly revolves around the area of finance. He holds a keen interest in financial inclusion and financial technology. He has presented research papers in several national and international conferences and published articles and papers in various reputed journals.

Amit Majumder, PhD, is presently working as Associate Professor of Commerce and PG Coordinator of Bijoy Krishna Girls' College, India. He is also a Visiting Faculty, Department of Commerce, University of Calcutta. He has authored 3 books from international publishers and contributed in 60 edited volumes, 50 nationally and internationally acclaimed peer-reviewed and referred journals. His areas of interests are strategic management, corporate governance, etc.

Prasenjit Makur is an Assistant Professor of Commerce at Calcutta Girls' College, Kolkata, West Bengal. He obtained his graduation and master's degrees from The University of Burdwan, India. He has more than seven years of teaching experience in the fields of accounting, finance, taxation, and economics and more than six years of research experience, with numerous publications in peer-reviewed national journals and books.

Enrico Musso is a Full Professor of Transport Economics at the Department of Economics of the University of Genoa, Italy, and Director of the Italian Centre of Excellence on Logistics, Transport, and Infrastructure). He is the Editor-in-Chief of the *International Journal of Transport Economics* and co-chair of the *Maritime Transport and Ports* group of the *World Conference on Transport Research Society*. He has led master's and PhD programmes and has been a visiting professor at several Italian and foreign universities. A former Senator of the Italian Republic, he is currently the President of Genoa Airport.

Riddhima Panda completed MSc in Economics from Calcutta University. She is working as an Assistant Professor at the Department of Economics, The Heritage College, Kolkata, West Bengal, India. Her research and teaching experience is more than four years. Her main area of interest of research is the study of socio-economic issues and also the issues of financial economics. She has published more than five papers in different reputed journals and book chapters.

Md. Zarif Rahman is a youth researcher specializing in peace and conflict studies, governance, education, and conflict mapping. He holds a BSS and MSS from the University of Dhaka and currently serves as a Research Associate at IID. Additionally, he is a member of the Bangladesh Police Reform Commission. Beyond his research work, he actively leads youth initiatives and contributes op-eds on contemporary issues.

Debdas Roy, PhD, is Associate Professor in the Department of English, Vidyasagar University, India. His areas of interest include gender and sexuality studies, Indigenous cultural studies, literature of the early modern period in England, and Indian English writings. He has some national and international publications to his credit which includes papers in journals of repute, articles in edited volumes, and edited books. Currently, he is the Director of an Indian Council of Social Science Research Minor Research Project (2023–2024).

Satyesh Chandra Roy, PhD, was Professor and Head, Department of Botany, University of Calcutta, India. Dr Roy was UGC Emeritus Professor in the University of Calcutta. He had more than 100 publications, published in both international and national journals. Twelve students got their PhD in various disciplines of Botany. He established the Protoplast Culture Laboratory in Calcutta. He worked on micropropagation of medicinal plants and the analysis and production of secondary metabolites through somaclonal variation in tissue culture.

Shubhamita Sarkar has passed MSc in Economics from the Vidyasagar University in 2024. She has earned a diploma in Data Science from the Department of Computer Science of the same university and possessed skills on handling complex data in the subjects like Economics and Business Studies. She has research interests on artificial intelligence, technological innovations, and environmental economics.

Vaishali Singh, PhD, is presently Assistant Professor of Public Policy at XIM University, Bhubaneswar, India. An alumna of the prestigious Peking University, China, where she earned a master's in Public Policy, she also holds a PhD from the University of Delhi. Her research focusses on comparative public policy and management, with a particular emphasis on inclusive development.

Ghirmai Tesfamariam Teame, PhD, is a distinguished scholar in the Department of Economics and Finance at the College of Business and Social Sciences, Adi-Keih, Eritrea. His research interests encompass environmental and natural resource economics, agricultural economics and rural development, and econometrics. He has a number of publications in internationally reputed journals.

Ashish Thakur is working as a Research Associate at VV Giri National Labour Institute (under Ministry of Labour and Employment, Government of India). Specializing in public policy and labour economics, he possesses expertise in statistical analysis and econometric modelling. With over four years of professional experience in the labour market domain, his areas of proficiency involve migration, employment and skills, demographics and the gig and platform economy. He has made significant contributions to five national and international projects, including International Labour Organization, BRICS Research Network, National Human Rights Commission, and Indian Council of Social Science Research.

Omar C. Vargas-Gonzàlez, PhD, is Professor, Research Assistant, and former Head of Computer Systems Department at Tecnológico Nacional de México Campus Ciudad Guzmán, Professor at Telematic Engineering at Centro Universitario del Sur Universidad de Guadalajara with a master's degree in Computer Systems. He has been trained in Innovation and Multidisciplinary Entrepreneurship at Arizona State University (2018) and a Generation of Ecosystems of Innovation, Entrepreneurship and Sustainability for Jalisco course by Harvard

University T.H. Chan School of Health. At present, he conducts research on diverse fields such as entrepreneurship, economy, statistics, mathematics and information and computer sciences.

José G. Vargas-Hernández, PhD, is presently a Research Professor, Instituto Tecnológico Mario Molina Pasquel y Henríquez, Unidad Académica Zapopan, Zapopan, México. He has a long career in Administrative and Management Sciences having more than 200 articles published in different journals and books and reports.

Serhat Yüksel, PhD, is an Associate Professor of Finance at Istanbul Medipol University, Istanbul, Turkey. He has more than 80 scientific articles, and some of them are indexed in Social Science Citation Index (SSCI). He is also editor of many different books published by Springer, Emerald, and IGI Global.

Foreword

New technologies have always been disruptive. Entire industries rise and fall with major technological advancements. The rise of the combustion engine, for example, led to the demise of the horse and buggy industry. Technological advancements create new winners and losers. Many classic industrial cities whose fortunes rose with manufacturing have either suffered major decline or transitioned to a post-industrial economy. The spatial, economic, political, and social implications of each historical epoch are immense. We live in an era of massive technological change that provokes fears of dystopia or blessings of a utopia. Some of those perceptions are coloured by science fiction films like Stanley Kubrick's *2001: A Space Odyssey*. The fear of the unknown and change drives perspectives about artificial intelligence (AI). This book fills a valuable niche by providing a wide range of perspectives on how AI is affecting global business and the implications for the broader society.

Too often, coverage of any new technology of advancement is dominated by a focus on Western economies. How will this affect Wall Street? Will new cures for cancer improve health disparities in the United States? While such topics have value, this book adds insights to our knowledge of how AI is impacting developing countries. Scholarship sometimes fails to capture the perspectives of change on rapidly growing countries. How is AI currently affecting the provision of education, healthcare, elections, human rights, economic development and labour, to name a few? As referenced above, technology creates new winners and losers. The potential of AI to improve living conditions, economic growth, life spans and quality of life in developing countries is both understudied and less known than in Western countries.

The pace of change associated with AI is staggering. A recent post on a World Bank blog pointed out:

> It took 75 years for fixed telephones to reach 100 million users globally. In contrast, mobile phones achieved this milestone in just 16 years, and the internet took only 7 years. The Apple store

> took 2 years and strikingly, ChatGPT reached this number in a mere two months. (Fan & Qiang, 2024)[1]

This is a radical change. The flow of information, ideas and knowledge creates opportunities for entrepreneurs seeking to improve the quality of life in more economically efficient ways. Several authors in this book highlight how AI is being used and the changes it imposes on society. The transformative power of this technology could catalyse tremendous growth and future prosperity.

Yet not all of the changes associated with AI are necessarily positive. The positive changes, while exciting, cannot mask potential downsides of rapid technological change. Section II of this book explores the social implications of AI growth – and there are many. The complexity of technological know-how threatens to galvanize societies into the technological 'haves' and 'have nots'. The productivity increases associated with AI could render today's highly skilled computer programmer obsolete – decimating a rising upper-middle class. Such disruptions would impact the stability and legitimacy of fragile nation-states.

We are on the cusp of undeniable change. How that plays out in developing countries remains unknown. However, *Artificial Intelligence in Business and Society: Global Insights* is a critical step to understanding and measuring those unknowns. My hope is that the readers will get immense scope of using the studies in their own areas of research and teaching, and the scholars contributing to this book will continue to empirically analyse how AI is impacting developing countries and continue to inform policymakers across the globe.

Kenneth Chilton, PhD
Professor
Department of Public Administration & Policy
Tennessee State University, USA

[1]Fan, Q., & Qiang, C. Z. (2024, June 3). *Tipping the scales: AI's dual impact on developing nations* [World Bank Blogs]. Digital Transformation. Retrieved February 21, 2025, from https://blogs.worldbank.org/en/digital-development/tipping-the-scales--ai-s-dual-impact-on-developing-nations

Preface

The world economy has been progressing towards a complete operational phase of technological tools in the last two to three decades. The growth of physical capital-induced growth and development of the nations is now the past events. The countries of today are inviting newer technologies for fast development of the economies as well as social changes. One such tool is the artificial intelligence (AI) which has the power of doing everything on its own without taking help of larger quantities of physical labour forces. There are so many good opportunities for this fast growth of technologies. Besides, there are black sides of it also. The world with rising unemployment problems will face the triggered rate of unemployment further after AI is invented on a larger scale. Therefore, its ramifications might fall upon the economy as well as different strata of the society.

Besides scientific areas of its uses, AI has a long list of areas in economics and society where it can have many positive effects. The effects are found in the growth, inequality, market power, productivity, employment, etc. Many researchers on economics have an idea that AI technology has a great economic potential as this technology is using neural networks and machine learning that can analyse a large number of complex data precisely in a short time and can make decisions and predictions. AI can impact education in many ways, including personalized learning, accessibility, language editing, reading comprehension, and automated grading. It helps to analyse medical records, identifying errors or potential risks such as misdiagnoses, incorrect treatments, or adverse events. This information can be used to help doctors prevent similar errors from happening in the future. Another way AI can be used is through clinical decision support. There have been so many instances of technological inventions and innovations in different social sectors till the end of the 20th century, but the new millennium has offered a phenomenal boost in the areas of AI where efforts are being made by the countries, mainly from the west, to reap the benefits in health services, education services, etc.

Under the background, the present edited book titled *Artificial Intelligence in Business and Society: Global Insights* throws light upon compiling studies related to the AI and its impacts upon business, economy, and society from a global perspective. As the researches in AI in social sciences are relatively new and scarce, there are thus limited data availabilities on several indicators of AI vis-à-vis economy, business, and society. The present book has strived to develop the book on the said contents as fine as possible to make it palatable to the readers in the related disciplines.

This book contains 16 chapters which are divided into two broad sections. Section I covers up the studies related to AI and its roles upon global business and economics containing seven chapters, and Section II captures the studies related to the AI and its implications with society covering nine remaining chapters. The brief objectives and outcomes of all the chapters are outlined below.

Chapter 1 investigates the impacts of AI on an economy, specifically Ghana, on long-run economic growth within the concept of human security with the intentions to test the hypothesis that there is a positive relationship between AI innovation, economic growth, and human security using the data sets of firms and industries from 2012 to 2022 and employing fixed effects and a generalized method of moments (GMM) estimation. The study reveals that there is a marginal significant relationship between AI innovation, processes of economic growth and human security in emerging economies such as Ghana who is a late starter to the evolution of such technological innovation.

Chapter 2, raising the necessity of AI in the banking industry in India, with banks leveraging AI for various functions such as fraud detection, customer service automation, creditworthiness evaluation, etc., assesses the effectiveness of public sector banks in promoting financial inclusion following the integration of AI into their operations employing data envelopment analysis. By analysing efficiency levels during the pre- and post-introduction of AI periods, the findings indicate a positive trend in overall technical efficiency over time, suggesting that AI adoption has contributed to enhanced resource utilization and operational effectiveness.

Chapter 3 seeks to determine the effect of AI on gross domestic product (GDP) growth of India for the year of 2022 and has selected terms of trade, human development index, and per capita real GDP for the year 2022 to understand its overall impact using secondary data. The results of the analysis show that terms of trade, global AI index, and human development index as explanatory variables significantly explain variation in per capita real GDP.

Chapter 4 examines the influence of AI adoption on employment across a range of skill levels in South Asian countries. Using correlational analysis, it looks at patterns in the relationship between AI preparedness and employment in different skill-level occupations. It draws attention to differences in workforce adaptation and the difficulties associated with changes in the labour market such as the possibility of employment polarization and widening gaps. The results highlight the significance of human resource investments, customized regulations, and regional collaboration in reducing workforce disruptions and utilizing AI's potential.

Chapter 5 intends to identify priority strategies for integrating microgrid systems with hospitals applying an AI-based multi-criteria decision-making method where literature-based criteria are weighted using the AI-based DEMATEL method. It is derived that the most important criterion that affects the process of integrating microgrid systems with hospitals is the initial investment cost. Similarly, it is seen that the criterion of having qualified personnel also contributes significantly to the process along with the integration of the AI approach with multi-criteria decision-making methodology.

Chapter 6 seeks to examine whether investments in AI have strong coherence with patents in AI sectors. If so, which sectors dominate the list and how they may impact upon incomes of the countries. The correlation, regression, and ranking exercises are done for the period 2010–2020 across a listed country of the world, and the results show that AI investments have a strong correlation with a number of patents, and an increase in AI investment leads to a significant increase in patents.

Chapter 7 analyses the emergent and disruptive digital technologies in an era of AI. It departs from the assumption that the emerging technologies create both opportunities and challenges with an impact on individuals, organizations, institutions, and society at large in terms of bias, surveillance, hacking, etc. using existing scientific literature. It concludes that control over the ethical disruption of digital technologies must require a digital conversation and leadership about acceptable ethical behaviours, under the assumption that digital transformation cannot be interrupted and must be guided by humans in following years of the near future.

Chapter 8 attempts to capture several aspects of AI such as AI-related education, role of the government towards AI, etc. The above-discussed areas by the help of a general equilibrium framework followed by a contingent valuation (CV) analysis, considering perception of stakeholders of higher education, regarding necessity of learning AI. The general equilibrium model depicts different outcomes regarding existence or abolishment of economic sectors in the presence of AI, under different conditions. By CV model, we consider the use-value of AI in regular life among the stakeholders of higher education. It shows that different socio-economic factors such as investments in infrastructure, teacher training, and the development of culturally appropriate AI solutions, etc. are significant behind one's willingness or non-willingness in learning AI.

Chapter 9 investigates the possible divergent impact of AI across countries and variations of AI tools across different occupations, education levels, and skills. Using the principal component analysis to estimate occupation-wise weights, a grand AI susceptibility index (AISI) score is computed in different occupations, and the study reveals that (i) the jobs are more threatened by AI in advanced economies (AEs) compared to emerging market and developing economies (EMDEs); (ii) occupations like managers, professionals, and clerical support workers are the most vulnerable (substitutable), whereas skilled agriculture, craft-related trade workers are the least susceptible to AI; and (iii) AI susceptibility increases with an increase in education levels.

Chapter 10 explores the impacts of AI on the arts and the humanities, highlighting possibilities, limitations, and pitfalls, through qualitative analysis. It reveals that while areas of the arts and the humanities like language teaching, choreography of dance, analysis of picture and field data, retrieval and restoration old yellowed manuscripts, interpretation of tangible and intangible historical pieces have possibilities of being greatly impacted by the use of such AI-assisted/driven delicate devices like Computer vision, algorithmic writing, and text mining tools like 'ChatGPT', 'Copy ai', 'Grammarly', 'Dall-e 3', 'Synthesia', etc., AI has not been able to effectively replace the 'artist' or the 'humanist' as the creator with

'God-like' creative potentialities. 'Inspiration' and 'the esemplastic imagination' of the creative artist remain anecdotal to AI.

Chapter 11 investigates how investments in healthcare that use AI affect the health outcomes of women in early adopter countries (the United States, the United Kingdom, Canada, France, Germany, China, Japan, and Israel) during 2014–2023 using the multivariate analysis of variance (MANOVA) to assess the cumulative effect of AI investments on health outcomes of women. It found that the *F*-value is low and not statistically significant, highlighting the fact that even in early adopter countries, investments in biotechnology, pharmaceuticals, and healthcare AI do not have a statistically substantial bearing on the overall health outcomes for women, making a disparity in gender. These findings show that to guarantee quantifiable and significant gains in health outcomes, AI investments in healthcare must take a more focussed and evidence-based approach.

Chapter 12 explores the long- and short-term dynamics of AI investment, healthcare expenditure, agricultural, and industry value-added on economic development of the BRICS countries (Brazil, Russia, India, China, and South Africa) between 2013 and 2023. Using panel fully modified ordinary least squares (OLS) and dynamic OLS pooled methods, it validated the results of the pooled mean group auto-regressive distributed lag (PMG/ARDL) model, which established that healthcare, industry value-added, and agricultural output across the BRICS economies significantly improve economic prosperity over time while AI investment shortens economic welfare. The study also confirms that healthcare is a homogeneous consequence of AI investment, and economic development is a homogeneous cause of AI investment.

Chapter 13 walks around the dual impact of AI on elections in South Asia, focussing on India, Pakistan, and Bangladesh using a qualitative approach. It reveals that during the pre-election phase, AI-enhanced personalized voter outreach and campaign strategies were effectively utilized, as evidenced in Pakistan and India, where political parties employed AI to target specific demographics with precision. However, it also fuelled disinformation, with PTI's AI-generated videos in Pakistan and deep-fake attacks against political figures in Bangladesh. In India, AI tools blurred the line between engagement and manipulation.

Chapter 14 focusses on the AI and human rights nexus in the way of 'how artificial intelligence may be the antagonist of human?' and 'how artificial intelligence may devastate human life by ruining rights', etc. Simultaneously, the question of the future identity of a human class called labour or farmer and the various righteous aspects of living a normal life with an unconscious machine within a single society is discussed. It reveals that AI would benefit human society in many ways, but there is a threat too which needs active cooperations from the part of the government institutions to mitigate them.

Chapter 15 presents a baseline for AI integration in urban mobility planning, with its role in closing socioeconomic gaps, enhancing efficiency in public transportation, and reducing greenhouse emissions. In follow-up studies, AI use in decarbonization in transportation, computerized fleet management, and resilient mobility infrastructure can be studied in relation to urban transit planning, in consonance with international objectives for sustainability. It has analysed the role of socio-demographic variables in mobility choices and the potential of AI. Results confirm that factors like gender, age, income, and place of residence are significant for evaluating the differences in mobility choices. Moreover, AI offers promising solutions for optimizing the efficiency and accessibility of urban transport services, anyway some limitations remain.

Chapter 16, the final chapter of this book, critically analyses possible roles of AI upon economy and social sectors relying on the available facts. It discusses that the concept of AI has been developed with the progress of computer technology and the development of machine learning and neural networks. It argues that AI has major positive and negative implications on the society, particularly in agriculture and in healthcare for medical professionals leading to the benefit of the society and human beings. But AI should be used with some ethical issues. There must have been some care and consideration so that privacy of citizens, freedom of individuals and fundamental rights, and unemployment problems are maintained.

The summary outcomes of all the covered studies show that AI has many economic and social benefits in countries and groups in the ways through increasing productivity in agriculture, industry and service sectors, tourism sector, hotel, space research, providing smart healthcare, and education services, helping election systems, etc. Besides, the studies were sceptical on the sustainability of the good effects. Though it might help in the short run, the long-run effects might be dangerous to the economy and society such as in reducing employment, numbing human brains and activities, human rights, among others. Thus, the studies recommended a sustainable use of such high-quality technology in human lives through proper managements from the parts of the governments in the countries in associations with private bodies.

The guts of this book may provide thought-infuriating solutions to the existing prospects and problems of the use of AI in business, economy, and the society, and there are immense possibilities of value addition to the existing literature in this area but further studies needed by the potential researchers. The readers and policymakers in the related fields would be enormously benefitted from the contents and materials of this book.

While executing the book project, the editor got marvellous supports from different angles of the academic and social world. The editor acknowledges the supports of the entire Emerald Team, the contributing authors, and the Foreword writer. Furthermore, the editor is beholden to his parents, wife, daughter, and other members of the family for their sacrifice and supports to uncover the volume. Nevertheless, the editor is exclusively accountable to any error that might still be left in this book.

Ramesh Chandra Das
Editor

Section I

Artificial Intelligence and Its Roles upon Global Business and Economics

Chapter 1

Implications of AI Innovation on Economic Growth and Human Security: A Panel Data Study of an Emerging Economy

Napoleon Kurantin

Ghana Armed Forces Command and Staff College, Teshie, Accra, Ghana

Abstract

The study investigates the application of artificial intelligence (AI) on economic growth and human security based on the application of panel data of an emerging economy with Ghana as a case study. The study aims to investigate and gauge the impact of AI on an economy specifically, on long-run economic growth within the concept of human security. The study intends to test the hypothesis that there is a positive relationship between AI innovation, economic growth and human security using the datasets of firms and industries from 2012 to 2022 and employing fixed effects and a generalised method of moments (GMM) estimation. GMM combines observed economic data with information in population moment conditions that results in estimates of the unknown parameters of an economic model. The study reveals that there is a marginal significant relationship between AI innovation, processes of economic growth and human security in emerging economies such as Ghana who is a late starter to the evolution of such technological innovation. It is expected that the study will contribute to the relevance of the application of AI innovation to stimulate gains to both the supply and demand sides in an emerging economy.

Keywords: AI innovation; economic growth; generalised method of moments; human security; panel data; Ghana

Artificial Intelligence in Business and Society: Global Insights, 3–18

Published under exclusive licence by Emerald Publishing Limited
doi:10.1108/978-1-83708-022-920261003

Introduction

The history of AI could be traced to McCathy in 1956 when he held the first academic conference on the subject. However, the effort, attempt and processes to understand if machines could truly think began early before 1956. Bush (1945), seminal work: *As We May Think*, proposed a system which amplifies humanity's knowledge and understanding. Going back five years, Alan (1950) espoused the notion of machines being able to simulate human beings with the ability to do intelligent things, for instance, playing chess.

Advances in computer science and digital technology including AI and machine learning have led to a plethora of their applications in sectors of the economy such as manufacturing, transportation, healthcare, finance, space science, agriculture, construction and education. The increased application of AI in human endeavours has opened questions as to whether AI technologies may have an impact on economic variables. According to the theories of neoclassical and endogenous economic growth models, technical change brings about increases in productivity, thus leading to a process of enhanced productivity and increased economic growth rates. Endogenous growth theory espouses the long-run economic growth rate attributable to forces that are particularly internal to the economic system with emphasis on those forces governing the opportunities and incentives to create technological knowledge (Das, 2025; Peretto, 1998; Romer, 1986, 1990; Solow, 1956). Thus, economic growth, to a large degree, is primarily attributed to internal and not external variables. The processes of economic growth are the result of investment in human capital, innovation and knowledge acquisition. The endogenous growth theory dwells on externalities and noted spillover effects of a knowledge-based economy which in turn leads to enhanced economic development. The theory equally stipulates that the long-run growth rate of an economy depends on policy measures. For instance, subsidies for the educational sector, particularly subsidies for research and development (R&D), serve as an incentive that increases the processes of innovation (Romer, 1994).

The simplest endogenous growth theory is presented by the AK model with constant-savings rate with assumed exogenous growth rate. Within the model, a single parameter usually A presents technological progress. Moreover, the model is based on the assumption that production functions do not exhibit diminishing returns to scale. This is based on the assumption that positive spillovers resulting from capital investment and enhanced technology lead to further improvement. In addition, agents within the model optimally determine the rate of consumption, saving and, thus, pointing out resource allocation to R&D leading to technological progress (Romer, 1994).

Among others, the central tenets of endogenous growth theory include government policy's ability to increase a country's growth rate if they lead to a more intense competition that stimulates product and innovation processes; there are increasing returns to scale from capital investment particularly in infrastructure and investment in education, health and telecommunications; continuous investment in human capital is a very important component of growth in an economy; and government policy should create the environment that ultimately serves as a source of new investment, job creation and technological innovation (Liberto, 2023).

A major criticism of the endogenous model is its failure to explain conditional convergence. Another critique of the model is the near impossibility to empirically verify its evidence; too much of it is involved in making assumptions about how unmeasurable things affected other unmeasurable things (Krugman, 2013).

The subject of this chapter is the identification of the role of technological changes in the most important theoretical approaches in aid of the processes of economic growth. According to Samuelson and Nordhaus, the aim is to employ a model of analysis with the essence of main growth theory approaches in the last 60 years to come to the answer to the question as to what the similarities and differences in the treatment of the category of technological changes in are traditional (neoclassical) and in modern theories. Henceforth, this is seen as important for the simple fact that economics lacks the necessary unified opinion regarding the classification of the most important growth and development theories, on the one hand, and the treatment of the key drivers of technological changes, on the other hand. In doing so, this chapter is fully aware of the fact that each growth theory has a certain value in respect to a specific time and place. Therefore, 'they are unsustainable as a universal explanation of economic development' (Samuelson & Nordhaus, 2009, p. 584). The above observations regarding the subject matter and goal of the study determine the corresponding structure of the work. After the introductory remarks, the second section presents the literature review with a focus on AI and the processes of economic growth. The third section presents the data requirement, research and methodological design. The fourth section dwells on the presentation of results and discussions and the last section emphasises the conclusion of the study and its inherit recommendations.

Literature Review

A working definition of the processes of 'development' is the expansion of citizens' freedom, political liberties, economic chances, social opportunities, transparency guarantees and protective security (Dusche, 2012). An enhancement of this definition is the explanation related to the concept of human security. According to Kofi Annan (2017), the late United Nations Secretary-General,

> human security, in its broadest sense, embraces far more than the absence of violent conflict. It encompasses human rights, good governance, access to education and health care and ensuring that each individual has opportunities and choices to fulfil his/her potential. Every step in this direction is also a step towards reducing poverty, achieving economic growth and preventing conflict. Freedom from want, freedom from fear, and the freedom of future generations to inherit a healthy natural environment – these are the interrelated building blocks of human and therefore, national security. (p. 1)

In accordance with a more inclusive approach to security, the United Nations Development Programme (UNDP, 1994) published seven pivotal areas involving health, economic, food, community, personal, political and environmental security, respectively.

In furtherance of this, some authorities view human security as enabling the conditions and environment that guarantees humans to be free from physical risk and physical danger, to live in a sustainable environment and to have economic welfare (de Sherbinim, 1996). Economic security is viewed on two levels involving micro and macro. Two aspects are accessed within the micro level; the institutional security of the market, requiring the existence of institutions that enable the successful functioning of a market economy. Henceforth, economists accept security of property rights and security of contracts as the relevant of these institutions. On the other hand, economic security relates to the individual based on security of employment and income (Adam & Limongi, 1993; Goldsmith, 1997). On the macro level, the policies formulated and implemented by the state to protect domestic markets are intended to enhance the economic security of the internal markets involving supply and effective demand. State strategic policies are intended to successfully develop new industries, penetrate world markets and enhance the nation's economic welfare (Liew, 2000).

Economic growth theory concerns itself with the issues of dynamic equilibrium, and efforts at researching reasonable answers to the questions as to the kind of use of available production factors and/or variables capable of providing sustainable increases in real gross domestic product (GDP) per capita in the long run (Sredojevic et al., 2016). Therefore, the application of production factors and their most efficient usage leads to the maximum economic growth rates (Cvetanovic et al., 2011a). In the true sense of the word, economic growth theory emerged in the mid-20th century with its identification and focus on technological change as the main and/or key variable of economic growth in worldwide economies. Neoclassicists were the first among their peers to vehemently bring to the fore the category of technological changes as the key imperative to economic growth; a number of empirical studies have buttressed this conclusion (Nelson & Winter, 1982; Solow, 1957).

Neoclassical growth theorists explain and predict that the rate of growth in poor developing economies is faster than rich developed economies. This stems from the fact that poor developing economies grow at a faster rate because they are further away from their steady state: a process referred to as absolute convergence (Sala-i-Martin, 1996). The main criticism of the neoclassicists is the failure to account for the question of how technological changes occur. This shortcoming of the neoclassical theory stems from the fact that technological changes within its growth model are of exogenous nature. Thus, a number of authoritative researchers on the sub-matter have tried to endogenise the processes of economic growth as attributed to technological changes (Petit, 1995).

The school of thought that emerged in the nineteenth-eighties to explain the origin of technological changes relative to the processes of economic growth is divided into endogenous theories and that of evolutionary-institutional theorists (Greenhalgh & Rogers, 2010). The endogenous and institutional-evolutionary theorists explain and attribute the phenomenon of economic growth to knowledge which thus leads to technological changes in the form of innovation. According to these schools of thought, the catalysts of an enhanced process of economic growth rates are technological spillover, R&D as well as international technological transfers (Sredojevic et al., 2016).

The endogenous growth model often starts with basic Cobb–Douglas functions extended to include human capital as an input of production:

$$Y = AK^{\alpha}L^{\beta}H^{\Upsilon} \tag{1}$$

where Y is the total output; K, the capital; L, labour and H, the human capital.

The identities α, β and γ represent the elasticities of output, labour and human capital (Cobb & Douglas, 1928; Hajkova & Humik, 2006). The level of knowledge: A represents the stock of ideas in an economy at a particular time period (Jones & Williams, 1998).

Equation 1 is divided by L to obtain the output per unit of labour. When the right side is multiplied by $\frac{L^{\sigma+\gamma}}{L^{\sigma+\gamma}} = \frac{L^{\sigma}}{L^{\sigma}}.\frac{L^{\gamma}}{L^{\gamma}} = 1$ based on an assumption of constant returns to scale: $\alpha + \beta + \gamma = 1$; the resultant is Equation 2:

$$\frac{Y}{L}A\left(\frac{K^{\sigma}}{L^{\sigma}}\right)\left(\frac{H^{\gamma}}{L^{\gamma}}\right) = A\left(\frac{K}{L}\right)^{\sigma}\left(\frac{H}{L}\right)^{\gamma} \tag{2}$$

As suggested by Cobb and Douglas (1928), per unit of labour variables are substituted by Greek letter (identities) as presented in Equation 3:

$$\gamma = Ak^{\sigma}h^{\gamma} \tag{3}$$

The available technology factor A as part of the knowledge stock at time t is a nonrival input (Romer, 1990). Collective efforts from the research fields result in Equation 4:

$$A = \delta R^{\vartheta} A \tag{4}$$

where R is the resources available for research.

This function is assumed to increase, leading to more ideas (Jones & Williams, 1998). However, depending on how previous knowledge impacts current research levels, Equation 4 could be increasing and/or decreasing in A. Related to this is the assumption that θ is equal to 1; an increase in R thus leads to an increase in new knowledge fields. The coefficient δ represents productivity (Jones & Williams, 1998; Romer, 1990). To calculate the growth rate, the natural log of Equation 3 results in Equation 5:

$$\Delta \ln y = \Delta \ln A + \sigma \Delta \ln k + \gamma \Delta \ln h \tag{5}$$

Y which is the growth rate is defined and thus presented as $g_y = \frac{\dot{y}}{y'}$ where $\dot{y} = \frac{dy}{dt}$

Henceforth, the growth rate could be expressed by:

$$g_y = \frac{dy/dt}{y} = \frac{d\ln y}{dt} = \frac{\ln y_t - \ln y_{t-s}}{s}$$

Dividing Equation 5 by changes in t results in the growth rate of Equation 6:

$$\frac{\dot{y}}{y} = \frac{\dot{A}}{A} + \alpha\frac{\dot{k}}{k} + \gamma\frac{\dot{h}}{h} \tag{6}$$

In addition, substituting Equation 4 for A in Equation 6 presents Equation 7:

$$\frac{\dot{y}}{y} = \frac{\delta R^{\theta} A}{A} + \alpha\frac{\dot{k}}{k} + \gamma\frac{\dot{h}}{h} \tag{7}$$

To conclude, the growth rate of y is presented as:

$$g_y = \delta R + \alpha gk + \gamma gh \tag{8}$$

The study focuses on the hypothesis that there is a significant positive relationship between AI innovation, economic growth and human security. AI patents published within a period are represented by the variable R as a proxy in the economy. This is slightly different from R as inputs and/or resources directed at research, for example, R&D expenditure as a share of labour's contribution to R&D (Griliches, 1988). This is succinctly put forward by Griliches (1998): the stochastic component of knowledge stock is captured to some extent by patenting, using patents may have some value added over the use of common research inputs as indicator of knowledge. Within this context, patents are seen as involving the type, inventiveness, quantity and the complexity of innovation created in a specified spatio-temporal frame (Griliches, 1988). It is assumed that continuous AI invention may exhibit increasing returns as it outpaces human intelligence, thus leading to technological singularity by extension, spurring economic growth (Aghion, 2018; Aghion & Howit, 1990, pp. 323–351).

As part of their criticism of the neoclassical theory, institutional and evolutionary growth theorists promote the concept of a national innovation system based on the assumption that economic growth is possible and enhanced with technological progress (Aghion & Howitt, 1992; Blanchard, 2005). Evolutionary–institutional theory of technological change identifies the determinants of the dynamics of technological changes as well as the innovation level of society as a whole. It is based on Schumpeter's theory of innovation as a key variable of economic growth with technological change as the main catalyst of an innovation

(Schumpeter, 1961; Todaro & Smith, 2011). The main point of reference is the analysis of the emergence and diffusion of technological changes at the company and/or micro level of reference (Dosi, 1982; Nelson, 1993).

The two main premises of the neoclassical approach: market equilibrium and perfect rationality of companies is criticised by Nelson and Winter (1982) relative to their goal of profit maximisation. Profit maximisation is related to innovation, a phenomenon that is opposite routine to prediction and certainty. Therefore, the phenomenon of innovation at the company/firm and/or national economy is identical to genetic mutation in the biological world leading to evolution. This brings to the fore a characteristic of technological changes relative to the social environment and the scientific system; scientific discoveries are among the direct results of co-evolution of scientific and technological knowledge and their practical application (Dosi, 1982). Related to this exposition are national innovation systems of the interaction of networks of public and private institutions that determine the origin, import, transformation and diffusion of new technologies (Freeman, 1987). The phenomenon of the national innovation system involves the interconnections and relationships of institutions researching, working on the creation and diffusion of scientific knowledge and technology within a sovereignty – national borders (Cvetanovic et al., 2011b).

The application of AI at such a starting point could be of relevance to developing countries at lower levels of economic development, who lack significant innovation potential. Thus, the ability to manage technological changes such as the adoption of AI is primarily an endogenous social process leading to sustainable development. There is a close nexus between scientific and technological advancement, development and human security both in terms of its positive and negative aspects, respectively. The fourth industrial revolution has led to new technologies expanding their applications rapidly among peoples of the world. Microsoft predicted that by 2025, 4.7 billion people will have access to the internet, and of this number, 75% of users will be in emerging economics (Burt et al., 2014; Ceyhan, 2002).

Technological advancement including the emergence of AI could create hitherto opportunities in the areas of governance, state-society relations, peace and conflict, international security, glocal governance and sustainable development within the framework of human security (Independent Commission on Multilateralism, 2016).

Human security, especially in the developing world, is threatened by disease, hunger, poverty, environmental degradation and more so; physical threats thus hinder processes of sustainable human development. The large majority of the world's population continues to face unacceptable depredation in access to water, food, healthcare, resources and basic security. Technology has the potential to ameliorate these conditions (Dowdeswell et al., 2006).

It's in light of this that the relevance of AI is brought to the fore as it holds the possibility of enabling the international community, governments and civil society to predict and prevent human insecurity. The application of AI in the domain of human security-related activities could greatly enhance knowledge, planning, development and empowerment (Ogata, 2015; Roff, 2017; Sane, 2008).

AI and Economic Growth

This section of the study provides a systematic review of the implications of AI on the processes of economic growth. Among others, AI is seen as having the capability of a machine to imitate intelligent human behaviour or an agent's ability to achieve goals in a wide range of environments (Aghion et al., 2017). Some observers have suggested that AI could become rapidly self-improving, leading to singularities that feature unbounded machine intelligence and/or unbounded economic growth in finite time (Good, 1965; Kurzweil, 2005; Vinge, 1993). As part of processes of economic globalisation, AI is viewed as an engine of productivity and economic growth and is able to increase the efficiency of production outlays and improve the decision-making process by analysing large amounts of data. Moreover, it is able to create new products and/or services, thereby spurring consumer demand and generating income and revenue streams (Szczepanski, 2019).

Nevertheless, AI could be highly disruptive on the economy and society at large. It is argued that it could lead to super firms involving hubs of wealth and knowledge that could lead to detrimental adverse effects on the wider economy, widen the ingenuity gap between less developed countries and that of advanced economies and lead to the demand for workers with AI skills while reducing others with far-reaching consequences for the labour market (Szczepanski, 2019).

Furthermore, AI has adverse effects on economic growth, including technological: some technological are yet to reach maturity stage to assess the economic benefits; legal: there remains insufficient regulation of AI ecosystem; socio-professional: the adverse effects of skills deficits and resistance to organisational change are very difficult to quantify; organisational: models related to AI in government and private sectors are still insufficiently integrated and institutional: the action and funding of public action on training relative to initial and continuous in AI targeted at reducing the digital divide are not equally promoted across economies and within economic sectors (Agrawal et al., 2019; Baldwin, 2019).

On the other hand, AI has the added advantage of stimulating economic growth by replacing labour with capital input which is an unlimited resource for the production of goods, services and ideas (Acemoglu & Restrepo, 2016; Aghion et al., 2017; Hemous & Olsen, 2014; Zeira, 1998). AI has the potential of automating 25% of the entire global labour market. AI is predicted to replace humans in 46% of administrative positions, 44% of legal jobs and 37% of architectural and engineering professions (Goldman, 2023). In the nutshell, AI could spur labour productivity growth and thus increase global GDP by 7% per year over a period of 10 years (Goldman, 2023). By harnessing the power of data analytics and algorithms, AI applications could help reduce fake transactions and better protect organisations from hackers as well as spearheading the fight against digital fraud (Trabelsi, 2024). The results of AI on economic growth are heterogeneous either as top-down based on value creation hypotheses and/or bottom-up by consulting users and experts. However, it is observed that AI technologies require adequate infrastructure, data availability and supplementary supportive policies which could vary across different economies and sectors (Agrawal et al., 2016, 2019). AI could significantly impact risk management across various industries and firms; it enhances risk assessment, prediction and mitigation processes (Trabelsi, 2024).

The effect and impact of AI on consumption are reflected in enhanced customisation, convenience, improved search and discovery, optimised pricing, predictive analytics, immerse experiences and increased security. Eight main areas impacted by AI include health: enhanced diagnosis enabled by data, identification diseases by the human genome, imaging and prediction; automative: smart cars and driver assistance; financial services: detection of fraud and the fight against money laundering; retailing: automated inventory and delivery management; communication and entertainment: content creation, etc.; manufacturing and production: optimisation of the supply chain and self-correction of production process; energy: optimised networks and storage operations that of smart infrastructure maintenance; logistics: traffic control and traffic jam reduction and enhanced road safety (Trabelsi, 2024). The construction of increasingly complex digital product and service transaction platforms serves as the basic structure of today's AI digital revolution: platforms that make it possible to reduce information asymmetries between different sectors of the economy at the micro and macro levels (Yang, 2022).

Data Requirement, Research and Methodological Design

One of the main shortcomings of a study of such nature within the context of a developing economy is the challenge of undertaking and/or performing an econometric analysis of obtained data to measure the level of AI relative to available panel dataset.

The dataset and associated information are based on secondary source outlay involving Google Patents Public Data, Ghana's Ministry of Information, the World Development Indices of the World Bank, Ghana's Registrar General's Department and Ghana's Ministry of Finance, respectively; use of panel datasets of firms and industries from 2012 to 2022. In addition, datasets and respective attributable information were equally sourced from the United Nation Department of Economic and Social Affairs Statistics Division.

Econometric models, as espoused by the following: Lach (1995), Wong et al. (2005), Kim et al. (2012), He (2019), Lu and Zhou (2021) and Lu (2021), are applied in this study. Therefore, from Equation 8 from the literature review, the stipulated econometric model for this study follows:

$$\text{Growth}_{it} = \varphi_0 + \varphi_1 \text{Growth}_{i,t-1} + \varphi_2 \text{GDP}pc_{i,t-1} + \varphi_3 \text{Patents}_{it} + \varphi X_{it} + \varepsilon_{it}$$

where Growth_{it} = annual average real GDP per capita growth rate of country *i* over period *t* (10 years). This is calculated by taking the divide of the difference between the natural log value of the real GDP per capita; using constant 2015 prices in US dollars (USDs); the natural log value of the initial real GDP by the number of years in period *t*. The identity Growth_{it} is equal to the instantaneous growth rate of the real GDP of a country/economy *i* in time *t*. To control any potential endogeneity as a result of an omitted variable, the variable growth rate is added in case there is an increased influence of the current growth rate relative to the lagged value involved.

$t - 1$ = Lagged real GDP per capita (10 years).

Parents$_{it}$ = Level of AI innovation within period t same as applied by Kim and Lee (2015).

X_{it} = Represents control variables: population growth; real gross capital rate per capita; real government expenditure growth rate per capita; trade openness; inflation; trade volume (exports plus imports) relative to GDP (Barro, 1997; Bassanini et al., 2001; Fan & Liu, 2021; Grier & Tullock, 1989). Furthermore, data are obtained from the Penn World Table (PWT) relating to years of schooling and returns to education as a proxy for human capital (Dasgupta & Stiglitz, 1988).

The panel data initially are integrated via ordinary least squares (OLS): a linear regression technique applied in the estimation of unknown parameters in a model. The applied OLS method minimises the sum of squared residuals (SSR), which is the difference between the actual values of the dependent variable and the predicted values from the model. The OLS results in the minimisation of the SSR as it optimises the noted values of the coefficients in a regression model. Hence, the total of the squares of the differences between the observed values and the values predicted by the model is as small as possible (Hutcheson & Sofroniou, 1999; Koteswara, 1970; Ryn, 1997). The Anderson–Hsiao (AH) and GMM estimation techniques are applied with the intend of minimising endogeneity issues such as bias resulting from reverse causality between growth rate and patents data (Arellano & Bond, 1991; Arellano & Bover, 1995; Blundell & Bond, 1998; Nickell, 1981).

Results and Discussion

This section of the study presents the obtained results and its corresponding discussion. It is hereby noted that due to issues of data availability, the unbalanced datasets depict the unequal number of observations (N) relative to the number of groups (n) of their corresponding variable as presented in Table 1.1, descriptive statistics of the applied panel data. As depicted in Table 1.1, the five-year growth rates averaged 0.975 with corresponding standard deviation of 3.34. The mean five-year real GDP per capita is 2,238 (USD). The population growth rate is 2.1% with a standard deviation of 1.21%. The gross capital formation per capita growth rate is 2.19%, 4.10% standard deviation. On the other hand, government expenditure per capita growth rate (%) is 19.57 with a standard deviation of 3.06. Human capital index growth rate (%) is 0.25 with a standard deviation of 0.38. AI patent per million people is 0.21 with a standard deviation of 275.88.

Following Table 1.1, Table 1.2 incorporates coefficients, thus presenting a summary of the economic performance measures including real GDP per capita and real GDP per capita growth rates, technological progress relative to AI and total patents per level of economic development. This is presented within a framework that measures countries with a real GDP per capita above USD 10,000 considered as advanced economics and those below this threshold as less developed

Table 1.1. Summary Statistics.

Variable	*N*	*n*	Mean	Standard Deviation
Real GDP per capita (USD)	1,080	200	2,238	2,066.38
Real GDP per capita growth rate (%)	1,834	200	0.975	3.34
AI patents per million people	504	105	0.21	275.58
Total patents per million people	504	104	8.6	11,875.65
Population	1,160	104	33,475,870	102,000.00
Population growth rate (%)	1,760	107	2.1	1.21
Gross capital formation per capita	1,825	107	2,353.040	2,457.01
Gross capital formation per capita growth rate (%)	1,824	107	2.19	4.10
Government expenditure per capita	1,825	107	2.96	1.65
Government expenditure per capita growth rate (%)	1,824	107	19.57	3.05
Human capital index	1,285	134	3.00	0.56
Human capital index growth rate (%)	1,276	134	0.25	0.38
Trade ratio to GDP (%)	1,638	176	70.12	36.37
Inflation (%)	1,725	107	31.9	15.7

Source: Author's compilation.

countries. Henceforth, high-income countries post higher technology output relative to patents per million people. China has the highest number of patents per million people which is attributable to an increased investment in R&D, foreign direct investment and subsidies (Chen & Zhang, 2019).

Estimation techniques applied panel OLS, fixed effects, AH and GMM. AH and GMM estimations are applied to minimise Nickell bias: a downward bias resulting in low *T* panels and originates in the connection between the lag-dependent variable and the fixed effects (Beck et al., 2014). The dependent variable real GDP growth rate per capita GMM resultant is 0.055, OLS is 0.035 and AH is 0.036. This lack of significance and, hence, a small magnitude of coefficients thus indicate a minimal impact of the first-order lagged growth. Gross capital formation and government expenditure growth rate portray significant positive effects. This implies that investment in physical capital and that of public infrastructure positively contribute to economic growth and an enhancement of human security. AI patents (4.11) have a minor significant impact on processes of economic

Table 1.2. Average Economic and Technology Output Across Classification.

Variable	Developed Economics	Developing Economics
Real GDP per capita (USD): five-year average	33,260.51	2,426.88
Real GDP per capita growth rate (5%), five-year average	1.12	1.27
AI patents per million people	280.85	4.11
Total patents per million people	25,775.75	674.21
N	602	1,346
n	81	143

Source: Author's compilation.

growth. This is buttressed by studies by Lu and Zhou (2021) and Yang (2022). Although Nguyen and Nadia (2022) argue that total patents do not display a significant impact on the long-run growth, information, communication and technology (ICT) does have a significant impact on economic growth as compared to other kinds of patents. Total innovation is significant at the 10% level in the OLS, fixed effects and AH; however, this is insignificant in the GMM. The application of the Sargan–Hansen test for overidentifying restrictions for the GMM model shows that AI and total patents are 0.315 and 0.461, respectively. Therefore, the null hypothesis stating that the instruments are valid is not rejected.

Ghana, like other emerging economies, could benefit from AI innovation as it drives long-run economic growth. The benefits could be accrued in sectors such as manufacturing, ICT, transportation, finance, increase precision and efficient application of physical capital and reduce defects and delays. The increased application of AI such as voice-to-text applications and speech recognition has enabled businesses to respond to customers in real time, increasing the volume of consumer transactions (Mou, 2019). Telecommunication businesses in Ghana have deployed AI to detect mobile money scam and fraudulent activities, preventing theft and loss.

Conclusion and Recommendations

The development and emergence of AI has been around since the 1970s. However, their application and impact has been pervasive in the last two decades; it is evidenced in the increased AI and total patent registration. The study sets out to determine the relationship between the level and adoption of AI and long-run economic growth based on the application of panel datasets. The study focuses on the hypothesis that there is a significant positive relationship between AI innovation, economic growth and human security. The study concluded that there is a marginal significant relationship between AI innovation, processes of economic growth and human security. For future research, it is recommended that an investigation into the empirical evidence of the explosion of AI invention, leading to technological singularity and economic growth and development. Henceforth, scholarly studies on human security and its relationships with science and technology such as AI are warranted and relevant and thus make a significant contribution to the literature of human security, economic growth and development.

References

Acemoglu, D. & Restrepo, P. (2018). "The Race between Man and Machine: Implications of Technology for Growth, Factor Shares, and Employment." American Economic Review *108*(6): 1488–1542.

Adam, P., & Limongi, F. (1993). Political regimes and economic growth. *Journal of Economic Perspectives*, *7*, 51–69.

Aghion, P. (2018). *Artificial intelligence and economic growth. The economics of artificial intelligence: An agenda*. University of Chicago Press. https://doi.org/10.3386/w23928

Aghion, P., & Howit, P (1990). A model of growth through creative destruction. *Econometrica*, *60*(2), 323–351.

Aghion, P., & Howitt, P. (1992). A model of growth through creative destruction. *Econometrrica*, *60*(2), 323–351.

Aghion, P., Jones, B., & Jones, C. (2017, October 10). *Artificial intelligence and economic growth* [NBER Working Paper No. 23928]. Northwestern University and NBER. chrome-extension //efaidnbmnnnibpcajpcglclefindmkaj/https://web.stanford.edu/~chadj/AI.pdf

Agrawal, A., Gans, J., & Goldfarb, A. (2016). The simple economics of machine intelligence. *Harvard Business Review*, *17*, 2–5.

Agrawal, A., Gans, J., & Goldfarb, A. (2019). Artificial intelligence: The ambiguous labour market impact of automating prediction. *Journal of Economic Perspectives*, *33*(2), 31–50. https://doi.org/10.3386/w25619

Alan, T. (1950). Computing machinery and intelligence. *Mind*, *49*, 433–460.

Annan, K. (2017, October 1). *Human security: An approach and methodology for business contributions to peace and sustainable development*. http://www.un.org/News/Press/docs/2000/20000508.sgsm7382.doc.html

Arellano, M., & Bond, S. (1991). Some tests of specification for panel data: Monte Carlo evidence and an application to employment equations. *Review of Economic Studies*, *58*(2), 277–297. https://doi.org/10.2307/2297968

Arellano, M., & Bover, O. (1995). Another look at the instrumental variable estimation of error-components models. *Journal of Econometrics*, *68*(1), 29–51. https://doi.org/10.1016/0304-4076(94)01642-D

Baldwin, R. (2019). *The globatics upheaval: Globalisation, robotics and the future of work*. Weidenfeld and Nicolson.

Barro, R. (1997). *Determinants of economic growth: A cross-country empirical study*. MIT Press. https://www.nber.org/system/files/working_papers/w5698/w5698.pdf

Bassanini, A., Stefano, S., & Philip H. (2001). *Economic growth: The role of policies and institutions. Panel data evidence from OECD countries*. OECD Publishing. https://doi.org/10.1787/18 51973

Beck, N., Katz, J., & Mignozzetti, U. (2014). Of Nickell bias and its cures: Comment on Gaibulloev, Sandler, and Sul. *Political Analysis*, *22*(2), 274–278. https://www.jstor.org/stable/24573226

Blanchard, O. (2005). *Makroekonomija*. Mate.

Blundell, R., & Bond, S. (1998). Initial conditions and moment restrictions and patents on long-term economic growth. *Journal of Econometrics*, *87*(1), 115–143. https://doi.org/10.1016/S0304-4076(98)00009-8

Burt, D., Kleiner, A., Nicholas, J., & Sullivan, K. (2014). Cyberspace 2025: Today's decisions, tomorrow's terrain. *Navigating the Future of Cybersecurity Policy*, *6*, 47.

Bush, V. (1945). As we may think. *The Atlantic Monthly*, 10–22.

Ceyhan, A. (2002). Technologisation of security: Management of uncertainty and risk in the age of biometrics. *Surveillance and Society*, *5*(2), 102–123.

Chen, Z., & Zhang, J. (2019). Types of patents and driving forces behind the patent growth in China. *Economic Modelling*, 294–302. https://doi.org/10.1016/j.econmod.2018.11.015 (2019)-80(C)

Cobb, C., & Douglas, P. (1928). A theory of production. *American Economic Review*, *18*, 139–165.

Cvetanovic, S., Mladenovic, I., & Nikolic, M. (2011a). Theoretical basis of the concept of national innovation systems. *Ekonomika, Journal for Economic Theory and Practice and Social Issues*, *57*(4), 14–23.

Cvetanovic, S., Obradovic, S., & Dordevic, M. (2011b). Hipoteza o konvergenciji u endogenim teorijama rasta. *Ekonomske Teme*, *49*(1), 1–13.

Das, R. C. (2025). Interrelationships among government participation, population and growth of per capita income: Inquiry on top twenty income-holding countries in the world. *Economies*, *13*(2), 46. https://doi.org/10.3390/economies13020046

Dasgupta, P., & Stiglitz, J. (1988). Learning-by-doing, market structure and industrial and trade policies. *Oxford Economic Papers*, *40*(2), 246–268. https://doi.org/10.1093/oxfordjournals.oep.a041850

de Sherbinim, A. (1996). Human security and fertility: The case of Haiti. *Journal of Environment and Development*, *5*, 28–39.

Dosi, G. (1982). Technological paradigms and technological trajectories: A suggested interpretation of the determinants and directions of technical change. *Research Policy*, *11*(3), 147–162.

Dowdeswell, E., Singer, P., & Daar, A. (2006). Increasing human security through biotechnology. *International Journal of Biotechnology*, *8*(1–2), 119–131.

Dusche, M. (2012). *Identity politics in India and Europe*. Sage.

Fan, D., & Liu, K. (2021). The relationship between artificial intelligence and China's sustainable economic growth: Focused on the mediating effects of industrial structural change. *Sustainability*, *13*(20), 2–15. https://doi.org/10.3390/su132011542

Freeman, C. (1987). *Technology policy and economic performance: Lessons from Japan*. Printer Publishers.

Goldman, S. (2023). The potentially large effects of artificial intelligence on economic growth. *Economic Research*, 12–33, (March 26).

Goldsmith, A. (1997). Economic rights and government in developing countries: Cross-national evidence on growth and development. *Studies in Comparative International Development*, *32*, 29–44.

Good, I. (1965). Speculations concerning the first ultraintelligent machine. *Advances in Computers*, *6*, 31–88.

Greenhalgh, C., & Rogers, M. (2010). *Innovation, intellectual property and economic growth*. Princeton University Press.

Grier, K., & Tullock, G. (1989). An empirical analysis of cross-national economic growth, 1951–1980. *Journal of Monetary Economics*, *24*(2), 259–276.

Griliches, Z. (1988). Patent statistics as economic indicator: A survey. *R&D and Productivity: The Econometric Evidence*, 287–347. https://doi.org/10.3386/w3301

Hajkova, D., & Humik, J. (2006). Cobb–Douglas production function: The case of a converging economy. *Czech Journal of Economics and Finance*, *57*(9–10), 465–476.

He, Y. (2019). The effect of artificial intelligence on economic growth: Evidence from cross-province panel data. *Korean Journal of Artificial Intelligence*, *7*(2), 9–12.

Hémous, D. & Olsen, M. (2022). The rise of the machines: Automation, horizontal innovation, and income inequality. *American Economic Journal: Macroeconomics, American Economic Association*, *14*(1), 179–223

Hemous, D., & Olsen, M. (2014). *The rise of the machines: Automation, horizontal innovation and income inequality* [CEPR Discussion Paper No. 10244].

Hutcheson, G., & Sofroniou, N. (1999). *The multivariate social scientist*. Sage Publications.

Independent Commission on Multilateralism. (2016). *The impact of new technologies on peace, security and development*. International Peace Institute. https://www.ipinst.org/2016/05/new-technologies-peace-development

Jones, C., & Williams, J. (1998). Measuring the social return to R&D. *Quarterly Journal of Economics*, *113*(4), 1119–1135.

Kim, Y., & Lee, K. (2015). Different impacts of scientific and technological knowledge on economic growth: Contrasting science and technology policy in East Asia and Latin America. *Asian Economic Policy Review*, *10*(1), 43–66.

Kim, Y., Lee, K., Park, W., & Choo, K. (2012). Appropriate intellectual property protection and economic growth in countries at different levels of development. *Research Policy*, *41*(2), 358–375. https://doi.org/10.1016/j.respol.2011.09.003

Koteswara, R. (1970). Testing for the independence of regression disturbances. *Econometrica*, *38*, 97–117.

Krugman, P. (2013, August 18). The new growth fizzle. *The New York Times*, 6. https://archive.nytimes.com/krugman.blogs.nytimes.com/2013/08/18/the-new-growth-fizzle/

Kurzweil, R. (2005). *The singularity is near*. Penguin.

Lach, S. (1995). Patents and productivity growth at the industry level: A first look. *Economics Letters*, *49*(1), 101–108. https://doi.org/10.1016/0165-1765(94)00618-C

Liberto, D. (2023, September 7). *Endogenous growth theory: Definition, history and criticism*. https://www.investopedia.com/terms/e/endogenousgrowththeory.asp

Liew, L. (2000). Human and economic security: Is there a nexus? *Research Gate*, 2–15. https://www.researchgate.net/publication/29452344_Human_and_Economic_SecurityIs_There_a_Nexus

Lu, C. (2021). The impact of artificial intelligence on economic growth and welfare. *Journal of Macroeconomics*, *69*(C), 103342–103362.

Lu, Y., & Zhou, Y. (2021). A review on the economics of artificial intelligence. *Journal of Economic Surveys*, *35*(4), 1045–1075.

Mou, X. (2019). *Artificial intelligence: Investment trends and selected industry uses*. World Bank Group. https://hdl.handle.net/10986/32652

Nelson, R. (1993). *National innovation systems: A comparative analysis*. Oxford University Press.

Nelson, R., & Winter, S. (1982). *An evolutionary theory of economic change*. Belknap Press/Harvard University Press.

Nguyen, C., & Nadia, D. (2022). The impact of ICT patents on economic growth: An international evidence. *Telecommunications Policy*, *46*(5), 102291.

Nickell, S. (1981). Biases in dynamic models with fixed effects. *Econometrica*, *46*(6), 1417–1426.

Ogata, S. (2015). Striving for human security. *United Nations Chronical*, *52*(2), 25–27.

Peretto, P. (1998). Technological change and population growth. *Journal of Economic Growth*, *3*, 283–311.

Petit, P. (1995). Employment and technical change. In P. Stoneman (Ed.), *Handbook of the economics of innovation and technical change* (pp. 12–36). Blackwell.

Roff, H. (2017, May 6). *Advancing human security through artificial intelligence*. International Security Department and US and the Americas Programme. https://www.chathamhouse.org/sites/default/files/publications/research/2017-05-11-ai-human-security-roff.pdf

Romer, P. (1986). Increasing returns and long-run growth. *Journal of Political Economy*, *94*, 1002–1037.
Romer, P. (1990). Endogenous technological change. *Journal of Political Economy*, *98*, S71–S102.
Romer, P. (1994). The origins of endogenous growth. *The Journal of Economic Perspectives*, *8*(1), 3–22. https://doi.org/10.1257/jep.8.1.3
Ryn, T. (1997). *Modern regression methods*. John Wiley and Sons.
Sala-i-Martin, X. (1996). The classical approach to convergence analysis. *Economic Journal*, *106*, 1019–1036.
Samuelson, P., & Nordhaus, W. (2009). *Economics*. McGraw-Hill.
Sane, P. (2008). *Human security: Approaches and challenges*. UNESCO Publishing.
Schumpeter, J. (1961). *The theory of economic development*. A Galaxy Book.
Solow, R. (1956). A contribution to the theory of economic growth. *Quarterly Journal of Economics*, *70*, 65–94.
Solow, R. (1957). Technical change and aggregate production function. *The Review of Economics and Statistics*, *39*(3), 312–320.
Sredojevic, D., Cvetanovic, S., & Boskovic, G. (2016). Technological changes in economic growth theory: Neoclassical, endogenous, and evolutionary-institutional approach. *Economic Themes*, *54*(2), 177–194. https://doi.org/10.1515/ethemes-2016-0009
Szczepanski, M. (2019). *Economic impacts of artificial intelligence (AI)*. European Parliamentary Research Service. chrome-extension://efaidnbmnnnibpcajpcglclefindmkaj/https://www.europarl.europa.eu/RegData/etudes/BRIE/2019/637967/EPRS_BRI(2019)637967_EN.pdf
Todaro, M., & Smith, M. (2011). *Economic development*. Addison-Wesley.
Trabelsi, M. (2024). The impact of corruption on economic growth: A nonlinear evidence. *Journal of Social and Economic Development*, 51–73. https://doi.org/10.1007/s40847-023-00301-9
UNDP. (1994). *Human development report*. Oxford University Press.
Vinge, V. (1993). The coming technological singularity: How to survive in the post-human era. In *Vision 21: Interdisciplinary science and engineering in the era of cyberspace* (pp. 11–22). https://ntrs.nasa.gov/citations/19940022855
Wong, P., Ho, Y., & Autio, E. (2005). Entrepreneurship, innovation and economic growth: Evidence from GEM data. *Small Bus Econ*, *24*(3), 335–350. https://doi.org/10.1007/S11187-005-2000-1
Yang, C. (2022). How artificial intelligence technology affects productivity and employment: Firm-level evidence from Taiwan. *Research Policy*, *51*(6), 14–36. https://doi.org/10.1016/j.respol.2022.104536
Zeira, J. (1998). Workers, machines and economic growth. *Quarterly Journal of Economics*, *113*(4), 1091–1117.

Chapter 2

Role of Public Sector Banks Toward Financial Inclusion in the Era of AI: An Efficiency Review Study

Sagnik Maity[a] *and Amit Majumder*[b]

[a]*Department of Commerce, University of Calcutta, West Bengal, India*
[b]*Department of Commerce, Bijoy Krishna Girls' College, West Bengal, India*

Abstract

The impact of artificial intelligence (AI) on the banking industry in India is increasingly pronounced, with banks leveraging AI for various functions such as fraud detection, customer service automation, creditworthiness evaluation, and personalized financial recommendations. This study employs data envelopment analysis (DEA) as a methodological approach to assess the effectiveness of public sector banks (PSBs) in promoting financial inclusion following the integration of AI into their operations. By analyzing efficiency levels during the pre- and post-introduction of AI periods, the research provides valuable insights into the evolving landscape of banking efficiency. The findings indicate a positive trend in overall technical efficiency (OTE) over time, suggesting that AI adoption has contributed to enhanced resource utilization and operational effectiveness. Moreover, the study underscores the significant potential for further improvements in efficiency, which could lead to advancements in financial inclusion initiatives. Unlike previous studies primarily focused on theoretical frameworks, this empirical examination offers practical, data-driven insights into the tangible impact of AI on PSBs in India.

Keywords: Public sector banks; data envelopment analysis; technical efficiency; artificial intelligence; financial inclusion; India

Artificial Intelligence in Business and Society: Global Insights, 19–36

doi:10.1108/978-1-83708-022-920261006

Introduction

AI is revolutionizing commercial banking by driving innovation, enhancing customer experiences, and optimizing operations (Subudhi, 2019). Banks leverage AI-powered algorithms in customer service, risk management, fraud detection, and marketing. AI-driven chatbots and virtual assistants, using natural language processing, provide continuous support, streamline processes, and improve accessibility (Elcholiqi & Musdholifah, 2020). AI also analyzes customer data to deliver personalized services, boosting satisfaction and loyalty. In risk management, machine learning algorithms assess credit risk, detect fraud, and manage operational risks, improving decision-making and reducing financial losses. Robotic process automation (RPA) automates repetitive back-office tasks like data entry and reconciliation, enhancing efficiency (Madakam et al., 2019). AI-driven cybersecurity solutions detect irregularities and prevent fraudulent transactions, safeguarding data and assets (Hassan et al., 2023). While AI enhances efficiency and customer centricity, responsible adoption prioritizing data privacy, transparency, and fairness is vital for maintaining trust (Vinoth, 2022).

AI significantly enhances the efficiency of PSBs by automating processes, streamlining workflows, and optimizing resource allocation. AI-powered tools like chatbots improve customer service by providing continuous support, reducing human workload, and enhancing accessibility, while AI-driven analytics personalize services and boost customer satisfaction (Subudhi, 2019). In risk management, machine learning algorithms detect anomalies and predict risks, enabling proactive mitigation. Additionally, AI and RPA improve back-office operations, reducing errors and accelerating processing for cost savings and higher productivity (Malini & Menon, 2017). By leveraging AI responsibly, PSBs can expand access to banking services in underserved areas, drive financial inclusion, stimulate economic growth, and promote sustainable development, positioning themselves for long-term success in the evolving banking landscape.

Literature Review

This section reviews literature in two key areas. The first explores the role of AI in public sector banking, highlighting its applications in streamlining operations, enhancing customer experiences, improving risk management, and fostering financial innovation. The second examines DEA as a tool for measuring banking efficiency, focusing on studies that evaluate PSBs' performance and the factors affecting it. By synthesizing insights from these domains, the authors provide a comprehensive understanding of the intersection between AI adoption and efficiency evaluation in PSBs.

AI in the Banking System

Studies on Global Aspects

In recent years, the banking industry has transformed with the adoption of AI. Königstorfer and Thalmann (2020) highlight AI's growing role in client engagement though it also points to a gap in its application in core banking operations such as lending, payment processing, and deposits, despite its potential to reduce losses, enhance security, and improve customer targeting. Jakšič and Marinč (2019) emphasize the enduring importance of relationship banking in managing information asymmetry amid FinTech advancements. Ashta and Herrmann (2021) discuss AI's evolution from rule-based systems to machine learning, highlighting cost reduction and differentiation benefits while stressing the need for risk mitigation. Manser Payne et al. (2021) examine AI-powered mobile banking's impact on service ecosystems, finding AI enhances transactional value propositions and identifying consumer satisfaction as vital for improving digital banking experiences.

Studies on Domestic Aspects

In the Indian banking sector, AI is driving significant operational transformations. Ashta and Herrmann (2021) highlight AI's potential to improve efficiency in areas like investments and microfinance by reducing costs and enhancing differentiation while stressing the importance of addressing challenges such as data integrity, algorithmic bias, and ethical considerations. Malali and Gopalakrishnan (2020) emphasize AI's transformative role in improving data analytics, customer service, and operational efficiency, predicting its pivotal role in delivering faster and more accurate banking services at lower costs. Suresh and Rani (2020) identify emerging AI trends in banking, including customer assistance, fraud reduction, voice-assisted banking, and management decision-making, emphasizing personal and societal impacts. Umamaheswari and Valarmathi (2023) highlight automation's advantages in boosting profitability, performance, and innovation while reducing reliance on human intervention, showcasing AI's potential to revolutionize the banking sector and enhance consumer experiences.

Studies on Efficiencies of the Banks

From these literature reviews, it is evident that AI has fundamentally transformed the core functions of the banking business. From innovative customer service to credit-related security, AI is increasingly integral to banking operations, and its adoption is expected to continue growing in the near future. Given the significance of measuring bank efficiency, it's essential to consider the insights provided by existing literature on this topic.

Studies on Indian banks highlight the evolution of efficiency over time. Bhattacharyya et al. (1997) assessed 70 commercial banks during liberalization, finding public banks most efficient, followed by foreign and private banks, with foreign banks improving and public banks declining. Saha and Ravisankar (2000) noted increased efficiency in PSBs from 1992 to 1995, analyzing outputs like branches and staff against inputs like deposits and advances. Das and Ghosh (2006) evaluated commercial banks (1992–2002) using DEA, finding medium-scale PSBs excelled in technological efficiency. Kumar and Gulati (2008) explored correlations between profitability, market share, and efficiency, analyzing OTE via Charnes, Cooper, and Rhodes (CCR) and Banker, Charnes, and Cooper (BCC) models and logistic regression. Maity and Sahu (2018) examined Pradhan Mantri Jan-Dhan Yojana's (PMJDY) impact on PSBs (2010–2018), showing improved efficiency post-implementation and highlighting its role in advancing financial inclusion.

Research Gap

From the literature review, it is evident that many PSBs use AI in their operations, aiming to increase efficiency. However, there is a lack of direct measures showing how AI enhances bank operations. To address this gap, this study focuses on examining the efficiency of PSBs with regard to financial inclusion, serving as the primary objective of this chapter.

Objective of This Study

The objective of this study is to measure the efficiency of PSBs before and after the introduction of AI.

Data

All the data utilized in this study were sourced from the Reserve Bank of India (RBI, 2024). Notably, the majority of banks commenced their implementation of AI starting from 2017. Consequently, data for the pre-introduction period were collected from 2011 to 2016, while data for the post-introduction period were collected from 2017 to 2022.

Variable Used in This Study

The current study employs a DEA methodology, which involves mindfully choosing input and output variables based on a thorough evaluation of existing literature. According to Cooper et al. (2007), the selection of inputs and outputs is contingent upon certain assumptions. One such assumption is:

$$n \geq (p \times q),$$

where n is the number of decision-making units (DMUs); p, the number of inputs; and q, the number of outputs.

As the number of PSBs exceeds six, the authors proceed with the data. The study utilized three inputs and two outputs to measure bank efficiency. Based on an extensive literature review, the chosen inputs were cash in hand (Alam & Rastgi, 2019), number of staff (Agarwala et al., 2023), and fixed assets (Maity & Sahu, 2020), while the selected outputs were advances and deposits (Agarwala et al., 2023; Maity & Sahu, 2020) for the DEA model.

Input Variables

(a) *Cash in hand*: Cash in hand remains a vital input in DEA models for PSBs, reflecting liquidity management and financial health. It ensures the ability to meet short-term obligations and supports lending activities. By integrating cash in hand with AI-driven analytics, PSBs can enhance DEA models' accuracy, optimize resource allocation, and adapt to market changes. Despite AI's transformative potential, cash in hand remains critical for assessing operational efficiency and financial sustainability.

(b) *Fixed assets*: In the era of AI, fixed assets in banks encompass both traditional infrastructure and digital technologies, such as AI platforms and data analytics systems, essential for modern banking operations. As an input variable in DEA models, fixed assets highlight the efficiency of AI investments in enhancing performance, customer experience, and risk management. This analysis helps optimize resource allocation and drive competitive advantages in the evolving digital banking landscape.

(c) *Number of staff*: In the AI era, the number of staff in PSBs reflects evolving workforce dynamics and the integration of AI technologies. While AI automates routine tasks and enhances efficiency, it necessitates upskilling employees for roles in data analysis, cybersecurity, and AI management. As an input variable in DEA models, staff numbers help evaluate AI's impact on workforce productivity, skillsets, and organizational strategies, guiding PSBs in workforce planning and adaptation to the digital banking landscape.

Output Variables

(a) *Advances*: AI is revolutionizing lending in PSBs by improving credit assessments, reducing processing times, and enhancing financial inclusion. AI analyzes diverse data, including non-traditional sources, to evaluate creditworthiness, enabling loans for underserved groups like small- and medium-sized enterprises (SMEs) and rural communities. Automation lowers costs and simplifies processes, while AI-driven chatbots enhance transparency and customer support, fostering inclusive growth in India.

(b) *Deposits*: AI boosts PSBs by driving deposit growth, enhancing efficiency, and promoting financial inclusion. AI-powered tools personalize services, streamline deposit processes, and improve accessibility for urban and rural populations. Chatbots offer 24/7 support, while AI strengthens fraud detection and risk management, fostering trust. By enhancing customer experiences and expanding access, AI helps PSBs serve underserved communities and drive economic growth in India.

Research Methodology

DEA, developed by Charnes et al. (1978), is a non-parametric method widely used in fields like economics, finance, and operations management to assess the relative efficiency of DMUs. It compares input–output relationships without assuming specific functional forms or distributions. DEA constructs a production or cost frontier from observed data, representing the maximum achievable output for given inputs. DMUs on the frontier are deemed efficient, while those below it are considered inefficient.

The two scaling techniques that are used in model 1 are CCR and BCC models. The DEA CCR model is a widely used method for assessing the relative efficiency of DMUs within a dataset (Charnes et al., 1978). In the CCR model, efficiency is determined by comparing each DMU's output to its input while considering the best-performing DMUs as benchmarks. On the other hand, the DEA BCC model is a variation of the DEA approach used to evaluate the relative efficiency of DMUs within a dataset (Banker et al., 1984). The BCC model, unlike the CCR model's assumption of constant returns to scale (RTS), allows for variable RTS, making it more flexible. It evaluates efficiency by assessing each DMU's output–input ratio while accounting for both technical efficiency and scale efficiency (SE).

Using this method, the most efficient DMUs are given a score of 1, while the least efficient ones receive a score close to 0. Consider a system with *n* DMUs, each with *p* number of inputs and *q* number of outputs. A test DMU0 ("0" indicates a focused DMU) has been given a relative efficiency score according to the following model:

$$\text{Max} \frac{\sum_{r=1}^{q} v_r y_{r0}}{\sum_{i=1}^{p} u_i x_{i0}}$$

Subject to,

$$\frac{\sum_{r=1}^{q} v_r y_{rj}}{\sum_{i=1}^{p} u_i x_{ij}} \leq 1; \quad (j = 1, 2, 3, \ldots, n), \ (i = 1, 2, 3, \ldots, p), \ (r = 1, 2, 3, \ldots, q), \tag{1}$$

$$u_i, v_r \geq 0.$$

In Equation (1)
y_{rj} = Output "*r*" produced by DMU "*j*."
v_r = Weight of the output "*r*."
x_{ij} = Input "*i*" employed by DMU "*j*."
u_i = Wight of the input "*i*."

The equation is converted into a linear programming scenario to find the efficiency score of the DMUs.

$$\text{Max} \sum_{r=1}^{q} v_r y_{ro}$$

Subject to,

$$\sum_{r=1}^{q} v_r y_{ro} - \sum_{i=1}^{p} u_i x_{ij} \leq 0; \ (j = 1, 2, 3, .., n), \tag{2}$$

$$\sum_{i=1}^{p} u_i x_{ij} = 1,$$

$$u_i \ , v_r \geq 0.$$

In this study, researchers utilized an output-oriented model for calculating bank efficiency. This approach is consistent with similar studies conducted by Agarwala et al. (2023) and Maity and Sahu (2018, 2020). Efficiency scores for banks are derived based on three key measures: OTE, which is calculated using the CCR model; pure technical efficiency (PTE), determined using the BCC model; and SE, calculated as the ratio of PTE and OTE.

Analysis of Results

Before conducting the DEA analysis, the authors first performed descriptive statistics to understand the nature of the data. The following are the descriptive statistics of the variables:

1. Cash in hand (2011–2016)
   - Mean: 1,518.36
   - Standard deviation: 2,939.35
   - Kurtosis: 18.36
   - Skewness: 4.28
   - Range: 17,406.78
   - Minimum: 1.99
   - Maximum: 17,408.77
2. Cash in hand (2017–2022)
   - Mean: 2,525.370571
   - Standard deviation: 4,299.986887
   - Kurtosis: 13.06127046
   - Skewness: 3.64364999
   - Range: 23,398.48
   - Minimum: 4.94
   - Maximum: 23,403.42
3. Number of staff (2011–2016)
   - Mean: 37,666.50
   - Standard deviation: 56,979.31
   - Kurtosis: 14.83
   - Skewness: 3.93
   - Range: 295,219
   - Minimum: 194
   - Maximum: 295,41
4. Number of staff (2017–2022)
   - Mean: 46,289.8381
   - Standard deviation: 56,669.27507
   - Kurtosis: 8.867077743
   - Skewness: 3.001674753
   - Range: 279,414
   - Minimum: 501
   - Maximum: 279,915
5. Fixed assets (2011–2016)
   - Mean: 2,426.65
   - Standard deviation: 2,399.61
   - Kurtosis: 6.88
   - Skewness: 2.37
6. Fixed assets (2017–2022)
   - Mean: 6,290.550095
   - Standard deviation: 9,004.37673
   - Kurtosis: 11.17763592
   - Skewness: 3.357552788

- Range: 14,270.50
- Minimum: 8.96
- Maximum: 14,279.46

7. Advances (2011–2016)
   - Mean: 215,701.9
   - Standard deviation: 293,638.1
   - Kurtosis: 16.70563
   - Skewness: 3.968797
   - Range: 1849211
   - Minimum: 88.53
   - Maximum: 1849299

9. Deposits (2011–2016)
   - Mean: 282089.5
   - Standard deviation: 354031.2
   - Kurtosis: 15.55141
   - Skewness: 3.785415
   - Range: 2240455
   - Minimum: 86.64
   - Maximum: 2240542

- Range: 49,861.06
- Minimum: 22.68
- Maximum: 49,883.74

8. Advances (2017–2022)
   - Mean: 349,492.5
   - Standard deviation: 49,619.81
   - Kurtosis: 10.68592
   - Skewness: 3.260354
   - Range: 2733390
   - Minimum: 576.32
   - Maximum: 2733966.6

10. Deposits (2017–2022)
    - Mean: 518,970.1478
    - Standard deviation: 724,127.8877
    - Kurtosis: 11.21729313
    - Skewness: 3.294138745
    - Range: 4,050,558.35
    - Minimum: 975.77
    - Maximum: 4,051,534.12

These statistics provide insights into the central tendency, variability, and range of values for each variable, facilitating a better understanding of the dataset before conducting the DEA analysis. Subsequently, the authors also conducted the isotonicity test to check for positive correlation between the inputs and outputs (Golany & Roll, 1989). The results indicate that all variables are positively correlated with each other.

OTE: As the isotonicity test gives the positive result, authors move to calculate the OTE scores of the DMUs. Table 2.1 shows the OTE scores calculated using the CCR model.

Table 2.1 displays the mean of the OTE scores for all PSBs from 2011 to 2016 and 2017 to 2022. Efficiency scores are calculated based on the CCR model, which assesses the efficiency of each PSB relative to others. Higher efficiency scores indicate better performance and efficient utilization of resources, with scores closer to 1 representing higher efficiency.

In the pre-introduction scenario, the mean OTE scores range from a minimum of 0.585 to a maximum of 1 among the PSBs, indicating varying levels of efficiency. Notably, IDBI Bank Limited stands out with a perfect score of 1, indicating consistent high efficiency across the six years examined. Similarly, Punjab and Sind Bank, Syndicate Bank, and Oriental Bank of Commerce exhibit mean OTE scores close to 1, reflecting high efficiency over the period. Among other notable

Table 2.1. OTE Scores of the DMUs.

DMUs	Mean of OTE Scores of DMUs from 2011 to 2016	Mean of OTE Scores of DMUs from 2017 to 2022
Allahabad Bank[a]	0.9024165	–
Andhra Bank[a]	0.858272	–
Bank of Baroda	0.96954	0.996692833
Bank of India	0.935934333	0.895635833
Bank of Maharashtra	0.743086167	0.9588195
Bharatiya Mahila Bank Ltd.[a]	0.585277333	–
Canara Bank	0.9027805	0.867597
Central Bank of India	0.5858945	0.757132833
Corporation Bank[a]	0.942003167	–
Dena Bank[a]	0.8041605	–
IDBI Bank Limited[b]	1	–
Indian Bank	0.922196667	1
Indian Overseas Bank	0.676563833	0.749877167
Oriental Bank of Commerce[a]	0.971228167	–
Punjab and Sind Bank	0.9941535	0.9777445
Punjab National Bank	0.749113	0.983541833
State Bank of India (SBI)	0.6480515	0.945312833
Syndicate Bank[a]	0.9948425	–
UCO Bank	0.964686833	0.781143833
Union Bank of India	0.985177667	1
United Bank of India[a]	0.730909833	–
Vijaya Bank[a]	0.870066833	–

Source: Authors' calculations.

[a]Banks that have been merged with other banks.

[b]Banks that have been converted into private banks.

performers, Union Bank of India, Bank of Baroda, and Corporation Bank demonstrate mean OTE scores above 0.9, indicating commendable efficiency levels. Conversely, Central Bank of India, Bharatiya Mahila Bank Ltd., and SBI display relatively lower mean OTE scores, suggesting potential areas for improvement in operational efficiency. Meanwhile, banks such as Bank of India, Canara Bank, and UCO Bank maintain consistency in their efficiency levels, boasting mean OTE scores above 0.9. However, Punjab National Bank and United Bank of India exhibit mean OTE scores below 0.8, suggesting a need to focus on enhancing operational efficiency compared to their peers. Overall, banks with consistently high or improving efficiency scores are likely implementing effective strategies, while those with declining scores may need to reassess their operations to remain competitive in the market.

In the post-introduction period, two banks, Indian Bank and Union Bank of India, achieved a perfect score of 1, indicating high efficiency in their operations following the introduction of AI. Additionally, five banks, namely SBI, Bank of Baroda, Bank of Maharashtra, Punjab and Sindh Bank, and Punjab National Bank, operate at 90% efficiency, reflecting commendable efficiency levels in their operations. However, the efficiency levels of the remaining banks are below 90%, suggesting potential inefficiencies in their allocation of resources or operational procedures despite the adoption of AI technologies. This indicates a need for these banks to reassess their strategies and processes to enhance their overall efficiency and competitiveness in the market.

Analyzing the table, the study observed trends in the mean output efficiency (OTE) scores of DMUs from 2011 to 2016 and 2017 to 2022. Notably, several banks show consistency or improvement in their efficiency over time. Bank of Baroda, Indian Bank, Punjab and Sind Bank, and Union Bank of India all demonstrate either stable or increased OTE scores, indicating sustained or enhanced operational efficiency. Conversely, some banks experience decreases in efficiency during the latter time period. For instance, Central Bank of India, Indian Overseas Bank, and UCO Bank show declines in their OTE scores, suggesting challenges or inefficiencies faced in converting inputs into outputs. Overall, these fluctuations in efficiency levels highlight the dynamic nature of the banking sector, emphasizing the need for ongoing efforts to optimize operational performance and adapt to changing market conditions.

PTE: The mean PTE scores for PSBs during the pre- and post-introduction periods of AI are presented in Table 2.2. These scores, calculated using the BCC model, offer insights into the relative efficiency of each PSB. A PTE score of 1 signifies complete technical efficiency, indicating optimal performance and resource utilization, while scores further from 1 indicate varying degrees of inefficiency.

From 2011 to 2016, several banks achieved a perfect PTE score of 1, including Bank of Baroda, Corporation Bank, IDBI Bank Limited, SBI, Syndicate Bank, UCO Bank, and Punjab and Sind Bank, demonstrating exemplary technical efficiency over the specified period. Banks with scores close to 1, such as Andhra Bank, Bharatiya Mahila Bank Ltd., Canara Bank, Indian Bank, Oriental Bank of Commerce, and Punjab National Bank, also showcased high levels of technical efficiency. Some banks exhibited PTE scores slightly below 1 but still relatively high, indicating a commendable level of technical efficiency with potential for further improvement. Examples include Bank of India, Indian Overseas Bank, and Union Bank of India. However, banks with PTE scores significantly below 1, such as Central Bank of India and United Bank of India, may need to focus on enhancing their technical efficiency to align with industry standards and best practices. With perfect efficiency scores, banks are performing effectively, but those with lower scores may need to improve their technical efficiency and competitiveness.

In the post-introduction scenario, the maximum levels of efficiency were demonstrated by Bank of Baroda, Indian Bank, SBI, Punjab National Bank,

Table 2.2. PTE Scores of the DMUs.

DMUs	Mean of PTE Scores of DMUs from 2011 to 2016	Mean of PTE Scores of DMUs from 2017 to 2022
Allahabad Bank[a]	0.925204	–
Andhra Bank[a]	0.9737745	–
Bank of Baroda	1	1
Bank of India	0.964487	0.925267667
Bank of Maharashtra	0.7271325	0.982007667
Bharatiya Mahila Bank Ltd.[a]	1	–
Canara Bank	0.988211	0.901365167
Central Bank of India	0.609827	0.761007833
Corporation Bank[a]	1	–
Dena Bank[a]	0.866222	–
IDBI Bank Limited[b]	1	–
Indian Bank	0.931075167	1
Indian Overseas Bank	0.699538	0.760861
Oriental Bank of Commerce[a]	0.980372333	–
Punjab and Sind Bank	0.999017	0.9874135
Punjab National Bank	0.917999667	1
SBI	1	1
Syndicate Bank[a]	1	–
UCO Bank	1	0.805694167
Union Bank of India	0.998335167	1
United Bank of India[a]	0.755216667	–
Vijaya Bank[a]	0.980559167	–

Source: Authors' calculation.

[a]Banks that have been merged with other banks.

[b]Banks that have been converted into private banks.

and Union Bank of India, indicating high efficiency in their operations. However, some banks exhibit fluctuations in their efficiency scores over the years. For instance, Bank of India's efficiency fluctuates, starting at 1 in 2017, decreasing to around 0.87 in 2020, and slightly improving in subsequent years. Furthermore, the efficiency of Bank of India, Bank of Maharashtra, Canara Bank, and Punjab and Sindh Bank exceeds 90%. However, the efficiency of the remaining banks is currently below 90%, suggesting potential inefficiencies in their resource allocation or operational processes that may need to be addressed.

Authors observe various trends from 2011 to 2016 and 2017 to 2022. Some banks exhibit consistent high efficiency across both time periods, maintaining PTE scores of 1, including Bank of Baroda and SBI. This indicates these banks are operating at maximum efficiency relative to their peers consistently. Meanwhile, Bank of Maharashtra notably increases its efficiency from 0.727 to 0.982, suggesting significant improvement in operational effectiveness. Conversely, UCO Bank experiences a decrease in efficiency from 1 to 0.806, indicating challenges or inefficiencies faced during the latter time period. Other banks such as Bank of India, Canara Bank, and Indian Overseas Bank show mixed trends with slight decreases or increases in their PTE scores. Overall, these shifts in efficiency levels highlight the dynamic nature of the banking industry and the importance of ongoing efforts to enhance operational performance.

Scale efficiencies: Table 2.3 presents SE, which assesses a bank's ability to operate optimally relative to other units in the dataset. SE values are computed by dividing the mean OTE scores by the mean PTE scores. An SE value of 1 indicates that the DMU operates as efficiently as its peers. SE values less than 1 suggest lower efficiency compared to peers, while SE values greater than 1 indicate higher efficiency than peers.

Throughout the study period, there were initially 21 PSBs operating in the Indian market, but by the end of the study, only 12 banks remained. The efficiency of these remaining 12 banks was compared for both the pre- and post-introduction periods to assess any changes over time.

During the period from 2011 to 2016, the analysis of SE reveals notable differences among the listed banks. Bank of Maharashtra stands out with the highest SE of 1.0219, indicating optimal resource utilization and operational efficiency. Conversely, SBI exhibits the lowest SE at 0.6481, suggesting potential inefficiencies in its resource allocation and management practices compared to other banks. Similarly, Punjab National Bank shows a relatively low SE of 0.8160, signaling possible inefficiencies in its operations. On the other hand, banks such as Indian Bank, Indian Overseas Bank, Punjab and Sind Bank, and Union Bank of India demonstrate SE values exceeding 0.96, indicating a relatively high level of efficiency in resource utilization. Canara Bank, Bank of Baroda, and Central Bank of India fall within the range of 0.91–0.97, suggesting moderate to high efficiency in their operations. The variation in SE values across these banks underscores differences in their operational processes, resource allocation strategies, and management efficiency. Overall, the SE analysis provides valuable insights into the operational performance and efficiency levels of these banks during the specified period.

During the period from 2017 to 2022, the SE analysis reveals a spectrum of performance among the listed banks. Indian Bank and Union Bank of India stand out with perfect SE values of 1, indicating optimal resource utilization and operational efficiency. Similarly, Bank of Baroda and Central Bank of India demonstrate very high SE values, with Bank of Baroda nearly reaching perfection at 0.9967, suggesting highly efficient operations. Other banks such as Indian

Table 2.3. Shortfall in Deposits, Advances, and Scale Efficiencies.

Banks	SE (2011–2016)	SE (2017–2022)	RTS	Shortfall Deposits	Shortfall Advances
Bank of Baroda	0.96954	0.996692833	Increasing	0	0
Bank of India	0.970396007	0.967974853	Decreasing	119,082.0766	66,193.48293
Bank of Maharashtra	1.021940522	0.97638698	Decreasing	8,339.101141	10,899.89701
Canara Bank	0.913550345	0.962536641	Increasing	95,077.89673	61,576.2257
Central Bank of India	0.960755263	0.994908068	Increasing	90,401.88419	113,748.2352
Indian Bank	0.99046425	1	Increasing	0	0
Indian Overseas Bank	0.967158086	0.985563942	Increasing	62,085.89135	66,699.0991
Punjab and Sind Bank	0.995131714	0.99020775	Decreasing	0	0
Punjab National Bank	0.816027529	0.983541833	Increasing	0	0
SBI	0.6480515	0.945312833	Increasing	0	0
UCO Bank	0.964686833	0.969528967	Increasing	62,132.79424	62,599.90679
Union Bank of India	0.986820558	1	Increasing	0	0

Source: Authors' calculations.

Overseas Bank, Punjab and Sind Bank, Punjab National Bank, and UCO Bank exhibit SE values above 0.98, indicating a relatively high level of efficiency in resource utilization. Canara Bank, Bank of Maharashtra, and SBI fall within the range of 0.945–0.976, suggesting moderate to high efficiency in their operations during the specified period. The variations in SE values across the banks highlight differences in operational processes, resource allocation strategies, and management efficiency. This analysis provides valuable insights into the performance and efficiency levels of these banks, offering opportunities for further examination and improvement in operational practices.

RTS: RTS is provided in Table 2.3; it gives insights into how a bank's output responds to a proportional increase in all inputs. If a bank exhibits "Increasing" RTS, it means that its output grows more than proportionally with an increase in inputs, indicating economies of scale. This suggests that as the bank expands its operations and invests more resources, it becomes increasingly efficient in generating output. Conversely, "Decreasing" RTS imply that output increases less than proportionally with input increases, signaling diseconomies of scale. In such cases, the bank may experience inefficiencies or operational challenges as it grows larger. Finally, "Constant" RTS indicates that output increases proportionally with input increases, suggesting a stable relationship between input and output. This implies that the bank maintains consistent efficiency levels regardless of changes in input levels, providing a balanced and sustainable operational framework. Understanding RTS is crucial for banks to optimize resource allocation, improve efficiency, and sustain long-term growth strategies.

The study has found from analysis the following:

- Banks such as Bank of Baroda, Indian Bank, Indian Overseas Bank, Punjab National Bank, SBI, UCO Bank, and Union Bank of India show increasing RTS for the period 2017–2022. This suggests that these banks are experiencing economies of scale, where increasing their inputs results in greater output increases, indicating efficient utilization of resources at a larger scale.
- Central Bank of India and Canara Bank also show increasing RTS for the later period, indicating efficiency gains from scaling up operations.
- However, Bank of India, Bank of Maharashtra, and Punjab and Sind Bank exhibit decreasing RTS during the 2017–2022 period, implying that increasing their scale of operations may lead to diminishing efficiency or diseconomies of scale.
- Punjab National Bank, despite having increasing SE in both periods, experienced a shift from decreasing to increasing RTS, suggesting improvements in efficiency despite scaling up operations.
- SBI shows a significant improvement in SE from the earlier period (2011–2016) to the later period (2017–2022), indicating enhanced operational efficiency over time.

Banks exhibiting increasing RTS typically operate efficiently, as their output grows more than proportionally with increases in inputs. This efficiency suggests that they are effectively utilizing resources and may find opportunities for further expansion or resource allocation. However, banks facing decreasing RTS may encounter challenges in maintaining efficiency as they scale up operations. These banks should consider reassessing their operational strategies to address inefficiencies and optimize resource utilization. By doing so, they can improve efficiency and avoid potential pitfalls associated with inefficient scaling, ensuring sustainable growth and operational effectiveness in the competitive banking industry.

Shortfall: Table 2.3 represents the shortfall in terms of deposits and advances, indicating the difference between actual deposits/advances and the optimal level according to the model. Among the 12 banks, 6 banks have no shortfall to report. However, banks like Bank of India, Canara Bank, and Central Bank of India exhibit significant shortfalls in both deposits and advances, suggesting a potential need for adjustments in their operations to align with the model's recommendations.

Findings

The analysis began with 21 banks in 2011, which decreased to 12 banks in 2022 due to mergers. In the CCR model, authors found that 33% of banks were efficient in the initial period, increasing to 50% in 2022. Interestingly, the mean efficiency score improved from 1 out of 22 banks being efficient in the pre-introduction of AI period to 2 out of 12 banks being efficient in the post-introduction period. This suggests that while mergers may have contributed to efficiency gains, the introduction of AI technologies may have also played a role in enhancing the overall efficiency of PSBs. These findings highlight the importance of both structural changes and technological advancements in driving efficiency improvements within the banking sector. In summary, the CCR model analysis provides valuable insights into the efficiency of PSBs, highlighting both strong performers and those with potential for improvement.

The observation that the BCC model demonstrates a decrease in the efficiency of banks from 61% in 2011 to 53% in 2022 suggests that while some banks may have become less efficient over time, there could be various factors at play influencing this trend. However, it is noteworthy that despite the decrease in overall efficiency, the mean of PTE scores improved from 31% in the pre-introduction period to 41% in the post-introduction period of AI. This indicates that although the overall efficiency of banks may have declined, there was an improvement in the technical efficiency component, which measures the efficiency of converting inputs into outputs while holding the scale of operations constant. These findings suggest that while there may be challenges impacting overall efficiency, such as changes in market dynamics or regulatory environments, the introduction of AI technologies may have positively impacted the technical efficiency of banks, enabling them to better utilize their resources and improve operational performance.

The analysis of SE reveals that out of the 12 banks considered, 9 banks have shown an improvement in their relative efficiency over the specified period. This improvement suggests that these banks have made strides in optimizing their resource utilization and operational processes, resulting in higher efficiency levels.

However, it's important to note that the remaining three banks have experienced a decrease in efficiency. These banks may benefit from further analysis to identify areas where operational improvements can be made to enhance their SE. This analysis could involve a detailed examination of their operational processes, resource allocation strategies, and management practices to pinpoint inefficiencies and implement targeted improvements.

By identifying and addressing areas of inefficiency, these banks can work toward enhancing their operational performance and ultimately improving their overall SE. This proactive approach can help them remain competitive in the market and better meet the evolving needs of their customers.

Conclusion and Policy Recommendations

The adoption of AI technologies has indeed had a positive impact on the efficiency of PSBs, as highlighted by the results obtained through the DEA methodology. By considering variables such as cash in hand, fixed assets, staff numbers, deposits, and advances, the study provides a comprehensive assessment of the banks' operational efficiency. The observed improvement in performance from the pre- to post-introduction of AI suggests that PSBs have become more proficient at utilizing their resources to generate deposits and advances, ultimately enhancing their overall efficiency. While AI implementation likely played a significant role in this improvement, other factors, such as bank consolidation through mergers, may have also contributed to the observed efficacy. With the reduction in the number of banks from 21 in 2011 to 12 in 2022, synergies resulting from mergers could have led to operational streamlining and efficiency gains. These findings underscore the importance of AI adoption and strategic restructuring in bolstering the efficiency of PSBs and enhancing their competitiveness in the dynamic banking landscape.

The advent of advanced technologies like AI, cloud computing, and blockchain has transformed traditional banking, optimizing processes, reducing costs, and enhancing customer satisfaction. AI-powered chatbots and virtual assistants revolutionize customer interactions by providing real-time assistance, automating tasks, and improving efficiency. While AI adoption enhances the efficiency of PSBs in India, it poses challenges like potential job losses. To address this, the government and RBI should invest in AI research and promote its use for efficiency and inclusion. Collaboration among policymakers, academics, and industry experts is essential to foster innovation and establish rules ensuring transparency, fairness, and data privacy.

References

Agarwala, N., Maity, S., & Sahu, T. N. (2023). Efficiency of Indian banks in fostering financial inclusion: An emerging economy perspective. *Journal of Financial Services Marketing*, 1–13. https://doi.org/10.1057/S41264-022-00203-7/TABLES/7

Alam, T., & Rastgi, R. (2019). Trend analysis of cost efficiency for the pharmaceutical industry: A DEA approach. *Management Science Letters*, *9*(5), 749–754.

Ashta, A., & Herrmann, H. (2021). Artificial intelligence and fintech: An overview of opportunities and risks for banking, investments, and microfinance. *Strategic Change*, *30*(3), 211–222.

Banker, R. D., Charnes, A., & Cooper, W. W. (1984). Some models for estimating technical and scale inefficiencies in data envelopment analysis. *Management Science*, *30*(9), 1078–1092.

Bhattacharyya, A., Lovell, C. A. K., & Sahay, P. (1997). The impact of liberalization on the productive efficiency of Indian commercial banks. *European Journal of Operational Research*, *98*(2), 332–345. https://doi.org/10.1016/S0377-2217(96)00351-7

Charnes, A., Cooper, W. W., & Rhodes, E. (1978). Measuring the efficiency of decision making units. *European Journal of Operational Research*, *2*(6), 429–444.

Cooper, W. W., Seiford, L. M., & Tone, K. (2007). *Data envelopment analysis: A comprehensive text with models, applications, references and DEA-solver software* (Vol. 2). Springer.

Das, A., & Ghosh, S. (2006). Financial deregulation and efficiency: An empirical analysis of Indian banks during the post reform period. *Review of Financial Economics*, *15*(3), 193–221. https://doi.org/10.1016/J.RFE.2005.06.002

Elcholiqi, A., & Musdholifah, A. (2020). Chatbot in Bahasa Indonesia using NLP to provide banking information. *IJCCS (Indonesian Journal of Computing and Cybernetics Systems)*, *14*(1), 91–102.

Golany, B., & Roll, Y. (1989). An application procedure for DEA. *Omega*, *17*(3), 237–250.

Hassan, M., Aziz, L. A.-R., & Andriansyah, Y. (2023). The role artificial intelligence in modern banking: An exploration of AI-driven approaches for enhanced fraud prevention, risk management, and regulatory compliance. *Reviews of Contemporary Business Analytics*, *6*(1), 110–132.

Jakšič, M., & Marinč, M. (2019). Relationship banking and information technology: The role of artificial intelligence and FinTech. *Risk Management*, *21*, 1–18.

Königstorfer, F., & Thalmann, S. (2020). Applications of artificial intelligence in commercial banks – A research agenda for behavioral finance. *Journal of Behavioral and Experimental Finance*, *27*, 100352. https://doi.org/10.1016/j.jbef.2020.100352

Kumar, S., & Gulati, R. (2008). An examination of technical, pure technical, and scale efficiencies in Indian public sector banks using data envelopment analysis. *Eurasian Journal of Business and Economics*, *1*(2), 33–69.

Madakam, S., Holmukhe, R. M., & Jaiswal, D. K. (2019). The future digital work force: Robotic process automation (RPA). *JISTEM – Journal of Information Systems and Technology Management*, *16*, e201916001.

Maity, S., & Sahu, T. N. (2018). Role of public and private sector banks in financial inclusion in India–an empirical investigation using DEA. *SCMS Journal of Indian Management*, *15*(4), 62–73.

Maity, S., & Sahu, T. N. (2020). Role of public sector banks towards financial inclusion during pre and post introduction of PMJDY: A study on efficiency review. *Rajagiri Management Journal*, *14*(2), 95–105. https://doi.org/10.1108/RAMJ-03-2020-0009

Malali, A. B., & Gopalakrishnan, S. (2020). Application of artificial intelligence and its powered technologies in the Indian banking and financial industry: An overview. *IOSR Journal of Humanities and Social Science*, *25*(4), 55–60.

Malini, A., & Menon, D. G. (2017). IEEE (Ed.). Technological innovations in the banking sector in India: An analysis. In *2017 International conference on technological advancements in power and energy (TAP energy)*. *IEEE Xplore*. (pp. 1–5).

Manser Payne, E. H., Peltier, J., & Barger, V. A. (2021). Enhancing the value co-creation process: Artificial intelligence and mobile banking service platforms. *Journal of Research in Interactive Marketing*, *15*(1), 68–85.

RBI. (2024). *Reserve Bank of India – Database*. https://www.rbi.org.in/scripts/bs_viewcontent.aspx?Id=2900

Saha, A., & Ravisankar, T. S. (2000). Rating of Indian commercial banks: A DEA approach. *European Journal of Operational Research*, *124*(1), 187–203. https://doi.org/10.1016/S0377-2217(99)00167-8

Subudhi, S. (2019). Banking on artificial intelligence: Opportunities & challenges for banks in India. *International Journal of Research in Commerce, Economics & Management*, *9*(7), 1–35.

Suresh, A., & Rani, N. J. (2020). Role of artificial intelligence (AI) in the Indian banking scenario. *Journal of Information Technology & Economic Development*, *11*(2), 1.

Umamaheswari, S., & Valarmathi, A. (2023). Role of artificial intelligence in the banking sector. *Journal of Survey in Fisheries Sciences*, *10*(4S), 2841–2849.

Vinoth, S. (2022). Artificial intelligence and transformation to the digital age in Indian banking industry – A case study. *Artificial Intelligence*, *13*(1), 689–695.

Chapter 3

Effect of Artificial Intelligence (AI) on GDP Growth of India in 2022: An Analysis

Suman Chakraborty[a] *and Riddhima Panda*[b]

[a]*Department of Economics, Raja Narendra Lal Khan Women's College, India*
[b]*Department of Economics, The Heritage College, India*

Abstract

In this present era, artificial intelligence (AI) is a buzz word. With the increase in hype for AI and its increasing rate of application worldwide, it has raised a debate on the impact of AI on increase in growth rate, productivity and unemployment. Having said that, studies have shown AI is still at an infant stage. With the increase in the ability to understand context and reply in human language, it has surely paved its way towards an impeccable journey of transforming an economy with the increase in productivity, gross domestic product (GDP) and economic growth. The advancement may cause some setbacks in terms of labour force participation with higher demand for labour with certain skill set to be able to work with AI and hence increasing the unemployment rate as well as creating a widening gap between developing and developed countries. In this chapter, we aim to determine the effect of AI on GDP growth of India for the year 2022 and have selected terms of trade (ToT), human development index (HDI) and per capita real GDP for the year 2022 to understand its overall impact using secondary data. The results of the analysis show that ToT, global artificial intelligence (GAI) index, and HDI as explanatory variables significantly explain the variation in per capita real GDP.

Keywords: AI; AI index; GDP; economic growth; productivity; unemployment

Artificial Intelligence in Business and Society: Global Insights, 37–47

Published under exclusive licence by Emerald Publishing Limited
doi:10.1108/978-1-83708-022-920261008

Introduction

AI is the theory of computer system that is capable of performing activity like humans. It is the science of machine that requires human intelligence such as visual, speech detection, translation of language, etc. The four main types of AI are reactive machines, limited memory machines, theory of mind and self-awareness. AI can help in boosting productivity and economic growth through technological revolution, yet there is a possibility that it could replace jobs, hence deepening the issue of unemployment and income disparity in the world economy.

According to the reports of International Monetary Fund (IMF), approximately 60% of the employment in advanced countries is exposed to AI. World economy has witnessed technological revolution from time to time but what set AI different from history is its ability to replace high-skilled jobs, thus making advanced nations more prone to the negative impact of AI than other emerging economies. Again, according to IMF, 40% of employment in developing countries and 26% of employment in low-income countries are exposed to the AI. Thus, the immediate risk from AI is less in these economies compared to the advanced countries. It also shows the lack of skilled workers and infrastructural development which fails to reap the benefit of AI, which could further worsen inequality among nations.

AI is integrated into business world undermining the need for policymakers. Thus, IMF has developed an AI preparedness index to estimate various categories such as human capital and labour market policies, digital infrastructure, innovation, ethics and various regulations. The human capital and labour market category evaluates years of schooling, migration related to employment and job opportunities. Adaptability to digital business world, strong governance and enforcement is assessed through regulations and ethics component of the AI preparedness index. Upon assessing 125 countries based on these four components of AI preparedness index, the result reveals that the wealthy nations are well equipped and ready to harness the benefit of AI compared to the low-income countries.

The highest scores on the countries were found to be in the United States, Singapore and Denmark on the basis of all the four components used to evaluate the AI preparedness index. According to the results assessed by IMF through the AI preparedness index, it can be concluded that wealthy and developed nations should strategise in developing solid policy frameworks for innovations and integration in AI to help nurturing a safe environment while keeping the public trust intact. Whereas in case of emerging and low-income economies, it is important to focus on investment in digitalisation and building a strong and competent workforce.

We know that an increase in investment in technological advancement such as computer, internet, venture capital, etc. shows an upward trend in the economic growth during the first decade of the present century. AI can also be compared in a similar way with facts and evidence that an investment made in this sector will give a boost to the economic growth with increase in the productivity of labour and capital in the future ahead. In a paper by (Nicholas, Christensen, Gallagher, Mate, Greg, 2016) opined that information technology (IT) investment, use of broadband, use of mobile phones and robotics are considered as four major benchmarks of technological advancement of AI which have shown some prominent economic impacts.

AI does not have predetermined future and can adapt to many directions. Apart from economic impact, AI can also impact other areas such as defence, culture as well as politics. We can try to balance the positive and negative impact of AI on macroeconomic areas such as labour productivity and growth. Despite the rapidly improving technical capabilities of AI, its adoption by businesses may continue to be slow and confined to large firms (Zolas et al., 2021). Moreover, the displaced worker can end up in less dynamic jobs enhancing the issue of underemployment and slowing down the overall economic progress in case of advanced countries. But there can be an alternate scenario if AI is used to upgrade the process of economic growth in places of requirement rather that substituting those jobs and labour force which are already skilled and showing progress. AI might be applied to a substantial share of the tasks done by most workers (Eloundou et al., 2023) and massively boost productivity in those tasks. Instead of treating AI as a substitute, AI can be complementary with the already existing skilled workers freeing them to work on creativity and innovation. This will result in a higher level of sustained economic growth in the world economy. This approach will even help in decreasing the income inequality in world economy instead of deepening income inequality by substituting jobs with AI. AI can be used as assistant in work and help employees to get better at their jobs and level up their efficiency.

Cornelli et al. (2023) have explored the link between AI investment and income inequality and explained that higher income households have seen an increase in share of income while low-income households have seen their share decrease. But their study has also revealed a shift to high-tech services resulted in greater productivity associated with AI investment. Kathuria et al. (2020) explained that there is a potential transformation in AI's ability to diffuse itself in diverse range of sectors starting from manufacturing, production lines, supply chain management, transforming quality control and high-quality customer engagement. It will also help in developing the sectors that have taken back seat such as agriculture sector in low-income countries especially will see a boost and hence economic growth. According to Chen et al. (2016), IT investment, use of broadband, use of mobile phones and robotics are considered as four major benchmarks of technological advancement of AI which have shown some prominent economic impact. Bamatraf et al. (2021) explained that traditionally economic growth model demonstrates the impact of capital, labour factors and technological progress as key determinants of economic growth, but in recent scenario, AI is a new factor of economic growth which acts as a catalyst in the process of economic growth.

Today's society has a variety of applications for AI. It is increasingly crucial in modern times because it can efficiently solve complex problems across multiple industries, including healthcare, entertainment, finance and education. AI is enhancing our daily lives, making them more convenient and efficient.

AI has the potential to automate a wide range of occupations, including intellectual positions, in contrast to earlier industrial revolutions. However, there aren't enough positions available to swiftly hire displaced workers without requiring extensive retraining. Advances in AI-based speech recognition have made personal assistants and automated voice searches useful. These systems include Google Now, Alexa, Cortana and Siri. AI will eventually replace workers in positions like personal assistants and foreign language translators as these technologies advance. Wall Street traders and other traditional high-paying occupations may also lose their employment.

The objective of numerous researchers, engineers and entrepreneurs has been to develop intelligence that is equivalent to human intelligence, either openly or implicitly. Human-like artificial intelligence (HLAI) offers advantages such as heightened productivity, more leisure time, and, most importantly, a deeper comprehension of our own minds. As technology improves, machines can replace human labour, leading to a decline in workers' economic and political influence and greater reliance on those who control the technology. Conversely, if AI is designed to enhance human abilities rather than replicate them, humans can maintain the ability to demand a portion of the value produced. Furthermore, augmentation leads to the development of new capabilities, products and services, ultimately creating significantly more value than HLAI alone. While both types of AI can be highly advantageous, there is currently a disproportionate emphasis on automation over augmentation among technologists, business leaders, and policymakers (Brynjolfsson, 2022).

The use of AI is expected to conserve resources and reduce the need for labour, which could diminish the competitive edge of numerous developing nations, weaken their trade conditions and possibly lead to a decline in their overall welfare. The emergence of natural monopolies is often associated with information technologies like AI, leading to a few dominant firms based in powerful countries but catering to the global economy. Typically, the market's selection of the speed and path of technological advancement is not ideal, presenting the opportunity to guide AI and other innovations in ways that enhance worldwide social well-being, such as environmental preservation and the creation of fulfilling job prospects (Korinek & Stiglitz, 2021).

There has been a great deal of research on AI and its impact on economy that is emerging with substantial benefit that could increase productivity and boost the GDP growth rate. As most of the research till date has mostly neglected the developing economies and stayed focused with developed economies and could not reflect properly the impact of macroeconomic components on GDP through development in AI. It is also important to establish the relation between microeconomic components of world with impact of AI, which is completely neglected and has not been made clear yet. Thus, making a conclusion and creating a negative impact of AI on GDP is not significant. An in-depth analysis with special emphasis on all aspects of components of society should be taken into consideration before concluding about the impact of AI on factor productivity, GDP growth, unemployment and economic growth.

Based on the above backdrop in this chapter, we are trying to analyse the relation between real GDP and investment in AI. GAI index score of different countries is taken as proxy in place of amount of AI investment.

Database and Methodology

Secondary data relating to per capita real GDP have been collected from Asian Development Bank (ABD) report, 2022. Data related to export and import are collected from International Financial Statistics (IFS, 2022). Here, we have selected 14 different countries on the basis of factors of economic growth and development of each country for the analysis of this chapter for the year 2022. These are Indonesia, India, Spain, Hong Kong, Japan, Australia, the United States, the United Kingdom, Denmark, Germany, Canada, Malaysia, Brazil and Norway. Simple statistical techniques have been used to analyse the existing chapter.

To examine the factor relationship of dependent and explanatory (independent) variables, regression analysis is used wherever it is necessary. Regression analysis is the most important way to estimate the exact relationship between a dependent variable and explanatory (independent) variables. Now, an equation of the multiple linear regression line can be written as $Y = (a + b_1X_1 + b_2X_2)$; here Y is the dependent variable and X_1 and X_2 are the explanatory variable. The adjusted R^2 and F of the estimated regression equation of this model are such that the relevant regression model is fitted to the data set.

To analyse the effect of AI on per capita real GDP through investment in artificial investment, we use the regression model. Here, we have taken per capita real GDP of 14 countries (RG) as a dependent variable and the components that can influence economic growth and development such as percentage of value of export to import (ToT), GAI index score, and HDI as explanatory variables for the selected countries.

In our analysis, we can write the regression model as

$$(\text{RG}) = \beta_0 + \beta_1\,\text{ToT} + \beta_2\,\text{GAI} + \beta_3\,\text{HDI} + e$$

where β_0 is the constant and β_1, β_2 and β_3 are the coefficients of the variables ToT, GAI index, and HDI, respectively. The above equation is estimated by ordinary least squares (OLS) method.

Status of Terms of Trade Across Different Selected Countries in the Year 2022

ToT for the year 2022 is calculated by taking the ratio of price of exports to price of imports. The selected 14 countries for the study are namely, Indonesia, Hong Kong, Japan, India, Spain, Australia, Norway, Brazil, Malaysia, the United States, Canada, Germany, the United Kingdom and Denmark.

The value of export for the year 2022 is maximum in case of Indonesia with \$2,85,83,16,400.00 followed by Japan with \$10,82,15,000.00, then India with export values \$3,64,86,200.00. India is followed by Hong Kong and the United States with respective export values \$51,13,200.00 and \$25,05,735.00. Export values in Denmark is less than that in Germany with \$16,00,740.23 and \$15,35,585.05, respectively. Norway with export value \$12,69,747.66 is followed by Malaysia, the

United Kingdom, Canada, Australia and Spain with respective export values as $11,26,660.80, $7,15,449.00, $6,88,343.50, $6,09,610.00 and $4,27,670.60. Brazil with $1,76,610.80 has lowest export value out of the selected 14 countries.

Import value is maximum in Indonesia with $2,41,57,60,100.00 followed by Japan, Germany and Denmark with import values $10,95,87,200.00, $1,410,944.45 and $1,362,719.25, respectively. Denmark is followed by Malaysia, India, Norway and Hong Kong with import values $1,043,918.16, $4,04,47,900.00, $987,479.48 and $49,97,388.00, respectively. Import value in the United States is less than that of Hong Kong followed by Canada, the United Kingdom, Australia and Spain. Import values in the United States in the year 2022 is $3,431,269.8 followed by $785,120.3, $753,962, $493,166 and $366,482.6, respectively. Brazil has the lowest import values with $175,561.4.

Value of export is more than the value of import in Indonesia and has the maximum ToT in the year 2022 among the 14 selected countries in this study with 118.3195467. It is followed by Norway, Australia, Denmark, Spain, Germany, Malaysia, Hong Kong and Brazil. It is observed that the value of export and value of import are least among the 14 countries selected for this study, but since the export and import values are approximately same, the ratio of export value to import value is 100.5977396 which is greater than the countries like Japan, the United Kingdom, India, Canada and the United States. The United States is with the minimum ToT because of greater disparity between the values of exports and imports. The value of imports in comparison to value of exports in the United States is much higher as a result the ratio of value of exports to that of the value of imports is less in the year 2022. The ratio of value of export to import in the year 2022 is 73.02646385.

Status of Real GDP Across Different Countries in the Year 2022

Real per capita GDP in the year 2022 is highest for Norway followed by the United States with $79,442.53345 and $62,789.12792, respectively. The third highest per capita GDP is $60,993.64125 in Australia followed by $60,345.55732 in Denmark. The United Kingdom is at the fifth position among the 14 countries selected with $47,923.48224 followed by followed by Canada, Hong Kong and Germany. Positions 9th, 10th, 11th and 12th are taken by Japan, Spain, Malaysia and Brazil, respectively. Last two positions are taken by Indonesia and India, respectively, with per capita real GDP 4,073.610494 and 2,089.734383.

Status of Human Development Index in the Year 2022

The estimates of HDI are collected from United Nations Development Programme (UNDP) report 2022. Among the 14 countries selected for the study, Norway ranks number 1 with HDI score 0.966. Norway has ranked second among all the countries of the world with an increase of 0.002 points in HDI score from 2021. Hong Kong is at number 2 among the 14 selected countries with HDI score of 0.956 in 2022. A decline can be seen in the HDI score from that of 2021 by 0.003 points followed by Denmark at position 3 with HDI score 0.95

in 2022 with a progress in HDI score by 0.005 points in 2022 from 2021. In the world list of HDI scores, Australia is at number 4 followed by Denmark at position 5. Germany is at number 4 in our study of 14 countries. Germany has ranked number 7 in the world report with an improvement of 0.002 points in its score from 2021. The HDI score of Germany in 2022 is 0.95 followed by Australia on the fifth position among the selected 14 countries with HDI score 0.946. There is a decline in the score of HDI by 0.003 points in 2022 from 2021. HDI score of the United Kingdom is less than that of Australia with HDI score 0.94 and is placed at number 6 and has shown a progress by 0.009 points than in 2021. Seventh place is occupied by Canada in our list of 14 countries for the study. The HDI score is 0.935 with a progress of 0.01 points followed by the United States at the eighth position and HDI score 0.927. In the world list, the United States is at number 20. The 9th and 10th positions are taken by Japan and Spain with HDI score 0.92 and 0.911, respectively, in 2022. HDI score of Japan and Spain is twenty-four and twenty-seven in the world list respectively followed by Malaysia and Brazil with HDI score 0.807 and 0.76, respectively. Thirteenth rank is given to Indonesia among the 14 countries selected for the study, and the HDI score is 0.713. It is at 112 in the world report. The lowest rank is given to India with HDI score 0.644. It ranks 134 in the world report.

Construction of Global Artificial Intelligence Index (GAI) and Its Status Among Different Selected Countries in the Year 2022

GAI assesses a nation's capacity for AI using an array of indicators. The index takes use of 111 indicators which have been collected from 62 governments and 28 various private and public data sources. These are broken down into seven smaller pillars: government strategy, research and development, talent, infrastructure and the operating environment. These metrics are grouped by associative themes around the three main pillars: investment, innovation and implementation.

AI is a powerful tool that can transform various sectors, including business, government and society. To measure a country's AI capacity, it is important to understand its ability to harness such power. The GAI index organises itself around the concept of capacity, which refers to the amount of something that a system can contain or produce. In essence, increased capacity means an increased ability to generate and maintain AI solutions both now and in the future. At a national level, greater adoption of AI results in more active systems, initiatives and personnel, and the quality of these factors is also improving.

The GAI index assesses capacity applying composite indicators, which combine a lot of data to a collection of numbers that effectively reflect the information's underlying complexity. It helps in evaluating the ability of a nation to set up, supervise and upkeep AI systems in a way that is fair, safe and productive. In the GAI index, the United States remains at the top, with China coming in second. This year, Singapore surpassed the United Kingdom, which dropped to the fourth place and secured the third place. The final country in the top five is Canada. Due to a number of variables, including highly skilled personnel, developments in AI research and innovation and significant private funding for AI start-ups, the United States obtained a perfect score of 100, excelling all the three main groups: Implementation, Innovation, and Investment. The United States has a highly skilled workforce that is dedicated to research and development in AI, making it a global leader in this area. Furthermore, the United States has a large number of AI start-ups that receive significant funding from private investors, which contributes to its top position in the ranking.

With an effective innovation component, China scored 62, while Singapore moved up to the third position thanks to clear government initiatives. Because of their inadequate infrastructure and low levels of investment, Nigeria, Sri Lanka and Kenya received the lowest scores. In the GAI index, the United States remains at the top, with China coming in the second place. This year, Singapore overtook the United Kingdom, which fell to the fourth place, to take the third place. The United States achieved a flawless 100, performing exceptionally in all three primary areas: implementation, innovation, and investment, due to numerous elements including well-trained professionals, progress in AI studies and creativity and substantial private investment.

China achieved a score of 62, demonstrating considerable strength in innovation, whereas Singapore's clear governmental endeavours elevated it to the third position. Nigeria, Sri Lanka and Kenya received the lowest scores because of insufficient infrastructure and minimal investment levels.

Singapore has been investing heavily in research and development in the field of AI, with its spending on AI research being 18 times larger than that of the United States in relation to GDP. The country also hosts at least 270 active AI start-ups per million people. The weightings for each pillar are distributed as follows: talent 15%, infrastructure 11%, operating environment 6%, research 26%, development 14%, government strategy 4% and commercial ventures 24%. The aim of weighting for completeness is to guarantee the dependability of the data utilised in establishing the overall scores of the GAI index, by lessening the influence of untrustworthy data on the rankings. The weightings for each pillar are as follows: talent 15%, infrastructure 11%, operating environment 6%, research 26%, development 14%, government strategy 4% and commercial ventures 24% (Table 3.1). The purpose of weighting for comprehensiveness is to ensure the reliability of the information used to determine the overall scoring of the GAI index, by reducing the impact of unreliable data on the rankings.

Results and Analysis of the Model

In this section, we analyse the impact of AI on per capita real GDP through multiple regression analysis. The regression equation concerning per capita real GDP (RG) as a dependent variable and ToT, GAI index, and HDI as independent variables shows that the variation in per capita real GDP (RG) is significantly explained by the value of ToT, GAI index, and HDI as explanatory variables to the extent of 80.68%; this means that the model has a very high predictive ability (Table 3.2).

Table 3.1. The Weightage of Pillars.

Pillars	Sub-pillars	Weightage	
Implementation	Talent	15%	Focuses on ability of skilled practitioner in artificial solutions
	Infrastructure	11%	Assesses the reliability and scale of access infrastructure from electricity and internet to supercomputing capabilities
	Opening environment	6%	Focuses on regulatory context and public opinion on AI
Innovation	Research	26%	Looks at the extent of specialist research and researchers, including number of publications and citations in credible academic journals
	Development	14%	Focuses on development of fundamental platforms and algorithms upon which innovative AI project relies
Investment	Government strategy	4%	Gauges the depth of the commitment from national governments to AI, investigating spending commitments and national strategies
	Commercial	24%	Focuses on the level of startup activity, investment and business initiatives based on AI

Source: Authors using Tortoise GAI index.

It is observed that coefficients of the variable values of GAI index and HDI are significant at 5%, and the coefficient of variable value of ToT is significant at 10% level of significance. The whole model's significance level is at 5% level of significance. Hence, it can be stated that the combined effects of the value of the explanatory variables, that is, ToT, GAI index, and HDI, in the model have significant effects on per capita real GDP in our study period 2022 (Table 3.2).

Table 3.2. Regression Results for the Year 2022.

Adjusted R^2	F Change	Significant F Change	Coefficients	Constant	Variables	t' Values	Significance
0.8068	19.10	0.0002	587.2146	−183,535.3	ToT	1.99	0.075
			573.6227		GAI	2.47	0.033
			159,225.3		HDI	4.77	0.001
Estimated regression equation: (RG) = 587.2146ToT*** + 573.6227GAI** + 159,225.3HDI* – 183,535.3							

Source: Authors' own calculations.

*, **, and ***, respectively, indicate the statistically significant results at 1%, 5%, and 10% levels of significance.

Conclusion

AI is a trendy term in the modern world. The discourse surrounding the effects of AI on growth rates, productivity, and unemployment has intensified due to the growing hype surrounding the technology and its growing global applicability. Nevertheless, research indicates that AI is still in its infancy. The improved capacity to comprehend context and respond in natural language has undoubtedly cleared the path for a flawless transformation of an economy marked by higher GDP, economic growth, and productivity. We are aware that throughout the first 10 years of the 21st century, there was an upward trend in economic growth, which was reflected in the increase in investments made in technological advancements such as computers, the internet, venture capital, etc. Similar comparisons can be made between AI and data, and evidence showing that investments in this field will undoubtedly drive economic growth in the future by raising capital and labour productivity. Robotics, mobile phone use, internet use and IT investment are four important indicators of AI's technological growth and have demonstrated some significant economic effects. However, because of the increased need for workers with a certain skill set to work with AI, this breakthrough may have some negative effects on labour force participation. As a result, the unemployment rate may rise and the gap between developed and developing nations may expand.

The use of multiple regression analysis to examine the effect of AI on real GDP per capita validates the hypothesis. The model has a very high predictive ability, as evidenced by the regression equation with per capita real GDP (RG) as the dependent variable and ToT, GAI index, and HDI as the independent variables. The results show that ToT, GAI index, and HDI as explanatory variables significantly explain the variation in per capita real GDP (RG).

References

Bamatraf, S., Amouri, L., El-Haggar, N., & Moneer, A. (2021). Exploring the socio-economic implications of artificial intelligence from higher education student's perspective. *International Journal of Advanced Computer Science and Applications, 12*(6), 369–376. https://doi.org/10.14569/IJACSA.2021.0120641

Brynjolfsson, E. (2022). The Turing trap: The promise & peril of human-like artificial intelligence. *Daedalus, 151*(2), 272–287.

Chen, N., Christensen, L., Gallagher, K., Mate, R., & Rafert, G. (2016). Global economic impacts associated with artificial intelligence. Analysis Group, 1–23.

Cornelli, G., Frost J., & Mishra, S. (2023). *Artificial intelligence, services globalisation and income inequality* [BIS Working Paper 1135]. Bank for International Settlements.

Kathuria, R., Kedia, M., & Kapilavai, S. (2020). *Implications of AI on the Indian economy* [Report 20-r-03]. Indian Council for Research on International Economic Relations (ICRIER).

Korinek, A., & Stiglitz, J. (2021). *Artificial intelligence, globalization, and strategies for economic development* [NBER Working Paper No. 28453]. NBER.

Zolas, N., Kroff, Z., Brynjolfsson, E., McElheran, K., Beede, D. N., Buffington, C., Goldschlag, N., Foster, L., & Dinlersoz, E. (2021). *Advanced technologies adoption and use by U.S. firms: Evidence from the annual business survey* [NBER Working Paper 28290]. National Bureau of Economic Research. https://www.nber.org/papers/w28290

Chapter 4

South Asian Labour Market Dynamics in the Era of Artificial Intelligence

Ashish Thakur

VV Giri National Labour Institute, Noida, India

Abstract

South Asia, with the largest workforce in the world, has started leading the way in the transformation of labour markets owing to the adoption of artificial intelligence (AI). The region's enormous youth population and glaring skill gaps, however, present serious issues that need intentional measures to match workforce capacities with the changing labour market. The influence of AI adoption on employment across a range of skill levels in South Asian countries is examined in this study. Using correlational analysis, it looks at patterns in the relationship between AI preparedness and employment in different skill-level occupations. The study draws attention to differences in workforce adaptation and the difficulties associated with changes in the labour market such as the possibility of employment polarization and widening gaps. The report also looks at how AI could encourage regional economic growth and highlights the necessity for reskilling programmes to deal with labour shifts brought on by AI adoption. The results highlight the significance of human resource investments, customized regulations, and regional collaboration in reducing workforce disruptions and utilizing AI's potential. In the AI-driven era, this research offers useful insights to support South Asian nations in achieving equitable growth and socioeconomic advancement.

Keywords: South Asia; artificial intelligence; employment; skill; job polarization; regional cooperation

Artificial Intelligence in Business and Society: Global Insights, 49–66

Published under exclusive licence by Emerald Publishing Limited
doi:10.1108/978-1-83708-022-920261011

Introduction

Technology has consistently been considered a force for development and capable of revolutionizing economies. The industrial revolutions of the previous centuries such as the mechanization of physical labour in the 18th century,[1] the emergence of regular wage employment in the 19th century[2] and digitization of manufacturing jobs in the 20th century[3] have had influence both positively and negatively on the employment of the low-skilled workers. Nevertheless, with the features of AI and digital technologies, the recent industrial revolution (fourth industrial revolution (IR4)) has become more complex and impacting even jobs at the higher end of the skill spectrum globally in both developed and developing economies.[4] This chapter examines the interaction of AI and labour market dynamics in the South Asian region.

The population of South Asian countries has been significantly restructured in terms of its distribution across a range of economic and non-economic activities in the present period of economic liberalization and changing demographics. In addition to the 712 million people (in the working-age group of 15+) who were employed in 2021,[5] South Asia is anticipated to have the largest supply of workforce in future years. Around 643 million individuals in the Asia-Pacific are between the ages of 15 and 24, making up around 53% of the world's young population. In 2021, there were 255 million youth in India alone, making up around 39% of the 643 million people living in the Asia-Pacific region. Furthermore, with approximately 100,000 youths joining the workforce every day, South Asia has the most noticeable youth labour force in the world and is home to nearly 1.92 billion people as of 2022.[6] Simultaneously, the skills gap is evident in South Asian nations due to the lack of knowledge and skills that young people possess for future work, as seen by low-quality education and inadequate vocational education.[7] To guarantee the expanding younger labour force's goals are fulfilled and that they become an essential factor in the country's economic growth, sufficient possibilities for earning a good and sustainable living must be offered. Despite providing a window of opportunity in the form of a more youthful, educated, and economically engaged labour force, the demographic makeup of the population may become a serious worry if adequate employment opportunities and developing skill demands are not made accessible to them. Hence, the study further looks

[1]https://users.nber.org/~confer/2006/SEGs06/allen.pdf

[2]https://inctpped.ie.ufrj.br/spiderweb/pdf_4/Great_Transformation.pdf

[3]https://academic.oup.com/qje/article-abstract/118/4/1279/1925105

[4]https://www.sciencedirect.com/science/article/pii/S2773207X24001386

[5]Author's calculation from World Population Prospectus 2022, Population Division, United Nations Department of Economic and Social Affairs (UN DESA).

[6]Author's calculation from World Population Prospectus 2022, Population Division, UN DESA.

[7]https://www.unicef.org/press-releases/more-half-south-asian-youth-are-not-track-have-education-and-skills-necessary

into the job polarization perspective, particularly in the case of India which is the most dominant region in terms of skills outlook.

Technology is the primary force behind improved efficiency and economic strength on a global scale.[8] Recent experience shows that AI and information and communication technology (ICT) can have an enormous positive multiplier effect on both the quantity and the quality of employment, even as it presents obstacles in the short run due to their labour-displacing repercussions.[9] To reap the full benefits from technological advancements and AI, significant efforts must be taken to raise the skill sets of both the current workforce and future employees, as the overall skill levels of South Asian nations remain relatively low. Hence, there is an urgent requirement for the policy ecosystem to facilitate, assess, and expand the institutional structures to impart skill development for improving the standard and certification systems as per the desired labour market demands, particularly in South Asia.

Objectives

Given that South Asia has the world's largest workforce, social and economic advancement requires the implementation of appropriate policies in addition to investments in human resources. In particular, considering the higher number of youth population and the existing skill mismatch, a significant change is required to match the skill level with the evolving nature of work.

1. To analyse the trend of different skill levels among South Asian nations while dealing with AI adoption rate in its job market using correlational analysis.
2. Examine the enduring effects of AI on the employment and regional cooperation scenario in South Asia, focusing on the transitioning of the job market and the likelihood of job polarization.
3. Analyse the capacity of AI to stimulate economic development and reskilling initiatives required by policymakers to address workforce changes induced by AI adoption in South Asia.

Literature Review

Automation and the constant division of labour have raised living standards and productivity in many sectors.[10] As automation grew, it reduced fears about job loss by raising the demand for skilled workers. But as a result of the division of labour, workers are forced to complete more frequent, specialized jobs rapidly and often

---

[8]https://rcc.harvard.edu/knowledge-technology-and-complexity-economic-growth#:~:text=Technological%20progress%20allows%20for%20the,used%20in%20production%20are%20complex

[9]https://www.intereconomics.eu/contents/year/2024/number/1/article/the-impact-of-artificial-intelligence-on-productivity-and-employment-how-can-we-assess-it-and-what-can-we-observe.html

[10]https://www.nber.org/system/files/working_papers/w24196/w24196.pdf

under pressure known as 'scientific management' or Taylorism, this method was created by Frederick Taylor to increase productivity but caused employees to lose interest in the finished product.[11] Notwithstanding these obstacles, specialization and automation have been important forces behind economic expansion by making it possible to produce items in predictable quantities and with consistent quality.[12]

The workforce became more educated as earnings expanded and educational attainment climbed as well. As this pattern developed, technology advanced more quickly, paving the way for the third industrial revolution (IR3), which was fuelled by the invention of computers. Technological advancements grew increasingly skill biased in the decades after the 1970s, increasing the need for individuals with medium- and high-skilled abilities while decreasing opportunities for people with only a primary school or less.[13] Work processes changed simultaneously, and manufacturing employment steadily decreased in all major industrialized economies.[14] The reason for this was the growing number of sophisticated devices and robots that replaced monotonous, regular work in industrial environments. According to the evidence that currently exists, the overall effect of robots on employment has been rather small and, in certain situations, even beneficial.[15] In contrast, the introduction of robots has had a considerably more noticeable negative impact on employment in emerging regions like South Asia, where a sizable section of labour has been displaced by automation. This disparity demonstrates the unequal effects of technological advancement, with emerging nations dealing with more difficulties in terms of automation-related job losses.[16]

Employment growth is impacted by automation in many ways. The displacement impact is the first way that new technologies directly displace workers by replacing their jobs with automation. However, automation also generates new employment.[17] Another one, since increased productivity fuels economic development (the productivity effect), automation creates a demand impact by reducing prices and raising disposable income throughout the economy.[18] These consequences don't happen simultaneously. Due to job displacement, automation initially tends to increase unemployment. On the other hand, unemployment tends

---

[11]https://www.researchgate.net/publication/327022222_Using_Taylorism_to_make_work_easier_A_work_procedure_perspective

[12]https://link.springer.com/article/10.1007/s13132-023-01183-2

[13]https://www.nber.org/reporter/2003number1/technology-and-inequality

[14]https://documents1.worldbank.org/curated/en/595681611845186942/pdf/The-Technology-Employment-Trade-Off-Automation-Industry-and-Income-Effects.pdf

[15]https://mitsloan.mit.edu/ideas-made-to-matter/a-new-study-measures-actual-impact-robots-jobs-its-significant#:~:text=Overall%2C%20robots%20have%20a%20mixed,jobs%20and%20other%20service%20jobs.%E2%80%9D

[16]https://www.wsj.com/world/asia/china-india-bangladesh-young-workers-unemployment-rates-a087d173

[17]https://www.mckinsey.com/featured-insights/future-of-work/jobs-lost-jobs-gained-what-the-future-of-work-will-mean-for-jobs-skills-and-wages

[18]https://www.mdpi.com/2071-1050/10/5/1661

to decline over time as prices and productivity throughout the economy adjust. While automation may cause short-term unemployment due to job displacement, its long-term effects often benefit the economy through higher productivity and increased demand, which can offset initial job losses.[19]

IR3 indicated the beginning of the digital age, which was defined by the broad adoption of the internet, and later the internet of things (IoT), as well as the use of information technology (IT) to automate industry.[20] Today, the world is on the verge of IR4, a transformative era marked by tremendous technological innovations and achievements. Unlike earlier revolutions, IR4 stands out for its pace, scope, and global influence, disrupting industries and removing traditional borders while fundamentally transforming systems throughout sectors, primarily driven by AI, machine learning (ML) and the transformative power of big data,[21] creating a critical potential for South Asia to capitalize on AI. It has the potential to transform precision agriculture and food production, promote socioeconomic advancement, strengthen law enforcement, and increase urban sustainability. To properly capitalize on these prospects, South Asia needs to boost investment in AI and big data advances while also developing the essential capacity and skills. This investment is critical for the region's ability to remain competitive in a fast-changing global economy while also addressing important issues.[22]

Methodology

This study uses a mixed-methods approach that combines qualitative and secondary quantitative data while making a correlational analysis between AI adoption and different skill levels of occupational employment using Oxford Insights and the ILOSTAT database for South Asian nations. To find further trends and effects of AI on the South Asian labour market, the study combines global databases, regional reports, and current literature from organizations like the Organisation for Economic Co-operation and Development (OECD), World Bank, and International Labour Organization (ILO). While accounting for regional peculiarities like informality and skill gaps, it places a strong emphasis on comparing automation and AI adoption patterns across industries.

AI and Employment Interaction

Since technological innovation increases the nation's ability to generate significantly more goods and services in terms of quantity and quality than human capacities, it is a significant driver of economic expansion on a global basis.

---

[19]https://www.sciencedirect.com/science/article/pii/S2590051X23000308#:~:text=Our%20most%20important%20findings%20suggest,work%20environment%20with%20new%20jobs.

[20]https://academic.oup.com/icc/article/28/5/1125/5193703

[21]https://www.sciencedirect.com/science/article/pii/S2090447924002612

[22]https://www.brookings.edu/articles/ai-in-the-global-south-opportunities-and-challenges-towards-more-inclusive-governance/

The employment of low-skilled workers has been impacted both favourably and unfavourably by the industrial revolutions of the past few centuries, including the mechanization of physical labour in the 18th century, mass production that raised wages and standards of living in the 19th century, and the digitization of manufacturing jobs in the 20th century.[23] Nevertheless, the latest industrial revolution (IR4) has become more complicated and is affecting even jobs at the higher end of the skill range globally due to the features of digital technology and AI.[24] There are numerous optimistic estimates about AI's growth potential. Over the next 10 years, the adoption of AI may boost global gross domestic product (GDP) by 7% and accelerate productivity growth by roughly 0.7%–1.3% points annually in the majority of emerging economies, according to Goldman Sachs.[25] However, in addition to earlier predictions of economic growth from more work automation, the McKinsey World Institute predicts that generative AI has the potential to boost the world economy by $17–$25 billion.[26]

The productivity bandwagon, a core belief that technological advancements and growing usage of AI boost productivity and raise wages and wealth, is the foundation for these techno-optimism projections.[27] With these optimistic trends, it is also important to remember that automation has some drawbacks both in the case of advanced and emerging economies. In 2019, the World Bank predicted that around 57% of jobs in OECD countries would be at risk due to the growing usage of automation.[28] AI's negative effects on employment, including job displacement and technological unemployment, have been shown in numerous studies. Repercussions of the labour market will affect workers through discrepancy, wage-push inflation, and a decline in tax revenue.[29] AI has the potential to deepen the global divide, which might harm South Asia's economy and relations with other countries.

Considering AI's benefits of increasing efficiency and productivity, the consequences on employment differ greatly around the globe based on industry emphasis and the degree of technology adoption. Nations with high incomes often gain from job enhancement, particularly in knowledge-driven sectors, while nations with poor infrastructure have a harder time keeping up with the rapid speed of automation. Nations like India, characterized by elevated youth unemployment rates, are especially susceptible to job displacement in industries like IT training

[23]https://www.thebritishacademy.ac.uk/publishing/journal-british-academy/9/the-holy-land-of-industrialism-rethinking-the-industrial-revolution/

[24]https://link.springer.com/article/10.1007/s10796-022-10308-y

[25]https://www.goldmansachs.com/insights/articles/generative-ai-could-raise-global-gdp-by-7-percent

[26]https://www.mckinsey.com/capabilities/mckinsey-digital/our-insights/the-economic-potential-of-generative-ai-the-next-productivity-frontier

[27]https://www.imf.org/en/Blogs/Articles/2024/01/14/ai-will-transform-the-global-economy-lets-make-sure-it-benefits-humanity

[28]https://www.worldbank.org/en/publication/wdr2019

[29]https://www.epi.org/publication/ai-unbalanced-labor-markets/

and content creation.[30] The disparity between existing skills and employment demands in these markets underscores the necessity for worker adaptation and ongoing upskilling. While AI and ML technologies transform businesses, the risk of job displacement in certain areas must be counterbalanced by initiatives to generate fresh, specialized positions, ensuring that economic growth is equitable and reliable for every worker.[31]

South Asia and Its Labour Market Scenario

According to the World Bank's measure, the majority of South Asian nations are still falling under the lower middle-income category, except for the Maldives, which has been placed in the upper middle-income group because of its smaller population and the fact that the majority of its economy relies on the service industry.[32] Afghanistan has dropped into the lower-income group in recent years as a result of political unrest and aggressive conditions.[33] The pandemic caused significant economic difficulties for South Asia, which led to a decline in GDP per capita during the year and an abrupt increase in the number of young populations falling into the Not in Education, Employment, or Training (NEET) category.[34]

Due to the significant impact of informality and the massive influx of labourers each year, South Asia's labour market dynamics are difficult to understand. Its population is considered to be the most densely and youthful globally with approximately 1.22 billion people worldwide between the ages of 15 and 24 years, accounting for nearly 16% of the total population in 2021. However, it is anticipated to rise by over 7% to 1.3 billion by 2030.[35] In contrast, 353 million people in the same age bracket live just in South Asia, making up about one-third of all youths worldwide.[36] The region's young population could offer a wealth of economic advantages by producing high-quality human capital that can make a significant contribution to economic growth. South Asia's youth population is the most worried about job opportunities. They have difficulty in finding decent employment due to labour market constraints on both the demand and supply sides. Even if they find employment, individuals will be working in the unorganized economy and won't be obtain a stable or well-paying job. A significant portion of these populations are already struggling with the additional burden caused by the pandemic, which will have an undesirable effect on their future capacity to earn a living and retain their current way of life.

---

[30]https://Pal, S. (2023). The future of India's IT sector: A study on automation, artificial intelligence and job displacement. *International Journal for Multidisciplinary Research*, *5*(3). https://doi.org/10.36948/ijfmr.2023.v05i03.3133

[31]https://www.nber.org/system/files/working_papers/w24196/w24196.pdf

[32]https://documents1.worldbank.org/curated/en/820841618502964506/pdf/Maldives-Systematic-Country-Diagnostic-Update.pdf

[33]According to World Bank's Income Group Classification.

[34]https://knowledge.unasiapacific.org/sites/default/files/2020-10/wcms_753369_1.pdf

[35]https://www.un.org/esa/socdev/documents/youth/fact-sheets/YouthPOP.pdf

[36]Author's calculation from World Population Prospectus 2022, Population Division, UN DESA.

Over the past several decades, the region has seen a fast expansion in its technological advancements, human capital, infrastructure, etc. The GDP per capita in South Asia increased by almost 600 dollars between 2013 and 2022 as a result of the region's fast economic expansion over the previous 10 years. However, while the labour force has somewhat grown, the number of youths with employment has declined by around 6 million.[37] In 2020, when the world economy collapsed by COVID-19, South Asia's unemployment rate hit an all-time high. By the year 2040, South Asia is expected to be the world's greatest source of youthful workers. However, it also anticipated that between 2020 and 2030, South Asia's young workers will be dropping out of formal school lacking the skills needed for the 21st century, which would make the region's problem much worse.[38] Besides this, the vulnerability of the workforce is also demonstrated by the unprecedented surge in NEET enrolment in recent years. As of 2022, there were over 115 million NEET youth in South Asia, a 16 million rise during the previous decade, even though the numbers varied greatly throughout the nations. Even the gender difference in NEET, which peaked during the pandemic year, is a significant cause for worry in South Asia. Therefore, one of the most important tasks for policymakers is to ensure that they find suitable and decent employment. About 18–20 million individuals in South Asia become working-age each year. It was projected that South Asia's job growth will almost decrease from 3% in 2022 to 1.6% in 2023. Compared to the nations of the global north, South Asian nations benefit from a demographic dividend. However, the region's resilient economic growth is seriously threatened by a sizable portion of youth who are NEET.[39]

Job Polarization

In many South Asian economies, particularly India, a phenomenon called job polarization, characterized by the simultaneous growth of high- and low-skilled jobs and a drop in middle-skill employment has become a major trend. Increasingly, routine middle-skill jobs like those in clerical or classical manufacturing are being automated or made outdated. As a result, there is a greater need than ever for highly skilled workers who can use and navigate these technical advancements. At the same time, low-skill jobs in labour-intensive sectors like construction continue to grow, often absorbing workers transitioning from the agricultural sector highlighting serious issues facing traditional industrial sectors which find it difficult to offer middle-skilled people sufficient employment opportunities.

According to research conducted between 1983 and 2012, automation in India's manufacturing sector has continued this trend. As industries have undergone technological change, demand has become skill biased, supporting workers with higher education and specific training. At the same time, agricultural

[37]https://www.emerald.com/insight/content/doi/10.1108/jes-01-2018-0013/full/html
[38]UNICEF (2019).
[39]https://www.ilo.org/sites/default/files/wcmsp5/groups/public/@dgreports/@dcomm/@publ/documents/publication/wcms_834081.pdf

workers who were unable to obtain middle-skill jobs because of technological challenges or a lack of necessary qualifications have moved to low-skill jobs in industries like construction. This dynamic is further complicated by the excess labour supply with secondary and tertiary education who are highly qualified for available low-skill positions but cannot meet the requirements of high-skilled roles. As a result, several middle-skilled workers have been forced to accept jobs in less demanding sectors which has increased job polarization and limited economic mobility within the labour force.[40] Another study examining urban India from 1983 to 2011 identified job polarization in the 1990s and 2000s, characterized by job creation in low- and high-skill positions and a decline in middle-skill jobs, attributed to automation and advances in technology in Indian industries.[41]

However, recent research indicates a more complex development of this pattern between 2012 and 2020. Throughout this time, there exists indications of 'mid-upgrading', with the majority of job growth being in low- to mid-level, high-paying positions which reflect the rise of employment in areas such as construction, wholesale and retail commerce, transportation, storage, and communication sectors. These sectors (which fall in between low- and medium-skilled occupations) have given workers new options, suggesting a partial reversal of the previous job polarization.[42] Although automation and technical advancements continue to have an impact on labour market interactions, this trend points to a more varied distribution of job opportunities, which may lessen some of the negative consequences of job polarization.

Cross Regional Analysis

Informality is a major global challenge attributed to a few reasons such as persistent inequality, sluggish economic growth, insufficient tax revenue, vulnerable employment circumstances, inefficient labour, and limited access to modern technology.[43] In South Asia, the prevalence of the informal sector contributes to low worker productivity, which in turn leads to a high rate of working poverty. While labour productivity has declined in the Maldives, it has grown at a reasonable rate in the other South Asian economies.[44]

A continuous and alarming trend in Southern Asia is revealed by the graph (Fig. 4.1), which analyses the percentage of informal employment across worldwide areas between 2014 and 2023. The region's rate of informal employment, which increased somewhat from 86.2% in 2014 to 87.2% in 2023, is still

---

[40]https://www.academia.edu/37709333/Job_Polarisation_in_India_Structural_Causes_and_Policy_Implications?

[41]https://papers.ssrn.com/sol3/papers.cfm?abstract_id=2850140

[42]https://www.econstor.eu/bitstream/10419/283099/1/1858878063.pdf

[43]https://openknowledge.worldbank.org/entities/publication/af6532f0-349a-5809-a9ba-d6e7abdb6018

[44]https://www.griffith.edu.au/__data/assets/pdf_file/0020/1935110/GAPSO2024-Policy-brief-Confronting-labour-market-challenges-in-South-Asia-An-SDG-perspective.pdf

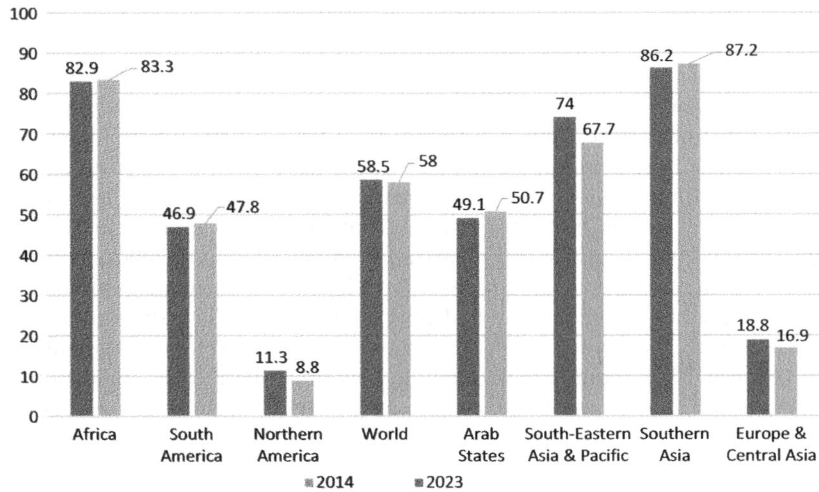

Fig. 4.1. Share of Informal Employment in Different Regions (%).
Source: ILOSTAT database.

distressingly high, demonstrating that despite economic advancement and shifting global dynamics, there are substantial structural obstacles to labour formalization. On the other hand, regions like Northern America (11.3%–8.8%) and Europe and Central Asia (18.8%–16.9%) have significantly improved their informality rates. These advancements highlight how strong institutional frameworks, economic diversification, and focused policies may effectively formalize the labour force. However, the growing informality in Southern Asia indicates that the workforce's move to formal employment has been hindered by economic progress and technological advancements. Adoption of AI is severely hampered in Southern Asia, particularly in rural areas with a lack of internet access and an inadequate digital infrastructure. Small- and medium-sized businesses, which make up the majority of the informal economy, have even less access to reasonable AI and ML technology. Furthermore, the majority of the workforce lacks the digital literacy and specialized training needed for AI- and ML-driven industries, creating a large skills gap. These issues are made worse by weak policy frameworks, poor regional coordination, and insufficient government funding for AI research, which delays the adoption of AI in the key industries. The manufacturing, textile, and agricultural sectors that make up the majority of the informal economy are especially susceptible to automation and job loss. At the same time, AI technologies can change the labour market by formalizing informal jobs, increasing productivity, and opening up new career paths. AI-powered platforms, for example, can improve supply chain transparency, facilitate improved adherence to labour laws, and link informal labour to formal markets. However, these benefits can only be achieved if Southern Asia overcomes its technological adoption.

To take leverage of AI's revclutionary potential, governments in Southern Asia have to make priority investments in digital infrastructure, such as increasing broadband access and developing AI research hubs, and skill development programmes with a focus on AI-related and digital capabilities. Public–private partnerships can be extremely beneficial in financing AI adoption for small firms, ensuring sustainability. In addition, policy frameworks must be improved to protect gig and platform workers, who becoming an increasingly important part of the AI-powered economy in this region. Regional collaboration and exchange of knowledge can also help countries move forward by allowing them to benefit from one another's gains.

Fig. 4.2 depicts the percentage of individuals utilizing the internet in various South Asian countries, compared to the global average of 59.3%. Within the region, Maldives leads with 79.10% internet penetration, closely followed by Bhutan at 76.85%, both exceeding the global average reflecting their focus on digital connectivity, which is supported by smaller populations and significant infrastructural investments. At 43.41%, India trails behind the worldwide average but outperforms most regional counterparts, indicating tremendous and unexplored opportunities for digital growth. Bangladesh (36.11%), Sri Lanka (36.18%), and Nepal (37.70%) have moderate internet adoption rates, highlighting the interplay of infrastructure progress and socioeconomic limits, while at the low end of the spectrum, Afghanistan (18.4%) and Pakistan (18.93%) have the region's lowest penetration rates, indicating political challenges and weak infrastructure. Despite excellent internet usage rates, the Maldives and Bhutan are slow to adopt AI technologies, which can be attributed to their fragile industrial bases, thereby reducing demand for advanced AI applications, as well as a shortage of skilled human

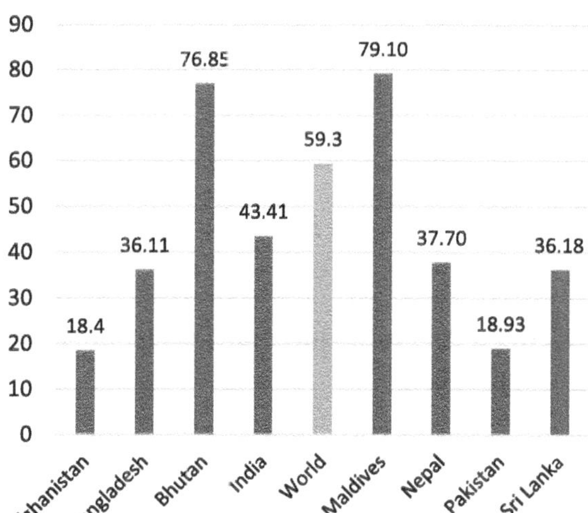

Fig. 4.2. Population Share Using Internet in South Asia 2020 (%).
Source: International Telecommunication Union (ITU), World Telecommunication/ICT Indicators Database.

capital to develop and deploy these technologies. Furthermore, these countries' small-scale economies are concentrated in certain industries, such as tourism, where AI adoption is still in its early stages. Other countries, notably India, are tapping into efforts such as the Production Linked Incentive (PLI) scheme to enhance technological capacities and AI integration, to boost productivity and industrial efficiency. Bangladesh, Sri Lanka, and Nepal are steadily eliminating obstacles to digital inclusion through smart infrastructure investments, as well as tackling affordability and literacy gaps. Meanwhile, Afghanistan and Pakistan confront more complicated difficulties, such as geopolitical instability and resource constraints, impeding significant progress towards AI technology adoption.

Due to the youth population and growing internet expansion, South Asia has tremendous potential for technological advancement. Alongside policies that promote the use of AI, governments must place a high priority on dependable and affordable access to the internet.

In addition, robotics is becoming easier to acquire owing to technological developments spearheaded by local entrepreneurs and collaborations with multinational corporations. Data from International Federation of Robotics (IFR), World Robotics 2024, demonstrates China leading with more than half of the global total which shows the annual installations of industrial robots in the 15 main markets for 2023. Together, the top five markets account for 79% of installations: China, Japan, the Republic of Korea, Germany, and the United States. Robot installations declined in many of the top nations, but it has increased significantly in Germany (+7%), India (+59%), Canada (+37%), and the United Kingdom (+51%) in the past few years. With 8,500 robotic implants in 2023, a phenomenal 59% growth, India ranked eighth globally. This becomes successful with the beneficial effect of strategies such as the PLI scheme and the India AI Mission programme that has promoted automation in key industries notably electronics, medicines, automobiles, etc. Considering its rapid expansion, India's robot density remains low as compared to advanced economies while indicating its huge potential in the sector of logistics, agriculture, healthcare, etc in upcoming years. However, obstacles such as scarcity of skilled workers, robotic specialists, and resistance to technology owing to job loss fears persist. Overcoming these challenges through comprehensive policies, skill enhancement, and industrial partnerships will empower India to bolster its manufacturing prowess and establish itself as a frontrunner in the global robotics sector.

Correlation Between AI Adoption and Different Skill-level Occupation in South Asia

South Asia is shifting towards service-based economies, with textiles and tourism contributing due to their unique strengths and geographic advantages. However, agriculture still plays a significant role in the region's economy. India has a booming IT-based services sector that accounts for over 50% of its GDP through software, and fintech services, while Bangladesh has emerged as a noteworthy industry-based economy in recent years. Despite being susceptible to environmental issues and worldwide disruptions, Nepal, Sri Lanka, and the Maldives prioritize tourism by utilizing their natural and cultural resources. Graphs below are the correlation analysis between the AI readiness score published by Oxford Insights evaluating the nation's preparedness to implement AI and different skill levels of occupation in which labour is employed in South Asian countries. With differing degrees of workforce, education level, technological preparedness, and economic growth, the South Asian region exhibits distinct patterns in the ways that AI adoption interplay with low-, medium-, and high-skilled workers. The scatter plots (Figs. 4.3–4.5) demonstrate a correlation between the percentage of employment in different skill levels of occupations (on the *Y* axis) and the AI Readiness Index (on the *X* axis) for several South Asian countries. Results show diverse correlational trends mainly attributed to structural and sector differences among the countries.

Fig. 4.3 shows the interaction between the AI Readiness Index and workers employed in highly skilled occupations. According to the data, the percentage of high-skilled jobs and AI readiness scores have a slightly negative relationship. Because of the strong technological infrastructure, focused policies, and investments that promote automation, innovation, and upskilling, countries like India, which are more prepared for AI, also have a lower percentage of their workers in high-skilled sectors. On the other hand, nations like Afghanistan exhibit low levels of AI readiness and low levels of high-skilled employment which are indicative of structural issues like unstable politics, inadequate educational systems, and slow adoption of new technologies. While outliers like the Maldives exhibit relatively high-skill employment despite moderate AI readiness, most South Asian countries, including Bangladesh, Pakistan, and Nepal, cluster in the lower-middle

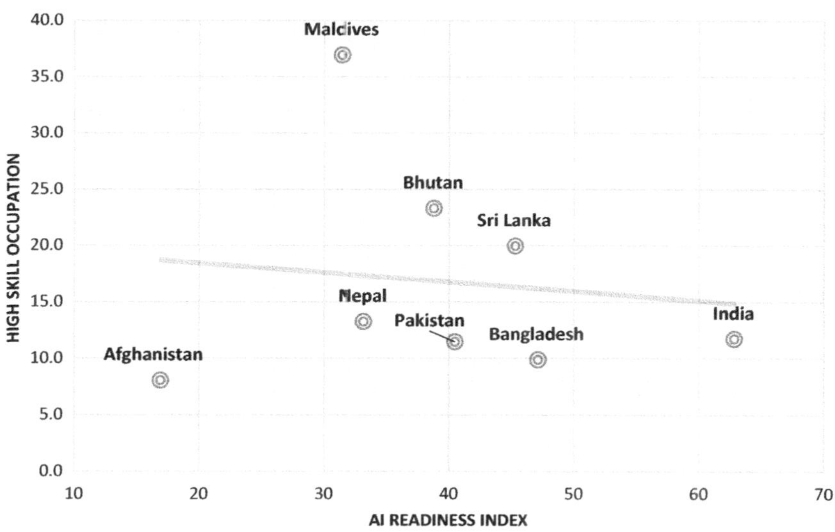

Fig. 4.3. Correlation Between the AI Readiness Index Score and the Proportion of Employment High-skilled Occupations. *Source*: ILOSTAT, ILO, and Government AI Readiness Index 2024, Oxford Insights. *Note*: Data on the various skill levels of South Asian nations are taken from the most recent years that are accessible (Nepal – 2017, Maldives – 2018, Afghanistan and Pakistan – 2021, Bangladesh and Sri Lanka – 2022, Bhutan and India – 2023).

range of both AI readiness and high-skill employment. This is probably because the Maldives' tourism-oriented economy places a strong emphasis on skilled management roles.

Similar to the above graphs, a negative trend is also reflected in the correlation (Fig. 4.4) between the AI Readiness Index score and the proportion of employment in medium-skilled occupations. Medium-skilled professions are more prevalent in nations with lower AI readiness scores, such as Afghanistan, Pakistan, and Bhutan. Because these economies are less vulnerable to automation and AI-driven developments, traditional services, manufacturing and agriculture continue to dominate. Due to the limited adoption of AI, medium-skilled professions in these nations might be involved in technical jobs, clerical work, and skilled physical labour that are mostly immune to automation.

On the other hand, nations with higher AI Readiness Index scores, such as Bangladesh and India, have a lower percentage of medium-skilled jobs reflecting the expanding use of AI technologies in these economies which frequently lead to the automation of medium-skilled, repetitive, rule-based professions. As a result, employees either upskill to fit into high-skill, technology-intensive positions or shift to low-skilled roles. To prevent workforce displacement and facilitate workers' transfer to high-skilled occupations, this trend highlights the necessity of targeted upskilling programmes in nations with greater AI preparedness. While preserving medium-skilled employment prospects, nations with low

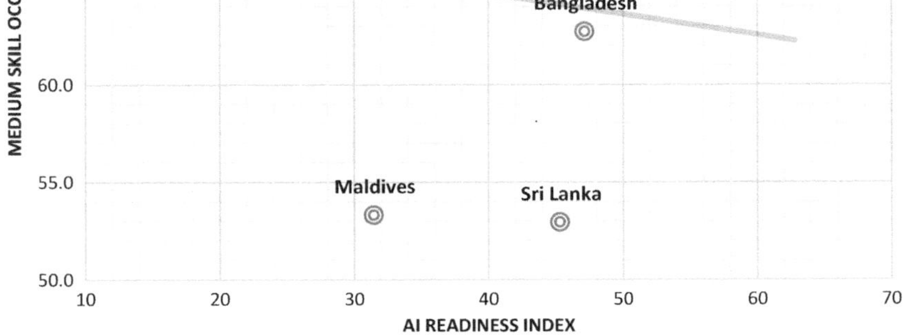

Fig. 4.4. Correlation Between the AI Readiness Index Score and the Proportion of Employment in Medium-skilled Occupations. *Source*: ILOSTAT, ILO, and Government AI Readiness Index 2024, Oxford Insights.*Note*: Data on the various skill levels of South Asian nations are taken from the most recent years that are accessible (Nepal – 2017, Maldives – 2018, Afghanistan and Pakistan – 2021, Bangladesh and Sri Lanka – 2022, Bhutan and India – 2023).

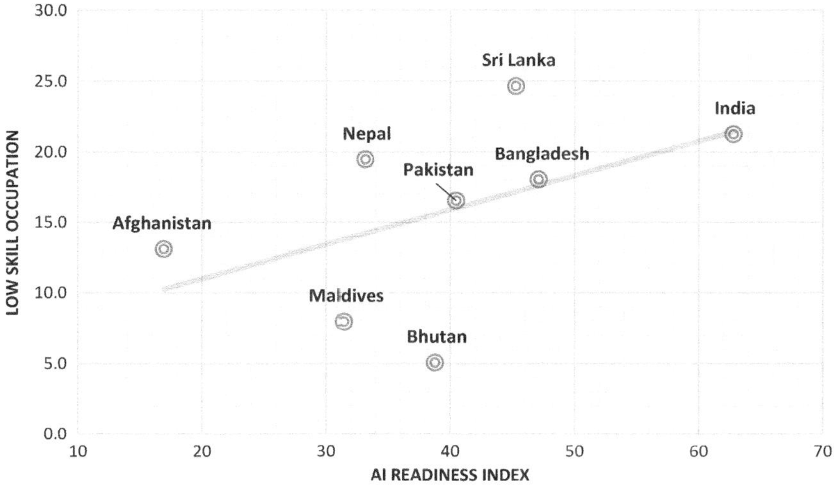

Fig. 4.5. Correlation Between the AI Readiness Index Score and the Proportion of Employment in Low-skilled Occupations. *Source*: ILOSTAT, ILO, and Government AI Readiness Index 2024, Oxford Insights. *Note*: Data on the various skill levels of South Asian nations are taken from the most recent years that are accessible (Nepal – 2017, Maldives – 2018, Afghanistan and Pakistan – 2021, Bangladesh and Sri Lanka – 2022, Bhutan and India – 2023).

AI readiness must concentrate on developing their technological capacities. Furthermore, the scatterplot (Fig. 4.5) shows that the percentage of employment in low-skilled occupations across South Asian countries is positively correlated with AI readiness scores suggesting a greater proportion of a nation's workforce works in low-skilled positions as its AI preparedness increases. Despite having greater AI preparedness, nations like Bangladesh and India have high rates of low-skilled jobs can be possibly related to the growing importance of gig and platform-based service industries, where AI technologies and digital platforms help create jobs in industries like domestic work, ride-hailing, and delivery services. Large sectors of the workforce are drawn to these positions since they usually do not require any higher qualifications or formal education[45] and have low entry hurdles, especially in emerging nations adjusting to AI-driven technological advancements.

Conclusion and Recommendation

This research investigates the relationship between labour markets in South Asia and AI capacity landscape. The variations in results highlight the complexities of analysing AI's influence in area with varying developmental stages and

[45]https://www.sciencedirect.com/science/article/pii/S0040162522006576#:~:text=Gig%20workers%20often%20acquire%20the,providing%20the%20necessary%20gig%20skills

technology integration. As a result, the research underlines the importance of standardized AI adoption for future investigations and more thorough insights into AI-influenced labour market dynamics. To overcome the skills gap, education systems in the region must be reoriented, emphasizing technical and vocational education and training (TVET) and apprenticeships system. Technological progress and education in AI and ML could offer significant opportunities for emerging South Asia to accelerate growth and enhance living standards through increased productivity driven by a larger workforce and the development of skills aligned with technology, including AI, digital competencies, advanced cognitive abilities, and soft skills. However, the current shortage of skilled workers in the region limits the technological adoption and generation of quality employment. As a result, suitable policy alternatives combining governments, businesses, and international organizations are required to manage the concerns related to technological adoption, skills mismatch, and job creation.

Furthermore, as AI becomes more prevalent in everyday activities, there are concerns regarding its management. Several regions around the world have made progress in the establishment of governing structures for AI, although South Asia remains largely undeveloped in this field having considerable obstacles as a result of weak monitoring and standards including the possible illicit use of AI, concerns about ethics, and lack of public assurance. As a result, the study suggests that South Asian countries should develop a collaborative and progressive policy for not only adopting but also regulating AI. The execution of National Employment Policies (NEMP) must be given top priority in the region, and National Education Policies (NEP) must be amended frequently to satisfy changing labour market demands. By encouraging inclusive and sustainable employment possibilities, especially for youth, NEMP should concentrate on boosting the establishment of quality jobs. By matching job creation tactics with the region's economic requirements and demographic trends, these policies can solve important issues like unemployment and skill gaps.

The labour market in South Asia may further gain significantly from the integration of NEMP with NEP. First of all, they will contribute to closing the skills gap, making youth more equipped for positions demanding higher level abilities. Subsequently, these policies will increase labour participation rates and advance gender equity by fostering inclusive opportunities. Third, it will promote innovation and entrepreneurship, which will help diversify the economy. At last, it will offer a methodical framework for addressing informal employment and advocate formalization which would improve social protections and job security.

References

Acemoglu, D. (2018). *Artificial intelligence, automation and work* [NBER Working Paper 24196]. National Bureau of Economic Research (NBER). https://ideas.repec.org/p/nbr/nberwo/24196.html

Acemoglu D. (2022). *Technology and inequality*. The Reporter, National Bureau Economic Research. https://www.nber.org/reporter/2003number1/technology-and-inequality

Bill, M., Müller, C., Kraus, W., Bieller, S., & International Federation of Robotics. (2024). World Robotics 2024. https://ifr.org/img/worldrobotics/Press_Conference_2024.pdf

Biven J., & Zipperer B. (2024). *Unbalanced labor market power is what makes technology – Including AI – Threatening to workers*. Economic Policy Institute. https://www.epi.org/publication/ai-unbalanced-labor-markets/

Brown S. (2020). *A new study measures the actual impact of robots on jobs*. Ideas Made to Matter. MIT. https://mitsloan.mit.edu/ideas-made-to-matter/a-new-study-measures-actual-impact-robots-jobs-its-significant#:~:text=Overall%2C%20robots%20have%20a%20mixed,jobs%20and%20other%20service%20jobs.%E2%80%9D

Chui, M., Hazan, E., Roberts, R., Singla, A., Smaje, K., Sukharevsky, A., Yee, L., & Zemmel, R. (2023). *The economic potential of generative AI: The next productivity frontier*. McKinsey & Company. https://www.mckinsey.com/capabilities/mckinsey-digital/our-insights/the-economic-potential-of-generative-ai-the-next-productivity-frontier

Filippucci, F. (2024). *The impact of Artificial Intelligence on productivity, distribution and growth: Key mechanisms, initial evidence and policy challenges* [OECD Artificial Intelligence Papers]. OECD. https://www.oecd.org/content/dam/oecd/en/publications/reports/2024/04/the-impact-of-artificial-intelligence-on-productivity-distribution-and-growth_d54e2842/8d900037-en.pdf

Georgieva, K. (2024). *AI will transform the global economy. Let's make sure it benefits humanity* [Blogs]. International Monetary Fund. https://www.imf.org/en/Blogs/Articles/2024/01/14/ai-will-transform-the-global-economy-lets-make-sure-it-benefits-humanity

Goldman Sachs. (2023). *Generative AI could raise global GDP by 7%*. Insights, Goldmansachs. https://www.goldmansachs.com/insights/articles/generative-ai-could-raise-global-gdp-by-7-percent

Guliyev, H. (2023). Artificial intelligence and unemployment in high-tech developed countries: New insights from dynamic panel data model. *Research in Globalization*, *7*, 100140. ISSN 2590-051X. https://doi.org/10.1016/j.resglo.2023.100140

Haleem, A., Javaid, M., Qadri, M. A., Singh, R. P., & Suman, R. (2022). Artificial intelligence (AI) applications for marketing: A literature-based study. *International Journal of Intelligent Networks*, *3*, 119–132. https://doi.org/10.1016/j.ijin.2022.08.005

Herrmann, A. M., Zaal, P. M., Chappin, M. M., Schemmann, B., & Lühmann, A. (2022). 'We don't need no (higher) education' – How the gig economy challenges the education-income paradigm. *Technological Forecasting and Social Change*, *186*, 122136. https://doi.org/10.1016/j.techfore.2022.122136

ILO. (2022). *World employment and social outlook: Trends 2022*. International Labour Organization. https://www.ilo.org/publications/flagship-reports/world-employment-and-social-outlook-trends-2022

ILO. (2023). *Tackling the COVID-19 youth employment crisis in Asia and the Pacific*. Co-publication of the Asian Development Bank and the International Labour Organization. https://knowledge.unasiapacific.org/sites/default/files/2020-10/wcms_753369_1.pdf

Khan, M. A., Naqvi, H. A., Hakeem, M. M., ud Din, G. M., & Iqbal, N. (2022). Economic and financial impact of the COVID-19 pandemic in South Asian. *Environmental Science and Pollution Research*, *29*, 15703–15712. https://doi.org/10.1007/s11356-021-16894-9

Kindberg-Hanlon, G. (2021). *The technology-employment trade-off, automation, industry and income effects* [Policy Research Working Paper 9529]. World Bank Group. https://documents1.worldbank.org/curated/en/595681611845186942/pdf/The-Technology-Employment-Trade-Off-Automation-Industry-and-Income-Effects.pdf

Li, L. (2022). Reskilling and upskilling the future-ready workforce for industry 4.0 and beyond. *Information System Frontiers, 13*, 1–16. https://doi.org/10.1007/S10796-022-10308-Y

Malik, S., Muhammad, K., & Waheed, Y. (2024). Artificial intelligence and industrial applications – A revolution in modern industries. *Ain Shams Engineering Journal, 15*(9), 102886. https://doi.org/10.1016/j.asej.2024.102886

McKinsey. (2017). *Jobs lost, jobs gained: What the future of work will mean for jobs, skills, and wages* [Report]. McKinsey Global Institute. https://www.mckinsey.com/featured-insights/future-of-work/jobs-lost-jobs-gained-what-the-future-of-work-will-mean-for-jobs-skills-and-wages

Mokyr, J. (2021). 'The Holy Land of Industrialism': Rethinking the Industrial Revolution. *Journal of The British Academy, 9*.

Nazmul, M., Hossain, A., & Islam, I. (2024). *Confronting labour market challenges in South Asia: An SDG perspective* [Policy Brief]. Griffith Aisa Pacific Strategic Outlook. https://doi.org/10.25904/1912/5203

Ndaguba, E., Nzewi, O., Ijeoma, E., & Sambumbu, M., & Sibanda, M. (2018). Using Taylorism to make work easier: A work procedure perspective. *South African Journal of Economic and Management Sciences, 21*. https://doi.org/10.4102/sajems.v21i1.2120

Okolo, C. T. (2023). *AI in the Global South: Opportunities and challenges towards more inclusive governance*. Brookings. https://www.brookings.edu/articles/ai-in-the-global-south-opportunities-and-challenges-towards-more-inclusive-governance/

Pal, S. (2023). The future of India's it sector: A study on automation, artificial intelligence and job displacement. *International Journal for Multidisciplinary Research, 5*(3). https://doi.org/10.36948/ijfmr.2023.v05i03.3133

Pantelimon, F.-V., Bologa, R., Toma, A., & Posedaru, B.-S. (2021). The evolution of AI-driven educational systems during the COVID-19 pandemic. *Sustainability, 13*(23), 13501. https://doi.org/10.3390/su132313501

Qin, Y., Xu, Z., Wang, X., Xu, Z., & Skare, M. (2024). Artificial intelligence and economic development: An evolutionary investigation and systematic review. *Journal of Knowledge Economy, 15*, 1736–1770.

Rahman, M. M., Rana, R. H., & Barua, S. (2019). The drivers of economic growth in South Asia: Evidence from a dynamic system GMM approach. *Journal of Economic Studies, 46*(3), 564–577. https://doi.org/10.1108/jes-01-2018-0013

Shah S. (2024). *India's economy in the era of AI, capital economics, capital economics*. https://www.capitaleconomics.com/publications/india-economics-focus/indias-economy-era-ai

Taalbi, J. (2019, October). Origins and pathways of innovation in the third industrial revolution. *Industrial and Corporate Change, 28*(5), 1125–1148. https://doi.org/10.1093/icc/dty053

UNICEF. (2020). "More than half of South Asian youth are not on track to have the education and skills necessary for employment in 2030," Press Release, United Nations Children's Fund https://www.unicef.org/press-releases/more-half-south-asian-youth-are-not-track-have-education-and-skills-necessary

World Bank. (2019). *The changing nature of work* [World Development Report]. World Bank Group. https://www.worldbank.org/en/publication/wdr2019

Chapter 5

Strategy Development with Artificial Intelligence-based Multi-criteria Decision-making Technique for Integration of Hospitals with Microgrids

Yaşar Gökalp[a], Serkan Eti[b], Hasan Dinçer[c] and Serhat Yüksel[c]

[a]*The School of Health, İstanbul Medipol University, İstanbul, Turkey*
[b]*IMU Vocational School, İstanbul Medipol University, İstanbul, Turkey*
[c]*The School of Business, İstanbul Medipol University, İstanbul, Turkey*

Abstract

Microgrid systems are defined as independent energy systems that integrate energy generation, storage, distribution, and consumption processes. Microgrid systems contribute to many aspects such as providing uninterrupted energy, environmental sustainability, controlling energy costs, and preparing for emergency scenarios. Hospitals, on the other hand, may have difficulty in tolerating energy interruption due to the nature of the healthcare services provided. Therefore, it is inevitable to integrate microgrid systems with hospitals. For this purpose, a set of criteria affecting the integration of hospitals and microgrid systems has been created based on the literature. The identified criteria are analyzed using the artificial intelligence (AI)-based spherical fuzzy (SF) The Decision Making Trial and Evaluation Laboratory (DEMATEL) method. The results of the analysis show that the most important criterion affecting the process of integrating microgrid systems with hospitals is the initial investment costs. The need for qualified personnel to use these systems also makes a significant contribution.

Keywords: Artificial intelligence; strategy development; decision-making; hospitals; microgrid

Artificial Intelligence in Business and Society: Global Insights, 67–80

doi:10.1108/978-1-83708-022-920261013

Introduction

Microgrid systems are independent energy systems that integrate the generation, storage, distribution, and consumption of energy. These systems are mostly designed to provide the energy needed by a specific region or facility (Hamanah et al., 2023). Apart from that, microgrid systems operate independently from traditional energy grids. Thanks to microgrid systems, the energy-supplied region can be protected from possible power outages (Zhen et al., 2023). In addition, these systems contribute to more efficient use of energy. Therefore, energy savings are achieved. Since microgrid systems are based on the use of renewable energy, they also contribute to reducing carbon emissions (Zou et al., 2023). These systems can be used in areas far from the main grid and in universities, as well as in hospitals. Hospitals are structures that need energy 24/7. The service provided must be uninterrupted (Hirwa et al., 2023). Microgrid networks can provide energy to hospitals during possible outages. Apart from that, it can contribute to reducing energy costs by providing energy savings for hospitals (Gökalp et al., 2022). However, many challenges affect the process of integrating microgrid systems with hospitals.

These challenges need to be minimized to increase the success of the integration process. First of all, since microgrid systems require advanced technology, the initial investment costs can be quite high (Chen et al., 2023). This can be quite challenging for hospitals with resource constraints. Apart from that, there is a need for qualified personnel who can use these systems that require advanced technology. A well-trained qualified staff can design the process and intervene immediately in case of possible malfunctions (Özdemirci et al., 2023). In addition, energy projects require many permits and licenses (Yoo & Jung, 2024). Therefore, disruptions in the necessary permitting processes can negatively affect the process. The equipment used in microgrid systems should be compatible with the equipment used in hospitals. Otherwise, it is not possible to ensure the sustainability of the system. These systems can sometimes be vulnerable to cyber-attacks (Koduru et al., 2023). This issue negatively affects the success of the system. Therefore, it is important to take the necessary security measures. Finally, microgrid systems require continuous maintenance (Arafat et al., 2024). This causes both additional costs and the need for personnel. Accordingly, this study aims to identify prioritized strategies for integrating microgrid systems with hospitals. The AI-based DEMATEL method was used in the process of determining the prioritized strategies. Literature-based criteria were weighted with this methodology. AI tools are developed through research and development efforts by public and private initiatives that have positive effects on economic, social, and environmental impacts. However, the primary goal of research and development activities is not economic growth, but rather obtaining patents for the invented products. It thus raises questions whether AI would work in an equitable manner to all corners of the society (Das, 2020; Das & Mukherjee, 2019).

The main contributions of this study are given below. (i) The AI approach is integrated with the multi-criteria decision-making methodology. Thanks to this method, it is possible to weigh experts according to their qualifications. Most of the methods used in the literature evaluate expert weights at the same level. However, experts may have different work experience and qualifications. In this study, a decision matrix is created by considering AI methodology to solve the related problem. (ii) This study also has some theoretical contributions. Hospitals are buildings that require uninterrupted energy. Therefore, it is inevitable to integrate them with microgrid systems. However, limited studies are addressing the integration of hospitals and microgrid systems. This adds another uniqueness to the study.

The second part of the study includes a literature review. The third section describes the methodology in detail. The fourth section consists of the findings of the study. The last section includes a discussion and conclusions.

Literature Review

One of the important criteria affecting the integration of microgrid systems with hospitals is the high initial investment cost (Hayashi et al., 2023). Microgrid systems require advanced technology. This situation makes the investments to be made costly (Chen et al., 2023). In addition, the costs of solar panels, wind turbines, batteries, and inverters used during the installation of microgrid systems are high. Furthermore, installation, assembly, and maintenance costs also affect these investments (Boonraksa et al., 2023). Lin et al. (2023) aimed to design a microgrid system for cotton farms in Australia. The research results emphasize the importance of the initial investment cost of this system to be installed for cotton farms. Owusu-Obeng and Schell (2023) examined microgrid investments through a case study in Ghana. It is stated that the costs of microgrid systems affect the investment decision.

Another criterion affecting the integration of microgrid systems with hospitals is the adequacy of the legal basis and incentive practices. The ease of obtaining the necessary licensing and permits for microgrid systems will contribute positively to the process (Naraindath et al., 2024). In addition, renewable energy projects bring with them environmental regulations (Dzwigol et al., 2023). Moreover, microgrid systems are usually installed by integrating them into existing energy infrastructure. At this point, obtaining infrastructure utilization permits also affects the process. Furthermore, the right incentive strategies facilitate the integration of microgrid systems and hospitals (An et al., 2023). Behrendt (2023) examined microgrid systems and European Union law. It is stated in the results of the study that legal uncertainties hinder the development of microgrid systems. Khubrani and Alam (2023) analyzed blockchain-based microgrid systems for secure energy production and distribution. As a result of the analysis, it is concluded that the adoption of renewable energy sources has become difficult due to legal and regulatory barriers.

Cybersecurity risks are another important factor affecting the integration of microgrid systems in hospitals (Pisla et al., 2023). Microgrid systems have remote management and monitoring capabilities. These features make microgrid systems a target for cyber-attacks. Apart from this, vulnerabilities in the software used in these systems are also a significant threat. Microgrid systems communicate with other systems in energy grids through networks. An attack on these networks can threaten the integrity of the system (Roux et al., 2023). Aghmadi et al. (2023) examined cyber security in microgrid systems. The results of the research emphasize cyber security measures for microgrid systems to be successful. Naraindath et al. (2024) investigated the improvement of cyber security in microgrid systems. It is stated that microgrid systems are vulnerable to harmful cyber-attacks.

Another influential factor is having qualified personnel who can use microgrid systems (Thiak & Hira, 2024). The correct design and installation of microgrid systems depends on the knowledge and experience of the personnel. Apart from this, the knowledge of the personnel plays an important role in the process of taking cyber security measures. In addition, personnel have an important role in the maintenance and repair processes of these systems. Therefore, it can be said that one of the aspects affecting the success of microgrid systems is having qualified personnel (Fishov et al., 2023). Costea and Orlando (2023) discussed the control and protection of a low voltage direct current (LVDC) microgrid. The importance of qualified personnel in microgrid systems is emphasized. Zafra-Cabeza et al. (2023) conducted a study aiming to develop a robust optimization for a possible fault that may occur in microgrid systems. It is underlined that the fault detection process should be carried out by qualified personnel.

As a result of the literature review, the following conclusions are reached:

(i) Microgrids are systems that include energy generation, storage, and distribution processes, usually operating independently in a specific region.
(ii) Hospitals are institutions that need uninterrupted energy as a requirement of the service provided.
(iii) Accordingly, it is necessary to integrate microgrid systems with hospitals.
(iv) However, many criteria affect the integration of microgrid systems with hospitals. Decision-makers can't respond to all these criteria at the same time.

Therefore, it is important to develop prioritized strategies by weighting the criteria affecting the integration of hospitals and microgrid systems according to their importance.

AI-based SF DEMATEL

In this study, it is aimed to determine the most appropriate strategy to be applied in the integration of microgrid networks to reduce power outages in hospitals. The DEMATEL method is preferred to quantitatively determine the importance levels of the strategies determined for this purpose (Özdemirci et al., 2023). Since the DEMATEL method is a method based on expert evaluation, fuzzy numbers are used to include uncertainties in the analysis. Fuzzy set theory is one of the current theories developed to measure uncertainty in mathematics (Dinçer, Yüksel, & Eti, 2023; Dinçer, Yüksel, Mikhaylov, et al., 2023). Another criticism in literature of expert evaluations is that they attribute equal importance to decision-makers.

The AI system is integrated into the model to take into account the difference in knowledge levels. Details of the AI-based SF DEMATEL method to be used in the study are given under this section (Eti et al., 2023).

First, the AI system needs to be built. Machine learning of the AI system, coded with TensorFlow and Keras libraries in Python open-code software, is performed iteratively with the training data set. After machine learning, the success of the AI system is tested (Kou, Dinçer, et al., 2024; Kou, Pamucar, et al., 2024). With the help of libraries, the number of neurons, activation function, number of layers, and optimization algorithm of the parameters are selected and added to the coding (Oflaz et al., 2023). The number of layers is an important factor that makes the model more complex and moves away from the linear structure. A total of nine-layer structure is constructed, including one input layer and one output layer. While the input layer consists of two neurons, expert opinion (Terms) and experience times (*d*), the output layer consists of components of SF numbers (μ, v, π). In other words, an output layer with three neurons is created; 64 neurons are added to each latent layer. Thus, a complex relationship network is obtained between input–output variables. The Sigmoid function in Equation (1) is preferred as the activation function. The main reason for this is that the output of the Sigmoid function is between 0 and 1 and supports fuzzy set theory.

$$S(x) = \frac{1}{1+e^{-ax}} \tag{1}$$

Among the optimization algorithms, the Adam algorithm detailed in Equations (2)–(6) is preferred because it provides efficiency in small data sets.

$$W_{t+1} = W_t - \frac{a}{\sqrt{\hat{S}_t + \varepsilon}} \hat{V}_t \tag{2}$$

$$\hat{V}_t = \frac{V_t}{1-\beta_1^t} \tag{3}$$

$$\hat{S}_t = \frac{S_t}{1-\beta_2^t} \tag{4}$$

$$V_t = \beta_1 V_{t-1} + (1-\beta_1)\frac{\partial L}{\partial w_t} \tag{5}$$

$$S_t = \beta_2 S_{t-1} + (1-\beta_2)\left.\frac{\partial L}{\partial w_t}\right]^2 \tag{6}$$

During the machine learning process, the Adam algorithm is repeated a specified number of iterations (epochs). In each epoch, the random data set obtained by simulation is used as the input variable. The output variable is calculated using Equations (7) and (8) and presented to the model.

Spherical Weighted Arithmetic Mean (SWAM)

$$=\left\{\left[1-\prod_{i=1}^{n}\left(1-\mu_i^2\right)^{w_i}\right]^{\frac{1}{2}},\prod_{i=1}^{n}v_i^{w_i},\left[\prod_{i=1}^{n}\left(1-\mu_i^2\right)^{w_i}-\prod_{i=1}^{n}\left(1-\mu_i^2-\pi_i^2\right)^{w_i}\right]^{\frac{1}{2}}\right\} \quad (7)$$

$$w_i=\frac{d_i}{\sum_{i=1}^{n}d_i} \quad (8)$$

The learning performance of AI is tested by ensuring that the Mean Squared Error (MSE) value given in Equation (9) is close to zero.

$$\text{MSE}=\frac{1}{m}\sum_{i=1}^{m}(Y_i-\hat{Y}_i)^2 \quad (9)$$

After the construction of the AI model, criterion evaluation is obtained with linguistic expressions appropriate to those in Table 5.1 required for DEMATEL analysis. In addition, the experience periods of the experts are collected.

Expert opinions and experiences are added to the system as input. As a result of the evaluation of the AI system, the AI-based initial direct matrix (D) given in Equation (10) is obtained.

$$D=\begin{bmatrix} 0 & \cdots & (\mu_{1n},v_{1n},\pi_{1n}) \\ \vdots & \ddots & \vdots \\ (\mu_{n1},v_{n1},\pi_{n1}) & \cdots & 0 \end{bmatrix} \quad (10)$$

According to the components of SF numbers, D is divided into three submatrices. Afterward, each submatrix is normalized by applying Equations (11) and (12).

$$X=sD \quad (11)$$

$$s=\min\left[\frac{1}{\max_i \sum_{j=1}^{n}|d_{ij}|},\frac{1}{\max_j \sum_{i=1}^{n}|d_{ij}|}\right] \quad (12)$$

Table 5.1. Linguistic Variable for Evaluation.

Terms	μ	v	π
Strong	0.85	0.15	0.45
Moderate	0.6	0.2	0.35
Weak	0.35	0.25	0.25
No influence	0	0.3	0.15

Source: Authors.

With the help of Equation (13), the total relationship matrix (T) is calculated for each submatrix. Afterward, the T matrix Euclidean normalization process is applied (Kou et al., 2023).

$$T = X*(1-X)^{-1} \tag{13}$$

Then, with Equations (14)–(16), the row (R) and column (C) sums of T are obtained. By applying Equation (17), the two sums are defuzzified.

$$r_i = \sum_{i=1}^{n} < \mu_{ij}^T, v_{ij}^T, \pi_{ij}^T > \tag{14}$$

$$c_j = \sum_{j=1}^{n} < \mu_{ij}^T, v_{ij}^T, \pi_{ij}^T > \tag{15}$$

$$e.g. < \mu_{11}^T, v_{11}^T, \pi_{11}^T > + < \mu_{12}^T, v_{12}^T, \pi_{12}^T > = \left[\left(\mu_{11}^T\right)^2 + \left(\mu_{12}^T\right)^2 - \left(\mu_{11}^T\right)^2\left(\mu_{12}^T\right)^2\right]^{0,5},$$

$$v_{11}^T v_{12}^T, \left[\left(1-\left(\mu_{11}^T\right)^2\right)\left(\pi_{11}^T\right)^2 + \left(1-\left(\mu_{12}^T\right)^2\right)\left(\pi_{11}^T\right)^2 - \left(\pi_{11}^T\right)^2\left(\pi_{12}^T\right)^2\right]^{0,5} \tag{16}$$

$$\text{Score} = (2\mu - \pi)^2 - (v - \pi)^2 \tag{17}$$

Finally, Equation (18) gives information about the weights of the criteria (w) (Yüksel et al., 2024).

$$w_i = \frac{R_i + C_i}{\sum_{i=1}^{n}(R_i + C_i)} \tag{18}$$

w values are ordered from largest to smallest, and this order shows the order of importance levels (Eti et al., 2024).

Analysis of Results

Using 1,000 data sets created by simulation, Equations (1)–(8) are applied and the AI model for the initial direct matrix is constructed. The learning process is carried out in 100 epochs, thus minimizing the amount of error. In other words, when it reaches a sufficiently large number of epochs, the iteration is stopped because the value in Equation (9) does not get any closer to zero. Since the final MSE value, which indicates learning success, is calculated as 0.02, it is stated that the AI system passed the test. After the AI system is established, the criteria set is determined. The strategies determined for the integration of microgrid networks are given in Table 5.2.

The criteria in Table 5.2 are evaluated by experts determined in accordance with the scale in Table 5.1. The experts' years of experience are 18, 25, and 26.

Table 5.2. Strategies for Microgrid Networks.

Strategies	Codes
Dimension of the initial investment cost	COST
Adequacy of legal basis and incentive practices	LEGAL
Qualified personnel familiar with the system	PERSONNEL
Difficulties in integration	CHALLENGE
Cyber security risks	SAFETY
Continuous maintenance and operation needs	MAINTENANCE

Source: Authors.

respectively, and they are managers with high field experience or academics with international publications. Evaluations collected from experts are summarized in Table 5.3.

The evaluations in Table 5.3 and the experience periods of the experts are integrated into the AI system. As a result of the AI process, D shown in Equation (10) in Tables 5.4 and 5.5. is obtained.

After the submatrices of D matrix are normalized with Equations (11) and (12), T is calculated with Equation (13) (Table 5.4). After calculating the information of row and column totals with Equations (14)–(16), the totals are defuzzified with Equation (17). Finally, Equation (18) is used, and the weights are computed. The weights of strategies are displayed in Table 5.5.

According to Table 5.5, the most important strategy in the integration of microgrid networks in hospitals is the size of the initial investment cost because the important weight of this criterion is determined as 0.245. The second calculated strategy is to have qualified personnel. The last strategy is that integration has difficulties.

Discussion and Conclusion

As a result of the analysis, the dimension of the initial investment cost is found as the most important criterion affecting the process of integrating microgrid systems with hospitals. The design, installation, and operation of microgrid systems require expertise. This expertise increases investment costs. In addition, they are systems that require relatively new technology. Accordingly, it can be said that investment costs are high (Boujoudar et al., 2023). Besides, the batteries required in storage processes also require high costs (Saini et al., 2023). Colucci et al. (2024) aim to develop strategies to minimize the cost of electricity in microgrid systems. It is argued that reducing battery costs in microgrid systems will increase the success of the system. Zhou and Xu (2023) conducted a cost–benefit assessment for a microgrid system in Northeast China. The results of the study indicate that the initial investment cost, operation and maintenance cost, and battery cost significantly affect the process. Li et al. (2023) and Dashtaki et al. (2023) stated that costs play an important role in the success of microgrid systems.

Table 5.3. Evaluation of Strategies.

	COST	LEGAL	PERSONNEL	CHALLENGE	SAFETY	MAINTENANCE
			Expert 1			
COST	–	3	3	3	2	3
LEGAL	1	–	0	2	2	3
PERSONNEL	1	3	–	3	3	3
CHALLENGE	2	1	1	–	0	0
SAFETY	2	3	3	1	–	0
MAINTENANCE	2	2	2	2	1	–
			Expert 2			
	COST	**LEGAL**	**PERSONNEL**	**CHALLENGE**	**SAFETY**	**MAINTENANCE**
COST	–	3	3	2	2	3
LEGAL	2	–	1	2	2	2
PERSONNEL	1	2	–	3	2	2
CHALLENGE	3	1	1	–	1	1
SAFETY	2	3	3	1	–	1
MAINTENANCE	1	2	3	2	2	–

(Continued)

Table 5.3. (*Continued*)

	Expert 3					
	COST	**LEGAL**	**PERSONNEL**	**CHALLENGE**	**SAFETY**	**MAINTENANCE**
COST	–	3	3	3	3	2
LEGAL	0	–	1	2	3	3
PERSONNEL	1	1	–	1	2	2
CHALLENGE	2	2	2	–	1	1
SAFETY	1	2	2	0	–	0
MAINTENANCE	2	1	3	2	2	–

Source: Authors.

Table 5.4. Initial Direct Matrix.

	COST			**LEGAL**			**PERSONNEL**			**CHALLENGE**			**SAFETY**			**MAINTENANCE**		
COST	0.00	0.00	0.00	0.85	0.15	0.45	0.85	0.15	0.45	0.80	0.16	0.47	0.71	0.18	0.46	0.80	0.16	0.47
LEGAL	0.41	0.25	0.28	0.00	0.00	0.00	0.27	0.27	0.22	0.60	0.20	0.35	0.71	0.18	0.46	0.80	0.16	0.47
PERSONNEL	0.35	0.25	0.25	0.70	0.19	0.48	0.00	0.00	0.00	0.78	0.17	0.49	0.74	0.18	0.47	0.74	0.18	0.47
CHALLENGE	0.71	0.18	0.46	0.45	0.23	0.30	0.45	0.23	0.30	0.00	0.00	0.00	0.27	0.27	0.22	0.27	0.27	0.22
SAFETY	0.54	0.21	0.33	0.80	0.16	0.47	0.80	0.16	0.47	0.30	0.26	0.23	0.00	0.00	0.00	0.20	0.28	0.19
MAINTENANCE	0.54	0.21	0.33	0.54	0.21	0.33	0.78	0.17	0.47	0.60	0.20	0.35	0.52	0.22	0.32	0.00	0.00	0.00

Source: Authors.

Table 5.5. Weights.

Strategies	Weights
COST	0.245
LEGAL	0.149
PERSONNEL	0.180
CHALLENGE	0.115
SAFETY	0.143
MAINTENANCE	0.168

Source: Authors.

The results of the analysis show that the second most important criterion affecting the integration of microgrid systems with hospitals is having qualified personnel who are familiar with these systems. The microgrid system should be designed according to the needs of the hospital. Accordingly, qualified personnel who know the requirements of the hospital are needed. Apart from that, these systems need regular maintenance. Qualified personnel familiar with the process can ensure that the problem is solved quickly in case of a possible failure (Sahoo et al., 2023). Rojek et al. (2023) conducted a study proposing an AI-based computational model for the sustainable transformation of energy markets. The results of the study emphasize the need for qualified personnel for the success of the model. Mudaheranwa et al. (2023) conducted a study to design microgrids for people living in remote areas in Rwanda. It is stated that the success of this design is related to qualified personnel and their performance.

This study aims to identify priority strategies for integrating microgrid systems with hospitals. To achieve this goal, an AI-based multi-criteria decision-making method is used. The literature-based criteria are weighted using the AI-based DEMATEL method. It is concluded that the most important criterion that affects the process of integrating microgrid systems with hospitals is the initial investment cost. Similarly, it is seen that the criterion of having qualified personnel also contributes significantly to the process. The main contribution of this study is the integration of the AI approach with multi-criteria decision-making methodology. Thanks to this method, expert weights can be determined according to their qualifications. Therefore, it can be said that the evaluation to be made is more appropriate. The main limitation of this study is that the evaluation is conducted specifically for hospitals. It is possible to make new evaluations by considering different sectors.

References

Aghmadi, A., Hussein, H., Polara, K. H., & Mohammed, O. (2023). A comprehensive review of architecture, communication, and cybersecurity in networked microgrid systems. *Inventions*, *8*(4), 84.

An, D., Yang, Q., Li, D., & Wu, Z. (2023). Distributed online incentive scheme for energy trading in multi-microgrid systems. *IEEE Transactions on Automation Science and Engineering*, *21*(1), 951–964.

Arafat, M. Y., Hossain, M. J., & Alam, M. M. (2024). Machine learning scopes on microgrid predictive maintenance: Potential frameworks, challenges, and prospects. *Renewable and Sustainable Energy Reviews*, *190*, 114088.

Bansal, R. C., Justo, J. J., & Mwasilu, F. (Eds.). (2023). *Modeling and control dynamics in microgrid systems with renewable energy resources*. Academic Press.

Behrendt, J. (2023). Microgrids and EU law: Three microgrid models to solve one regulatory puzzle. *Energy Policy*, *177*, 113483.

Boonraksa, T., Pinthurat, W., Wongdet, P., Boonraksa, P., Marungsri, B., & Hredzak, B. (2023). *Optimal capacity and cost analysis of hybrid energy storage system in standalone DC microgrid*. IEEE Access.

Boujoudar, Y., Azeroual, M., Eliysaouy, L., Bassine, F. Z., Albarakati, A. J., Aljarbouh, A., Knyazkov, A., Moussaoui, H. E., & Lamhamdi, T. (2023). Fuzzy logic-based controller of the bidirectional direct current to direct current converter in microgrid. *International Journal of Electrical and Computer Engineering*, *13*(5), 4789–4797.

Chen, B., Jiang, J., & Shao, Y. (2023, February). Integrated scheduling and control system of microgrid based on dynamic programming algorithm. In *2023 IEEE international conference on integrated circuits and communication systems (ICICACS)* (pp. 1–5). IEEE.

Colucci, R., Mahgoub, I., Yousefizadeh, H., & Al-Najada, H. (2024). *Survey of strategies to optimize battery operation to minimize the electricity cost in a microgrid with renewable energy sources and electric vehicles*. IEEE Access.

Costea, S. D., & Orlando, S. (2023, October). LVDC microgrid topology, control and protection in the EU funded project Hyperride. In *2023 IEEE PES innovative smart grid technologies Europe (ISGT EUROPE)* (pp. 1–6). IEEE.

Das, R. C. (2020). Interplays among R&D spending, patent and income growth: New empirical evidence from the panel of countries and groups. *Journal of Innovation and Entrepreneurship*, *9*, 18. https://doi.org/10.1186/s13731-020-00130-8

Das, R. C., & Mukherjee, S. (2019). Do spending on R&D influence income? An enquiry on the world's leading economies and groups. *Journal of the Knowledge Economy*, *11*, 1295–1315. https://doi.org/10.1007/s13132-019-00609-0

Dashtaki, A. A., Hakimi, S. M., Hasankhani, A., Derakhshani, G., & Abdi, B. (2023). Optimal management algorithm of microgrid connected to the distribution network considering renewable energy system uncertainties. *International Journal of Electrical Power & Energy Systems*, *145*, 108633.

Dinçer, H., Yüksel, S., & Eti, S. (2023). Identifying the right policies for increasing the efficiency of the renewable energy transition with a novel fuzzy decision-making model. *Journal of Soft Computing and Decision Analytics*, *1*(1), 50–62.

Dinçer, H., Yüksel, S., Mikhaylov, A., Muyeen, S. M., Chang, T., Barykin, S., & Kalinina, O. (2023). CO_2 emissions integrated fuzzy model: A case of seven emerging economies. *Energy Reports*, *9*, 5741–5751.

Dzwigol, H., Kwilinski, A., Lyulyov, O., & Pimonenko, T. (2023). Renewable energy, knowledge spillover and innovation: Capacity of environmental regulation. *Energies*, *16*(3), 1117.

Eti, S., Dinçer, H., Yüksel, S., & Gökalp, Y. (2023). Analysis of the suitability of the solar panels for hospitals: A new fuzzy decision-making model proposal with the T-spherical TOP-DEMATEL method. *Journal of Intelligent & Fuzzy Systems*, *44*(3), 4613–4625.

Eti, S., Yüksel, S., Dinçer, H., Kalkavan, H., Hacioglu, U., Mikhaylov, A., Danish, M. S. S., & Pinter, G. (2024). Assessment of technical and financial challenges for renewable energy project alternatives. *Cleaner Engineering and Technology*, *18*, 100719.

Fishov, A., Osintsev, A., Ghulomzoda, A., Marchenko, A., Kokin, S., Safaraliev, M., Dmitriev, S., & Zicmane, I. (2023). Decentralized emergency control of AC power grid modes with distributed generation. *Energies*, *16*(15), 5607.

Gökalp, Y., Yüksel, S., & Dinçer, H. (2022). Balanced scorecard-based cost analysis of service industry using a novel hybrid decision making approach based on golden cut-oriented bipolar and q-ROF sets. *Journal of Intelligent & Fuzzy Systems*, *43*(4), 4709–4722.

Hamanah, W. M., Hossain, M. I., Shafiullah, M., & Abido, M. A. (2023). *AC microgrid protection schemes: A comprehensive review*. IEEE Access.

Hayashi, R., Takano, H., Nyabuto, W. M., Asano, H., & Nguyen-Duc, T. (2023). Bilevel optimization model for sizing of battery energy storage systems in a microgrid considering their economical operation. *Energy Reports*, *9*, 728–737.

Hirwa, J., Zolan, A., Becker, W., Flamand, T., & Newman, A. (2023). Optimizing design and dispatch of a resilient renewable energy microgrid for a South African hospital. *Applied Energy*, *348*, 121438.

Khubrani, M. M., & Alam, S. (2023). Blockchain-based microgrid for safe and reliable power generation and distribution: A case study of Saudi Arabia. *Energies*, *16*(16), 5963.

Koduru, S., Machina, V. S. P., & Madichetty, S. (2023). Cyber attacks in cyber-physical microgrid systems: A comprehensive review. *Energies*, *16*(12), 4573.

Kou, G., Dinçer, H., & Yüksel, S. (2024). Pattern recognition of financial innovation life cycle for renewable energy investments with integer code series and multiple technology S-curves based on Q-ROF DEMATEL. *Financial Innovation*, *10*(1), 1–22.

Kou, G., Pamucar, D., Dinçer, H., Deveci, M., Yüksel, S., & Umar, M. (2024). Perception and expression-based dual expert decision-making approach to information sciences with integrated quantum fuzzy modelling for renewable energy project selection. *Information Sciences*, *658*, 120073.

Kou, G., Pamucar, D., Dinçer, H., & Yüksel, S. (2023). From risks to rewards: A comprehensive guide to sustainable investment decisions in renewable energy using a hybrid facial expression-based fuzzy decision-making approach. *Applied Soft Computing*, *142*, 110365.

Li, X., Chen, L., Hao, Y., Wang, Z., Changxing, Y., & Mei, S. (2023). Sharing hydrogen storage capacity planning for multi-microgrid investors with limited rationality: A differential evolution game approach. *Journal of Cleaner Production*, *417*, 138100.

Lin, Y., Wang, J., Zhang, J., & Li, L. (2023). Microgrid optimal investment design for cotton farms in Australia. *Smart Grids and Sustainable Energy*, *9*(1), 5.

Mudaheranwa, E., Ntagwirumugara, E., Masengo, G., & Cipcigan, L. (2023). Microgrid design for disadvantaged people living in remote areas as tool in speeding up electricity access in Rwanda. *Energy Strategy Reviews*, *46*, 101054.

Oflaz, F., Yüksel, S., Dinçer, H., & Eti, S. (2023). A novel fuzzy decision-making methodology for ranking energy storage investments in emerging economies. *Decision Analytics Journal*, *9*, 100345.

Owusu-Obeng, P. Y., & Schell, K. R. (2023). Bi-level goal programming model for simultaneous microgrid investment and tariff design: A case study in the Volta Region of Ghana. *Renewable Energy Focus*, *47*, 100511.

Özdemirci, F., Yüksel, S., Dinçer, H., & Eti, S. (2023). An assessment of alternative social banking systems using T-spherical fuzzy TOP-DEMATEL approach. *Decision Analytics Journal*, *6*, 100184.

Pisla, M. A., Stanculescu, M., Porumb, R. F., Enache, B. A., & Seritan, G. C. (2023, March). Microgrid cyber security enhancement considerations. In *2023 13th International symposium on advanced topics in electrical engineering (ATEE)* (pp. 1–5). IEEE.

Rojek, I., Mroziński, A., Kotlarz, P., Macko, M., & Mikołajewski, D. (2023). AI-based computational model in sustainable transformation of energy markets. *Energies*, *16*(24), 8059.

Roux, R., Olwal, T. O., & Chowdhury, D. S. (2023). Software defined networking architecture for energy transaction in smart microgrid systems. *Energies*, *16*(14), 5275.

Sahoo, S., Jena, N. K., Anurag, A., Naik, A. K., Sahu, B. K., & Sahu, P. C. (2023). Frequency regulation of microgrid using fuzzy-logic based controllers. In N. Nayak (Ed.), *Proceedings of the 2023 International Conference in Advances in Power, Signal, and Information Technology (APSIT)* (pp. 120–123). *IEEE*. https://doi.org/10.1109/APSIT58554.2023.10201752

Saini, V. K., Kumar, R., Al-Sumaiti, A. S., & Panigrahi, B. K. (2023). Uncertainty aware optimal battery sizing for cloud energy storage in community microgrid. *Electric Power Systems Research*, *222*, 109482.

Thiak, S., & Hira, A. (2024). Strategic options for building a new electricity grid in South Sudan: The challenges of a new post-conflict nation. *Energy Research & Social Science*, *109*, 103417.

Yoo, Y., & Jung, S. (2024). Modeling forecast errors for microgrid operation using Gaussian process regression. *Scientific Reports*, *14*(1), 2166.

Yüksel, S., Eti, S., Dinçer, H., Gökalp, Y., Yavuz, D., Mikhaylov, A., & Pinter, G. (2024). Prioritizing the indicators of energy performance management: A novel fuzzy decision-making approach for G7 service industries. *Environmental Research Communications*, *6*(1), 015003.

Zafra-Cabeza, A., Marquez, J. J., Bordons, C., & Ridao, M. A. (2023). An online stochastic MPC-based fault-tolerant optimization for microgrids. *Control Engineering Practice*, *130*, 105381.

Zhen, J., Huang, S., Jia, X., & Du, H. (2023, May). Transient stability evaluation of ındependent microgrid based on message passing graph neural network. In *2023 6th International conference on electronics technology (ICET)* (pp. 861–866). IEEE.

Zhou, J., & Xu, Z. (2023). Optimal sizing design and integrated cost-benefit assessment of stand-alone microgrid system with different energy storage employing chameleon swarm algorithm: A rural case in Northeast China. *Renewable Energy*, *202*, 1110–1137.

Zou, W., Li, J., Yang, Q., Wan, X., He, Y., & Lan, H. (2023). A real-time energy management approach with fuel cell and battery competition-synergy control for the fuel cell vehicle. *Applied Energy*, *334*, 120667.

Chapter 6

Coherence Between Investment in Artificial Intelligence, Patent Seeking, GDP, and Employment: A Cross-country Analysis

Shubhamita Sarkar and Ramesh Chandra Das

Department of Economics, Vidyasagar University, India

Abstract

The new millennium has witnessed so many developments in the front of science and technology with the aim of promoting growth in a sustainable manner. The use of technological devices in the production process has minimized the uses of the traditional factors leading to low price production in certain products. But the latest development in the technological arena has been the use of artificial intelligence (AI) which has made life so simple and fast and made all the three production sectors, agriculture, industry, and service, highly AI dependent in many developed countries. The countries with the help of both public and private investments have sought patents in the several heads of AI besides other sectors' patents. This chapter examines whether investments in AI have strong cohesion with patents in AI sectors, gross domestic product (GDP), and employment of the countries using correlation and regression analysis for the period 2010–2020 across a listed country of the world. The observations are that the United States has the highest number of patents across most sectors, indicating strong innovation and technological development in various fields of AI followed by China and others. The correlation analysis shows that in most of the countries, AI patents maintain positive associations with GDP of the countries, but in some countries, the association is negative when the growth of GDP is concerned. Further, with respect to total employment, we find a few countries where AI patents maintain positive coherence, but in most of the countries, AI patents lead to low growth of employment, in concrete terms, negative growth of employment.

Keywords: AI; R&D; investment; patent; GDP; employment; correlation

Artificial Intelligence in Business and Society: Global Insights, 81–94

doi:10.1108/978-1-83708-022-920261015

Introduction

The new millennium has witnessed so many developments in the front of science and technology with the aim of promoting growth in a sustainable manner. The uses of physical factors like the traditional and human labour force, traditional and modern capitals, among others, have faced diminishing returns leading to retardation in growth and development of the countries in particular and the whole world in general. The use of technological devices in the production process has minimized the uses of the traditional factors leading to low price production in certain products which are mostly in the manufacturing and service sectors. But the latest development in the technological arena has been the use of AI which has made life so simple and fast and made all the three production sectors, agriculture, industry, and service, highly AI dependent in many developed countries. The countries with the help of both public and private investments have sought patents in the several heads of AI besides other sectors' patents.

Today, the world is well-acquainted with the term AI. AI is a branch of computer science focused on developing systems that can perform tasks typically requiring human intelligence. These tasks include learning, reasoning, speech recognition, and converting speech to text using natural language processing.

The craving to develop AI did not originate in the 21st century, it has been a fascination across many generations throughout history. When we look back to ancient times, there were many polymaths who attempted to create different types of automatons. Among these polymaths, some are famous for their creations, such as Al-Jazari's floating boat, Archytas' dove, Vaucanson's digesting duck, and Leonardo Da Vinci's knight, among many others. We can say that the idea of a machine being able to function on its own is ancient. AI has covered a long journey to come into existence in this world.

Turing (1950), a famous mathematician and scientist, published his research paper 'Computing Machinery and Intelligence' to help in decoding the Nazi's Enigma code during World War II. Six years later, in 1956, John McCarthy, known as the father of AI, coined the term 'Artificial Intelligence'. His seminal article (McCarthy, 1959) has changed the world of AI in a short span. The journey to develop a system capable of performing like a human was not easy. Scientists from different countries faced many challenges along the way, but now we stand in an era where humanoids and the first robot citizen named Sophia (2016) have been successfully created. She has the ability to see and replicate emotions, as well as communicate.

In 2019, Google's AlphaStar reached grandmaster status in the video game Starcraft II, outperforming all but 2% of human players. OpenAI (2021) started beta testing GPT-3, a model that uses deep learning to create code, poetry, and other such language and writing tasks. OpenAI (2022) developed DALL-E, which can process and understand images well enough to produce accurate captions, moving AI one step closer to understanding the visual world.

AI is basically categorized into two types: Weak AI and Strong AI. Weak or Narrow AI is designed to perform specific tasks with focus and training. We see applications of Weak AI in systems like Apple's Siri, Amazon's Alexa, IBM

Watson, and autonomous vehicles. Strong AI has two components: Artificial General Intelligence (AGI) and Artificial Super Intelligence (ASI). Their intelligence levels are equal to human intelligence and are currently theoretical.

AI has now become a part of our day-to-day activities. It is used in various fields like healthcare, agriculture, banking, corporate sectors, and more. Banking is one of the most crucial sectors in the development of an economy. The banking system operated traditionally, resulting in more time and money spent, but now banks and many financial institutions are adopting modern technologies that help in cyber-security and fraud detection, data collection and analysis, customer experience, and smoothly carrying out other activities. EVA, the chatbot system adopted by HDFC Bank, is a proof that the banking system is gradually accepting AI applications. Similarly, we can see the applications of AI in agriculture and other fields. AI applications in agriculture include crop disease detection, automated weed control systems, livestock health monitoring, precise irrigation systems, drone-assisted aerial surveillance, and more. As we can see the positive side of AI, there must also be some negative aspects. As Google CEO, Sundar Pichai said in a 2018 town hall event in San Francisco that the invention of AI has caused more upheaval than the invention of fire. The increased use of AI and automation raises the chances of job loss in the economy, as machines can work continuously without getting tired. Developing and maintaining AI is extremely expensive. AI lacks emotions and cannot think outside the box, as they lack the creativity and intuition that human beings possess. Ethical issues such as unjustified actions, opacity, bias, moral responsibility, and discrimination arise from the use of AI and are matters of serious concern. According to the International Monetary Fund (IMF) report, 40% of jobs will be affected by AI. Therefore, we need effective policies to balance the gap caused by job losses due to the intervention of AI.

Thus, within the complex and uncertain scenarios on the impacts of AI, the aim of this chapter is to examine how AI investment influences GDP, the number of AI patents, and the employment across some selected countries of the world. By analysing the data from 2010 to 2020, this study tries to understand whether AI investment leads to economic growth, encourages innovation, and affects job markets.

Literature Review

The study reviews some of the available literature on the associations or impacts of AI with several areas like banking, employment, GDP and its growth, etc. to find the untouched areas where the present study can intervene.

Banking Sector

Padmanabhan and Metilda (2021) explored the implementation of AI and its effect on the banking sector. They concluded that after adopting these technologies, customers could enjoy banking services anytime and anywhere, though it comes at a cost to the banking sector. Shetty et al. (2022) studied how the banking system implements AI in their traditional systems and how the different age groups of bankers and customers reacted after the implementation. They concluded that customers aged 18–25 were strongly in favour of the implementation of AI in banks, while those below 18 and above 60 show less interest. Similarly, bankers aged 21–30 strongly support AI in banks and enjoy the benefits after its implementation. Vijaya Lakshmi (2024) explored the impact and implementation of AI in Hyderabad's banking and financial services sector and found that while most customers are satisfied with the services provided by advanced technologies, some customers found AI to be of little use to them. AI is not only helpful for banking customers but also benefits the banking sector in many ways. Kaur et al. (2020) studied the impact of AI on the modern banking system and how it has transformed banking practices. They observed that the application of these modern technologies had significantly changed the face of banking in India. There is another interesting work by Karthiga et al. (2024) who studied the impact of AI on the banking system. The study has concluded that AI has the potential to transform the future of banking in India. With the help of chatbots, machine learning algorithms, and other advanced technologies, banks can generate new ideas and serve their customers more intelligently and efficiently. With the advancement of technology, our financial activities are now just a fingertip away. With a single click, we can transfer money to any corner of the world. Vinoth and Chandran (2022) studied the impact of AI on the banking system and its effect on our daily lives. They revealed that in the future, the Indian banking system would become more advanced with the increasing application of more developed and smarter AI technologies.

Agriculture Sector

Dharmaraj and Vijayanand (2018) studied the role of AI in the agricultural sector and provided an extensive examination of the integration and application of AI technologies in the agricultural sector, emphasizing how these advancements are transforming farming practices. Elbaşi et al. (2023) studied the significant impact that AI has on modern agriculture and concluded that due to the increasing global population and the subsequent rise in food demand, the adoption of AI technologies has become necessary in this field. AI applications in agriculture are categorized into three main areas: soil and crop monitoring, predictive analytics, and agricultural robotics. By focusing on these three areas, productivity will improve. Awais et al. (2023) studied how AI can enhance soil analysis to achieve sustainability in agriculture. The study pointed out the limitations of traditional methods and encouraged the use of AI-driven approaches, which help to obtain accurate data on soil analysis and enable efficient irrigation. Karmokar et al. (2015) studied a system which is designed to identify the leaf diseases by the help of image processing and neural network techniques. The study concluded that the proposed Too Long Didn't Read (TLDR) system is the first initiative of its kind in Bangladesh for tea leaf disease recognition. The method is effective, low-cost, and non-destructive, requiring only digital photographs of tea leaves to identify diseases. The system can help in taking preventive measures to save tea production from extensive damage. Munnisunkar et al. (2022) discussed how technological advancements in the agricultural sector have historically reduced labour demand while increasing productivity. The study provides examples from the United States and Europe, where labour demand in agriculture has declined, but AI-driven job opportunities are emerging. The study predicted that the loss of manual jobs and other farming challenges should be addressed through significant investment in AI. Ryan (2023) examined the societal and ethical impacts of AI in agriculture, identifying key themes like transparency, fairness, and sustainability. While AI can enhance sustainable farming and productivity, it also poses challenges such as trust, privacy, and farmers' autonomy. The study stresses the importance of transparent and fair AI systems that respect privacy and support all farming communities.

Impact of AI on GDP Growth

Mou (2019) explained that AI was transforming industries and boosting global economic growth, especially in the United States and China, with China receiving 75% of global AI funding in early 2018 due to strong government support. Emerging markets, despite their potential, receive less investment. AI is used in various fields like energy, healthcare, education, manufacturing, finance, and transportation. While AI brings many benefits, it also poses challenges like job loss and uneven investment. Emerging markets could greatly benefit from AI, especially in agriculture and finance. Continued investment in AI is crucial for tackling global challenges. Vijayakumar (2021) studied AI's impact on US economic growth from 2010 to 2020, finding immediate benefits in the Life Sciences and long-term gains in Physical Sciences and Engineering. Private investment is crucial for growth, and policymakers should account for both short-term and long-term effects while addressing income inequality. Parteka and Kordalska (2023) analysed the relationship between advancements in AI and economic productivity in Organisation for Economic Co-operation and Development (OECD) countries as well as some non-OECD countries. After their rigorous analysis, they found no significant evidence of a link between technological innovation in AI and macroeconomic productivity growth.

GDP is one of the most important indicators to measure the growth rate of a country. By analysing the growth rate, we can determine which countries are more inclined to utilize technological advantages. According to Jaromir Vrbka (2016), the GDP of Eurozone countries can be predicted using AI, especially neural networks. The study analyses GDP data from 1960 to 2015 and forecasts the GDP of Eurozone countries up to 2050. The predictions made by AI are much more accurate and easier to calculate than those made using conventional statistical and mathematical models. Gonzales (2023) applies fixed effects and the generalized method of moments to analyse the impact of AI on long-term GDP growth. The study shows that AI patents are more effective in promoting GDP growth than other types of patents. As AI patents increase, AI innovation rises, resulting in improved productivity in the economy and enhanced quality of services.

Impact of AI on Employment

Damioli et al. (2023) studied the impact of AI technologies on employment, mainly focusing on the supply side. The study has found that these technologies are labour-friendly and will help improve employment in the long run. Employment has become a major concern for many countries, especially those with large populations such as China and India. The employment rate has decreased in low-skill-level jobs due to the adoption of technology in various sectors. Loong et al. (2021) primarily examined the impact of AI on the labour market in the Chinese economy. They found that AI was transforming the working system from traditional methods to more flexible working arrangements, which may pose a high risk for low-skill-level employment. However, high-tech and innovative sectors may see new job opportunities. Therefore, Chinese labour laws should design policies to help secure the position of low-skill-level workers. Sholler and MacInnes (2022) also examined and expressed concern about the impact of AI on employment and income disparities. The implementation of AI technologies may benefit high-skilled workers but reduces opportunities and leads to job losses for low- and medium-skilled workers due to automation. They suggest that policies should be implemented to ensure that the benefits of AI technologies are more evenly distributed across the workforce.

Impact of AI on Research and Development (R&D)

Aloun (2024) studied the impact of AI on patents and significant changes AI is bringing to the global patent system. The study concludes that the integration of AI into the patent system is inevitable and will lead to significant changes in how patents are examined, granted, and enforced.

Giczy et al. (2022) have studied how AI impacts R&D and introduced a new dataset designed to identify AI inventions within patent documents. The study finds that the creation and public release of the Artificial Intelligence Patent Dataset (AIPD) is a significant step forward in AI research. The dataset enables a more detailed analysis of AI's role in innovation, providing a valuable tool for policymakers and researchers to explore the determinants and effects of AI inventions.

Baruffaldi et al. (2020) focus on the development of AI through multiple data sources. This paper shows the rapid growth of AI technologies across the globe. Benassi et al. (2019) studied about the patenting activity at the European Patent Office (EPO) related to Fourth Industrial Revolution (4IR) technologies. The paper shows how companies increasingly specialize in specific technological areas and how patent applications have grown rapidly, with 4IR-related filings constituting a significant portion of overall patent activity at the EPO. Although there have been some studies in the area that R&D does not necessarily impact GDP, rather they are targeted for patent seeking (Das, 2020; Das & Mukherjee, 2019).

Objectives of the Study

The present chapter seeks to examine whether investments in AI have strong cohesion with patents in AI sectors, GDP, and employment of the countries. If so, how it may impact incomes, employment, and number of AI patents of listed countries of the world.

Data Descriptions

The analysis is based on secondary data regarding private AI investment, number of AI patents, GDP, and employment across listed countries over different years. AI investment refers to the allocation of resources, including capital, time, and expertise, into AI-driven technologies to enhance. GDP at purchaser's prices is the sum of gross value added by all resident producers in the economy plus any product taxes and minus any subsidies not included in the value of the products. It is calculated without making deductions for depreciation of fabricated assets or for depletion and degradation of natural resources. Data are in constant 2015 prices, expressed in US$. The number of AI patents of the country shows the innovation capacity in the AI technologies. Similarly, employment in a country refers to the total number of people engaged in economic activities within that country. Eleven countries are considered for the study, so far as availability of the data is concerned, countries like Canada, China, France, Germany, Japan, Italy, India, Japan, Singapore, South Korea, United Kingdom, and the United States. The data on AI investment, measured in constant 2021 US$, are taken from 'Our World in Data' (https://ourworldindata.org), and the data on GDP, measured in constant 2015 US$, are taken from the World Bank (https://databank.worldbank.org/source/world-development-indicators). The data on annual AI-granted patents by industry (sum of 10 different fields such as banking and finance, industry and manufacturing, energy management, physical science and engineering, security, life science, transportation, business, telecommunications, and personal device and computing) are taken from (https://ourworldindata.org) for the list countries for time period of 2010–2020. The employment data for this study have been sourced from World Bank's World Development (https://databank.worldbank.org/source/world-development-indicators).

Methodology

Data on AI investment, GDP, AI patents, and employment across selected countries have been compiled from credible sources. The relations between AI investment and GDP and AI patents and employment are analysed using the product–moment correlation coefficients to determine whether AI investments are positively or negatively associated with these factors using the following formula:

$$R = \frac{\sum \left(x_i - \bar{x}\right)\left(y_i - \bar{y}\right)}{\left[\sum \left(x_i - \bar{x}\right)^2\right]\left[\sum \left(y_i - \bar{y}\right)^2\right]}$$

where R is the correlation coefficient; x_i y_i, the individual data points for the variables X and Y; $\bar{x}, \bar{y}$ the mean of the variables X and Y, and Σ the summation across all data points.

Then, the values are tested by t statistics for statistical significance where the expression is:

$t = R\sqrt{\frac{(n-2)}{(1-R^2)}}$ with $n - 2$ degrees of freedom, here the number of observations is 11 so $(n - 2) = 9$; the table value of $t = 2.101$ for 5% level of significance. If the t-value is more than 2.101, then it is said that the said correlation is statistically significant.

After that, the regression exercise has been done between total AI investment and the number of patents, AI investment and GDP, and AI investment and employment for each country.

Regression equations are:

$$\text{AI patents} = \alpha + \beta \text{ AI investment} + \varepsilon \quad (1)$$

$$\text{GDP} = a + b \text{ AI investment} + \theta \quad (2)$$

$$\text{Employment} = p + q \text{ AI investment} + \varnothing \quad (3)$$

where α, a, and p are the intercepts; β, b, and q, are the regression coefficients; AI investment is the independent variable, and ε, θ, and $\varnothing$ are the error terms in Equations (1), (2), and (3), respectively. AI patents, GDP, and employment are the dependent variables in Equations (1), (2), and (3), respectively. The above three regression analyses are done for all the individual countries.

Analysis of Results

The study first presents the descriptive statistics, mainly the mean and standard deviation, of all the four indicators which are shown in the upper panel of Table 6.1. Then, the correlation results are shown using the formula as given in the 'Methodology' section and are shown in the lower panel of Table 6.1.

The number of AI patents shows a country's innovation capacity in AI technologies, and AI patents cover a range of industries, including agriculture, manufacturing, healthcare, and so on. From the upper panel of Table 6.1, it is observed that countries such as the United States, China, Japan, and South Korea have shown highest number of AI patents on an average for the entire period of the study, indicating that these countries have strong R&D efforts. On the other hand, countries such as China, the United States, and the South Korea have shown positive associations of AI investment with GDP growth. One of the biggest debates surrounding AI is its impact on employment. While AI increases efficiency and reduces costs, it also raises concerns about job displacement. The correlation analysis between AI investment and employment presents mixed results; it displaces labour in the labour surplus economy China.

The correlation coefficient between AI investment and the number of AI patents is positive for all the listed countries except Italy. The above results show

Table 6.1. Results of Mean (Standard Deviation), Correlation Coefficient, and Corresponding Estimated t-Value.

Country	AI Investment		AI Patent		GDP		Total Employment	
	Mean	Standard Deviation	Mean	Standard Deviation	Mean	Standard Deviation	Mean	Standard Deviation
Canada	8.59E+08	6.35E+08	239.55	170.27	1.55E+12	9.3E+10	1.2E+07	362,926.561
China	5.97E+09	6.24E+09	5,146.55	4,931.48	1.11E+13	2.4E+12	5.1E+08	9,228,830.815
France	6.57E+08	3.66E+08	24.73	22.95	3.43E+12	1.7E+11	1.5E+07	108,875.4346
Germany	6.57E+08	3.66E+08	162.09	140.70	2.44E+12	8.7E+10	2.5E+07	1,162,679.918
Italy	40,789,240	31,754,866	9.45	7.44	2.89E+12	1.7E+11	1.1E+07	338,261.9087
India	5.25E+09	6.27E+09	76.91	93.24	2.11E+12	4.2E+11	2.4E+08	5,386,663.188
Japan	4.83E+08	4.19E+08	971.64	897.53	1.87E+12	5.3E+10	3.9E+07	1,671,122.912
South Korea	2.75E+08	2.52E+08	1,689.00	1,664.44	4.41E+12	1.3E+11	1.7E+07	894,058.0729
Singapore	4.48E+08	7.25E+08	55.00	48.86	1.47E+12	1.3E+11	2,250,533	153,388.5349
United Kingdom	1.75E+09	1.11E+09	112.00	88.93	3.06E+11	3.5E+10	2E+07	942,088.8714
United States	3.42E+10	3.1E+10	5,766.55	4,789.24	1.82E+13	1.3E+12	9.4E+07	3,764,933.089

(Continued)

Table 6.1. (*Continued*)

	Correlation Results		
Country	**AI Investment and AI Patent**	**AI Investment and GDP**	**AI Investment and Employment**
Canada	0.45 (1.52)	0.65(2.58)*	0.47(1.62)
China	0.88 (5.47)*	0.89 (5.17)*	−0.82 (−4.32)*
France	0.57 (2.10)	0.52 (1.85)	0.19 (0.59)
Germany	0.56 (2.04)	0.75 (3.38)*	0.72 (3.14)*
Italy	−0.13 (−0.39)	−0.55 (−1.97)	0.19 (0.57)
India	0.21 (0.66)	0.59 (2.19)*	0.38 (1.22)
Japan	0.30 (0.95)	0.44 (1.46)	0.30 (0.95)
South Korea	0.92 (7.04)*	0.74 (3.31)*	0.60 (2.22)*
Singapore	0.51 (1.77)	0.71 (3.04)*	0.59 (2.17)*
United Kingdom	0.39 (1.28)	0.43 (1.42)	0.77 (3.57)*
United States	0.76 (3.53)*	0.88 (5.64)*	0.73 (3.20)*

Source: Authors' own computations.

Note: E+ means the values will precede before the decimal points with zeros depending upon the number after E+ with one less zero (e.g. the coefficient for Canada is 8.59E+08 means 859,000,000.00). (−) signs indicate that variables are negatively correlated, and (+) signs indicate that the variables are positively correlated.

*Significant correlation coefficient at 5% level of significant.

that the AI investment has a positive impact on patent registration. Higher AI investment encourages companies and institutions to develop new AI technologies which leads to generate more patent applications. Most of the countries show a positive relation between AI investment and the number of patents, except in few cases like Italy, where the correlation is negative. The United States leads in AI patents, followed by China. The correlation coefficient between AI investment and the GDP is positive in most countries, indicating that as AI investment increases, GDP also tends to grow except Italy. Italy shows a negative and insignificant correlation coefficient, whereas Canada, China, France, Germany, India, South Korea, Singapore, and the United States show a significant positive correlation between the AI investment and GDP, but out of this, only the United States and China show a strong relationship between AI investment and GDP. In countries like Germany, South Korea, and the United States, AI investment has led to job creation, particularly in high-tech companies, but in case of China, the correlation between AI investment and employment is negative, which indicates that AI investment creates an inverse effect on the job markets in China. It may lead to job losses in that sectors which depend on manual labour.

Now coming to the impact of analysis of AI investment upon number of AI patents, GDP, and employment which is done by the regression exercise, the results are shown in Table 6.2.

Table 6.2 presents the regression results exploring number of patents, GDP, and employment as the dependent variables and AI investment as the only independent variable. The positive signs of the regression coefficient are observed in all the selected countries except Italy. The United States, China, and South Korea show the higher values of the regression coefficients, suggesting that increased AI investment is strongly correlated with the patent numbers. In case of GDP as the dependent variable, all the selected countries show a positive sign except Italy, which means AI has a positive impact on the economic growth in most of the countries particularly in the United States, China, and South Korea. For employment, the results are mixed. Countries such as Germany, South Korea, and the United States show positive results, but in case of China, there are negative impacts of AI on employment, which means AI investment may be replacing traditional jobs rather than creating new employment opportunities.

Concluding Observations

In our journey to examine the associations and impacts of AI investments upon patents, GDP, and employment for a listed country for the period 2010–2020, the results show that the United States shows highest number of patents, indicating that it is focusing on innovation and technological development in various fields of AI from the above observations. After the United States, China has the second-highest number of patents. European countries such as Germany and France have a moderate level of patents. Fewer patents have been filed in India and Italy. The correlation analysis shows that in most of the countries, AI investment maintains positive associations with AI patents and GDP of the countries, but in some countries, the association is negative when the growth of GDP is

Table 6.2. Results of Regression Exercise.

Dependent Variable: AI Patent, GDP (Constant 2015 US$), and Employment									
Independent Variable: AI Investment									
Country's Name	AI Patents			GDP			Employment		
	Constant	Regression Coefficient	R^2 Value and *p*-Value)	Constant	Regression Coefficient	R^2 Value (*p*-Value)	Constant	Regression Coefficient	R^2 Value (*p*-Value)
Canada	139.71	1.16E−07	0.20 (0.16)	1.47E+12	92.35	0.42 (0.03)	11,894,422	0.000258	0.23 (0.14)
China	128.36	8.41E−07	0.77 (0.0004)	9.19E+12	328.78	0.78 (0.0002)	5.22E+08	−0.00175	0.64 (0.002)
France	8.22	2.51E−08	0.33 (0.06)	2.38E+12	91.84	0.27 (0.10)	15,330,688	4.25E−05	0.04 (0.57)
Germany	63.27	1.51E−07	0.32 (0.07)	3.26E+12	255.68	0.56 (0.01)	23,746,116	0.001619	0.52 (0.01)
Italy	10.18	−1.79E−08	0.02 (0.71)	1.89E+12	−527.55	0.30 (0.08)	11,125,942	0.001098	0.03 (0.58)
India	64.60	2.34E−09	0.05 (0.53)	1.96E+12	29.26	0.35 (0.06)	2.39E+08	0.00023	0.14 (0.26)
Japan	766.09	4.26E−07	0.09 (0.37)	4.36E+12	93.21	0.19 (0.18)	37,659,071	0.002462	0.71 (0.00)
South Korea	257.78	5.2E−06	0.85 (0.00)	1.39E+12	284.87	0.55 (0.01)	16,184,659	0.001513	0.35 (0.05)
Singapore	39.72	3.41E−08	0.26 (0.11)	2.9E+11	34.86	0.51 (0.01)	2,194,429	0.000125	0.34 (0.06)
United Kingdom	80.32	1.81E−08	0.15 (0.23)	2.82E+12	39.89	0.18 (0.19)	19,165,727	0.000391	0.59 (0.01)
United States	2,211.41	1.04E−07	0.58 (0.01)	1.7E+13	35.05	0.78 (0.00)	91,741,521	7.81E−05	0.53 (0.01)

Source: Authors' own computations.

Note: E− means the values will proceed after the decimal points with zeros depending upon the number after E− with one less zero (e.g. the coefficient for Canada is 1.16232E−07 means −0.0000001162). *Significant regression coefficient at 5% level of significance. At 5% level of significance with degrees of freedom 9, the *t* statistics value is 2.101.

concerned. Further, with respect to total employment, we find a few countries where AI investment maintains positive coherence, but in most of the countries, AI investment leads to low growth of employment, in concrete terms, negative growth of employment.

Therefore, AI investment is good for GDP, and it has a significant impact on GDP growth and innovation, as reflected in the increasing number of AI patents. However, it has various effects on employment through country and industry. The policymakers of the countries should think of the labour layoffs due to AI investment and to frame alternative policies such as workforce reskilling and job transition programmes towards absorbing the surplus of displaced labours in other sectors. To achieve a sustainable economic growth, countries should adopt AI in different fields while ensuring that employment opportunities should not be harmed. Governments and industries should work together to balance the technological advancements with sustainable economic policies, ensuring that AI benefits society as a whole.

References

Aloun, D. M. (2024). The impact of Artificial Intelligence on patents. *International Journal of Recent Research in Social Sciences and Humanities*, *11*(2), 63–72.

Awais, M., Naqvi, S. M. Z. A., Zhang, H., Li, L., Zhang, W., Awwad, F. A., Ismail, E. A. A., Khan, I., Raghavan, V., & Hu. J. (2023). AI and machine learning for soil analysis: An assessment of sustainable agricultural practices. *Bioresources and Bioprocessing*, *10*, 90. https://doi.org/10.1186/s40643-023-00710

Baruffaldi, S., van Beuzekom, B., Dernis, H. & Harhoff, D. (2020). Identifying and measuring developments in artificial intelligence: Making the impossible possible. www.oecd-ilibrary.org

Benassi, M., Grinza, E., & Rentocchini, F. (2019). The rush for patents in the fourth industrial revolution: An exploration of patenting activity at the European Patent Office. *SSRN Electronic Journal*. https://doi.org/10.2139/ssrn.3414338

Damioli, G., Roy, V. Van, Vertesy, D., & Vivarelli, M. (2023). AI technologies and employment: Micro evidence from the supply side. *Applied Economics Letter*, *30*(6), 816–821. https://doi.org/10.1080/13504851.2021.2024129

Das, R. C. (2020). Interplays among R&D spending, patent and income growth: New empirical evidence from the panel of countries and groups. *Journal of Innovation and Entrepreneurship*, *9*, 18. https://doi.org/10.1186/s13731-020-00130-8

Das, R. C., & Mukherjee, S. (2019). Do spending on R&D influence income? An enquiry on the world's leading economies and groups. *Journal of the Knowledge Economy*, *11*, 1295–1315.

Dharmaraj, V., & Vijayanand, C. (2018). Artificial intelligence (AI) in agriculture. *International Journal of Current Microbiology and Applied Sciences*, *7*(12), 2122–2128.

Elbaşı, E., Mostafa, N., Al Arnaout, Z., Zreikat, A., Cina, E., Varghese, G., Shdefat, A., Topcu, A., Abdelbaki, W., Mathew, S., & Zaki, C. (2023). Artificial intelligence technology in the agricultural sector: A systematic literature review. *IEEE Access*, *11*, 171–202.

Giczy, A. V., Pairolero, N. A., & Toole, A. A. (2022). Identifying artificial intelligence (AI) invention: A novel AI patent dataset. *The Journal of Technology Transfer*, *47*, 476–505. https://doi.org/10.1007/s10961-021-09900-2

Gonzales, J. T. (2023). Implications of AI innovation on economic growth: A panel data study. *Economic Structures, 12*(13). https://doi.org/10.1186/s40008-023-00307-w

Karmokar, B. C., Ullah, M. S., Siddiquee, M. K., & Alam, K. M. R. (2015). Tea leaf diseases recognition using neural network ensemble. *International Journal of Computer Applications, 114*(17), 27–30.

Kaur, N., Sahdev, S. L., & Sharma, D. (2020). Banking 4.0: The influence of artificial intelligence on the banking industry & how AI is changing the face of modern day banks. *International Journal of Management, 11*, 577–585.

Karthiga, R., Ananthi, S., Kaur, R., Das, D. K., Natarajan, S. & Dhinakaran, D. P. (2024). Impact of Artificial Intelligence in the banking sector. *YUGATO, 76*(1).

Loong, Z., Ai, X., Huang, T., & Xiang, S. (2021). The impact of AI on employment and the corresponding response of PRC labor law. *Journal of Chinese Human Resources Management, 12*(2), 69–94.

McCarthy, J. (1959). Programs with common sense. Her Majesty's Stationery Office (H.M.S.O.) (Ed.). In *Teddington conference on the mechanization of thought processes* (pp. 300–307). National Physical Laboratory in Teddington, England.

Mou, X. (2019). Artificial intelligence: Investment trends and selected industry uses. *International Finance Corporation, 8*(2), 311–320.

Munnisunkar, S., Nel, L.., & Diederichs, D. (2022). The impact of artificial intelligence on agriculture labour in Europe. *Journal of Agricultural Informatics, 13*(1), 46–54.

OpenAI. (2021). *OpenAI scholars 2021: Final projects.* https://openai.com/index/openai-scholars-2021-final-projects/

Sophia. (2016). Sophia-a humanoid robot, https://en.wikipedia.org/wiki/Sophia_(robot)

Padmanabhan, V., & Metilda, V. P. (2021). An impact of artificial intelligence in Indian banking industries. *International Research Journal of Education and Technology, 1*(4), 39–45.

Parteka, A., & Kordalska, A. (2023). Artificial intelligence and productivity: Global evidence from AI patent and bibliometric data. *Technovation, 124*, 1–14.

Ryan, M. (2023). The social and ethical impacts of artificial intelligence in agriculture: Mapping the agricultural AI literature. *AI & Society, 38*, 2473–2485.

Shetty, S. K., Spulbar, C., Birau, R., & Filip, R. D. (2022). Impact of artificial intelligence in banking sector with reference to private banks in India. *Physics AUC, 32*, 59–72.

Sholler, D., & MacInnes, I. (2022). *The economic impact of AI on employment and income disparities*. 31st European conference of the International Telecommunications Society (ITS): 'Reining in digital platforms? Challenging monopolies, promoting competition and developing regulatory regimes', Gothenburg, Sweden, June 20–21. https://hdl.handle.net/10419/265669

OpenAI. (2022). Artificial Imagination, https://time.com/collection/best-inventions-2022/6225486/dall-e-2/

Turing, A. M. (1950). Computing machinery and intelligence. *Mind, 49*, 433–460.

Vijayakumar, H. (2021). The impact of AI-innovations and private AI-investment on U.S. economic growth: An empirical analysis. *Reviews of Contemporary Business Analytics, 4*(1), 14–32.

Vijaya Lakshmi, B. (2024). A study on artificial intelligence in banking sector. *International Journal of Creative Research Thoughts (IJCRT), 12*(1), 381–386. http://www.ijcrt.org/papers/IJCRTZ020043.pdf

Vinoth, S., & Chandran, P. (2022). Artificial intelligence and transformation to the digital age in Indian banking industry – A case study. *Turkish Online Journal of Qualitative Inquiry (TOJQI), 13*(1), 689–695.

Vrbka, J. (2016). Predicting future GDP development by means of artificial intelligence. *Littera Scripta, 9*(3), 154–167.

Chapter 7

Disruptive Digital Technologies in Emerging Artificial Intelligence: A Critical Analysis

José G. Vargas-Hernández[a], *Omar C. Vargas-Gonzàlez*[b], *Selene Castañeda Burciaga*[c] *and Omar Alejandro Guirette Barbosa*[c]

[a]*Postgraduate and Research Division. Instituto Tecnológico Mario Molina Pasquel y Henríquez, Unidad Académica Zapopan, Zapopan, Jalisco, Mexico*
[b]*Instituto Tecnológico de México, Campus Cd. Guzmán, Jalisco, México*
[c]*Universidad Politécnica de Zacatecas, Zacatecas, México*

Abstract

Machine learning in artificial intelligence (AI) tools, such as the ChatGPT, can offer prompt responses with an unforeseen combination of innovative and valuable texts produced from digital traces, with the likelihood of an exceptionally low selection subject to quality data sources and training. These traces require a knowing subject to interpret, analyze, and validate the outcomes. This chapter analyzes the emergent and disruptive digital technologies in an era of AI. It departs from the assumption that the emerging technologies create both opportunities and challenges with an impact on individuals, organizations, institutions, and society at large in terms of bias, surveillance, hacking, etc. using existing scientific literature. It concludes that control over the ethical disruption of digital technologies must require a digital conversation and leadership about acceptable ethical behaviors, under the assumption that digital transformation cannot be interrupted and must be guided by humans in the following years of the near future.

Keywords: Machine learning; artificial intelligence; ChatGPT; employment; digital trace; digital transformation

Artificial Intelligence in Business and Society: Global Insights, 95–109

doi:10.1108/978-1-83708-022-920261017

Introduction

I Can Do Everything for You

Human development in recent decades has been accompanied by emergent and rapid disruptive technological changes leading to a growing proliferation of digitized devices and services. Emergent and disruptive digital technologies have become intrinsic to our current way for life and will be part of our future lifestyle, from mundane routines and activities to improvement of productivity, contributing to manage the requirements of an economic growth in a more competitive and dynamic environment and evaluating the balance of power for a more collective security.

AI has a significant impact on individuals, organizations, and societies by offering systematic capabilities of learning and reasoning based on inputs and the differences with the expected outputs, predicting and adapting to changes in the socio-ecosystems from its received external environment stimulus. AI is a digital transformation led by emerging technologies that have burst into all fields and sectors worldwide leading to benefits in terms of agility, efficiency, transparency, and social welfare, so it can be said that emerging and disruptive digital technologies play a leading role in our environment and can do everything for us!

Smart Life on Everything

AI, internet of things (IoT), blockchain, and ChatGPT, among others, are emergent and disruptive digital technologies that aid human beings and societies in quick and efficient way to increase economic productivity, support the social well-being by providing a more educated, productive, and healthier lifestyle of individuals, anticipate and prevent responses to crisis and disasters, absorbing shocks, etc. (Sharifi et al., 2021). An increased level of research in chatbots designed to respond to queries of the user by mapping the best possible response in real-time feedback is based on adopted language models and deep learning to address natural language processes (NLPs) (Kushwaha & Kar, 2021; Lokman & Ameedeen, 2018).

The Evolution of Emerging and Frontier Technologies

The pace of change is likely to accelerate because of the "frontier technologies" that are redefining our world, taking advantage of digitization and connectivity, including AI, big data, blockchain, the IoT, three-dimensional (3D) printing, robotics, drones, biotechnology, and nanotechnology. Emerging and disruptive technologies evolution has become the buzzword of the current economic and productivity growth, geopolitical landscape, and security architecture, to build resilience leading to conclude that there is a strong link between them. The design of future digital technologies is bound to change the technological socio-ecosystem and the society at large.

Organizations and states remain the major actors in technological innovation designing and implementing policies, strategies, tactics, and instruments, although the leading technological edge is currently and will be led in the future by private firms, university research centers, and academia while extending the possibility to involve the whole of society approach in operations. The emerging technologies create both opportunities and challenges with an impact on individuals, organizations, institutions, and society at large in terms of bias, surveillance, hacking, etc. Digital technologies enhance economic, societal, and socio-ecological resilience in terms of health, education, connectivity, communication, etc.

Innovation and competition are the drivers of an emerging and disruptive digital technologies raising challenges and threats based on dynamic and organic processes that require creative destruction of established technologies and industries that takes considerable time in revealing its true features and ultimate effects (Schumpeter, 1949, 1994). Thus, the organic process of creative destruction applies to a new cycle of emerging and disrupting digital technologies that will win the competition leading to the entire transformation of the technological socio-ecosystem.

A positive impact of these technologies is the promotion of resilience with the identification of maintenance needs by inspecting critical infrastructure leading to respond to the emergencies with assistance of recovery efforts in crises and disasters, for example.

Why Is the Digital Era Going Wrong? Who Controls the Future?

Any emergent technological outcome is a neutral tool before receiving connotations depending on how it is being used. However, in this era of emerging and disruptive digital technologies, we are witnessing heated debates on legal frameworks, standards, recommendations, methods, practices, problems, etc., marked by lack of agreement among the main actors due to divergent interests for control without a clear how to provide solutions.

Emerging and disruptive digital technologies such as big data, biotechnologies, quantum, and autonomous systems require separate international standardization principles of responsible use, which may require various regulatory levels in the space domains. However, the debate on whether ChatGPT's use must be restricted, legislated, and regulated is split. Technological innovation must be stalled by global standards to ensure performance and interoperability between the different emerging technological socio-ecosystems. In the elaboration of this, standards must be driven by global governance mechanisms with the participation of other sectors such as private sector and academia.

Obviously, it is difficult to know how far human evil can go, incapacity and stupidity. Suffice it to remember that the largest sources of profit are related to death: war and drugs. Thus, the human being does not seem very trustworthy, as stated by Marín (2023).

What Is the Focus of AI?

The focus of emerging and disruptive digital technologies has been on automation and not in creating jobs must be amended. AI has been focused on automation, and this focus should be changed to the net increase of jobs and job creation. The focus of long-term AI directions must have an impact on the greatest value of implementation by augmenting people in the jobs, enrichment of jobs and tasks, reimagine and redefine old tasks to create new job activities, and transform culture to adapt AI threats into new opportunities.

Warnings of job losses confuse AI with automation overshadowing the augmentation benefit of a combination and complementation of human and AI, where both combine and complement each other. AI has already a negative impact on the workplace by applying to highly repeatable routine tasks requiring copious quantities of data observations and decisions to be analyzed searching for patterns. Applying AI to less-routine with low repeatability and more varied tasks is yielding higher benefits in job creation and greater value. Applying AI to nonroutine tasks tends to combine and complement humans and machines each other to perform more efficiently than either human experts or AI-driven devices and machines working alone.

Investments in AI-enabled technologies must evaluate the jobs lost, job creation, and transformation of co-working collaboration and decision-making processes between workers and digital technologies. Technological innovations are associated with a transition period of job loss followed by a recovery. Jobs affected by AI vary across industry sectors, with manufacturing and service areas such as education and healthcare hit the hardest. While AI eliminates many middle- and low-level positions, it also creates new opportunities for highly skilled management roles as well as some entry-level and low-skilled jobs.

Research suggests that consumers still prefer the interaction with a knowledgeable human salesperson than using AI in more specialized areas who make a significant impact on customer satisfaction. These efforts of applying AI and robotics in retailing to replace human tasks prove not to be successful to eliminate this job at all despite that operational activities are disrupted, reducing labor, making labor savings, and prompting to reinvest in training to enhance customer experience and satisfaction, creating higher value.

The impact of AI and digital technologies in outsourcing is pressured to fundamental changes aimed to reinvent and invest on business models with the symbiosis of human activities instead of only automating practices to create new business opportunities. Improvement of nonroutine work by applying AI and robotics must concentrate on leveraging knowledge of digital technologies about general purpose tools to be incorporated into work processes leading to develop a competitive relationship of intelligent employee–robot automation processes to identify and optimize labor-intensive and repetitive activities currently performed by humans.

Automation, robotics, AI, and other digital technologies have a multiplier effect which requires to redefine and create more jobs to create higher value than displacing and killing them, to the extent that it should augment the workforce, increasing the productivity and quality of their work, freeing up time to be employed on more strategic priorities. AI, robotics, and other digital technologies improve the productivity of many jobs that already have become a positive motivator. AI, robotics, and automation in manufacturing as in any other sectors, rather than removing humans from task processes, contribute to augment customer experiences of workers leading to improve productivity by reducing costs, reducing frictions in value chains, optimizing supply chains, and creating higher value opportunities.

ChatGPT Could Make These Jobs Obsolete

The subtitle of this section is taken from Mitchell (2023) in a recent article of analysis, which I borrowed because it is very illustrative of the situation. Concerned with the emergence of a disruptive tool ChatGPT capabilities, a surprising intelligent chatbot upended from and based on AI, which since its release on November 30, 2022, proving to be a tool with capabilities to perform complex tasks and simplify them (Biswas, 2023). Higher education, finance and banking, hospitality and tourism, and information technology industries are sectors in which AI and its most recent tool ChatGPT are enhancing business management and marketing activities, among others (Yogesh et al., 2023).

A competitive battle is taking place among AI chatbots already released — such as ChatGPT, Google's Bard, Microsoft's Bing, ChatSonic, and Ernie developed by China's Baidu — which is leading many employees to feel anxious or fearful about losing their jobs. OpenAI-powered ChatGPT and released GPT-4 are fueling fear among the informational technologies due to the replacement of programmers and other informational technology professionals by current ongoing massive layoffs (Biswas, 2023). OpenAI's ChatGPT extends the capabilities through the integration of natural language models and deep learning based on a generative pre-training transformer (GPT) architecture (Radford et al., 2018) of neural networks aimed to predict the sequence of words in human interactions through generative and discriminative algorithms (Vaswani et al., 2017) used to generate responses to queries that resemble a human expert. The ChatGPT system is designed on a huge data set and continually improves itself using a simple text prompt to generate the ability to work through any problem and answer to any question with certain varying accuracy depending on its task. Experts and analysts are warning that the improvement of these and other capabilities of the ChatGPT tool could spell doom for numerous job fields in industry.

According to the analysis of Biswas (2023) by April 2023, 503 technological companies worldwide have laid off 139,165 employees in 2023, in part due to the release of the AI chatbot. However, other analysts, such as Goldman Sachs, are more pessimistic concluding that at least 300 million jobs are getting obsolete and replaced. Technology engineering and software design has undergone massive staff layoffs at Silicon Valley (Fig. 7.1). Large firms like Microsoft have announced a large investment in the revolutionary technology of AI replacing a substantial portion of its global well-paid white-collar workforce while leaving many employees and industries currently vulnerable, from the financial, healthcare, and publishing sectors. Microsoft has already laid off thousands of workers (Mitchell, 2023).

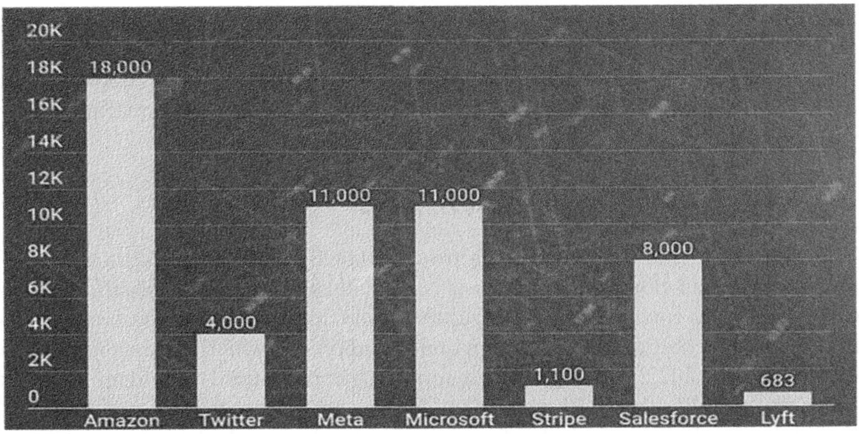

Fig. 7.1. The Job Losses Across Silicon Valley. *Source*: Potter (2023).

Major corporations such as Microsoft have laid off 10,000 employees while simultaneously investing in a partnership with OpenAI to advance artificial intelligence innovations across a broad range of products intended to stimulate growth (Potter, 2023). Other technological firms going through the layoff of white-collar employees to achieve cost-cutting measures include Amazon, Facebook, Apple, and Meta (Fig. 7.1).

Technology analysts and experts are warning that the AI tool ChatGPT is making white-collar jobs obsolete and putting millions of people out of work (Potter, 2023). Humans must learn how to harness ChatGPT as a mind-blowing tool of the AI technology which is rocking practices on the academia and social media and leading to the risk that jobs in certain sectors can be supplemented and even replaced such as high education, financial services, journalism, software design engineering, and graphics, etc., just to mention some of the affected sectors. However, the efficient performance of ChatGPT in finding answers to complex questions and providing solutions to difficult problems across many work tasks and professional fields demonstrates its wide applicability.

There are some job roles that AI is not able to replace in the current and future scenarios. Some of these jobs analyzed by Biswas (2023) are programming, hardware technology, network engineering, cyber security analysis, risk analysis, project management, and information technology training, among others. Using ChatGPT is transforming the nature of work, in terms of knowledge, capabilities, competencies, and roles of employees. Due to the disruptions already created, ChatGPT as it stands today has been already banned or blocked the access in some schools concerned over cheating actions.

Consequences of Automation for Jobs, Wages, and Inequality

Automation reduces human intervention in job performance by creating machines capable of replacing human attributes in the execution of more complex and repetitive operations with more certainty and security to work more efficiently by reproducing human tasks and leading to fully substitute workers in some cases.

Regarding research on the effects of automation, many studies forecast that in the following years, there will be a huge job destruction, reduction of wages, and thus an increasing level of inequality (Fig. 7.2).

Automation is often associated with job destruction. Automation of tasks will change with advances in AI (Acemoglu et al., 2022). Following automation is a decline in routine jobs (Acemoglu et al., 2020; Humlum, 2020). Research on automation documents that it is easier to implement in routine tasks (Levy & Murnane, 2003).

Digital automation technologies tend to expand the tasks performed by the efficient capital, while displacing jobs of certain worker groups for which they have comparative advantage or by reducing the relative and real wages of workers specialized in routine tasks in manufacturing industries undergoing digital automation, such as the blue-collar jobs and clerical workers. In contrast, workers with postgraduate studies not displaced from their jobs have wage gains. Wage inequality is rising sharply among the worker groups specialized in routine tasks of industries in economies experiencing rapid automation over the last decades (Acemoglu & Restrepo, 2022).

Wage inequality is the result of task displacement, rather than productivity growth and overall capital intensity. According to Acemoglu and Restrepo (2022), task displacement of workers driven by automation from employment opportunities has a defined role in the surge of wage inequality over the last decades. A model designed and developed by Brito and Curl (2020) with data from 1984 to 2016 demonstrates that the most important consequence of automation is to lower the share of workers in real wages of medium-skilled and low-skilled jobs in domestic production which has steadily declined. Task allocation to diverse types of capital, labor, and automation technologies expands tasks performance of capital at the expense of workers. Tax displacement leads to increase in wage inequality.

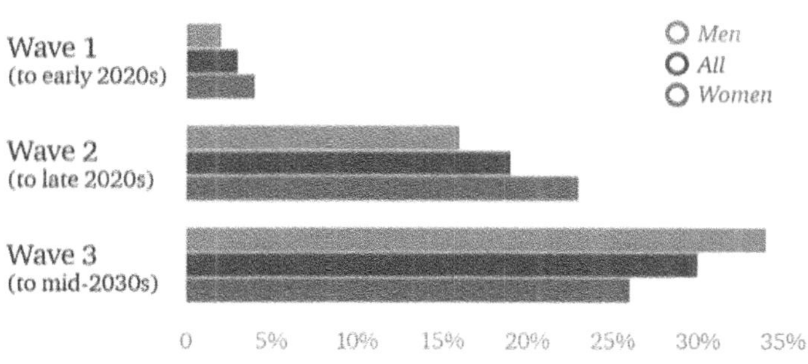

Fig. 7.2. Existing Jobs at Potential Risk of Automation. *Source*: PwC estimates based on Organisation for Economic Co-operation and Development (OECD) Programme for the International Assessment of Adult Competencies (PIAAC) data median values for 29 countries.

The Potential of Generative AI

AI may reverse the trends of slowing global productivity, increasing the gap of inequality, and diminishing the worker power, undermining advancement of living standards. Productivity is barely growing and will continue for some years due to economic and geopolitical uncertainty and the rising capital costs leading to holdback increases in economic growth and wages while widening the gap of inequality. Workplace shifts due to pandemic and investments into generative AI eventually will produce compelling results unleashing an era of productivity growth despite that it will take more than a decade to reap the benefits. There is an optimism on the use of digital technologies for the creation and development of new business models and workers switching tasks and jobs to yield better results in increasing productivity, augmenting wages, and reducing the inequality wage gap. The implementation of the diverse tools of AI in the productivity revolution will take a long-term period to pay off (Strauss, 2023).

AI tools like ChatGPT are easy to adopt ensuring integration with other everyday use apps, which can amplify inequality of resource access leading to asymmetric use and marginalizing groups that will not have represented data (Chen & Wellman, 2004; Weissglass, 2022). Gopinath (2023) from the International Monetary Fund foresees a boost of economic growth and benefits workers raising productivity by automating cognitive tasks and giving rise to new higher-productivity tasks to perform with machines taking care of routine and repetitive tasks. Humans could spend more time on being creative innovators and analytical people. AI can spread the knowledge of experienced and productive workers.

The potential of generative AI as more tools are developed brings about sweeping changes to the global economy, driving about 7%, or almost $7 trillion increase in global gross domestic product (GDP) lifting productivity growth by about 1.5 percentage points over a 10-year period. Generative AI tools could enhance productivity at office, sales, design building, manufacturing parts, improving healthcare in patient diagnosis, cyber fraud detection, etc. benefiting the global economy. The impact of AI on labor productivity depends on its capacity and the adoption period. The contribution of AI to labor productivity is subject to its ability and the adoption stage leading to the effect of AI adoption on the annual growth of labor productivity, given a 10-year period of adoption.

Surveillance Intensifies

A negative impact of the emerging technologies may be the empowerment of malicious actions and the erosion of individual privacy.

Actions to Redirect Technological Innovation and Change

Changing the Narratives

At the international level, the discussion on the standardization in the present of future digital technologies exists between communities considering that the measures must be evolutive, and most of the times, the narratives collide leaving space to black swan scenarios and uncertainties lurking back.

Some of the issues that must be considered during changing the stories are the optimism instead of realism on technological dominance plans for countries, administration, rules, and standards, values of competition and cooperation, congruent planning coordination, patterns of interaction between governments, tech companies, start-ups, research scientists and scholars, world market demand, lack of protocols, revenues, etc., to accomplish operational needs, challenge issues, create benefits for participating actors and significant impact for society as a whole.

Focusing on Machine Learning and Intelligence Instead of Machine Usefulness

AI systems are characterized as machine-based systems with certain varying levels of autonomy which give support to humans in their objectives and tasks, making predictions, recommendations, decisions, etc., using data analytics also referred as big data based on a massive amount of alternative data sources. AI and machine learning in several industries build applications to take advantage of connections between AI and machine learning, helping the companies to transform their processes and products. Machine learning algorithms are forms of AI increasingly applied in use experience with big data automatically to learn and improve predictability in performance without human programming (OECD, 2021). AI and machine learning are used today in various applications. Machine learning models trends are AI techniques increasingly utilized in the use experience of big data automatically to learn and increase predictability in performance without programming (OECD, 2021). AI and machine learning today are utilized in numerous applications.

AI and machine learning are utilized to maximize retailers' stock, in healthcare organizations in image processing for improved identification of cancer; in banking and finance, to identify fraud, predict risk, and financial pre-emptive advice; in sales and marketing, for predicting sales, campaign optimization, sentiment analysis, etc.; in cyber security, to protect organizations and their clients by detecting anomalies; in customer services, chatbots and cognitive search to gauge the intent of customers, virtual assistance, and question answering; in transportation, to optimize routes for efficiency, predictive analysis, traffic forecasting, etc.; in production, applied to predictive maintenance and efficiency of operations, etc.

Behind the scenes, the engine of machine learning attempts to reinforce known patterns in the member's behavior and adjust accordingly when the member changes patterns (Burns, 2023). The "Chat Generative Pre-Trained Transformer" (ChatGPT) is a tool of AI, with usefulness as a machine to overcome resistance to change resulting from the implementation process of digital innovations. As with most tools of AI, ChatGPT sometimes works great and simply fine, becoming an especially useful learning machine to provide support to human tasks.

Enhancing Human Capabilities

The relationship between humans and the AI ecosystem is one of enhancement of human capabilities and not replacement. AI can be leveraged to enhance cognitive functions and human behavior in the analysis, interpretation, and decision-making. However, the digital traces of AI require a knowing subject to interpret, analyze, and validate the outcomes.

Humans are uniquely adapted to constantly create, becoming good at it, but when it comes to analyzing, interpreting, and understanding data, the larger the data set becomes, the worse humans perform (Williams, 2023). Humans visualizing data miss the smaller trends that have been averaged out besides that are innately biased through past experiences and preexisting assumptions such as spotting correlations to assume causations. While AI takes care of the details of data analysis and interpretation, humans can concentrate on creating what he/she does best, making best decisions and empowering to implement them, driving behavior change, improving the abilities to inspire, and creating habits and true accountability. It is difficult to hold accountability in AI systems for any errors and problems with generated content because they lack awareness and consciousness as humans have.

Humans have a limited ability to scale by only focusing on one item at a time, while in comparison, AI does not have limitations regarding scalability processing thousands of tasks in a fraction of a second. Thus, humans can have AI scalability as a trait.

Creating Countervailing Powers

The new frontier digital technologies from AI to quantum information science with no clear definition that makes it challenging to standardize and regulate because of the worldwide competition of major players to have the largest world market share (Neaher et al., 2021). both risks and responsibilities will enable to bring more value in the digital technologies field by producing more benefits to the participants. The new regulations and standards for the new and disruptive digital technologies will need to come out of a creative destruction of outdated advances that bring about a general scientific revolution to fully come to effect to develop no longer emergent the emerging technologies. This is contended by Kuhn (1962, p. 11) who claimed that men whose research is conducted on common paradigms are bound by the same rules and standards for scientific practice. A new model of cooperation in partnerships between governments and firms sharing by ensuring proper alignment of interest involving the society at large.

Alignment Ethics

It is difficult to imagine how far the evil and stupidity of the human being can go. The rise of ChatGPT and their effects on individuals and society is an opportunity to discuss ethical issues when using these and other similar tools. In the field of AI, alignment ethics aims to steer AI systems toward ethical principles based on humans' intended goals and preferences. An AI system is considered ethically aligned if it advances the intended objectives of human development. Preceded debates are conducted with moral and ethical considerations on specific technologies, as, for example, the Ethics of AI Recommendation of UNESCO.

AI is a digital technology different from all previous technologies including neural networks, deep learning through algorithms, and automatic learning, which have presented new and different risks and ethical concerns (Blackman, 2020) considering that humans have control over the machines, turning on and turning off. Humans need to make decisions on what is an acceptable behavior in the use of digital technologies and more precisely on the tools of AI, to design, enact, and enforce policies.

Avoiding Biases on Data and Models of AI

AI is already here to stay forever and from ethical alignment to be used responsibly which requires the commitment to act and behave ethically at every turn. The increasing use of AI has risen significant ethical alignment concerns sparking debates regarding issues from human data privacy to the use of algorithms in chatbots and ChatGPT that not only perpetuates but tend to emphasize religious, ethnic, racial, gender, and other biases. The ethics of responsible AI has an orientation from utilitarianism to justify some threats posed by tools such as the ChatGPT and similar chatbots that include black-box algorithms to validate copyright, infringement discrimination and biases, vulgarity, plagiarism, fake media, fabricated unauthentic textual content, among others.

These ethical issues are being already reported by academics, organizations, and institutions worried with these developments, and some measures are being proposed to deal with them. Among other measures to put into place and enforce to mitigate the negative effects are the claims of disclosing data collected and transparency of what is done with that data, to establish committees dedicated to overseeing the use of AI, to identify intelligent agents and chatbots as non-human entities, etc. (Carufel, 2019).

Ways to Conduct Additional Training

Academic, institutional, and organizational leaders are worried and concerned about the effect of AI replacing the workforce and the ways to conduct additional training to employees that are rightly worried about being displaced from their jobs. Organizations adopting AI must understand, analyze, manage, assess, and mitigate risks, monitor, and evaluate ethical reviews and bias screening considering the evolution of algorithms in nature which require training on the heterogeneous algorithm models that possess high velocity and variability. The diverse ways to conduct additional training are an issue that raises ethical concerns.

Permission to Use Millions of Words and Material on AI Training

Reputation and legal risks of AI are using copyrighted or offensive content, loss of privacy, spreading false information, fraudulent transactions, lack of transparency, misuse, bias, etc. Regarding the integrity issues, to identify the actual scriptwriter by comparing the text created by ChatGPT is still elusive now. There are many legal concerns and issues around copyright and ownership of content generated by AI.

Laws and regulations are concerned with these ethical issues dealing with the content created by learning machines which create legal disputes over the ownership of rights to use and profit from the generated content. However, generative AI content poses an elevated risk for intellectual property rights and copyright protection, which has serious implications for research to avoid potential infringement caused by the use. OpenAI has already declared that it does not take any responsibility for any infringement that may occur.

Long-term Implications of AI Are Not Clear

AI risk management frameworks must consolidate in the long term the ethical theory to integrate socially responsible judgments leading to ensure reasoned, purposeful, cautious, and ethical leverage alignment to generative AI models. Identification of AI and management risks leads to design and implement ethical models to be used long term to determine a path (Ashok et al., 2022). Utilitarianism is an ethical approach used in decision-making based on the positive and negative impact of actions that do best good and least harm to individuals, organizations, and environment (Bohm et al., 2022).

Perspectives on Future Jobs in the Era of AI

Without a doubt, AI has had a great impact on the development of society; in this regard, it is possible to glimpse a new paradigm regarding the use of new technologies. Therefore, studies must be directed at aspects that include a comprehensive vision between these technologies and the human being, since they must be complementary to their development and not only see them as competition.

After the above and articulating a policy on in which direction research on AI ought to be oriented, De La O-Miranda and Cortés-Campos (2023) are attended to, who expound that emerging technology such as the metaverse aims to transform the way companies, organizations, and people interact globally. Technology of this nature is based on the creation of the internet and its reach. The metaverse is a virtual world with significant contribution to the economy, society, and education. The metaverse can break down physical boundaries, so it promotes international interaction and is huge in potential in many fields, which can revolutionize the way people live and work.

Conclusions

Machine learning in AI tools, such as the ChatGPT, can offer prompt responses with an unforeseen combination of innovative and valuable texts produced from digital traces, with the likelihood of an exceptionally low selection subject to quality data sources and training. These traces require a knowing subject to interpret, analyze, and validate the outcomes. As a stochastic and algorithm parrot, most of the tools of AI are unconscious and not be able to produce self-knowledge, which by themselves do not constitute meaningful, valid, and legitimated scientific knowledge.

The development of ethical codes, law, and regulations for the governance of generative AI systems is required, aimed to minimize ethical concerns such as discrimination, false data and information, plagiarism, copyright infringement, etc. Further, questions regarding the copyright ownership, intellectual property rights, regulations for acceptable use norms, etc. are issues that must be raised, discussed, analyzed, and addressed.

Research and practice must be extended to explore innovative approaches for using AI tools and other digital disruptive and breakthrough technologies for finding solutions to all ills leading to potential enhancement of human development, creating social and environmental benefits, and increasing productivity. These opportunities to conduct future research call for more transdisciplinary approaches with implications in educational programs that must be challenged using an ethical perspective of digital technologies and AI tools aimed to benefit humanity.

References

Acemoglu, D., Hazell, J., & Restrepo, P. (2022). Artificial intelligence and jobs: Evidence from online vacancies. *Journal of Labor Economics*, *40*, S293–S340.

Acemoglu, D., Lelarge C., & Restrepo, P. (2020). Competing with robots: Firm-level evidence from France. *AEA Papers and Proceedings*, *110*, 383–388.

Acemoglu, D., & Restrepo, P. (2022). Tasks, automation, and the rise in U.S. wage inequality. *Econometrica*, *90*(5), 1973–2016.

Ashok, M., Madan, R., Joha, A., & Sivarajah, U. (2022). Ethical framework for artificial intelligence and digital technologies. *International Journal of Information Management*, *62*, Article 102433.

Biswas, S. (2023, April 2). *ChatGPT: 7 IT jobs that IA can't replace*. https://www.geeksforgeeks.org/chatgpt-7-it-jobs-that-ai-cant-replace/

Blackman, R. (2020, October 15). *A practical guide to building ethical IA*. https://hbr.org/2020/10/a-practical-guide-to-building-ethical-ai

Bohm, S., Carrington, M., Cornelius, N., de Bruin, B., Greenwood, M., Hassan, L., & Shaw, D. (2022). Ethics at the centre of global and local challenges: Thoughts on the future of business ethics. *Journal of Business Ethics*, *180*(3), 835–861.

Brito, D., & Curl, R. F. (2020). *Automation does not kill jobs. It increases inequality* [Baker Institute Report No. 11.06.20]. Rice University's Baker Institute for Public Policy.

Burns, E. (2023). *Machine learning*. TechTarget network. https://www.techtarget.com/searchenterpriseai/definition/machine-learning-ML

Carufel, R. (2019, December 18). *Companies embrace AI, but execs cite challenges on alignment, ethics*. Agility PR Solutions. https://www.agilitypr.com/pr-news/public-relations/companies-embrace-ai-but-execs

Chen, W., & Wellman, B. (2004). The global digital divide–within and between countries. *IT & Society*, *1*(7), 39–45.

De La O-Miranda, D., & Cortés-Campos, A. (2023). El metaverso como tecnología disruptiva a la disposición de la metodología de enseñanza en las instituciones de educación superior. *Innovaciones Educativas*, *25*(Especial), 78–87. https://doi.org/10.22458/ie.v25iEspecial.4819

Gopinath, G. (2023, June 5). *The power and perils of the "artificial hand": Considering IA through the ideas of Adam Smith speech to commemorate 300th anniversary of Adam Smith's birth University of Glasgow.* International Monetary Fund. https://www.imf.org/en/News/Articles/2023/06/05/sp060523-fdmd-ai-adamsmith?cid=em-COM-123-46688

Humlum, A. (2020). *Robot adoption and labor market dynamics* [Working paper]. University of Chicago.

Kuhn, T. (1962). *The structure of scientific revolutions.* University of Chicago Press.

Kushwaha, A. K., & Kar, A. K. (2021). *MarkBot – A language model-driven chatbot for interactive marketing in post-modern world.* Retrieved January 31, 2023, from https://doi.org/10.1007/s10796-021-10184-y

Levy, D. H. F., & Murnane, R. J. (2003). The skill content of recent technological change: An empirical exploration. *The Quarterly Journal of Economics, 118*(4), 1279–1333. http://www.jstor.org/stable/25053940

Lokman, A. S., Ameedeen, M. A. (2019). Modern Chatbot Systems: A Technical Review. Arai, K., Bhatia, R., and Kapoor, S. (Eds.). In Proceedings of the Future Technologies Conference (FTC) 2018. *Advances in Intelligent Systems and Computing, 881.* Springer, Cham. https://doi.org/10.1007/978-3-030-02683-7_75

Marín, F. M. (2023). *De las humanidades digitales a la Inteligencia artificial general.* University of Texas at San Antonio.

Mitchell, A. (2023, January 25). ChatGPT could make these jobs obsolete: 'The wolf is at the door.' *New York Post.* https://nypost.com/2023/01/25/chat-gpt-could-make-these-jobs-obsolete/

Neaher, G., Bray, D., Mueller-Kaler, J., & Schatz, B. (2021). *Standardizing the future: How can the United States navigate the geopolitics of international technology standards?* [Atlantic Council Report].

OECD. (2021). *Artificial intelligence, machine learning and big data in finance: Opportunities, challenges, and implications for policy makers.* https://www.oecd.org/finance/artificial-intelligence-machine-learning-big-data-in-finance.pdf

Potter, W. (2023, January 27). *'This is not crying wolf … the wolf is at the door': Fears AI could make white collar jobs obsolete as Microsoft pumps multibillion-dollar investment into ChatGPT after laying off 10,000 workers.* Dailymail.com. https://www.dailymail.co.uk/news/article-11683901/ChatGPT-make-white-collar-jobs-obsolete-Microsoft-pumps-billions-AI.html

Radford, A., Narasimhan, K., Salimans, T., & Sutskever, I. (2018). *Improving language understanding with unsupervised learning* [Technical report]. OpenAI.

Schumpeter, J. (1949). *The theory of economic development, an inquiry into profits, capital, credit, interest and the business cycle.* Harvard University Press.

Schumpeter, J. (1994). *Capitalism, socialism and democracy.* Routledge.

Sharifi, A., Khavarian-Garmsir, A. R., & Kummitha, R. K. R. (2021). Contributions of smart city solutions and technologies to resilience against the COVID-19 pandemic: A literature review. *Sustainability, 13*, 1–28.

Strauss, D. (2023, June 4). Generative AI's 'productivity revolution' will take time to pay off. *Financial Times.* https://www.ft.com/content/21384711-3506-4901-830c-7ecc3ae6b32a

Vaswani, A., Shazeer, N., Parmar, N., Uszkoreit, J., Jones, L., Gomez, A. N., & Polosukhin, I. (2017). *Attention is all you need. Advances in neural information processing systems.* Proceedings of the 31st conference on neural information processing systems, Long Beach, CA, USA. https://proceedings.neurips.cc/paper/2017/file/3f5ee243547dee91fbd053c1c4a845aa-paper.pdf

Weissglass, D. E. (2022). Contextual bias, the democratization of healthcare, and medical artificial intelligence in low- and middle-income countries. *Bioethics, 36*(2), 201–209.

Williams, J. (2023). How AI will enhance human capabilities. *Forbes*. https://www.forbes.com/sites/forbescommunicationscouncil/2018/03/19/how-ai-will-enhance-human-capabilities/?sh=1d37cd1e366f

Yogesh, K., Kshetri, N., Hughes, L., Slade, E. L., Jeyaraj, A., Kar, A. K., Baabdullah, A. M., Koohang, A., Raghavan, V., Ahuja, M., Albanna, H., Albashrawi, M. A., Al-Busaidi, A. S., Balakrishnan, J., Barlette, Y., Basu, S., Bose, I., Brooks, L., Buhalis, D., …, Wright, R. (2023). "So, what if ChatGPT wrote it?" Multidisciplinary perspectives on opportunities, challenges, and implications of generative conversational AI for research, practice, and policy. *International Journal of Information Management*, *71*, 102642. https://doi.org/10.1016/j.ijinfomgt.2023.102642; https://www.sciencedirect.com/science/article/pii/S0268401223000233

Section II

Artificial Intelligence and Implications to Society

Chapter 8

Artificial Intelligence and the Future of Education in Developing Economies: Theories and Empirics

Nilendu Chatterjee[a], Tonmoy Chatterjee[b] and Ghirmai Tesfamariam Teame[c]

[a]*Department of Economics, Bankim Sardar College, India*
[b]*Department of Economics, Bhairab Ganguly College, India*
[c]*Department of Economics, College of Business and Social Sciences, Eritrea*

Abstract

Artificial intelligence (AI) and application of its various aspects have been increasingly becoming a necessity for every stakeholder in education. The rapid application of AI in every sphere of life has made it an interesting element in education, and the pace at which such application has been growing, it is certainly going to become compulsory for everybody – whether it is teachers or students. But in developing economies is it possible to educate everyone with AI and its application? What role can the government play in this regard? What role can the families play? Or, why is it necessary to learn AI for the stakeholders? What impact can it have on the labour market? All these things need to be understood and investigated. This study looks to capture all the aspects of the above-discussed areas by the help of a general equilibrium framework followed by a contingent valuation (CV) analysis, considering the perception of stakeholders of higher education, regarding the necessity of learning AI. The general equilibrium model depicts different outcomes regarding existence or abolishment of economic sectors in the presence of AI, under different conditions. By CV model, we consider the use-value of AI in regular life among the stakeholders of higher education. It shows different socio-economic factors are significant behind one's willingness or non-willingness in learning AI. Consideration of different stakeholders and policy-setters of higher education in developing

Artificial Intelligence in Business and Society: Global Insights, 113–126

doi:10.1108/978-1-83708-022-920261019

economies under one umbrella and analysing the overall impact in a single study is unique and deserves significance.

Keywords: Artificial intelligence; developing economies; higher education; general equilibrium; CV analysis

Introduction

AI is generally believed as the ability of machinery tools, software to perform tasks like humans and reduce workloads as well as save time (Wartman & Combs, 2018). Hence, it is the imitation of human behaviour which is superfast and skilled by various programmes or software (Mohammed & Watson, 2019). Going beyond the initial thinking about its application in doing difficult works, AI has been getting into every activity of our regular lives, and the pace of such entry is very fast, and in the coming years, the use of AI is only going to increase by leaps and bounds. AI is not only the new electrifying lifeline of the present age, but it is also the most potential factor that will decide the fates of the economies in the ages of fourth and fifth industrial revolutions. That is why economies like China have been investing huge money in the development of AI which is expected to increase its gross domestic product (GDP) by 26% by the year 2030 (Golic, 2019; Mou, 2019). North American economies are expected to experience a growth of above 14% in GDP (PwC, 2017). These figures are self-explaining about the inevitable importance of AI in the coming days, and education which forms the very basis of development AI and the economy actually guides the development of AI and industrial revolution. The full-fledged development and use of AI will change many social orders – be it workplace, be it education or be it administration. The growth and use of AI in every sphere of lives will leave no choice for the education sector but to accept it (Ng, 2017).

It is undeniable that life has become fast, and for the sake of maintaining pace, education also has to become fast. Does it mean fast classes or a system that generates fast results? Or, does it mean teachers should be teaching fast? One has to accept that as we move from industry 4.0 to industry 5.0, we need an education system that complements these industrial developments and that needs a more skilful education system – be it teacher, be it students, be it curriculum – everything needs to be compatible with the needs of the market. The questions which arise are is it sufficient to have skills, critical thinking ability, metacognition skills? Or, should we go for a completely different system that has never been seen or thought of before? Or, should it be the mix of the both? The answer lies in the fact that to an extent AI can help education that will differentiate human beings from robots and having social emotions and values. This extent of opportunities provided by AI will decide its extent of application in the field of education, even to the extent of replacing teachers (Felix, 2020).

Different studies of AI on education have valued its role differently. Studies suggest that good teachers will always exist, even if AI takes full charge of things in education, AI will make teaching more individualistic. With AI, teachers will be focusing more on improving students' communication ability, affective intelligence, etc. Teachers will focus on improving creativity, and AI will make both teachers and students 'more human'; it will improve the quality of teachers, learning experiences, and research outcomes and reduce everyone's work pressure (Haseski, 2019; Manyika et al., 2017). But the opposite views are there as well, studies believe AI will bring a downfall in the quality of teachers and students and shifting the workload to the computers or software will do no good for either of the two, and therefore, the future of education is in danger (Humble & Mozelius, 2019). Hence, the best way is to develop an education environment where both the students and teachers will go hand in hand with these supporting structural developments like AI, without losing their own intellect (Wogu et al., 2018). As AI is being used more in education, there are significant changes being witnessed in this arena. AI can improve the reach of education, and it can make education accessible for the poor, and thus, it can be inclusive for all (Pedro et al., 2019). The personalized learning for both students and teachers can effectively develop because of the uses of AI, and it improves the level of learning, although it is accepted that quality education needs active human involvement and not full dependency on machines (Grosz & Stone, 2018). AI can be helpful in reducing the routine, repetitive tasks of the teacher and concentrate more on improvement in teaching, while the secondary tasks of repetitive works can be done by AI-based software which will essentially implement the dual-teacher model where the mix of both human and AI can go along (Pedro et al., 2019).

In developing economies, AI and its various applications can really have a deep as well as changing effect on education and rest of the sectors. But there are lack of enough studies on this aspect that combine both theory and empirics. This study focuses on that lacuna and looks to fill it.

The present study is organized as follows: The second section discusses about the benefits and challenges of using AI in developing economies. The third section is dedicated for the discussion of a general equilibrium model by which we shall show what impact AI can have on education and other sectors in the developing economies. The fourth section is for explaining the logit regression that we have performed on AI based on views of stakeholders in higher education. The final section concludes the study with possible policy suggestions.

AI in Developing Economies – Benefits and Challenges

AI has the potential to significantly impact education in developing economies, offering innovative solutions to long-standing challenges and creating new opportunities for learning and growth. This transformative technology can revolutionize the educational landscape in various ways, addressing issues of access, quality, and equity. The following points elucidate the potential benefits and challenges of implementing AI in education within developing economies:

1. AI can adapt to individual student needs, providing tailored content and pacing. This approach allows students to learn at their own speed, focusing on areas requiring more support and advancing through well-understood

concepts. AI algorithms can analyse students' performance data in real time, adjusting content difficulty and type to optimize learning outcomes.

2. AI-powered educational tools can reach remote areas, bridging geographical gaps in education access. In regions where physical schools are scarce or difficult to reach, AI-driven online learning platforms can provide quality education to students in rural or isolated communities, potentially reducing educational disparities between urban and rural areas.
3. AI translation tools can help overcome language obstacles in multilingual societies. In countries with diverse linguistic landscapes, AI can facilitate the translation of educational materials into local languages, making content more accessible to a wider range of students. This capability extends beyond simple text translation, as AI can also provide real-time audio translations during lectures or video content, ensuring that language differences do not hinder the learning process.
4. AI can assist teachers with administrative tasks, allowing more time for student interaction. By automating routine activities such as grading, attendance tracking, and lesson planning, AI frees up valuable time for teachers to focus on direct student engagement, mentoring, and addressing individual learning needs.
5. AI solutions may provide affordable alternatives to traditional educational resources. In developing economies where educational budgets are often constrained, AI can offer cost-effective ways to deliver high-quality educational content. This includes digital textbooks that can be easily updated and distributed, virtual laboratories for science experiments, and interactive simulations for complex concepts.
6. AI can help prepare students for future job markets by teaching digital literacy and technological skills. As the global economy becomes increasingly digitized, AI-powered education can ensure that students in developing countries acquire the necessary skills to compete in the international job market. This includes not only technical skills related to AI and data science but also soft skills such as critical thinking, problem-solving, and adaptability.
7. AI can analyse educational data to inform policy decisions and resource allocation. By processing vast amounts of data on student performance, attendance, and engagement, AI can provide valuable insights to policymakers and educational administrators. AI can also predict future trends in education, allowing policymakers to proactively address potential challenges and opportunities.
8. AI can provide more accurate and fair evaluations of student performance. AI-powered assessments can adapt in real-time, providing a more comprehensive and nuanced evaluation of student knowledge and skills. These assessments can go beyond traditional multiple-choice questions, incorporating interactive elements, open-ended responses, and even practical demonstrations of skills.
9. AI can supplement human instruction in areas with insufficient qualified teachers. In regions facing a shortage of trained educators, AI-powered tutoring systems can provide additional support to students, ensuring they

receive guidance and instruction even when human teachers are not available. These AI tutors can offer personalized assistance, answer questions, and provide explanations on a wide range of subjects, helping to fill gaps in educational coverage.

10. AI platforms can facilitate lifelong learning opportunities beyond formal education. These platforms can offer personalized learning paths based on an individual's career goals, current skill set, and learning preferences. This continuous learning approach is particularly valuable in developing economies, where rapid economic changes may require workers to frequently update their skills.

While the potential benefits of AI in education are significant, several challenges need to be addressed:

(i) Lack of reliable internet and electricity in some areas may hinder AI implementation. Many AI-powered educational tools require consistent internet connectivity and power supply, which may not be available in all parts of developing countries. Addressing these infrastructure gaps is crucial for ensuring equitable access to AI-enhanced education.

(ii) Ensuring equitable access to AI-powered education tools across socioeconomic groups is crucial to prevent exacerbating existing inequalities. There is a risk that only affluent students or those in urban areas may benefit from AI in education, potentially widening the gap between privileged and underprivileged groups.

(iii) Protecting student information and ensuring ethical use of educational data is essential. As AI systems collect and analyse large amounts of student data, there are concerns about privacy, data security, and potential misuse of information. Developing robust data protection policies, implementing secure data storage and transmission protocols, and educating students and parents about data rights are crucial steps in addressing these concerns.

(iv) Ensuring AI systems are culturally relevant and sensitive to local contexts is necessary for effective implementation. AI educational tools developed in one cultural context may not be directly applicable or appropriate in another. There is a need for localization of content, adaptation of teaching methods to align with local pedagogical approaches, and consideration of cultural nuances in language and communication styles.

(v) Preparing educators to effectively integrate AI tools into their teaching practices is crucial for successful implementation. Many teachers in developing economies may lack familiarity with AI technologies or may be hesitant to incorporate them into their teaching. Comprehensive training programmes are needed to help teachers understand the potential of AI in education, learn how to use AI tools effectively, and develop strategies for blending AI-enhanced learning with traditional teaching methods.

(vi) Ensuring the accuracy and reliability of AI-generated educational content is vital for maintaining educational integrity. As AI systems become more involved in content creation and curation, there is a need for rigorous quality control measures to prevent the spread of misinformation or biased content.

(vii) Maintaining essential human elements in education while leveraging AI benefits is important for holistic learning experiences. While AI can provide personalized learning and instant feedback, it cannot fully replace the social and emotional aspects of human interaction in education. Finding the right balance between AI-driven instruction and human teaching is crucial for developing well-rounded students.

(viii) Addressing potential biases in AI algorithms and ensuring fair treatment of all students is crucial for equitable education. AI systems may inadvertently perpetuate or exacerbate existing biases related to gender, race, socioeconomic status, or other factors. Rigorous testing and auditing of AI algorithms for bias, as well as diverse representation in AI development teams, are necessary to mitigate these risks.

(ix) Ensuring that AI educational systems can keep pace with evolving technologies and job market demands is essential for long-term relevance. The field of AI is rapidly advancing, and educational systems need to be flexible enough to incorporate new technologies and adapt to changing skill requirements in the job market.

(x) Developing appropriate policies and regulations to govern the use of AI in education is necessary to ensure responsible and ethical implementation. This includes establishing guidelines for data collection and use, setting standards for AI educational tools, and defining the roles and responsibilities of various stakeholders in AI-enhanced education.

Theoretical Background

Here, we consider an economy which consists of three sectors, say, *Formal Less advanced Sector* (Sector 1), *Informal Advanced Sector* (Sector 2) and *Formal Advanced Sector* (Sector 3). It is to be noted that Sector1 produces X_1 by employing AI augmented labour (I) and capital (K). Similarly, Sector 2 is also producing X_2 by using I and K. However, Sector 3 uses I and K along with output of Sector 2, that is, X_2 to produce X_3. Apart from these, the usual competitive conditions remain intact following Jones (1965, 1971) and Beladi and Marjit (1992). From the competitive equilibrium condition in the product market of the three sectors, we get the following three equations, that is, Equations (1)–(3).

$$a_{I1}R + a_{K1}r = P_1 \tag{1}$$

$$a_{I2}R + a_{K2}r = P_2 \tag{2}$$

$$a_{I3}R_S + a_{23}P_2 + a_{K3}r\beta = P_3 \tag{3}$$

where P_i represents the international price of commodity i, $i = 1, 2, 3$. R represents the rate return to I, and R_S represents the rate return to the labour engaged in Sector 3. It is to be noted that $R_S > R$, that is, rate of return to the labour in Sector 3 is unionized. Again, r represents return to K, and β shows the productivity of AI augmentation in Sector 3. Moreover, $a_{ij}s$ are depicted as unit demand of input i in Sector j. Here, for simplicity, we assume that Sectors 1 and 2 are using variable coefficient technology, whereas Sector 3 uses fixed coefficient technology, that is, a_{I3}, a_{23}, and a_{K3} are fixed.

The full employment condition in the AI augmented labour (I) market as well as the fact that efficiency of I depends on the output of Sector 2, that is, X_2, is expressed by the following equation, namely, Equations (4)–(6).

$$a_{I1}X_1 + a_{I3}X_3 + a_{I2}X_2 = I\varepsilon(X_2) \tag{4}$$

where ε measures production efficiency of I. Perfect mobility of capital between Sector 1 and Sector 2 is given by the following equation.

$$a_{K1}X_1 + a_{K2}X_2 = K \tag{5}$$

The product of Sector 3, that is, X_3 is prepared with the help of the output of Sector 2, is expressed by the following equation.

$$a_{23}X_3 = X_2 + X_2^* \tag{6}$$

Case 1: Sector 1 Vanishes and Sector 2 Exists

Given the assumption that the rise in R is more in Sector 2 than in Sector 1, we come across a new equational structure which can be written as:

From the competitive equilibrium condition in the product market of the two sectors, we get the following two equations, that is, Equations (2) and (3).

$$a_{I2}R + a_{K2}r = P_2 \tag{2}$$

$$a_{I3}R_S + a_{23}P_2 + a_{K3}r\beta = P_3 \tag{3}$$

Full employment of the labour market is written in terms of expression (7),

$$a_{I3}X_3 + a_{I2}X_2 = I\varepsilon(X_2) \tag{7}$$

Perfect mobility of capital between Sector 1 and Sector 2 is given by Equation (8).

$$a_{K2}X_2 = K \tag{8}$$

The product of Sector 3, that is, X_3 is prepared with the help of the output of Sector 2, is expressed by Equation (6).

$$a_{23}X_3 = X_2 + X_2^* \tag{6}$$

Now, we see that an increase in K causes r to fall. This will lead to an increase in the AI augmented wage of labour (R) and a fall in P_2. A reduction in r causes a_{K2} to go down and thus X_2 to go up. Again, a rise in R and fall in r lead to an increase in $I\varepsilon(X_2)$. Following this from Equation (7), we find another increase in X_3. These results give us the following proposition.

> *P1*. A regime change from international capital immobility to international capital mobility resulting in (i) abolition of the less advanced sector and survival of both informal and formal advanced sectors and (ii) leads to an increase in the levels of output of both the surviving advanced sectors.

Case 2: Sector 2 Vanishes and Sector 1 Exists

Given the assumption that the rise in R is more in Sector 1 than in Sector 2, we come across a new equational structure which can be written as:

From the competitive equilibrium condition in the product market of the two sectors, we get the following two equations, that is, Equations (1) and (9).

$$a_{I1}R + a_{K1}r = P_1 \tag{1}$$

$$a_{I3}R_S + a_{K3}r\,\beta = P_3 \tag{9}$$

Full employment of the labour market is written in the form of Equation (10).

$$a_{I1}X_1 + a_{I3}X_3 = I \tag{10}$$

Perfect mobility of capital between Sector 1 and Sector 2 is given by the following equation:

$$a_{K1}X_1 = K \tag{5.2}$$

Now, we see that an increase in K causes r to fall. This will lead to an increase in the AI-augmented wage of labour (R). A reduction in r causes a_{K1} to go up and thus X_1 to go down (from Equation 10). Again, a rise in R and fall in r lead to a fall in $a_{I1}X_1$ and a_{I3}, which in turn leads to increase in increase in X_3 (from Equation (9)). These results give us the following proposition:

P2. A regime change from international capital immobility to international capital mobility resulting in (i) abolition of the informal advanced sector and survival of both formal less advanced and formal advanced sectors and (ii) leads to an increase in the level of output of formal advanced sector and fall in the output level of less advanced sector.

Empirical Analysis – Logit Model

For this analysis, we have collected data from 860 people associated with higher education; out of them, 445 are students, and rest of the 350 are teachers and 65 are educational administrators. The survey was conducted in June 2024. Since the survey was conducted by online mode, the respondent's identity as well as replies were unknown to us – which establishes the application of randomness in the survey process. The data were collected across six higher education institutes, three each from rural and urban areas. Since the sample size covered students and teachers from both urban and rural backgrounds, it effectively establishes the robustness of the study because of its wider coverage and reflection of the reality across different segments of the society. Even if our questionnaire contained several questions on education, socio-economic aspects, the main question was whether the respondent feels the necessity of learning and applying AI in education. This implies that our dependent variable *Y* was binary, since the respondent had to give the reply either in YES or NO. The replies were then converted into binary settings by assigning 1 to YES and 0 to NO. Since we have performed logistic regression analysis and used the logit of *Y*, it makes our dependent variable *Y* categorical. Hence, if the learning as well as application of AI in the education increases the utility of the respondent, then one can expect a positive reply, that is, a YES can be expected, else the reply is NO when it is not affecting the utility. Hence, for the sake of estimating the willingness among the stakeholders of higher education to learn and use AI, application of logistic regression is necessary. Hence, the dependent variable (*Y*) of our logit model is of the following form.

$l_n \frac{P_i}{(1-P_i)}$, where *Pi* is the probability of replying with a YES or the willingness of learning AI and (1 − *Pi*) is the probability of replying with a NO where the respondent does not consider AI as an important tool to learn and apply. Pi represents the probability of Y=1 and the opposite, that is, $Y = 0$ is represented by (1 − *Pi*). One has to note that the form of the dependent variable is thus representing the log-odds ratio which is the ratio of the two probabilities – a YES and a NO. As people are more willing to learn AI for higher education, the log-odds ratio will go up and vice-versa. The independent variables used in our study are shown in Table 8.1, which we have selected mostly based on literature survey and as per need of the study (Chatterjee, 2017, 2019, 2022).

Table 8.1. Independent Variables.

Financial condition	Monthly income of the family from all sources
Sex	Dummy variable. 0 for males, 1 for females, 2 for others
Caste	Dummy variable. 0 for general caste, 1 for OBC, 2 for SC, 3 for ST
Area of living	Dummy variable. 0 for urban, 1 for rural
Profession of respondent	Dummy variable. 0 for students, 1 for teachers, 2 for administrators
Infrastructure	Dummy variable. 0 for not a problem, 1 for if it is a problem
Cost-effectiveness	Dummy variable. 0 for yes, 1 for no
Workload reducing	Dummy variable. 0 for yes, 1 for no
Government's initiatives	Dummy variable. 0 for required, 1 for not required
Purpose of learning	Dummy variable. 0 for present learning, 1 for staying updated, 2 for future labour market
Course requirement	Dummy variable. 0 for yes, 1 for no

Source: Authors.

One can notice the fact that several socio-economic conditions have been used as dummy variables in this study because such conditions do influence the decision of an individual.

Out of 860 respondents, 559 replied positively with a YES and 301 responded with a NO. It implies that around two-third of the respondents are in favour of learning and applying AI in higher education. Our sample size for the urban area was 495 and that for the rural area was 365, including all three forms of respondents associated with higher education. In the urban area, we found 136 respondents with a negative reply, and in the rural area, this number was 165. Hence, in the rural area, a higher proportion of people replied negatively. These respondents who replied with a NO can be classified as 'protestors', but they cannot be eliminated from the analysis because any change in higher education caused by AI is going to have an impact on these people as well. There could be workings of several factors simultaneously behind the reply of an individual but few of them may be significant and few may be not from the sense of statistics. We need to estimate the significance or insignificance of each of the independent factors or variables. For doing it, this study employs the logit analysis. The regression results of the analysis are reported below.

Table 8.2 is self-explanatory in many respects, irrespective of significance or non-significance of the factors. AI, being a new concept, is believed to be cost-incurring; hence, higher the income, higher is the tendency for learning AI; this similar thinking of the respondents gets reflected in the question of

Table 8.2. Logit Analysis Estimating Preference for AI.

Variables	**Coefficients**	**Marginal Effects (d *Y*/d*X*)**
Financial condition	0.00288* (3.29)	0.00059* (3.81)
Sex	0.00779 (0.47)	0.00825 (0.20)
Caste	−0.00425** (−1.99)	−0.00873** (−2.07)
Area of living	−0.00818* (−7.01)	−0.00841* (−6.48)
Profession	−0.00248* (−7.24)	−0.00520* (−8.66)
Infrastructure	0.05207* (8.24)	0.08024* (8.89)
Cost-effective	−0.00245*** (−1.81)	−0.00288*** (−1.84)
Workload reducing	0.00880* (8.27)	0.00897* (9.27)
Government's initiatives	0.00648* (4.99)	0.00759* (5.91)
Purpose of learning	−0.00781* (−4.88)	0.00826* (−8.22)
Course requirement	0.00221** (1.98)	0.00412** (2.00)
Constant	8.2126* (5.27)	
Log-likelihood	199.288	
Likelihood Ratio (LR) chi-square	289.24	
Probability > chi-square	0.000	
Pseudo R^2	0.8834	
Total no. of observations	860	

Source: Computed by authors.

Note: The values in the parentheses for both coefficient and marginal effects are the *t*-values.

*Significant at 1% levels; **significant at 5% levels; and ***significant at 10% levels.

cost-effectiveness. People believe it is not cost-effective. Sex is insignificant which implies AI is important for all – irrespective of the gender. Caste has a negative sign before it, which implies the fact that as we move from the people of general caste to that of scheduled caste and others, the eagerness of learning AI falls – which could be because of the fact that people of these castes live in poor financial condition, and they believe AI is a costly thing to learn; therefore, their replies are reflecting that thinking. Urban people are keener in learning AI than their rural counterparts which could be because of the relatively better financial condition of the urban people. Students have more eagerness in learning AI as seen from the question on profession, as we move to the teachers and administrators, the willingness drops. Almost similar sort of outcomes can be seen when it comes to the question of purpose of learning. One can see that people are responding in favour of learning AI to be ready for the requirements of the future labour market requirements than for present conditions. This implies the fact that people believe that learning AI is good for future and perhaps that is why the relatively aged people – teachers and administrators – are less willing in learning AI. A few things which are accepted by all are the time-saving aspect of AI, the need for the governments' initiatives, and the need for better infrastructure for its smooth implementation – respondents accepted the fact that it saves hours and government initiatives are needed for its proper implementation and acceptance across different stakeholders of higher education. Another thing that the stakeholders believe is that there is a need for incorporating AI in curricula because incorporating as a part of syllabi can help in its acceptance as well as spread; hence, incorporating as a part of course is the need of the hour. The pseudo-R^2 of our analysis is above 88% which is really high, and the mean variance inflationary factor (VIF) of our variables is 3.22, which implies that the issue of multicollinearity is not a problem in our analysis because it is within the tolerable limit of 5. Along with the estimation of variables, we have found out the marginal effects of each of the variables which shows the proportionate change in the willingness to learn AI for higher education due to the proportionate change in the respective independent factor, holding other factors unchanged – this analysis also follows the same significance levels of variables like that of the main analysis. A majority of our variables are significant at either 1% or 5% level, only one is insignificant – that too carries significance.

Conclusion

The study has several aspects – it combines a theory-based model that shows why it is necessary to learn as well as implement AI in education – without which there is a chance of getting abolished in the near future. The ground-level reality combining the views of the stakeholders of higher education – students, teachers, administrators – is even more interesting because it covers both the urban and rural population, and it points out to a few important things such as government initiative, cost aspect, and purpose of learning. These things say that it is important to make AI an integral part of the education system and that too by means of government's initiative by means of education policy; better infrastructural condition as well as by making it cost-friendly. For maximizing the potential of AI in education, a collaborative approach involving governments, educational institutions, technology companies, and local communities is necessary. This should include investments in infrastructure, teacher training, and the development of culturally appropriate AI solutions. Additionally, policies must be put in place to ensure equitable access to AI-powered education and to address ethical concerns surrounding data use and privacy.

Governments can play a crucial role by creating supportive policy environments, allocating resources for AI in education initiatives, and establishing regulatory frameworks that promote innovation while protecting student interests. This may involve developing national AI strategies for education, creating incentives for private sector involvement in educational technology, and fostering partnerships between local and international institutions to share knowledge and best practices. Educational institutions need to be proactive in embracing AI technologies, adapting their curricula, and teaching methods to incorporate AI-enhanced learning experiences. Institutions should also engage in research and pilot projects to evaluate the effectiveness of AI in various educational contexts and contribute to the growing body of knowledge in this field. As AI technologies continue to evolve, their potential to transform education in developing economies will only grow. This, in turn, can lead to improved learning outcomes, enhanced skill development, and greater economic opportunities for individuals and communities. The integration of AI in education is not just about technological adoption; it represents a fundamental shift in how we approach teaching and learning. However, realizing this potential requires a thoughtful, inclusive, and ethical approach that places the needs and rights of learners at the centre of all AI initiatives in education.

In conclusion, while AI presents significant opportunities for transforming education in developing economies, its successful implementation requires careful consideration of local contexts, ethical implications, and long-term sustainability. By addressing the challenges and leveraging the strengths of AI in education, developing economies can create more resilient, adaptive, and inclusive educational systems that empower learners and contribute to broader social and economic development goals. The journey towards AI-enhanced education is complex and ongoing, but with collaborative efforts and a commitment to equity and quality, it holds the promise of revolutionizing learning experiences and outcomes for millions of students in developing economies.

References

Beladi, H., & Marjit, S. (1992): Foreign capital and protectionism. *Canadian Journal of Economics*, 25, 233–238.

Chatterjee, N. (2017). Willingness to pay for drinking water in some selected dryland areas of West Bengal: A contingent valuation approach. *Vidyasagar University Journal of Economics*, *XIX*, 14–37.

Chatterjee, N. (2019). Use of renewable resources and sustainable livelihood in Indian Sunderbans: An attempt through contingent valuation method. *Vidyasagar University Journal of Economics*, *XXII*, 98–117.

Chatterjee, N. (2022). Households' willingness to pay for improved water supply system in the dryland areas of West Bengal – An estimation using double-bounded dichotomous-choice model. *Economic Affairs*, *67*(5), 787–795. https://doi.org/10.46852/0424-2513.4.2022.12

Felix, C. V. (2020). The role of the teacher and AI in education. In E. Sengupta, P. Blessinger, & M. S. Makhanya (Eds.), *International perspectives on the role of technology in humanizing higher education* (Innovations in Higher Education Teaching and Learning, Vol. 33, pp. 33–48). Emerald Publishing Limited. https://doi.org/10.1108/S2055-364120200000033003

Golic, Z. (2019). Finance and artificial intelligence: The fifth industrial revolution and its impact on the financial sector. *Zbornik Radova Ekonomskog Fakulteta u Istočnom Sarajevu*, *19*, 67–81.

Grosz, B. J., & Stone, P. (2018). A century-long commitment to assessing artificial intelligence and its impact on society. *Communications of the ACM*, *61*(12), 68–73.

Haseski, H. I. (2019). What do Turkish pre-service teachers think about artificial intelligence? *International Journal of Computer Science Education in Schools*, *3*(2), 3–23. https://doi.org/10.21585/ijcses.v3i2.55

Humble, N., & Mozelius, P. (2019, October). Artificial intelligence in education – A promise, a threat or a hype? Proceedings of the European conference on the impact of artificial intelligence and robotics 2019 (ECIAIR 2019), Oxford, UK (pp. 149–156). Academic Conferences and Publishing International Limited.

Jones, R. W. (1965). The structure of simple general equilibrium models, *Journal of Political Economy*, 73, 522–557.

Jones, R. W. (1971). A three-factor model in theory, trade and history. In J. Bhagwati, et al., (Eds.). *Trade, Balance of Payments and Growth, North- Holland*, pp. 3–21.

Manyika, J., Chui, M., Miremadi, M., Bughin, J., George, K., Willmott, P., & Dewhurst, M. (2017). *A future that works: Automation, employment, and productivity*. McKinsey Global Institute.

Mohammed, P. S., & Watson, E. N. (2019). Towards inclusive education in the age of artificial intelligence: Perspectives, challenges, and opportunities. In J. Knox, Y. Wang, & M. Gallagher (Eds.), *Artificial intelligence and inclusive education. perspectives on rethinking and reforming education*. Springer, 1–19 https://doi.org/10.1007/978-981-13-8161-4_2

Mou, X. (2019). *Artificial intelligence: Investment trends and selected industry uses* (EMCompass No. 71). World Bank Group.

Ng, A. (2017, January 25). *Artificial intelligence is the new electricity*. Speech presented at Stanford MSx. https://www.youtube.com/watch?v=21EiKfQYZXc.

Pedro, F., Subosa, M., Rivas, A., & Valverde, P. (2019). *Artificial intelligence in education: Challenges and opportunities for sustainable development*. UNESCO.

PwC. (2017). *Sizing the prize What's the real value of AI for your business and how can you capitalise?* https://www.pwc.com/gx/en/issues/analytics/assets/pwc-ai-analysis-sizing-the-prize-report.pdf

Wartman, S. A., & Combs, C. D. (2018). Medical education must move from the information age to the age of artificial intelligence. *Academic Medicine*, *93*(8), 1107–1109.

Wogu, I. A. P., Misra, S., Olu-Owolabi, E. F., Assibong, P. A., & Udoh, O. D. (2018). Artificial intelligence, artificial teachers and the fate of learners in the 21st century education sector: Implications for theory and practice. *International Journal of Pure and Applied Mathematics*, *119*(16), 2245–2259.

Chapter 9

Impact of Artificial Intelligence on the Future of Education, Skill Development and Job Market: Blessing or a Curse

Rajib Bhattacharyya[a] *and Kaushiki Banerjee*[b]

[a]*Department of Economics, Goenka College of Commerce and Business Administration, India*
[b]*Department of Economics, Barasat Government College, India*

Abstract

Of late, there has been a revolutionary shift in technology, digitalization and machine learning which has opened up a new frontier of 'generative artificial intelligence' (AI), across the globe. AI basically refers to a spectrum of interrelated machine learning technologies applied to solve problems inspired by human intelligence. *Future of Jobs Report* (May 2023) has predicted a churn in the structure and composition of the labour market. One may decompose the effect of this AI into three broad dimensions: a displacement effect, a productivity effect and a reinstatement effect. The present chapter attempts to investigate the possible divergent impact of AI across countries (developed, developing and emerging nations) and variations of AI tools across different occupations, education levels and skills. Using the Organisation for Economic Co-operation and Development (OECD) data (Programme for the International Assessment of Adult Competencies (PIAAC) survey) and World Bank data (Skill Measurement Programme (STEP) survey), an occupation-wise AI Susceptible Index (AISI) has been constructed. Principal component analysis (PCA) is applied to estimate occupation-wise weights. Further, grand AISI scores are computed in different occupations. A higher score suggests a bigger possibility of adoption of AI. The study reveals that (i) the jobs are more threatened by AI in advanced economies (AEs) compared to emerging market and developing economies (EMDEs); (ii) occupations like managers, professionals and clerical support workers are the most vulnerable

Artificial Intelligence in Business and Society: Global Insights, 127–147

doi:10.1108/978-1-83708-022-920261021

(substitutable), whereas skilled agriculture and craft-related trade workers are the least susceptible to AI; and (iii) AI susceptibility increases with increase in education levels.

Keywords: Labour market; Artificial Intelligence Readiness Index; AI Susceptible Index; principal component analysis; skills development; education

Introduction

Of late, health, economic and geopolitical volatility combined with growing social and environmental pressures have created divergent labour market outcomes between developed and developing nations. Rapid changes in consumer and worker expectations, the urge for green and energy transition have led to major structural and sectoral shifts in the composition of the workforce – stimulating new occupations and skills but at the same time depressing some traditional jobs. According to the *Future of Jobs Report* (May 2023) by the World Economic Forum, 'Employers anticipate a structural labour market churn of 23% of jobs in the next five years'. According to this study, due to the rapid application of AI, 69 million new jobs are expected to be created, whereas the expected job loss is about 83 million. This corresponds to a net decrease of 14 million jobs or 2% of current employment. A higher-than-average churn has been noted in the supply chain and transportation and media, entertainment and sports industries, but in the case of retail and wholesale manufacturing of consumer goods, a lower-than-average churn has been noticed. A report by Investment Bank Goldman Sachs states that AI could replace the equivalent of 300 million full-time jobs. In the United States and Europe, it would probably replace a quarter of work tasks but at the same time will lead to new job creation and a productivity boom.

There are many ways to define AI, but one simple definition is 'intelligence demonstrated by machines' (Wikipedia, 2020). A leading textbook in the field defines it more precisely as machines thinking and/or acting humanly and/or rationally (Russell & Norvig, 2010). 'AI' represents a range of technologies using a variety of computational methods, particularly machine learning, which involves computerized learning processes inspired by human intelligence (Walsh et al., 2019). AI can analyse large data sets via learning processes that are supervised (i.e., learning guided by a human) or unsupervised (i.e., machine autonomous learning from the data; Walsh et al., 2019). Common methods that are often referred to as AI also include natural language processing (e.g., analysis and generation of text) and pattern recognition (e.g., identifying associations in data sets; Walsh et al., 2019).

But will AI be a blessing or a curse on the future job market? Will it throw out a permanent section of the existing who are no longer employable because their jobs are being done by computers? Will artificially developed machine intelligence someday take over the world and control the creators who made them? Or will AI and robotic technology usher in a golden age of human leisure and prosperity?

Historical Evolution of AI

AI is the latest form of machine-made application performing human activities using the advanced intelligence of science and engineering. Though the history of AI traces back to the 1950s of the work by Alan Turing, the coining of the term AI goes in the name of a group of computer scientists along with Marvin Minsky of MIT. A famous paper titled 'Steps Toward Artificial Intelligence' was published (Minsky, 1961). The next few decades witnessed rapid advancement in AI. The first wave focused on breaking down complex operations into smaller components and the second wave stressed mainly on encoding specialized human expertise into rules for the machine to follow. But by the mid-1980s, the progress of innovations slowed down and this field experienced, what is commonly known as, 'AI winter'. But again, there was an upsurge of interests since 2000, particularly due two three important changes: (a) data explosion, (b) tremendous growth of computing power and (c) application of new algorithms (particularly algorithms like 'neural networks' and 'deep learning'). The first practical signs of labour market churn were experienced when the best human players of the TV game show were beaten by IBM's Watson programme. Next in 2015, Google's AlphaGo beat a grand master of the game of Go (more complex than chess), and in 2017, it went on to beat the number one-ranked human player of the game.

The latest development that has taken place since 2018 is the transition of specialized AI (or sometimes referred to as narrow or weak AI performing predominantly specific programmes) to generalized AI (referred to artificial generalized intelligence, AGI). The AGI has been developed with a view to achieving a long-term perspective of the ability to undertake a wide range of tasks (Malone et al., 2020; Russell & Norvig, 2010). Of late, the introduction of OpenAI in 2020, in the form of a natural language model, technically known as the generative pre-trained transformer (GPT-3), is capable of performing a wide range of tasks for which it was not explicitly trained. The four major fields of AI are (i) machine learning, (ii) computer vision, (iii) natural language processing and (iv) robotics.

Reasons for Increasing Interest in AI in Education

To improve the teaching-learning process, the educators seek a safe, effective and scalable technology-enhanced 'automation based on association' or AI, being fully aware of the possible dangers of data privacy and security risks. There are three main reasons for addressing AI education:

(a) AI may provide an effective means of enhancing educational services at a larger scale and lower cost.
(b) Proper awareness and evaluation of potential system risks and concerns of job loss needs to be addressed for long-run sustainability.
(c) Due attention must also be placed on possible unintended or unexpected consequences of AI.

Factors Responsible for Advancement in AI

The rapid advancement in AI is made possible due the following factors:

(i) A significant drop in the cost of computation has led to a huge increase in computing power and storage capacity (e.g., cloud storage).
(ii) Rapid progress in scientific knowledge, information and communication technology (ICT) and widespread adoption of internet facilities has made it easy to use and store digital information necessary to develop tools based on AI principles.
(iii) Drastic fall in capital costs of digital technology has resulted in the removal of barriers to new start-ups and allowed new players to enter the market with adequate supply of highly educated software engineers.

Decomposition of Effect of AI in Three Broad Dimensions

Schumpeter developed the concept of 'creative destruction' for decades, and history shows that whenever new technologies were introduced, it had created disruptions, at least in the short run, in the labour market due to displacement of traditional workforce by newer ones. One may decompose the effect of this new technology on the future of education, skill development and job market into three broad dimensions: *a displacement effect*, a *productivity effect* and a *reinstatement effect* (Acemoglu & Restrepo, 2018; Chiacchio et al., 2018).

When a firm introduces automation into its operation, the labour market impact depends on its three-dimensional effects: (a) the displacement effect, where there is a direct substitution of existing jobs and tasks by a new set of workers; (b) the productivity effect, due to improvement in productivity which stems from the boost in demand for labour both due to a drop in prices and an increase in disposable income; and (c) a reinstatement effect or sometimes called skill-complementarity effect, where human and machine complement each other, there is an increase in jobs and tasks necessary to use, run and supervise the new machines. In the initial stages, the first effect dominates, which causes huge unemployment in the labour market. But in later stages, there are chances of the second and third effects to gain strength, and in that situation, the adverse situation may turn around (Autor et al., 2006; ILO Report, 2015). At the final phase, higher productivity results in the increase in demand which is uniformly distributed across sectors, irrespective of the extent to which these are being automated. In effect, less employment will be created in sectors with higher degrees of automation compared to those that do not benefit from automation. This will manifest in polarization of jobs and an increase in income inequality (Bessen, 2019).

Literature Survey

Technological advancement has historically contributed to economic growth (Romer, 1990; Solow, 1957) but has been debated widely because of its strength to substitute human labour. The widespread digitalization and use of AI technologies in recent times has once again fuelled up this debate. AI has complemented many occupations thereby raising labour productivity, but at the same time, some occupations are threatened by labour displacement due to substation of human skills by machines powered by AI (Acemoglu & Restrepo, 2018; Lane & Saint-Martin, 2021). Most of the researches measuring the impact of use of AI on occupations predominantly focus on the United States (Acemoglu et al., 2020; Brynjolfsson et al., 2018; Felten et al., 2019; Fossen & Sorgner, 2021; Frey & Osborne, 2017). Some of the studies are also based on OECD countries (Arntz et al., 2016; Georgieff & Hyee, 2021). The pioneer work by Felten et al. (2019), who developed a measure namely AI Occupational Impact (AIOI), investigated the impact of AI on labour polarization and wages. Then, Felten et al. (2021) constructed an index to measure the impact of AI on occupations, viz., AI Occupational Exposure (AIOE) measure based on US database O*NET (Occupational Information Database). O*NET is a rich database of detailed work activities corresponding to all the occupation codes which are being used by Felten et al. (2021) to estimate the likelihood of the major activities in a given occupation to be performed by AI without human intervention which in turn provides the degree of labour substitutability of a job by AI. But AI technology may also be complementary to human work. Hence, a modified version of AIOE has been proposed by Pizzinelli et al. (2023) is the complementarity-adjusted AI Occupational Exposure (C-AIOE). C-AIOE captures to what extent the exposure to AI of occupations is mitigated by their potential for complementarity which is known as labour augmenting technological progress (Fellner, 1967). The impact has been studied on a combination of advanced (the United Kingdom and the United States) and developing countries (Brazil, Colombia, South Africa and India). In contrast to Felten et al. (2021), they suggested that the jobs which are typically highly exposed to AI also have the largest opportunity to be complemented by AI (e.g., high-skilled occupations). But certain jobs, clerical support occupations, have greater exposure but low complementarity makes them more vulnerable to job destruction. Jobs in the United States and the United Kingdom are both high exposure and high complementarity, whereas in developing countries, less than 40% of the occupations have high exposure with a fraction of low level of complementarity.

A few researches also evaluate the impact of AI and robotization on employment in developing countries (Aly, 2022; Carbonero et al., 2020). Carbonero et al. (2023) estimated occupation-wise suitability of jobs for machine learning to thwart light on the extent of 'destructive digitalization' versus 'transformative digitization' in case of Lao People's Democratic Republic (PDR) and Vietnam using semantic textual similarities (SBERT) method. Sentence-BERT (SBERT) is a variant of BERT (Bidirectional Encoder Representations from Transformers). Copestake et al. (2023) measured the impact of AI on service-led growth in India using data on AI-related job postings, showing that AI jobs augment salary of the individuals, but it has the potential to replace high-skilled occupations.

Objectives of the Study

The present paper attempts to investigate the possible divergent impact of AI across countries (developed, developing and emerging nations) and variation of AI tools across different occupations, education levels and skills.

Data and Methodology

To measure suitability of jobs for AI, the micro-level data-measuring skills of individual workers in different countries are considered. In this regard, two different data sets are used, viz, World Bank's Skill Measurement Programme (STEP)[1] focusing on lower- and middle-income countries and OECD's Programme for the International Assessment of Adult Competencies (PIAAC)[2] focusing on developed regions. Here, only those adults who were found to be employed have been included. In these data sets, questions measuring different skills required to perform a given task in a particular occupation are provided. Skill ranges from reading, writing, problem-solving to manual skills. Since the thrust of this chapter is to measure susceptibility of an occupation to AI (i.e. machine learning), we focus on specifically those skills where possibility of adoption of AI is higher. Here, AI-powered robotic technology is outside the purview of the present analysis. The present analysis has included those human skills which are more susceptible to AI like (i) reading, (ii) writing, (iii) numeracy and (iv) use of ICT. Therefore, occupations where usage of these four skills are higher, they would be more threatened by labour displacement. Both the surveys have provided a score for these four skills based on several questions regarding how different tasks are performed using these skills in a particular occupation. The responses are coded in different Likert scales. To formulate AISI, first of all, after quantifying each of the skill variables, they have been normalized using the following formula making them comparable across all dimensions in both the surveys.

$$S_{ijk} = \frac{\text{Actual}S_{ijk} - \text{Min}S_{ijk}}{\text{Max}S_{ijk} - \text{Min}S_{ijk}} \tag{1}$$

where i stands for the ith nation, $i = 1,2, \ldots, 27$; j is the jth skill corresponding to kth occupation (j =1,2,3,4); (k = 1,2,…,10). The skill indicators are denoted by S_1 = ICT skill, S_2 = numeracy skill, S_3 = reading skill, S_4 = writing skill. The data are based on 27 countries classified as (i) AEs (here 12 representative countries) and (ii) EMDEs (here 15 representative countries) as classified in World Economic Outlook (2023).

To formulate the index, occupation-wise weights of these four skills are estimated using PCA. Since the usage of skills varies across occupations, suitability of a skill to AI will also vary across occupations. Thus, these weights are endogenous and should be determined by PCA. Since in the data set, the responses are received from a unit level, thus upon normalizing, the mean value of the skill indicator corresponding to a particular occupation in a particular country is taken as the representative value for the occupation in that country for PCA. The benefit of using PCA is that it helps in identifying significant skill indicators along

[1]Can be accessed from the website of World Bank, https://microdata.worldbank.org/index.php/catalog/2994/get-microdata.

[2]Can be accessed from the website of OECD, https://webfs.oecd.org/piaac/puf-data/.

with their weights, and a sub-index for AI susceptibility is formulated for each of the occupation categories across countries. Following Nunnally and Bernstein (1994), the significant skill indicators are chosen after performing Student's *t*-test.

$$t = \frac{r\sqrt{(n-2)}}{\sqrt{(1-r^2)}} \tag{2}$$

where *r* is the factor loadings and *n* is the number of observations.

Thus, across countries, an occupation-wise sub-index-measuring AI susceptibility is constructed considering four skill indicators. The higher value of the index implies greater chance of adoption of AI in that occupation. Thus, the formula for *k*th occupation in *i*th country will be

$$\text{Occup}_{k,\,i} = \frac{\sum_{j=1}^{4} w_{kij} S_{kij}}{\sum_{j=1}^{4} w_{kij}} \tag{3}$$

The aggregate AISI will give an idea of the extent to which the country is susceptible to adoption of AI. The aggregate AISI is formulated by *weighting the occupation-level AISI sub-index* to the prevalence and importance of each occupation in that country which is measured by the employment share in each occupation in the country (Guarascio et al., 2023).

$$\text{AISI}_i = \frac{\sum_{k=1}^{10} (\text{empshare}_{k,i} \times \text{Occup}_{k,i})}{100} \tag{4}$$

The value of the index ranges from 0 to 1 where higher the value of AISI, the greater is the chance of adoption of AI in that country. For the present analysis, occupation categories are chosen from International Standard Classification of Occupations (ISCO-08). ISCO-08 classifies jobs in 10 major groups, viz, (i) managers, (ii) professional, (iii) technicians and associate professionals, (iv) clerical support workers, (v) service and sales workers, (vi) skilled agriculture, forestry and fishery workers, (vii) craft-related trade workers, (viii) plant and machine operators and assemblers, (ix) elementary occupations and (x) armed forces occupations.

Following the same methodology, the impact of adoption of AI on different levels of education is estimated across countries. In this case, the education levels are classified as (i) primary, (ii) lower secondary, (iii) upper secondary and (iv) tertiary. Once again, PCA is performed to construct the index corresponding to each education category where significant skill indicators and their corresponding weights are determined by PCA.

Impact of AI on Skill, Education and Job Market

There are two polar opposite views regarding the future impact of AI on the labour market. One extreme view suggests that it will result in a jobless future (e.g., Ford, 2015; Susskind, 2020; West, 2018), while commentators on the other extreme believe that the oncoming AI will enrich labour productivity and work experience (e.g., McKinsey Global Institute, 2017). Due to limited availability of data on the application of AI in the labour market, the assessments may vary or may be inconclusive. One of the largest data sources is the 'Burning Glass Technologies' or sometimes referred to as 'Lightcast data' (https://lightcast.io/).

Various Measurements Related to AI

Various measures are used from time to time to assess the impact of AI on jobs. First, AIOI was used by Felten et al. (2018, 2019). The AIOI measure links specific applications of AI and occupations. Second, suitability for machine learning (SML) index was developed by Brynjolfsson et al. (2018, 2019). Third, AI exposure score was created by Michael Webb (2020), which was constructed to measure the 'exposure' of various occupations to a particular technology.

World Labour Demand for AI Jobs and Geographical Distribution

If we choose the percentage of all jobs that require some AI application in total jobs over time as the metrics of labour demand for AI jobs, then the three leading nations are the United States (2.1%), Canada (1.5%) and Spain (1.3%). AI Hiring Index portrays the rate of hiring of AI workers as the percentage of LinkedIn members with AI skills on their profile or working in AI-related occupations who added a new employer in the same period the job began, divided by the total number of LinkedIn members in the corresponding location. The relative AI Hiring Index (2022) identifies top 15 geographic locations.

AI Readiness Index (AIRI)

In many countries of the world, the government is trying to regulate, improve and provide a digital platform to AI (like the European Union's AI Act, Digital Platform Government in Republic of Korea, etc.) and ensure the delivery of AI as a 'public service'. The AIRI attempts to examine country-wise readiness of the government to deliver AI as public services. The AIRI ranks 193 countries on the basis of three pillars: (a) government (b) technology and (c) data and infrastructure, across 10 dimensions and 39 indicators. The first pillar depends on vision, governance and ethics, digital capacity and adaptability of the government. The second pillar depends on human capital, innovation capacity and maturity, and the third pillar is determined by data representation, data availability and infrastructure. The total scores and the rankings of our representative 27 countries are shown in Table 9.1.

Empirical Analysis

Table 9.2 depicts the result of PCA. Here, for each of the 10 occupations, the list of significant skill indicators is obtained along with their factor loadings. For

Table 9.1. AIRI.

	2023 Ranking	Country	Total Scores
AEs	1	United States	84.80
	2	Singapore	81.97
	3	United Kingdom of Great Britain and Northern Ireland	78.57
	6	France	76.07
	7	Republic of Korea	75.65
	9	Japan	75.08
	11	Denmark	73.91
	13	Norway	72.71
	14	Sweden	72.55
	15	Austria	72.37
	30	Israel	65.46
	31	Czech Republic	65.17
EMDEs	16	China	70.94
	38	Russian Federation	62.92
	40	India	62.58
	41	Chile	61.95
	45	Hungary	60.66
	47	Türkiye	60.51
	53	Colombia	57.85
	59	Viet Nam	54.48
	60	Ukraine	53.29
	68	Mexico	50.37
	85	Armenia	45.22
	95	Sri Lanka	41.89
	99	Georgia	41.27
	101	Kenya	40.19
	136	Lao PDR	33.05
	141	Ghana	32.58

Source: Government AIRI (2023), Oxford Insights.

Table 9.2. Results of PCA of Occupation (Category-wise) and Aggregate AISI Score Across Countries.

Occupations	Skill Indicators (Factor Loading)			
	ICT Tools	Numeracy	Reading	Writing
Armed forces	0.481601***	0.097148	0.619048***	0.612701***
Managers	0.404904***	0.491337***	0.538232***	0.552221***
Professionals	0.425397***	0.337529***	0.564593***	0.621568***
Technicians and associate professionals	0.355331***	0.517312***	0.549105***	0.551917***
Clerical support workers	−0.473851**	0.5783***	0.216582	0.627795***
Service and sales workers	0.531792***	0.35104***	0.551435***	0.538412***
Skilled agriculture, forestry and fishery workers	0.5219482***	0.456306***	0.5003672***	0.5186401***
Craft-related trade workers	0.5323707*	0.3916022***	0.5340161***	0.52731***
Plant and machine operators and assemblers	0.536646***	0.5090695***	0.5535096***	0.3827354***
Elementary occupations	0.5076515***	0.447606***	0.5268915***	0.5141246***

Country	Agg AISI Score (Rank)	Country	Agg AISI Score (Rank)
EMDEs		**AEs**	
China	0.446078 (17)	Austria	0.551222 (6)
Hungary	0.474385 (16)	France	0.522923 (11)
Mexico	0.51886 (13)	Czech Republic	0.542513 (7)
Russia	0.492694 (15)	Denmark	0.525417 (10)
Chile	0.522336 (12)	Israel	0.534785 (8)
Kenya	0.204314 (25)	Japan	0.49621 (14)
Turkey	0.424994 (18)	Korea Republic	0.594976 (1)
Georgia	0.253509 (21)	Norway	0.553024 (5)
Ghana	0.197953 (26)	Singapore	0.573447 (4)
Lao PDR	0.173326 (27)	Sweden	0.532531 (9)
Sri Lanka	0.215782 (24)	United Kingdom	0.580524 (3)
Ukraine	0.339487 (19)	United States	0.591355 (2)
Vietnam	0.234759 (22)		
Armenia	0.217743 (23)		
Colombia	0.311278 (20)		

Source: Authors' estimation.

***, ** and * imply significance at 1%, 5% and 10% levels, respectively.

armed forces, ICT, reading and writing skills are significant and numeracy skills is not significant. Thus, an index for armed force occupation is constructed using these three significant skill indicators. Here, the factor loadings of the significant skill indicators are used as weights (Table 9.2). For managers, professionals and technicians, all the four skill indicators are significant, but for clerical support workers, only numeracy and writing skills appeared to be significant. Thus, the occupation-wise sub-index for susceptibility to AI is obtained (see Appendix).

The sub-index for ISCO-08 occupations across countries is presented in Table 9.3. It is evident from Table 9.3 that occupations like skilled agriculture, craft-related trade workers and elementary occupations are least susceptible to the adoption of AI as the AI susceptible skills, that is, reading, writing, numeracy and ICT, are least used in these occupations. But occupations like managers, professionals and clerical support workers are the most vulnerable as the skills used are highly substitutable to AI and can be replaced by AI. Also, occupations like service and sales workers and plant and machine operators are threatened as the possibility of job substitution by AI exists to some extent in these occupations, but these occupations have medium exposure to AI as compared to occupations like managers, professionals and clerical support workers. It is apparent from the index values for all the occupation categories that the index has typically higher values for (i) manager, (ii) professionals and (iii) clerical support workers and medium range values for (iv) technicians, associate professionals and (v) service and sales workers. The index values are in the lower range for the rest of the occupations. This pattern of variation in AISI index across occupations is similar across the countries. Only the index scores higher for AEs because these countries are technologically already more advanced and use of AI has been widespread compared to EMDEs.

Here, higher rank (positional value) implies greater risk of AI susceptibility in aggregate in a nation. It is evident from the country rankings that the AEs are among the top scorers indicating huge spurt in technology, and also demographic factors causing shrinking adult workforce have already necessitated these countries to adopt a labour-saving technology. Rapid mechanization was already taking place, and now the substitution of human skills by AI is making these countries more affected by advancement in AI. Thus, the jobs are more threatened by AI in AEs compared to EMDEs. It is found that Korea (Republic) is the most affected one by AI (0.594976) followed by the United States whereas Lao PDR is the least affected one (0.173326). It is obvious because Korea (Republic) has the largest share of AI patents in the world, and the United States is also the leading developer of AI technologies. Even Singapore has also grown in share of users of AI at work in the world with 68% already implemented AI at work (Gillespie et al., 2023). It is also evident from our result that jobs are the most susceptible to AI in these nations. In AEs, the share of workers in occupations like professionals, managers or in retail occupations is higher which also has greater exposure to AI. Thus, higher potential for AI complementarity in certain occupations coupled with a major share of employment in those occupations has led AEs more susceptible to AI. This result is also supported by the recent researches

Table 9.3. Occupation-wise AI Susceptibility Index Across Countries.

Country	Index									
	Manager	Professionals	Technicians and Associate Professionals	Clerical Support Workers	Service and Sales Workers	Skilled Agriculture, Forestry and Fishery Workers	Craft-related Trade Workers	Plant and Machine Operators and Assemblers	Elementary Occupations	Armed Forces
EMDEs										
China	0.580014	0.637514	0.505058	0.587383	0.350371	0.165327	0.27161	0.284626	0.257053	–
Hungary	0.623175	0.641583	0.570062	0.504468	0.442161	0.33132	0.41186	0.29177	0.329241	0.432283
Mexico	0.669697	0.721375	0.645417	0.618654	0.507486	0.654568	0.567192	0.504188	0.463475	0.360382
Russia	0.565105	0.559664	0.576975	0.537904	0.450467	0.61828	0.42568	0.409564	0.346839	0.585724
Chile	0.619529	0.688048	0.674979	0.624139	0.455578	0.40786	0.523613	0.365509	0.459729	0.670865
Kenya	0.483113	0.649056	0.592132	0.480311	0.201611	0.419271	0.205286	0.209022	0.097106	0.26098
Turkey	0.523095	0.562284	0.520224	0.580616	0.451442	0.119182	0.411827	0.287399	0.293927	0.462597
Georgia	0.424141	0.459625	0.451193	0.449031	0.232852	0.334117	0.141948	0.115885	0.080752	0.442547
Ghana	0.461596	0.512697	0.426962	0.479982	0.151934	0.162651	0.206333	0.220375	0.117824	–
Lao PDR	0.431165	0.453723	0.472869	0.540783	0.227682	0.107768	0.187361	0.21517	0.15624	0.363378
Sri Lanka	0.397555	0.513546	0.377341	0.454803	0.230328	0.114902	0.176537	0.118765	0.106572	0.317506
Ukraine	0.540823	0.619423	0.449641	0.535475	0.255453	–	0.217685	0.229245	0.102536	0.413624
Vietnam	0.565807	0.651474	0.565566	0.532321	0.226747	0.165647	0.214253	0.180768	0.132068	0.597244
Armenia	0.548564	0.521213	0.428702	0.542785	0.221793	0.111639	0.224477	0.162455	0.084226	0.480011
Colombia	0.451125	0.626775	0.474145	0.554752	0.304886	–	0.257799	0.203726	0.160726	0.159732

(Continued)

Table 9.3. (*Continued*)

Country	Index									
	Manager	Professionals	Technicians and Associate Professionals	Clerical Support Workers	Service and Sales Workers	Skilled Agriculture, Forestry and Fishery Workers	Craft-related Trade Workers	Plant and Machine Operators and Assemblers	Elementary Occupations	Armed Forces
AEs										
Austria	0.686662	0.67243	0.633593	0.589829	0.452631	0.368693	0.467892	0.40338	0.416213	0.692305
France	0.645861	0.633958	0.570937	0.514457	0.47391	0.419188	0.48153	0.354333	0.37834	0.662354
Czech Republic	0.665984	0.63159	0.64904	0.599271	0.520849	0.400675	0.475096	0.395197	0.386631	0.396319
Denmark	0.668762	0.638489	0.627932	0.578984	0.48188	0.440001	0.489733	0.433573	0.387045	0.62581
Israel	0.582616	0.612123	0.580884	0.46783	0.394179	0.3671	0.514789	1.433904	0.217571	–
Japan	0.680102	0.638401	0.642658	0.523656	0.47535	0.35303	0.505169	0.416194	0.346268	0.499733
Korea (Republic)	0.639556	0.696905	0.661263	0.689151	0.535201	0.347674	0.562511	0.451842	0.425965	0.844269
Norway	0.659326	0.655162	0.643424	0.54234	0.434523	0.389099	0.492692	0.494902	0.369561	–
Singapore	0.640925	0.693503	0.63032	0.521287	0.449374	–	0.503649	0.483267	0.432319	0.627356
Sweden	0.652095	0.627046	0.61016	0.513574	0.406603	0.44949	0.441479	0.358475	0.285833	0.518927
United Kingdom	0.656415	0.701034	0.673638	0.576004	0.4766	0.363413	0.536643	0.473855	0.409837	0.729919
United States	0.700671	0.70443	0.660204	0.600847	0.507436	0.51307	0.530932	0.45893	0.34384	0.805815

Source: Authors' estimation.

Note: '–' indicates missing values. The index for Ukraine, Colombia and Singapore for the occupation of skilled agriculture, forestry and fishery workers cannot be obtained due to lack of data. Following the same reason, indexes for China, Ghana, Denmark and Norway for the occupation armed forces cannot be obtained.

which posit that AEs are facing the highest risk of job loss due to the use of AI (OECD Employment Outlook, 2023).

Among the emerging economies, China has rapidly adopted AI technology in its economy and also dramatically reduced employment share in agriculture in recent times. Needless to say, the country is having tremendous potential for implementation of AI with demand for AI growing rapidly. But due to lack of skilled AI developers, the demand–supply mismatch is causing China to have a medium impact of AI. Still the jobs are cushioned to some extent to the possible threats of AI in China (AISI score 0.446078). Also emerging economies like Mexico, Chile and Hungary are facing some risk (if not as high as the advanced world) due to the adoption of AI as these countries are also developing AI technologies at a faster pace; the jobs are having increasing exposure to AI as suggested by their AISI scores. The rest of the EMDEs are comparatively less susceptible to the adoption of AI having scores less than 0.4. Since the majority of employment in many of these countries are still in traditional sectors, like agriculture, forestry, fishing, craft-related trade works, elementary occupations, so complementarity is low and also advancement in AI technology is slow.

Table 9.4 shows the result of PCA for education where factor loadings for the four skill indicators are provided. Factor loadings of all the four skill indicators are significant across four education categories. Thus, the index is formed considering all the indicators, and the index values for all the education categories are shown in Table 9.4. Across nations, with the rise in education level, gradually the scores are rising, implying AI susceptibility increases with education level. Thus, the more educated labour force (i.e. tertiary or upper secondary level) is more adversely affected by AI adoption compared to the less educated workforce (i.e. primary or lower secondary) as the former work in skilled (*white-collar*) occupations work which can be more easily be replaced by AI technology compared to the latter. Low-educated workers are still concentrated more in traditional occupations where manual skills are more used than intelligence (like numeracy, technology skills) which are not complementary to AI. The trend observed is similar in both (i) AEs and (ii) EMDEs.

Table 9.4 also reports the aggregate AISI w.r.t. education for the countries and ranks 27 countries based on the score. It is observed that all the AEs are facing greater vulnerability to AI as the share of educated workers (i.e. tertiary and upper secondary) is higher in the labour force in these nations and also these countries are more advanced in using AI technology. Particularly, the United States (highest AISI score) being the largest developer of AI, and also supply of workers completing tertiary level of education is high, thus making the nation the most susceptible to AI. Also, Singapore and Korea (Republic) have made remarkable progress in developing AI technology and produced the greatest share of college graduates; thus, these nations will also bear the brunt of the adoption of AI. The emerging economies are less susceptible to AI compared to AEs. But among the emerging countries, China, Chile, Hungary and Mexico have potential for the adoption of AI which may put the skilled workers at stake. China is one of the leading developers of AI, but it has a shortfall of supply of skilled AI professionals making the country still less vulnerable to AI. But in other developing

Table 9.4. Education Category-wise Result of PCA and Aggregate AISI Score Across Countries.

Education Level	Factor Loadings			
	ICT Tools	Numeracy	Reading	Writing
Primary	0.519177***	0.450878***	0.528578***	0.497765***
Lower secondary	0.503733***	0.436408**	0.522674***	0.531614***
Upper secondary	0.493074***	0.464137***	0.518146***	0.522474***
Tertiary	0.458175***	0.445285***	0.55706***	0.530548***

Country	Primary	Lower Secondary	Upper Secondary	Tertiary	Agg Index (Rank)
China	0.168123	0.336039	0.458095	0.636477	0.444942 (16)
Hungary	0.3641	0.4275	0.474803	0.63723	0.515609 (15)
Mexico	0.460671	0.657279	0.599708	0.71693	0.565896 (11)
Russia	0.097351	0.578175	0.505925	0.568391	0.380705 (18)
Chile	0.491194	0.653981	0.542491	0.664129	0.56329 (12)
Kenya	0.138612	0.340985	0.315661	0.685741	0.301503 (22)
Turkey	0.309008	0.405351	0.438195	0.56838	0.413935 (17)
Georgia	0.097346	0.177868	0.206179	0.396804	0.2696 (24)
Ghana	0.213974	0.277608	0.236673	0.239574	0.193644 (27)
Lao PDR	0.159673	0.242569	0.297039	0.491469	0.204632 (26)
Sri Lanka	0.091675	0.178977	0.308809	0.532085	0.221848 (25)
Ukraine	0.075282	0.155312	0.26203	0.512558	0.380065 (19)

Vietnam	0.145925	0.247228	0.310469	0.62291	0.279655 (23)
Armenia	0.132404	0.163216	0.242071	0.468235	0.302944 (21)
Colombia	0.186296	0.311978	0.325598	0.538219	0.335235 (20)
Austria	0.23638	0.563667	0.582087	0.671945	0.574263 (10)
France	0.519066	0.657969	0.538182	0.640291	0.581442 (8)
Czech Republic	–	0.599273	0.571982	0.667327	0.592462 (6)
Denmark	0.299848	0.566811	0.543219	0.648473	0.58202 (7)
Israel	0.651393	0.503265	0.498249	0.616656	0.530102 (14)
Japan	0.278485	0.64649	0.504516	0.608603	0.561531 (13)
Korea Republic	0.35884	0.566207	0.549567	0.673438	0.616009 (3)
Norway	0.370306	0.609374	0.542244	0.650104	0.592676 (5)
Singapore	0.35857	0.646745	0.533645	0.686264	0.632093 (2)
Sweden	0.4599	0.571176	0.522245	0.613891	0.576699 (9)
United Kingdom	0.514097	0.674546	0.56757	0.627107	0.607652 (4)
United States	0.542955	0.580286	0.581778	0.695024	0.644543 (1)

Source: Authors' estimation.

Note: '–' indicates missing value.

countries, the share of the labour force completing tertiary education is low, and also the AI sector is less developed in these countries due to a lack of digital infrastructure further reducing the threats of use of AI.

Conclusion

The present study has tried to examine empirically the differential impact of AI across two sets of nations, the AEs and the EMDEs, in respect of the labour market, skill development and educational levels. The Government AIRI (2023) and AISI provide similar results. With regard to the three pillars, (a) government (b) technology and (c) data and infrastructure, the AEs shows more readiness than the EMDEs (outlier being China). The jobs are more threatened by AI in AEs compared to EMDEs. Out of a set of 27 representative nations, it is found that Korea (Republic) is the most affected one by AI (0.594976) followed by the United States, whereas Lao PDR is the least affected one (0.173326). Occupations like managers, professionals and clerical support workers are the most vulnerable (substitutable), whereas skilled agriculture and craft-related trade workers are the least susceptible to AI and (iii) AI susceptibility increases with the increase in education levels. Hence, automation, machine learning, computer vision and robotics are expected to bring about a demographic change in the composition of the labour force in the years to come.

References

Acemoglu, D., Autor, D., Hazell, J., & Restrepo, P. (2020). *AI and jobs: Evidence from online vacancies* [NBER Working Paper No. 28257]. NBER.

Acemoglu, D., & Restrepo, P. (2018). The race between man and machine: Implications of technology for growth, factor shares, and employment. *American Economic Review*, *108*(6), 1488–1542.

Aly, H. (2022). Digital transformation, development and productivity in developing countries: Is artificial intelligence a curse or a blessing? *Review of Economics and Political Science*, *7*(4), 238–256.

Arntz, M., Gregory, T., & Zierahn, U. (2016). *The risk of automation for jobs in OECD countries: A comparative analysis* [OECD Social, Employment and Migration Working Paper No. 189]. OECD Publishing.

Artificial Intelligence Index Report. (2022). Human-centred Artificial Intelligence (HAI). Standford University [Available at https://hai.stanford.edu/ai-index/2022-ai-index-report]

Autor, D. H., Katz, L. F., & Kearney, M. S. (2006). The polarisation of US labour market. *American Economic Review*, *96*(2), 189–194.

Bessen, J. (2019). Automation and jobs: When technology boosts employment. *Economic Policy*, *585*, 589–626. https://scholarship.law.bu.edu/faculty_scholarship/815

Brynjolfsson, E., Mitchell, T., & Rock, D. (2018). What can machines learn, and what does it mean for occupations and the economy? *American Economic Association Papers and Proceedings*, *108*, 43–47.

Brynjolfsson, E., Rock, D., & Syverson, C. (2018). Artificial intelligence and the modern productivity paradox: A clash of expectations and statistics. In *The Economics of Artificial Intelligence: An Agenda*, 23–57. University of Chicago Press.

Carbonero, F., Davies, J., Ernst, E., Fossen, F. M., Samaan, D., & Sorgner, A. (2023). The impact of artificial intelligence on labor markets in developing countries: A new method with an illustration for Lao PDR and urban Viet Nam. *Journal of Evolutionary Economics, 17*, 1–30. https://doi.org/10.1007/s00191-023-00809-7

Carbonero, F., Ernst, E., & Weber, E. (2020). *Robots Worldwide: The Impact of Automation on Employment and Trade*. IAB Discussion Paper No. 7–2020. Institute for Employment Research, ZBW – Leibniz Information Centre for Economics, Kiel, Hamburg. [Available at https://www.econstor.eu/bitstream/10419/224602/1/vfs-2020-pid-40084.pdf]

Chiacchio, F., Petropoulos, G., & Pichler, D. (2018). *The impact of industrial robots on EU employment and wages – A local labour market approach* [Working Paper 25186]. Bruegel.

Copestake, A., Marczinek, M., Pople, A., & Stapelton, K. (2023). *AI and services-led growth: Evidence from Indian job adverts*. Article on Ideas for India.

Fellner, W. (1967). Measures of technological progress in the light of recent growth theories. *The American Economic Review, 57*(5), 1073–1098.

Felten, E. W., Raj, M., & Seamans, R. (2019). *The occupational impact of artificial intelligence: Labor, skills, and polarization* [Working paper]. https://doi.org/10. 2139/ssrn.3368605

Felten, E. W., Raj, M., & Seamans, R. (2021). Occupational, industry and geographic exposure to artificial intelligence: A novel dataset and its potential uses. *Strategic Management Journal, 42*(12), 2195–2217.

Fossen, F. M., & Sorgner, A. (2021). Digitalization of work and entry into entrepreneurship. *Journal of Business Research, 125*, 548–563. https://doi.org/10.1016/j.jbusres.2019.09.019

Ford, M. (2015). The rise of the robots: Technology and the threat of mass unemployment. *International Journal of HRD Practice, Policy and Research*, 2016, *1*(1), 111–112. [Available at https://www.ijhrdppr.com/wp-content/uploads/2016/03/IJHRD-Vol-1-No-1-Final.pdf]

Frey, C. B., & Osborne, M. A. (2017). The future of employment: How susceptible are jobs to computerization? *Technological Forecasting and Social Change, 114*, 254–280.

Future of Jobs Report. (2023, May). World Economic Forum.

Gillespie, N., Lockey, S., Curtis, C., Pool, J., & Akbari, A. (2023). Trust in artificial intelligence: A global study. The University of Queensland and KPMG Australia. doi: 10.14264/00d3c94.

Georgieff, A., & Hyee, R. (2021). *Artificial intelligence and employment: New cross-country evidence* [OECD Social, Employment and Migration Working Paper No. 265]. OECD Publishing.

Government AI Readiness Index. (2023). Oxford Insights. https://oxfordinsights.com/wp-content/uploads/2023/12/2023-Government-AI-Readiness-Index-1.pdf

Guarascio, D., Reljic, J., & Stollinger, R. (2023). *Artificial Intelligence and Employment: A Look into the Crystal Ball*. LEM Papers Series 2023/34, Laboratory of Economics and Management (LEM), Sant'Anna School of Advanced Studies, Pisa, Italy.

ILO Report. (2015). *World employment and social outlook 2015: The changing nature of jobs*. https://www.ilo.org/global/research/global-reports/weso/2015-changing-nature-of-jobs/WCMS_368626/lang-en/index.htm

International Monetary Fund. (2023). World economic outlook: Navigating global divergences (October). IMF eLibrary. https://www.elibrary.imf.org/downloadpdf/display/book/9798400235801/9798400235801.pdf

Lane, M., & Saint-Martin, A. (2021). *The impact of artificial intelligence on the labour market: What do we know so far* [OECD Social, Employment and Migration Working Paper No. 256]? https://doi.org/10.1787/7c895724-en

Malone, T. W., Rus, D., & Laubacher, R. (2020, December 17). *Artificial intelligence and the future of work* [Research brief]. MIT Work of Future.

McKinsey Global Institute. (2017). https://www.mckinsey.com/featured-insights/future-of-work/jobs-lost-jobs-gained-what-the-future-of-work-will-mean-for-jobs-skills-and-wages.

Minsky, M. (1961, January). *Step towards artificial intelligence*. Proceedings of the IRE.

Nunnally, J. C., & Bernstein, I. H. (1994). *Psychometric theory*. New York: McGraw-Hill.

OECD. (2023). *OECD Employment Outlook 2023: Artificial Intelligence and the Labour Market*, OECD Publishing, Paris, https://doi.org/10.1787/08785bba-en.

Pizzinelli, C., A. Panton, M. M. Tavares, M. Cazzaniga, and L. Li, (2023). *Labor market exposure to AI: Cross-country differences and distributional implication* [IMF Working Paper 23/216]

Romer, P. M. (1990). Endogenous technological change. *Journal of Political Economy*, *98*(5), 71–102.

Russell, S. J., & Norvig, P. (2010). *Artificial intelligence: A modern approach* (3rd ed.). Prentice Hall, Pearson.

Solow, R. M. (1957). Technical change and the aggregate production function. *The Review of Economics and Statistics*, *39*(3), 312–320.

Susskind, D. (2020). *A world without work: Technology, automation and how we should respond*. London: Penguin Books Limited, 326.

Walsh, T., Levy, N., Bell, G., Elliott, A., Maclaurin, J., Mareels, I., & Wood, F. (2019). *The effective and ethical development of artificial intelligence: An opportunity to improve our well-being*. Australian Council of Learned Academies. https://acola.org/wp-content/uploads/2019/07/hs4_artificial-intelligence-report.pdf

Webb, M. (2020). *The impact of artificial intelligence on the labor market*. Unpublished manuscript, Stanford.

West, D. (2018). *The future of work: Robots, AI, and automation*. Washington, DC: Brookings Institution Press.

Wikipedia, (2020). https://en.wikipedia.org/wiki/Artificial_intelligence

Appendix

$$\text{Occup}_{k=\text{Armed force}} = \frac{(0.481601 \times S_{1ij}) + (0.619048 \times S_{3ij}) + (0.612701 \times S_{4ij})}{0.481601 + 0.619048 + 0.612701} \quad (1)$$

$$\text{Occup}_{k=\text{Manager}} = \frac{(0.404904 \times S_{1ij}) + (0.491337 \times S_{2ij}) + (0.538232 \times S_{3ij}) + (0.552221 \times S_{4ij})}{0.404904 + 0.491337 + 0.538232 + 0.552221} \quad (2)$$

$$\text{Occup}_{k=\text{Prof}} = \frac{(0.425397 \times S_{1ij}) + (0.337529 \times S_{2ij}) + (0.564593 \times S_{3ij}) + (0.621568 \times S_{4ij})}{0.425397 + 0.337529 + 0.564593 + 0.621568} \quad (3)$$

$$\text{Occup}_{k=\text{Tech}} = \frac{(0.355331 \times S_{1ij}) + (0.517312 \times S_{2ij}) + (0.549105 \times S_{3ij}) + (0.551917 \times S_{4ij})}{0.355331 + 0.517312 + 0.549105 + 0.551917} \quad (4)$$

$$\text{Occup}_{k=\text{Clerk}} = \frac{(-0.473851 \times S_{1ij}) + (0.5783 \times S_{2ij}) + (0.627795 \times S_{4ij})}{0.5783 + 0.627795 - 0.473851} \quad (5)$$

Chapter 10

Possibilities, Limitations and Pitfalls of Application of AI in the Arts and the Humanities: A Qualitative Study

Debdas Roy

Department of English Literature, Language and Cultural Studies, Vidyasagar University, India

Abstract

This chapter explores the impacts of artificial intelligence (AI) on the arts and the humanities (A&H), highlighting possibilities, limitations and pitfalls. The study reveals that while areas of the A&H like language teaching, choreography of dance, analysis of picture and field data, retrieval and restoration of old yellowed manuscripts and interpretation of tangible and intangible historical pieces have possibilities of being greatly impacted by the use of such AI-assisted/driven delicate devices like Computer vision, algorithmic writing and text mining tools like 'ChatGPT', 'Copy ai', 'Grammarly', 'Dall-e 3', 'Alli AI', 'Jasper', 'Midjourney', etc., AI has not been able to effectively replace the 'artist' or the 'humanist' as the creator with 'God-like' creative potentialities. 'Inspiration' and 'the esemplastic imagination' of the creative artist remain anecdotal to AI. The core creative and expressive aspects of the A&H remain outside the purview of AI. Using qualitative research methodology, this chapter agrees with the view that AI has not only greatly impacted many areas of the A&H but also has created many possibilities among the students, researchers, teachers and entrepreneurs in the field of the aforementioned faculties. However, the possibilities this wonderful tool has created will be translated into reality and will help human civilization to advance towards its desired goals, only if we are aware of the pitfalls of the use of AI and make judicious use of this latest invention of science and technology.

Keywords: AI; data analysis; text mining; choreography; esemplastic imagination; sculptor; superman; dehumanization

Artificial Intelligence in Business and Society: Global Insights, 149–162

doi:10.1108/978-1-83708-022-920261023

Introduction

Despite sharing many similarities in terms of disciplines, cultural concerns, thinking, creative process, etc., the A&H have different foci, methods and emphases. For example, the arts (e.g. painting, sculpture, etc.) focus on the creative and expressive aspects of human culture, such as the form and style, while the Humanities (e.g. literature, linguistics, etc.) focus on analytical aspects. While the arts include painting, drawing, sculpting, music, dance and theatre, the Humanities include literature, language, philosophy, history, anthropology, political science, sociology, linguistics, religious studies, etc. Before we delve into a discussion of the possibilities, limitations and pitfalls of the application of AI in the fields of A&H, it is worth remembering that AI existed in ancient times also, though in a different form. In Greek mythology, Daedalus constructed automated 'humanoid statues' (Brynjolfsson, 2022, p. 272). Yanshi's leather man mentioned in Chinese texts, the bronze Talus of the Argo-nautica and the towering clay *Mokkerkalfe* of Norse mythology, the picture of the chariot pulled by horses made of metal as mentioned in the Rig Veda, the machines that can make music and dance as mentioned in the Yajur Veda, the Brahmastra, the *Vimanas*, flying machines that were powered by mercury and controlled by the mind as mentioned in the Mahabharata, the mechanical man and various automata mentioned in *Yantra Sarvasva*, a book written by Bharata Muni in the second century BCE, the automated machines and the *chakravala* (a mechanical calculator that could solve complex algebraic equations) that could perform mathematical calculations as mentioned by Brahmagupta, a renowned mathematician of the eighth century in India – all these are examples of AI in ancient times (Kumararaja, 2023). There is no point in dismissing these ancient humanoid machines as 'myths' because myths are also accounts of superhuman people or activities which ostensibly existed or were performed in reality but which sound incredible because they are remote from us in terms of time, space and culture. In some ways, technology and mythology are not as apart as they appear to be. The relation of technology with mythology is just like the relation between the Unimate[1] and the biohybrid robots.[2] Both belong to the same line of gradual development that began with the automated water wheel. The line has been so extended that it tends to be disconnected from the 'old' and the 'ancient', but the difference is not of kind but of degree.

However, the AI as we understand today is one of the latest developments in the field of systemic technology and programming to have taken the world of knowledge by storm. Since the beginning of modernity, Industrial Revolution,

[1]The first commercial, digital and programmable robot built by George Devol in 1954 and named the Unimate. It was used to lift pieces of hot metal from die-casting machines at plants.

[2]Machines that combine biological components with synthetic materials to create improved performance or features. These robots can be used in a variety of biomedical applications, including diagnostics, targeted drug delivery, tissue engineering and minimally invasive surgeries.

globalization, etc., the fields of education including A&H and the systems of creation and transmission of knowledge-information have been increasingly impacted by computational technologies and their applications (Rahayu & Pujiyono, 2017). AI is one of the latest developments in the field of systemic technology and programming to have revolutionized the world of knowledge and information technology. Researchers and professionals are working on it and are exploring new possibilities. There have been successful attempts in AI research fields to simulate human reasoning processes. Its capacity to draw inferences from vast materials of data has been its greatest strength. Forms of AI are operating to boost creativity of computers, to filter knowledge, to perform various tasks (e.g. search) independently and accurately, to create online platforms, to create robots and machines that can perform as intelligently as the humans, to diagnose diseases, to forecast about a great number of things including how the humans may behave in a given situation and so on. Human-like AI is augmenting productivity, creating leisure for human beings and doing what is understood to be the workings of the human mind. AI has profound economic implications too. What the invention of the steam engine and electricity had done to the industrial economy in Victorian England, the invention and widespread application of AI has the potentiality to do the same thing to the economy of current times. Automation has offered added incentives to business executives, technologists and policymakers, among others. The disciplines belonging to science have joined hands with AI and have made great strides forward. In such a situation, the disciplines belonging to A&H cannot remain aloof from the impact of AI. AI has burst into the forefront of popular consciousness in such a way that the A&H people are acquainted with generative AI tools and language models like 'ChatGPT', 'Copy ai', 'Grammarly', 'Dall-e 3', 'Alli AI', 'Jasper', 'Midjourney', 'descript', 'personal AI', 'AI art generators', 'Synthesia', etc. Thus, based on qualitative research, this chapter purports to engage with the possibilities and the limitations the interface between AI and A&H generates in the present times. Many scholars are exploring this area. For example, Zargar (2023) has engaged with the impact of AI on literature, human intellect and knowledge acquisition. Jebaselvi et al. (2024) have explored the rise of AI in English Language and Literature. Ghafar et al. (2023) is concerned with the review of literature on the impact of AI on English Language Learning. Premkumar (2024) has discussed the emerging trends and implications of AI in literary creation and criticism. Raj et al. (2023) have focussed on exploring applications, implications and ethical considerations of AI in English literature. Thus, from this brief and select review of literature, it is evident that scholars are exploring the relation between AI and English literature and criticism. The impact of AI on A&H is an area which still largely awaits exploration. This relative gap in research has sparked interest in me to focus on the interface between AI and the A&H.

Methodology

Critical and in-depth examination of the relevant library resources, encounter with the relevant available texts, consulting reference books, periodicals and earlier related research form the bedrock of this study. Qualitative analysis forms one of the bases of this study. The study has consulted relevant literature to inquire how the language departments having focus on cultural studies and how the departments that take students away from the four walls of the classroom to the fields where the endangered communities of peoples live, take the help of AI to analyse pictures, texts, old manuscripts, tangible folk cultural heritage, etc. By examining non-numerical data, the study has found out that being led by their mentors, students in different A&H departments collect data in the form of field stories, riddles, proverbs, saga of life, memoirs, poems, rhymes, songs, mantras, pieces, etc. and translate those data into local, national and international languages. AI helps a lot in translating, documenting and interpreting tangible cultural heritage.

Possibilities

It has been found that some areas of A&H have been positively impacted by AI. For example, AI has been giving potential benefits to Anthropologists (a discipline that involves the humanities, social sciences and natural sciences) in the analysis of data, especially in the area of expert-system development. Researchers are uploading facts and principles, and out of those, expert analyses are being made by AI. According to Meyer Fortes (1983) one of the main concerns of the Anthropologists is to evolve the rules which are of cardinal importance to man and his existence in society. The discipline studies the systems of rules; their establishment, observance and enforcement in the face of breach; and their adaptation to changing circumstances that are characteristic of societies or of a range of societies, and AI has much to offer in these endeavours (Chablo, 1996, p. 553). Some specific benefits are (i) knowledge elicitation techniques for use in the field; (ii) software for the analysis and cross-referencing of field notes; (iii) software for the extraction of significant social rules and cognitive categories and their graphic representation; (iv) techniques for assembling and comparing complete sets of rules, kinship relations or taxonomies held by individuals with the object of determining the total knowledge and the core culture of a group; (v) software to assess the completeness and consistency of elicited rule systems; and (vi) to identity what features of taxonomies, kinship patterns, etc., are common. In archaeology, AI is extensively used in recognition of images (Table 10.1) and relics found during excavation, and AI helps in matching humans belonging to ancient times and relatively modern times.

In the Field Data Documentation

In recent times, AI has introduced new means of protecting and studying cultural and historical artefacts. With the growth of digital technologies, AI is playing a pivotal role in preserving and making accessible our endangered cultural heritage (Mostafa, 2024). For example, AI has been playing a great role in inventorying and inventory management. It is reshaping the preservation and restoration of cultural heritage using 'Computer vision' and 'Natural Language Processing' (NLP) devices. AI-supported 'Computer vision' is performing tasks like 'object

Table 10.1. A Comparative Analysis of Potentialities of Human Power and AI Power.

Year	**Parameters**											
	Reading Comprehension		**Image Recognition**		**Language Understanding**		**Handwriting Recognition**		**Speech Recognition**		**Predictive Reasoning**	
	Human	**AI**	**Human**	**AI**	**Human**	**AI**	**Human**	**AI**	**Human**	**AI**	**Human**	**AI**
1998	00	−100	00	–	00	–	00	−100	00	−100	00	–
1999	00	–	00	–	00	–	00	–	00	–	00	–
2000	00	–	00	–	00	–	00	–	00	–	00	–
2001	00	–	00	–	00	–	00	–	00	–	00	–
2002	00	−48.0	00	–	00	–	00	−48.0	00	–	00	–
2003	00	−26.2	00	–	00	–	00	−26.7	00	–	00	–
2004	00	–	00	–	00	–	00	–	00	–	00	–
2005	00	–	00	–	00	–	00	–	00	–	00	–
2006	00	−25.3	00	–	00	–	00	−25.3	00	–	00	–
2007	00	–	00	–	00	–	00	–	00	–	00	–
2008	00	–	00	–	00	–	00	–	00	–	00	–
2009	00	–	00	−100	00	–	00	–	00	–	00	–
2010	00	−20	00	–	00	–	00	−20	00	–	00	–
2011	00	–	00	–	00	–	00		00	−65.6	00	–
2012	00	−4.00	00	−44.2	00	–	00	−4.00	00		00	–

(Continued)

Table 10.1. (*Continued*)

Year	Parameters											
	Reading Comprehension		Image Recognition		Language Understanding		Handwriting Recognition		Speech Recognition		Predictive Reasoning	
	Human	AI	Human	AI	Human	AI	Human	AI	Human	AI	Human	AI
2013	00	−1.33	00		00	–	00	−1.33	00	−53	00	–
2014	00	–	00	−6.80	00	–	00		00	−27.8	00	–
2015	00	–	00	0.69	00	–	00		00	−8.71	00	–
2016	00	–	00	6.62	00	–	00	–	00	−1.24	00	–
2017	00	–	00		00	–	00		00	0.41	00	–
2018	00	2.67	00	11.69	00	−100	00	2.67	00	1.66	00	–
2019	00	–	00	9.52	00	3.73	00	–	00	–	00	−100
2020	00	18.85	00	16.45	00	11.94	00	–	00	–	00	–
2021	00	–	00	–	00		00	–	00	–	00	−80.5
2022	00	–	00	–	00	16.67	00	–	00	–	00	−30.6
2023	00	–	00	–	00	–	00	–	00	–	00	−0.62
Growth from start to end data		118.8		116.4		116.6		102.6		101.6		99.38

Source: www.ourworldindata.org/artificial-intelligence

Note: For each capability, the first year always shows a baseline of –100, even if better performance was recorded later that year. It is noteworthy that in each of the parameters, AI has equalled and subsequently surpassed humans in terms of performance after a certain period.

detection'. Machines are given eyes by 'Computer vision' with which the machine can see, observe and comprehend its surroundings with more accuracy than human vision is capable of (Vina, 2024). In imitation of human vision, 'Computer vision solutions' aim to distinguish objects, calculate distances and detect movements. However, unlike the humans, who have a lifetime of experiences to help them see and understand, 'Computers vision' relies on vast amounts of data, high-definition cameras and complex algorithms. Naturally, the accuracy with which 'Computer vision' can interpret data is more accurate and less time-consuming than human vision. Let us try to define the functioning of 'Computer vision' with some concrete examples. Suppose a field researcher has captured the rare moments of a dancer who is the last surviving representative of the community who have invented the dance form. After taking the photograph, he is trying to interpret the rare dance form for those in the society where many people are interested in that dance. Human vision will look at the picture with the 'eyes'. Eyes will send signals to the brain, and the brain will send results and will interpret that the dance is 'graceful' and 'exciting'. Let 'Computer vision' look at the same picture of dance. 'Computer vision' also has 'eyes' and 'brain'. But the result will be much different. 'Computer vision' will come out with 'pose estimation' at different points of time during the dance. It will measure 'the distance from the performer and the viewers' from the photograph. It will also instantly 'compare' the rare dance form with some other folk dance forms and will also be able to say how old the dance form is on the basis of that comparison. Thus, the AI-enabled 'Computer vision' will help the researchers in the relevant field of the arts to reconstruct the 'history' and 'characteristics' of that particular dance form. Let us take another example. A researcher in the field of folk literature has found a yellowed rare manuscript of folk drama. Beating the human eye, 'Computer vision' will be able to count the number of words in the manuscript, the time period of composition of the old manuscript, the age of the flat material (palm leaves, parchment chapter, etc.) on which the manuscript has been written, etc., within the fraction of a second. A researcher in history, to cite yet another example, has come across a rare piece of black granite with inscriptions on it. The piece of stone is so eroded that the inscriptions on it are not decipherable. It is here that AI will come forward. An AI-enabled 'vision' will come out with reliable conclusions about the ancient time it belonged to, the name of the civilization, the ingredients of the stone, the longevity and the orthographic text of the inscription on the stone. All these are not only treasures in research but also valuable historical records that offer insights into past societies, cultures and technologies. Their preservation ensures that future generations can learn from and appreciate the richness of human history. Thus, AI technologies have emerged as powerful tools in this direction. Through methods like 'object detection', AI can identify and document features of cultural artefacts with remarkable precision, aiding in their protection and study. These fields are reshaping how historical artefacts and artworks are documented, restored and accessed. Computer vision allows AI to enhance the cataloguing and restoration of cultural heritage by accurately identifying damaged pieces, which are then repaired by technicians. Meanwhile, AI-driven NLP may enable the translation and digitization of ancient texts, preserving linguistic heritage and making it accessible for research and education worldwide. Bradford and Côté-Laurence (1995) have demonstrated that the software named CorX (an acronym for ChoReographiceXpert system) is a 'rule driver', which is a special kind of expert system that applies dance rules non-deterministically for composing dance choreography. Early AI works on dance choreography included text editors for dance notation systems (Calvert, 1986; Dransch et al., 1986; Herbison-Evans, 1988). It used scores written in an existing dance notation to drive an animation (Calvert et al., 1986). More recent work has tended to design tools to assist the choreographic process (Bente, 1989; Bradford & Cate-Laurence, 1991; Schiphorst et al., 1990).

In the Field of Personalized Tutoring

Personalized tutoring has been a practice in the field of education since ancient times. The craze is no less these days. AI may play a major role in personalized tutoring in the field of arts. This is not to say that there are no good teachers now. Even if there are good teachers, it is found that some learners miss some points or fail to understand the points made by the teacher. He needs the lesson to be repeated umpteen times which is not possible for a teacher who must complete his or her assignment. AI may be helpful in this regard. AI-enabled personalized tutoring is available at all levels. All students including the below average ones are using AI for learning experience. Its advantage is that it is scalable and user-friendly.

In the Field of Teaching and Learning of Language

Authors like Li (2020), Mukhallafi (2020), Zhu (2017) and Wang (2019) are of the opinion that AI with its computer-assisted language learning process, data management technology, NLP system, digital proficiency, adaptive system for arranging, organizing and choosing content diversified instrumental methods and teaching strategies, etc. has revolutionized the teaching and learning of English as a foreign language. For example, the integration of visuals, voice and text in an intelligent gadget makes English language learning more stereoscopic and visual. As Ribeiro (2020) has said that the most important practical use of AI for English language instructors is in English language teaching (ELT). AI has created a scope for immersion learning in which learners employ all of their senses to simultaneously train their proficiency in English as per the occupational demands. AI is playing a great role in speech recognition (Table 10.1) and in the teaching of pronunciation.

Test scores of AI systems in five parameters vis-àvis human performances are shown in the table. In each parameter, the initial performance of the AI is set to –100 and human performance is used as a baseline, set to zero. When the AI's performance crosses the zero line, it scores more points than humans. It is observed from the table that AI takes around 18 years to make at par with human power in reading comprehension, image recognition and handwriting recognition. Thus, there is still a gap between the AI power and human power so far as components of language are concerned. The study has computed the growth (or progress) rates of all the parameters from their starting years to the end years (refer to the last row of the table). It is observed that reading comprehension has the highest progress rate of 118.8% of the AI to catch up with the human powers, but language understanding has fastest growth of power with six years (2018–2023) to reach 116% followed by predictive reasoning which has the growth rate of 99% as it attained the rate in just five years (2019–2023).

In the Field of Publishing and Authoring Books

The study finds that the publishing houses of A&H are making extensive use of AI. They are using AI-driven writing assistants. Authors of books on A&H are using writing assistants, which provide real-time suggestions for improving style, grammar and coherence. Some authors are using AI for generating initial drafts, which are then refined through human inputs. Errors tend to elude the eyes of the chapter-writers in the field of A&H. Unlike the researchers in sciences and social sciences, a researcher and a writer in the A&H deal with more number words and less amount of data than a researcher in science. While composing something using a great number of words, authors tend to skip words, mistype words, commit grammatical errors and create complicated and convoluted constructions. AI can help authors greatly in this field. For example, if the author opens any word document with Google docs which is an AI-supported computer tool, he or she will be able to give us more accurate and fault-free texts. AI has revolutionized the way literature is created, consumed and understood. For example, a researcher in the field of A&H has to analyse a vast number of unstructured documents, websites, social media and other unstructured text for the purpose of research. AI-enabled 'text mining' which is the process of extracting meaning from unstructured text data can greatly help. Text mining is a computational process that uses NLP, machine learning (ML) and other techniques to analyse text data.

Limitations

While exploring the relation between the A&H and the AI, it is not good to gloss over the fact that at the bottom there is an antithetical relation between the A&H and the AI. This apparently polar relation stems from some millennium-long, justified, undying notions about 'creativity' within the A&H. For example, literature (including imaginative works like poetry, drama, fiction, etc.), the visual and graphic arts (including painting, drawing, drawing, design and other forms expressed on flat surfaces), the plastic arts (sculpture, modelling), the decorative arts (enamelwork, furniture design, mosaic, etc.), the performing arts (theatre, dance, music), music (as composition), architecture (often including interior design), etc. are thought to be basically 'inspirational' (Plato, 1997), 'mimetic' (Aristotle, 1984, 2019), 'imaginative' (Kant, 2000), 'sublime' (De Quincey, 1827; Longinus, 1995), 'spontaneous', 'intentional' (Stokes, 2008, p. 119), 'original' (i.e., not copied), 'agential', 'visionary', 'surprising' and so on. On the other hand, AI is held to be 'artificial', 'intelligent' (Ahmet, 2018; Campesato, 2020; Wang, 2019;

Whitby, 2009), 'simulated', 'technological', 'computational' (Cheng & Day, 2014), 'filtered and processed' (Rahman, 2009, p. 343), 'robotic' (Karsenti, 2019), 'mechanical', 'analytical', 'software and device-based' (Mehrotra, 2019), 'task-based', 'goal-oriented' (Joshi, 2019, p. 4) and so on. Hence, there is a tension in their relationship. Though partially reconciled to the necessities and inevitabilities of the need of AI in the fields of A&H, many people are still assailed by doubts and dilemmas regarding the use of AI in the field under question. The apprehensions arise out of the two words – 'artificial' and 'intelligence' – which are thought to be at variance with 'intuition' and 'emotion' which constitutes the soul of the A&H. It is thought that AI cannot be a substitute for the creative 'inspiration', the 'human consciousness' and 'unpremeditated' qualities which inform any creative piece of writing. English poet Samuel Taylor Coleridge (1817) in his *Biographia Literaria* has said that creativity inspired by 'the esemplastic Imagination' is 'God-like'. The meaning of the word 'esemplastic' is 'unifying' and 'moulding' into something new. It can reconcile the opposites of light and shade, reason and imagination, the natural and the supernatural, etc. It has the unique capacity to fuse disparate elements into a new combination and to create something which never existed on the earth. Thus, creativity is a repetition in the finite self of the 'infinite I AM'. Thus, there is justification in the doubt among many people belonging the A&H that 'a *device* (emphasis mine) that juxtaposes things and functions like a person' (Joshi, 2019, p. 4) and 'a *mind* (emphasis mine) that fuses things and creates an organic whole' are two different things. Despite being used in the writing process, AI tools have not been able to replace the author as the creator. Brainstorming is not synonymous to creativity and conceptualizing. William Wordsworth has said that poetry is a spontaneous overflow of 'powerful feelings' and AI is not capable of 'feelings'. AI can edit, polish, streamline, revise and enhance textual quality. AI has much impact on the 'end-product', but it has little contribution in the formation of the 'creative embryo'. The organically related coordinates of themes, ideas, forms and expressions that constitute the life-breath of any piece of literature or any piece of art are not prompted by the AI. It only shapes and curates, whereas imagination moulds, modifies and unifies in undying combinations. A&H as a 'conduit of human expression and cultural preservation' (Zargar, 2023) holds a unique position in the cultural history of human beings. AI has hardly been able to capture that position. The beliefs, struggles and aspirations literature reflects and the quality of the artist as a 'seer' ('vates') into the womb of futurity inspired by the 'law of probability and necessity' (Aristotle) are beyond the reach of AI. Even the nuanced emotion which forms the basis of human communication is beyond the reach of AI.

Pitfalls

The application of AI in the field of A&H has created some pitfalls also. The application of AI may be most welcome in one country, but it may be fatal for another. For example, there are some advanced countries in the world which do not have enough professional mentors to meet the requirements of the number of teachers for the in-person classes. In those countries, AI-monitored virtual classrooms are the most appropriate. But in countries like India, Sri Lanka, Bangladesh and Pakistan, the picture is different. To cite another example, art workers and artisans are losing 'political and economic bargaining power' and are becoming increasingly dependent on those who control technology (Brynjolfsson, 2022, p. 272). A sculptor is likely to lose his or her earnings if an AI-driven chisel replaces the human hand, and the artisan is bound to accept the terms and conditions of those who have mastered the use of AI technology. It is noticeable that in the last five years, there has been a significant stagnation in the field of recruitment of A&H graduates in job sectors. The AI-driven teaching and learning process is replacing the qualified graduates. Nowadays app-based teaching and learning has become so rampant that it is grabbing the 'market'. Human beings have been partially rendered useless on account of mass skill automation engineered by AI which has threatened the universal basic income. Mitra (2023) has opined that we may enter a 'post-work world' in future (Sramana Mitra [2023, 44:14]). A new kind of binary is round the corner – the species called 'man' and the species called 'superman'. This triumph of 'intelligence' and 'superman' was sensed by the eminent English litterateur Shaw, G. B. (1903). *Man and Superman: A Comedy and a Philosophy*. London: Brentano's. Based on AI, a new evolution in the field of A&H is afoot. The new 'superman' is apparently performing all the functions that an artist can do and that too with more accuracy. People have begun to believe that AI can write plays like William Shakespeare, it can compose songs like Rabindranath Tagore, it can sculpt like Michelangelo, it can plan and design an edifice like Ustad Ahmad Lahori, it can paint like Pablo Picasso and so on. The future will say if such beliefs are supported or not, but a new danger in the form of a new binary is round the corner. The species called 'man' falls into two binaristic categories – 'common man' and 'AI-enabled man'. A teacher of English is going to be of two categories – 'AI-enabled English Teacher' and 'the ordinary English Teacher'. This will be a blatant dehumanization. It will not be a good sign if the human value is measured in terms of the capacity for 'mechanical production'. This will drastically alter human relationships, and the present cyber will give place to the 'age of AI superman', much like the Anthropocene. Yet another pitfall we should be aware of is the tendency of researchers not to use their 'mind' and to get things done by the AI. If one click brings the world on the screen, who will care to put in labour and effort? This tendency to 'search' by the 'machine' instead of the 'mind' may bring in mutation in the human genes and may gradually render the human mind incapable of any 'thinking' and 'creating'.

Conclusion

Thus, the study of the interface between the AI and the A&H reveals that there are some possibilities, limitations and pitfalls. There is a moral question involved. We must support the view that AI and human beings are different. One need not necessarily replace the other, just as an automated chisel used by the sculptor to remove the inessential elements from a block of stone does not replace the creative hand of the sculptor. Nor does an 'intelligent' natural language processor should replace the language instructor and skill developer who puts the processor to a good use for the benefit of the students. Thus, AI should 'accelerate the skill development process' (Ghafar et al., 2023, p. 18). It should 'assist human thought' (Sridhar, 2018). In the context of, for example, ELT in the classroom, it is not a question of if a teacher is required in the classroom, but if the teacher requires AI to enhance the effectiveness and quality of his/her teaching. What is required is an AI-based language teaching model. Thus, this chapter understands the function of AI in the creation, exploration and dissemination of knowledge of the A&H. Since we are concerned with the application of AI in the A&H, we may mention the deplorable condition of the graduates from the arts faculties in colleges and universities in the developing and underdeveloped countries. A great number of qualified youth are running from pillar to post for a small job. In such a condition, the application of AI will drastically reduce the required number of professionals in the education sector, and it will lead to more suicide of youths. If AI is used in replacing human labour instead of augmenting it, AI will be dangerous and a luxury in these countries. In countries like India, AI should be used in getting those things done which are beyond human labour.

References

Ahmet, C. (2018). *Artificial intelligence: How advance machine learning will shape the future of our world*. Independently published.

Aristotle. (1984). *The complete works of Aristotle: The revised Oxford translation* (J. Barnes, Ed.). Princeton University Press.

Aristotle. (2019). *Nicomachean ethics* (Terrence Irwin, Trans.). Hackett Publishing.

Bente, G. (1989). Facilities for the graphical computer simulation of head and body movements. *Behavior Research Methods, Instruments, & Computers*, *21*(4), 455–462.

Bradford, J. H., & Cate-Laurence, P. (1991). Animate tokens, their design and application. *Leonardo*, *24*(5), 557–562.

Bradford, J. H., & Côté-Laurence, P. (1995). An application of artificial intelligence to the choreography of dance. *Computers and the Humanities*, *29*(4, August), 233–240. https://www.jstor.org/stable/30204501

Brynjolfsson, E. (2022). The Turing trap: The promise & peril of human-like artificial intelligence. *Daedalus*, *151*(2, Spring), 272–287. https://www.jstor.org/stable/10.2307/48662041

Calvert, T. W. (1986). Toward a language of movement. *Computers and the Humanities*, *20*(1), 35–43.

Calvert, T. W., Lee, C., Ridsdale, G., Hewitt, S., & Tso, V. (1986). The interactive composition of scores for dance. *Dance Notation Journal*, *4*(2), 35–40.

Campesato, O. (2020). *Artificial intelligence, machine learning, and deep learning*. Stylus Publishing.

Chablo, A. (1996). What can artificial intelligence do for anthropology? *Current Anthropology*, *37*(3, June), 553–555. https://www.jstor.org/stable/2744556

Cheng, S. M., & Day, M. Y. (2014, November 21–23). *Technologies and applications of artificial intelligence*. In Proceedings of the 19th international conference, TAAI, Taipei, Taiwan. Springer.

Coleridge, S. T. (1817). *Biographia literaria*. Rest Fenner.

De Quincey, T. (1827). On murder considered as one of the fine arts. *Blackwood's Magazine*, *21*(122, February), 199–213.

Dransch, D. O. K., Beatty, J. C., & Ryman, R. S. (1986). *Choreo-Scribe: A graphics editor to describe body position and movement using Benesh movement notation* [Computer Science Technical Report CS-86-48]. University of Waterloo.

Fortes, M. (1983). *Rules and the emergence of society* (occasional chapter 39). Royal Anthropological Institute.

Ghafar, Z. N., Salh, H. F., Abdulrahim, M. A., Farxha, S. S., Arf, S. A., & Rahim, R. I. (2023). The role of artificial intelligence technology on English language learning: A literature review. *Canadian Journal of Language and Literature Studies*, *3*(2), 17–31. https://doi.org/10.53103/cjlls.v3i2.87

Herbison-Evans, D. (1988). Dance, video, notation and computers. *Leonardo*, *21*(1), 45–50.

Jebaselvi, C. A. E., Mohanraj, K., & Anitha, T. (2024). The rise of ai in English language and literature. *Shanlax International Journal of English*, *12*(2), 53–58.

Joshi, A. V. (2019). *Machine learning and artificial intelligence*. Springer Nature.

Kant, I. (2000). *Critique of the power of judgment* (P. Guyer, Ed., E. Matthews, Trans.). Cambridge University Press.

Karsenti, T. (2019). Artificial intelligence in education: The urgent need to prepare teachers for tomorrow's schools. *Formation et Profession*, *27*(1), 105. https://doi.org/10.18162/fp.2019.a166

Kumararaja, K. (2023, March 30). *Artificial intelligence in ancient India*. https://medium.com/@kumararaja/artificial-intelligence-in-ancient-indiaa66dbd937286#:~:text=Indian%20philosophers%20and%20scholars%20also,in%20the%202nd%20century%20BCE

Li, R. (2020). Using artificial intelligence in learning English as a foreign language: An examination of IELTS Liulishuo as an online platform. *Journal of Higher Education Research*, *1*, 85–89. https://doi.org/10.32629/jher.v1i2.178

Longinus. (1995). *On the sublime* (J. Henderson, Ed., pp. 143–308). Harvard University Press.

Mitra, S. (2023, March 11). *India's prospects in the age of AI*. Ramakrishna Mission Institute. www.youtube.com

Mehrotra, D. D. (2019). *Basics of artificial intelligence & machine learning*. Notion Press.

Mostafa, I. (2024). *AI in art and cultural heritage conservation*. https://www.ultralytics.com/blog/ai-in-art-and-cultural-heritage-conservation

Mukhallafi, T. R. A. (2020). Using artificial intelligence for developing English language teaching/learning: An analytical study from university students' perspective. *International Journal of English Linguistics*, *10*(6), 40. https://doi.org/10.5539/ijel.v10n6p40

Plato. (1997). *Plato: Complete works* (J. M. Cooper & D. S. Hutchinson, Eds.). Hackett Publishing.

Premkumar, B. (2024, July–August). The impact of artificial intelligence on literary creation and criticism: Emerging trends and implications. *International Journal of Language, Literature and Culture (IJLLC)*, *4*(4), 27–41.

Rahayu, S., & Pujiyono, W. (2017). Media Pembelajaran Kecerdasan Buatan Pokok BahasanMetode Pelacakan Menggunakan Multimedia Pada E-Learning. *JSTIE (JurnalSarjana Teknik Informatika) (E-Journal)*, *5*(1), 136–145. https://doi.org/10.12928/jstie.v5i1.10824

Rahman, S. M. (2009). *Methods and applications for advancing distance education technologies: International issues and solutions*. IGI Global. https://www.researchgate.net/publication/234655269_Methods_and_Applications_for_Advancing_Distance_Education_Technologies_International_Issues_and_Solutions.

Raj, A. V. T., Udayakumar, U., & Saravanan, D. (2023, July). Integrating artificial intelligence in English literature: Exploring applications, implications and ethical considerations. *Indian Journal of Advanced Research in Science, Communication and Technology (IJARSCT)*, *3*(1), 11–15.

Ribeiro, R. (2020). *Artificial intelligence in English language learning*. https://www.cambridge.org//elt/blog/2020/03/09/artificial-intelligence-english-language-learning/

Schiphorst, T., Calvert, T., Lee, C., Welman, C., & Gaudet, S. (1990). Jane Carrasco Chew and John Whiteside (Eds.). Tools for interaction with the creative process of composition. In *Proceedings of CHI '90: The ACM conference on computer-human interaction* (pp. 167–174). New York: Association for Computing Machinery.

Shaw, G. B. (1903). *Man and Superman: A Comedy and a Philosophy*. London: Brentano's.

Sridhar, G. S. (2018). *Artificial Intelligence: Way to Future*. https://books.google.co.in/books/about/ARTIFICIAL_INTELLIGENCE_WAY_TO_FUTURE.html?id=h7VIDwAAQBAJ&redir_esc=y

Stokes, D. R. (2008). A metaphysics of creativity. In K. Stock & K. Thomson-Jones (Eds.), *New waves in aesthetics* (pp. 105–124). Palgrave-Macmillan.

Vina, A. (2024). "Exploring How the Applications of Computer Vision Work." https://www.ultralytics.com/blog/exploring-how-the-applications-of-computer-vision-work.

Wang, R. (May 18–19, 2019). *Research on artificial intelligence promoting English learning change*. In Proceedings of the 3rd international conference on economics and management, education, humanities and social sciences (EMEHSS 2019), Suzhou City, China. https://doi.org/10.2991/emehss-19.2019.79

Whitby, B. (2009). *Artificial intelligence*. The Rosen Publishing Group, Inc.

Zargar, N. A. (2023, August). The impact of artificial intelligence on literature, human intellect, and the balance of knowledge acquisition. *Journal of Emerging Technologies and Innovative Research (JETIR)*, *10*(8), 1–4. https://www.jetir.org/view?chapter=JETIR2308371

Zhu, D. (June 25–26, 2017). *Analysis of the application of artificial intelligence in college English teaching*. In Proceedings of the 2017 2nd international conference on control, automation and artificial intelligence (CAAI 2017), Sanya, China. https://doi.org/10.2991/caai-17.2017.52

Chapter 11

Early Adopters of AI and Gender Disparities in Health Outcomes

Vaishali Singh

School of Governance and Public Affairs, XIM University, Bhubaneswar, India

Abstract

While artificial intelligence (AI) has the potential to improve healthcare delivery and outcomes for all individuals, including women, there are several areas where gender disparities persist, and AI may be involved in mitigating or exacerbating them. Amid the ever-increasing pervasiveness of AI in the health sector, it is imperative to examine how AI intersects with gender disparities in health outcomes globally, especially in the early adopter countries. Gender disparities in health outcomes are a crucial concern that gets manifested in differences in health status, access to healthcare, and health-related experiences between men and women. Gender disparities in health outcomes highlight unequal distributions of health resources, opportunities, and risks based on gender. This study looked at how investments in healthcare that uses AI affect the health outcomes of women in early adopter countries (the United States, the United Kingdom, Canada, France, Germany, China, Japan, and Israel) between 2014 and 2023. Multivariate analysis of variance (MANOVA) was used to assess the cumulative effect of AI investments on health outcomes of women. The study found that the F-value (4.139) is low and not statistically significant ($p = 0.376$), highlighting the fact that even in early adopter countries, investments in biotechnology, pharmaceuticals, and healthcare AI do not have a statistically substantial bearing on the overall health outcomes for women, making gender disparity in the countries. These findings show that in order to guarantee quantifiable and significant gains in health outcomes, AI investments in healthcare must take a more focused and evidence-based approach.

Keywords: Gender disparity; health outcomes; AI; MedTech; early adopters; MANOVA

Artificial Intelligence in Business and Society: Global Insights, 163–178

doi:10.1108/978-1-83708-022-920261025

Introduction

The latter half of the 20th century marked the advent of research into artificial intelligence (AI) in healthcare (Pauker et al., 1976; Shortliffe et al., 1973). While early efforts were primarily research-oriented, AI has now transitioned into practical applications, reshaping the healthcare landscape. As a rapidly advancing and powerful technology, AI holds immense potential to revolutionize patient care by boosting satisfaction, enhancing treatment quality, and streamlining operational efficiency (Davies, 2019; Wahl et al., 2018; Sharma et. al., 2022). Though the findings are not always consistent, AI is already showing its potential to revolutionize healthcare by saving healthcare workers' time and advancing patient outcomes (Alowais et al., 2023; Gala et al., 2024). AI is improving healthcare by making processes like screening and diagnosis easier, and it may continue to do so in the future. Health professionals generally concur that AI could be a catalyst in routine care due to its ability to improve diagnostic precision, identify public health threats, combat antimicrobial resistance, provide advanced tools to healthcare professionals, and advance personalized medicine with better patient monitoring (Jiang et al., 2017; Vijayan et al., 2022).

Three main factors account for the expanding potential of AI applications across a range of clinical domains: First, the exponential growth of electronic health data, which serves as the basis for AI algorithms, and recent notable advancements in computing and machine learning technology have made it easier to develop complex algorithms and implement them practically at the bedside (Bohr & Memarzadeh, 2020; Yu et al., 2018). Additionally, the rise of several startup businesses alongside well-established industry titans is indicative of the democratization of AI (Li et al., 2024; Young, 2022). Healthcare is one of the most interesting industries for AI usage because of the immense bulk of health data and the difficulties mentioned above. Due to data availability and pressing needs, the COVID-19 pandemic has further expedited the use of AI applications in healthcare (Oliveira Hashiguchi et al., 2021).There is an urgent need for change since health systems are facing more and more problems, and AI offers a possible way to make healthcare systems safer and more effective (Ayers et al., 2023).

Early Adopters of AI in Healthcare

Since 2016, investment in healthcare AI initiatives has increased at a faster rate than in other areas of the global economy (Buch et al., 2018). The need to invest in healthcare stems from the trend of rising costs of healthcare everywhere. Longer life expectancies, an increase in the prevalence of chronic illnesses, and the constant progress of overpriced new remedies all support this trend (Li et al., 2019). Due to aging populations, the burden of age-related illnesses is rising, especially in wealthier nations. There is a 25% lifetime risk of stroke and a 50% lifetime risk of cancer (Fontana, 2009). The increasing incidence of these costly diseases, increased access to healthcare, and notable developments in pharmaceutical and technological disease treatment are all contributing to the sharp increase in costs (Norbeck, 2013). Therefore, it should come as no surprise that experts see a bleak future for the viability of healthcare systems worldwide. Therefore, to maintain the sustainability of our healthcare systems, it is imperative that we provide high-quality treatment while also reducing expenses. AI forebodes to enhance healthcare and reduce expenses (Higgins & Madai, 2020). Its primary components are deep artificial neural networks (ANNs), which use layers of linked "neurons" to resemble brain-like structures. Personalized care, improved monitoring, fewer errors, and cheaper expenses are all promised by using machine learning in the medical field (Saha et al., 2020). AI systems can reduce diagnostic and therapeutic mistakes by analyzing massive datasets from clinical trials, diagnostic data, and medical records to anticipate health outcomes and offer real-time recommendations on health risks (Yoldemir, 2020). AI supports research to comprehend illness processes and optimal therapies, helps manage and alleviate treatment-related problems, and offers assistance throughout active treatment phases (Bajwa et al., 2021). AI-based decision support arrangements have been demonstrated to enrich diagnostic performance and lessen the strain of medical practitioners, especially in imaging (e.g., magnetic resonance imaging (MRI) and mammography). In the healthcare industry, the developed nations have leveraged their advancements in technology and the funding options to move faster in product and service innovations in healthcare (Kelly & Young, 2017).

The rapid advancements in AI have revolutionized the healthcare industry, with many early adopter nations leading the charge in integrating AI-enabled technologies into their medical systems (Bresnick, 2017; Singhal & Carlton, 2019). Early adopters of AI technology stand to gain economic and geopolitical dominance (Feijóo et al., 2020). Countries may position themselves as leaders in AI development and application by influencing worldwide AI policies and practices and setting global standards thanks to this early integration. Advances in AI do help early adopter countries more, mostly in the form of increased economic development, improved operational efficiency, and competitive advantages across a range of industries (Earley, 2020; Enholm et al., 2022). By improving a number of areas, including manufacturing, logistics, healthcare, education, and energy, early AI adoption may greatly increase a country's gross domestic product (GDP) (Wolff et al., 2020). AI that is adopted early on also fosters innovation and increases human potential. AI may be integrated into a variety of industries to help individuals and organizations create customized solutions that stimulate economic development and innovation (Sharma, 2024). As an illustration, the united parcel service (UPS) shows how AI may enhance environmental sustainability, save costs, and streamline business operations (Farlow et al., 2023). These advancements provide nations that are quicker to embrace AI technology with a competitive edge. These countries' leadership in the field of AI is further cemented by their crucial involvement in establishing international AI standards and regulations. AI investment in healthcare is advancing rapidly in early adopter nations, with significant potential to transform healthcare delivery and outcomes. According to Mou (2019), AI has the ability to advance predictive maintenance, power transmission, drug research and diagnostic processes, learning environments, and product design. Costs might be cut and operational efficiency greatly increased with the practice of AI.

With strategic goals established by the administrative directive "Maintaining American Leadership in Artificial Intelligence" to expedite AI research and development, the United States has achieved notable advancements in AI healthcare (Robert, 2019). In terms of research and contributions to AI in healthcare, the United States is likewise at the forefront (Secinaro et al., 2021). China has a well-thought-out plan that involves significant infrastructure expenditures, with the goal of becoming a worldwide leader in AI by 2030. But there are still issues such as inadequate regulatory rules and a lack of comprehensive planning (Robert, 2019). The government of Japan has made significant investments in AI through initiatives such as the Cross-Ministerial Strategic Innovation Promotion Program (SIP) for an "Innovative AI Hospital System." However, these investments' ethical issues are not well addressed (Halamka, 2019; Ishii & Kimura, 2020; Katirai, 2023). Through the "AI in Health and Care Award" initiative, the National Health Service (NHS) is aggressively using AI into healthcare in the United Kingdom. This program encourages the creation and assessment of AI tools that enhance clinical judgment, operational effectiveness, and diagnostic computed tomography (CT) scan analysis, patient outcome prediction, and patient care pathway optimization are all being done with AI techniques (Bodenheimer & Sinsky, 2014; Blease et al., 2019). Israel's strong tech environment and access to medical data have made it a leader in healthcare AI. Israeli businesses are creating AI-assisted diagnostics, tailored treatment regimens, and early illness diagnosis (Tessler et al., 2024). Hospitals are adopting AI to improve individualized treatment plans and expedite hospital operations, while startups like Zebra Medical Vision are employing AI for radiography. Acute care may now be provided to patients in their homes thanks to "hospital-at-home" models being advanced in Canada (Pelletier et al., 2024). Early health issue identification is made possible by AI-powered remote monitoring devices that track patient vitals in real time. This strategy enhances patient treatment for those living in rural locations while simultaneously lowering hospital bed occupancy. Clinical decision assistance, cost reduction, and healthcare system management optimization are more uses of AI. France has embraced AI in healthcare, emphasizing rehabilitation technology like exoskeletons that use AI to help paralyzed individuals move (Laï et al., 2020). Leading the charge in this endeavor are businesses such as Wandercraft. In order to improve patient care, France is also encouraging AI applications in clinical data platforms and reproductive therapies that use AI to glean insights from patient information. The development and use of AI in fields including imaging, clinical trials, and patient care are Germany's main priorities (Weinert et al., 2022).

AI Investment in Healthcare and Impact on Health Outcomes for Women

There is a clear enthusiasm around the use of AI in medical well-being. However, alongside this enthusiasm, it's important to be aware of the restrictions and difficulties that can prevent AI-driven healthcare from being widely adopted and providing equal advantages. The exclusionary character of AI systems is a major obstacle (Sloane, 2024). AI models are frequently created and trained on datasets that don't accurately reflect a variety of demographic groups, especially underrepresented groups like women, members of ethnic minorities, and residents in low-income areas (Acemoglu, 2021). Existing health inequalities may be exacerbated by healthcare algorithms that perform worse for certain populations as a result of this exclusionary bias. For example, medical AI systems that were mostly trained on data from men would not be able to identify the signs of conditions like heart attacks that manifest differently in women. To solve this problem and guarantee fair healthcare results, a more inclusive approach to data collecting and model building is needed. Large sums of money are being invested in AI development by nations like China, the United States, and the United Kingdom that are early users of AI in the medical field. The promise to save medical expenses, improve diagnostic precision, and offer forecasting capabilities that might stop disease outbreaks justifies this funding increase (Parikh & Helmchem, 2022; Ramezani et al., 2023). With a projected 28% annualized growth rate (compound annual growth rate (CAGR)) globally, AI in healthcare is expected to develop at an astounding rate, highlighting the significant business opportunity of AI-driven health technology (Väänänen et al., 2021). However, unless diversity is given top priority in the utilization of AI technology, the returns on these expenditures will be modest.

The effect of AI on health impacts warrants more investigation, especially for women. There is a presumption regarding the positive and progressive impact of AI in healthcare in bettering health outcomes. However, the field of AI can also exacerbate the existing disparities or even not be cost-effective in the long term (Donia & Shaw, 2021). According to a Pew study, 60% of Americans believe they would feel uneasy if their personal healthcare specialist used AI to diagnose illnesses and suggest treatments; just 39% said they would feel at peace with this. One contributing element to these opinions is the general public's lack of conviction that applying AI to medicine and health will result in better health outcomes. Only 38% of 11,004 US adults surveyed by the Pew Research Center between December 12 and 18, 2022, believe that using AI to diagnose illnesses and suggest treatments would improve patients' overall health outcomes, while 33% believe that it would have the opposite effect and 27% say it wouldn't make much of a difference. According to 71% of respondents, they would not wish to utilize AI for their personal mental health assistance. According to research, healthcare algorithms frequently lack adequate gender representation and that may result in significant variations in the standard of treatment that women get (Noble, 2018; Tufekci, 2015). AI models for breast cancer diagnosis, for instance, have shown remarkable results; yet, there are still gaps in areas like maternity health, reproductive health, and women's mental healthcare. Since these fields are frequently neglected or underfunded in the context of larger healthcare innovation, they demand particular attention (Rahkovsky et al., 2021). This crucial gap may be filled by making sure AI technologies are programmed on sex-disaggregated evidence and are cognizant of the particular health requirements of women (Buslón et al., 2023; Connell, 2012; King et al., 2018; Lau et al., 2023; Manandhar et al., 2018).

Rationale and Objectives of the Study

The goal of this chapter is to identify the gendered effects of AI-led healthcare by investigating how these technologies change women's health outcomes between 2014 and 2023.

Methods

This panel data study looked at eight countries that are often recognized as early adopters of AI to investigate the association between AI investment in healthcare and women's health outcomes on important metrics. The research covers the following countries: the United States, the United Kingdom, Canada, France, Germany, Israel, Japan, and China. The study period covers data from 2014 to 2023 ensuring a decade-long analysis. The information on AI investments in healthcare came from the OECD.AI, which calculates venture capital (VC) financial investment in AI and data enterprises globally using data from private sources like Preqin, which is then processed by the Jožef Stefan Institute's AI lab in Slovenia and analyzed by the Organisation for Economic Co-operation and Development (OECD). Preqin is a private corporation that was established in 2003 and gathers information about funds, fund managers, and private equity deals. The data on health outcomes were sourced from the Health, Nutrition, and Population Statistics in the World Bank data repository.

Variables

The study explores the relationship between investments in AI within healthcare, drugs, and biotechnology (independent variable) and several key health outcomes (dependent variables). The independent variable is measured as the total investments in AI in healthcare, drugs, and biotechnology, expressed in USD millions. The dependent variables include the adolescent fertility rate, defined as the number of newborns per 1,000 females aged 15–19, and the maternal mortality ratio, which reflects the number of maternal deaths per 100,000 live births within 42 days of pregnancy termination. Additional dependent variables are mortality from cardiovascular diseases (CVDs), cancer, diabetes, or chronic respiratory diseases (CRDs), quantified as the proportion of 30-year-olds who would die before age 70 from these conditions under existing mortality patterns, and survival to age 65, which represents the proportion of newborns expected to live to age 65 based on current death rates. Further health outcomes include life expectancy at birth for females, measured as the average number of years a newborn is expected to live under current mortality trends, and the lifetime risk of maternal death, defined as the probability of a 15-year-old female eventually dying from maternal causes under constant reproduction and mortality rates. To account for economic factors, GDP per capita is included as a control variable, representing the national output divided by the midyear population.

Statistical Analysis

Descriptive statistics, including means, standard errors, medians, and interquartile ranges, were calculated for each variable. After adjusting for GDP per capita, partial correlations between sum of AI investment in healthcare, drugs, and biotechnology and each dependent variable (adolescent fertility rate, maternal mortality ratio, mortality from CVD, cancer, diabetes, or CRD, survival to age 65, life expectancy at birth, lifetime risk of maternal death) were calculated. The combined effects of AI investments on the dependent health outcome variables were evaluated using MANOVA, and the individual effects of AI investments on each dependent variable – with GDP per capita included as a control factor – were evaluated using the univariate analyses of variance (ANOVAs). The criterion for analytical significance was set at $p < 0.05$. SPSS (version 25) was used for all statistical analyses.

Results and Discussion

An overview of the distribution of the study's important variables is provided by the descriptive statistics in Table 11.1.

Healthcare, pharmaceutical, and biotechnology investments in AI: The average investment is 1,140.2 units (no currency is given), but the high standard deviation (2,705.01) indicates significant variability. The range is noteworthy, ranging from −109.00 (which can suggest a loss or negative cash flow) to 17,939, which indicates that certain nations or organizations have large investments in contrast to others. Indicators of health: The sample's comparatively low teenage fertility rates are indicated by the range of 2.72–24.04, with a mean of 9.95. With a low of 3.00 and a maximum of 32.00, the maternal mortality ratio (mean = 10.78) likewise shows significant variability (SD = 7.54). The mean mortality rate from diabetes, cancer, CVD, or CRD is 8.51, with a considerable degree of variability (SD = 1.85). With little fluctuation, the survival rate to age 65 is high (mean = 92.56), suggesting that the majority of the population lives to this age. With little variation (SD = 2.15), the life expectancy at birth is around 83.65 years. As is typical for the majority of industrialized regions, the lifetime risk of maternal mortality is extremely low (mean = 0.02). With a range of 7,532.8 to 65,020.4, GDP per capita exhibits significant variability (mean = 39,308, SD = 13,387.16).

Several significant linkages are shown by the partial correlations between AI investments and health outcomes as given in Table 11.2. Although it may appear contradictory, investments in AI show a moderately favorable link with the teenage fertility rate ($r = 0.408$, $p < 0.001$). This relationship may be influenced by indirect or contextual variables. The maternal mortality ratio and AI investments show a robust favorable association ($r = 0.667$, $p < 0.001$), signifying that higher investments are associated with higher maternal mortality. However, this association may be muddled by the level of development or health priorities of a given nation. In a similar vein, there is a substantial positive link between AI investments and mortality from diabetes, cancer, cardiovascular illness, or

Table 11.1. Summary of Descriptive Statistics.

Variables	*N*	**Mean**	**Standard Deviation (SD)**	**Minimum**	**Maximum**
Investments in AI in healthcare, drugs, and biotechnology	80	1,140.2	2,705.01	−109.00	17,939
Adolescent fertility rate	80	9.95	4.48	2.72	24.04
Maternal mortality ratio	80	10.78	7.54	3.00	32.00
Mortality from CVD, cancer, diabetes, or CRD	80	8.51	1.85	5.70	12.00
Survival to age 65	80	92.56	1.53	89.00	94.97
Life expectancy at birth	80	83.65	2.15	79.30	87.71
Lifetime risk of maternal death	80	0.02	0.01	0.00	0.04
GDP per capita	80	39,308	13,387.16	7,532.8	65,020.4

Source: Author.

Table 11.2. Summary of Partial Correlation Results.

Independent Variable	Dependent Variable	Correlation (r)	p-Value
Investments in AI in healthcare, drugs, and biotechnology	Adolescent fertility rate	0.408	0.000
	Maternal mortality ratio	0.667	0.000
	Mortality from CVD, cancer, diabetes, or CRD	0.548	0.000
	Survival to age 65	0.113	0.322
	Life expectancy at birth	−0.592	0.000
	Lifetime risk of maternal death	0.673	0.000

Source: Author.

CRD ($r = 0.548$, $p < 0.001$), which may point out that larger investment is focused on areas with higher rates of these diseases. Conversely, there is no significant correlation between investments and survival to age 65 ($r = 0.113$, $p = 0.322$). AI investments and life expectancy at birth are found to be adversely correlated ($r = -0.592$, $p < 0.001$), indicating that investments may be focused on regions with lower life expectancy. Furthermore, there is a high positive link between investments and the lifetime risk of maternal mortality ($r = 0.673$, $p < 0.001$), which is surprising considering that AI investments are often made with the goal of enhancing health outcomes. As part of initiatives to address pressing health issues, this association could indicate a targeted distribution of AI investments in areas with greater risks to maternal health.

The impacts of GDP per capita and AI investments on important health outcomes were investigated using the univariate ANOVA. The findings as given in Table 11.3 show that the teenage fertility rate is not significantly impacted by either GDP per capita ($F = 5.211$, $p = 0.263$) or AI investments ($F = 4.139$, $p = 0.376$). Similarly, neither GDP per capita ($F = 0.108$, $p = 0.797$) nor AI investments ($F = 13.460$, $p = 0.214$) substantially affect the maternal mortality rate. While AI investments ($F = 20.637$, $p = 0.174$) and GDP per capita ($F = 39.645$, $p = 0.100$) have very high F-values for mortality from CVD, cancer, diabetes, or CRD, these impacts are still statistically insignificant. AI investments ($F = 2.095$, $p = 0.508$) and GDP per capita ($F = 6.628$, $p = 0.236$) do not significantly affect longevity to age 65. GDP per capita has a strong correlation with life expectancy at birth ($F = 166.342$, $p = 0.049$), whereas AI investments do not substantially predict life expectancy at birth ($F = 102.011$, $p = 0.079$). Neither GDP per capita ($F = 0.498$, $p = 0.609$) nor AI investments ($F = 9.343$, $p = 0.256$) significantly affect lifetime risk of maternal death. The impact of GDP per capita on life expectancy at birth was the sole significant predictor found in the ANOVA overall ($p = 0.049$), indicating that greater GDP per capita is linked to longer life expectancies.

Table 11.3. Univariate ANOVA and MANOVA Results.

Univariate ANOVA			
Dependent Variable	**Independent Variable**	***F*-Value**	***p*-Value**
Adolescent fertility rate	Investments in AI in healthcare, drugs, and biotechnology	4.139	0.376
Adolescent fertility rate	GDP per capita	5.211	0.263
Maternal mortality ratio	Investments in AI in healthcare, drugs, and biotechnology	13.460	0.214
Maternal mortality ratio	GDP per capita	0.108	0.797
Mortality from CVD, cancer, diabetes, or CRD	Investments in AI in healthcare, drugs, and biotechnology	20.637	0.174
Mortality from CVD, cancer, diabetes, or CRD	GDP per capita	39.645	0.100
Survival to age 65	Investments in AI in healthcare, drugs, and biotechnology	2.095	0.508
Survival to age 66	GDP per capita	6.628	0.236
Life expectancy at birth	Investments in AI in healthcare, drugs, and biotechnology	102.011	0.079
Life expectancy at birth	GDP per capita	166.342	0.049
Lifetime risk of maternal death	Investments in AI in healthcare, drugs, and biotechnology	9.343	0.256
Lifetime risk of maternal death	GDP per capita	0.498	0.609

MANOVA					
Independent Variable	**Wilks' Lambda**	*F*	**Hypothesis df**	**Error df**	***p*-Value**
Investments in AI in healthcare, drugs, and biotechnology	0.003	4.139	77.000	1.000	0.37

Source: Author.

The cumulative impact of AI investments on all dependent variables is evaluated using the MANOVA as given in Table 11.3. A tiny percentage of the overall variance cannot be explained by the independent variable, according to the Wilks' lambda ($\lambda = 0.003$); however, this might also be a sign of overfitting. With $p = 0.376$, the F-value ($= 4.139$) is not statistically significant and is low. This suggests that investments in biotechnology, pharmaceuticals, and healthcare AI do not, taken together, have a statistically significant multivariate impact on the aggregate health outcomes.

The present study demonstrates that AI investments in healthcare in early adopter nations are not making a difference in the overall health outcomes related to women. The study analyzed the data from 2014 to 2023 covering a full decade of AI investments. While there has been a lot of buzz and excitement about the ability of AI in healthcare diagnosis and healthcare management (Morley et al., 2021), the evidence suggests that there are certain barriers in the effective use of AI to positively impact health outcomes, especially for women. In the early adopter nations, the AI-led healthcare is much more advanced than in other developing nations, and despite the advancements in AI innovations, the health outcomes for women remain unchanged. The findings of this study call for a rethinking of the ongoing trend of massive VC investments in AI-led healthcare.

AI is often exaggerated in its potential to enhance the efficiency and reduce the costs of healthcare. Hospitals have to deal with high up-front costs, disrupted workflows, and unmeasured return on investment (ROI). In reality, the AI systems are constantly changing and require constant monitoring, education, and personalization (He et al., 2019). While AI can improve administrative processes, it is not clear if it will impact therapeutic effectiveness and patient outcomes (Topol, 2019). Even so, ROI is yet to be recognized in areas like women's health that require long-term proof of benefits (Obermeyer et al., 2019). For instance, incompatibility of AI systems with the current electronic health records (EHRs) often bars smooth deployment from taking place (Corrêa et al., 2023; Thiru et al., 2003). Information from clinical settings' electronic health records may be imprecise, lacking, altered in ways that compromise its significance, unrecoverable for study, of unclear origin, lacking in level of detail, and inconsistent with research procedures (Blumenthal & Tavenner, 2010; Rosenbaum, 2015). Moreover, because most AI models are developed in controlled environments that do not reflect the complexity of healthcare delivery in real life, contextualizing them to specific hospital settings remains challenging (Hersh et al., 2013). This underscores the fact that AI solutions need to be co-designed with physicians and other stakeholders to ensure usability and adoption (Wiens et al., 2019). Co-design not only ensures that the end user will be aligned with clinical needs but also increases acceptance and confidence by including end users at every stage of development.

AI models need high-quality diverse data, and in the case of medicine, mistakes within the records can create a problem in health equity, misdiagnosis, and inappropriate treatment recommendations. Over the years, women in general, especially those who are pregnant, have traditionally been excluded from clinical studies due to liability and harm concerns. The modern-day AI datasets, which also underrepresent women, have continued this trend. Doctors and other medical professionals are often unwilling to rely on AI recommendations, especially in high-risk contexts, such as cancer detection or surgery (Schulz et al., 2017). This has been proven by many research studies that AI models operate as "black boxes," providing answers without proper logic. This minimizes the direct impact of AI on health outcomes. Once touted as an innovation in AI-based cancer, the IBM Watson Health project failed to deliver positive results in real-world clinical settings. It was difficult to tailor the system to different healthcare environments, and variations between what the program proposed and standard clinical practices (Ross & Swetlitz, 2017) are also some of the reasons. Only a few AI technologies are put to extensive testing in the real world, which only increases the skepticism of health professionals. This underlines the gap between in-trial performance and actual performance.

While there is a considerable market for women's health that cannot be ignored, there are few investors in this area. Frost & Sullivan (2020) projected that by 2025, the femtech market—including software, diagnostics, goods, and services focused on women's health—will reach a value of $50 billion. Only in 2022, femtech companies were given an amount as small as just 3% of world financing for digital health startups (Kemble et. al., 2022). Due to their larger markets and more lucrative use cases, "big-ticket" ailments like cancer and heart disease are typically the focus of AI developers and funders (Omaleki & Reed, 2019). Although affecting billions of women around the world, menstrual health, endometriosis, and menopause are sometimes considered "niche" issues. Underinvestment in women's health reflects systemic prejudices and lost opportunities for social and economic advancement. For health outcomes to improve for women, evidence-based investments are needed to leverage the potential of AI in improving health outcomes.

Conclusion

Healthcare AI has received billions of dollars from governments, tech corporations, and VC firms. However, rather than developing AI solutions that tackle the most pressing patient needs, a large portion of this investment is allocated toward commercially successful items like wearable health devices, AI-driven scanning tools, and hospital workflow optimization. The results of the study reveal that in the early adopter countries, investments in biotechnology, pharmaceuticals, and healthcare AI do not have a statistically substantial bearing on the overall health outcomes for women, causing gender disparity in the countries.

It points out that funding for AI, R&D is now unduly focused on fields like robotic surgery and imaging technologies that have strong commercial benefits and recommends that there is a need to invest R&D funds in illnesses and health issues that have a significant societal effect, such as primary care access, mental health, and maternity health to be used in an equitable manner to reduce gender disparity in the health sector.

References

Acemoglu, D. (2021). *Harms of AI* [Working Paper Series]. https://doi.org/10.3386/w29247

Alowais, S. A., Alghamdi, S. S., Alsuhebany, N., Alqahtani, T., Alshaya, A. I., Almohareb, S. N., Aldairem, A., Alrashed, M., Saleh, K. B., Badreldin, H. A., Al Yami, M. S., Al Harbi, S., & Albekairy, A. M. (2023). Revolutionizing healthcare: The role of artificial intelligence in clinical practice. *BMC Medical Education*, *23*, 689. https://doi.org/10.1186/s12909-023-04698-z

Ayers, J. W., Poliak, A., Dredze, M., Leas, E. C., Zhu, Z., Kelley, J. B., Faix, D. J., Goodman, A. M., Longhurst, C. A., Hogarth, M., & Smith, D. M. (2023). Comparing physician and artificial intelligence chatbot responses to patient questions posted to a public social media forum. *JAMA Internal Medicine*, *183*(6), 589. https://doi.org/10.1001/jamainternmed.2023.1838

Bajwa, J., Munir, U., Nori, A., & Williams, B. (2021). Artificial intelligence in healthcare: Transforming the practice of medicine. *Future Healthcare Journal*, *8*(2), e188–e194. https://doi.org/10.7861/fhj.2021-0095.

Blease, C., Kaptchuk, T. J., Bernstein, M. H., Mandl, K. D., Halamka, J. D., & DesRoches, C. M. (2019). Artificial intelligence and the future of primary care: Exploratory qualitative study of UK general practitioners' views. *Journal of Medical Internet Research*, *21*(3), e12802. https://doi.org/10.2196/12802

Blumenthal, D., & Tavenner, M. (2010). The "meaningful use" regulation for electronic health records. *The New England Journal of Medicine*, *363*(6), 501–504. https://doi.org/10.1056/NEJMp1006114

Bodenheimer, T., & Sinsky, C. (2014). From triple to quadruple aim: Care of the patient requires care of the provider. *Annals of Family Medicine*, *12*, 573–576.

Bohr, A., & Memarzadeh, K. (2020). The rise of artificial intelligence in healthcare applications. A. Bohr & K. Memarzadeh (Eds.). In *Artificial intelligence in healthcare* (pp. 25–60). Elsevier. https://doi.org/10.1016/b978-0-12-818438-7.00002-2

Bresnick, J. (2017, July 24). Artificial intelligence in healthcare market to see 40% CAGR surge. HealthITAnalytics. https://healthitanalytics.com/news/artificial-intelligence-in-healthcare-market-to-see-40-cagr-surge

Buch, V., Ahmed, I., & Maruthappu, M. (2018). Artificial intelligence in medicine: Current trends and future possibilities. *British Journal of General Practice*, *68*(668), 143–144. https://doi.org/10.3399/bjgp18X695213.

Buslón, N., Cortés, A., Catuara-Solarz, S., Cirillo, D., & Rementeria, M. (2023). Raising awareness of sex and gender bias in artificial intelligence and health. *Frontiers in Global Women's Health*, 4, 970312, 1–8. https://doi.org/10.3389/fgwh.2023.970312

Connell, R. (2012). Gender, health and theory: Conceptualizing the issue, in local and world perspective. *Social Science & Medicine*, *74*(11), 1675–1683. https://doi.org/10.1016/j.socscimed.2011.06.006

Corrêa, F. F., Carrilho, T. R. B., Bonilha, E. A., Keller, V. N., Melo, T. C., Kac, G., & Diniz, C. S. G. (2023). Analysis of the quality of prenatal data of pregnant women attended at healthcare services in the city of São Paulo between 2012 and 2020. *Brazilian Journal of Epidemiology*, *26*, e230051. https://doi.org/10.1590/1980-549720230051

Davies, S. (2019). Artificial intelligence in global health. *Ethics & International Affairs*, *33*, 181–192. https://doi.org/10.1017/S0892679419000157

Donia, J., & Shaw, J. A. (2021). Co-design and ethical artificial intelligence for health: An agenda for critical research and practice. *Big Data & Society*, *8*, 20539517211065248

Earley, S. (2020). *The AI-powered enterprise: Harness the power of ontologies to make your business smarter, faster, and more profitable*. LifeTree Media.

Enholm, I. M., Papagiannidis, E., Mikalef, P., & Krogstie, J. (2022). Artificial intelligence and business value: A literature review. *Information Systems Frontiers*, *24*(5), 1709–1734.

Farlow, A., Hoffmann, A., Tadesse, G. A., Mzurikwao, D., Beyer, R., Akogo, D., Weicken, E., Matika, T., Nweje, M. I., Wamae, W., Arts, S., Wiegand, T., Bennett, C., Farhat, M. R., & Gröschel, M. I. (2023). Rethinking global digital health and AI-for-health innovation challenges. *PLOS Global Public Health*, *3*(4), e0001844, 1–12. https://doi.org/10.1371/journal.pgph.0001844

Feijóo, C., Kwon, Y., Bauer, J. M., Bohlin, E., Howell, B., Jain, R., Potgieter, P., Vu, K., Whalley, J., & Xia, J. (2020). Harnessing artificial intelligence (AI) to increase well-being for all: The case for a new technology diplomacy. *Telecommunications Policy*, *44*, 101988. https://doi.org/10.1016/j.telpol.2020.101988.

Fontana, L. (2009). Modulating human aging and age-associated diseases. *Biochimica et Biophysica Acta 1790*(10), 1133–1138. https://doi.org/10.1016/j.bbagen.2009.02.002

Frost & Sullivan. (2020). *Women's health market potential and growth opportunities*. Frost & Sullivan Market Report.

Gala, D., Behl, H., Shah, M., & Makaryus, A. N. (2024). The role of artificial intelligence in improving patient outcomes and future of healthcare delivery in cardiology: A narrative review of the literature. *Healthcare*, *12*(4), 481. https://doi.org/10.3390/healthcare12040481

Halamka, J. (2019). *Japan to emerge as the leading learning lab for digital health innovation*. Healthcare IT News.

He, J., Baxter, S. L., & Xu, J. (2019). The practical implementation of artificial intelligence technologies in medicine. *Nature Medicine*, *25*, 30–36 https://doi.org/10.1038/s41591-018-0307-0

Hersh, W. R., Weiner, M. G., Embi, P. J., Logan, J. R., Payne, P. R., Bernstam, E. V., Lehmann, H. P., Hripcsak, G., Hartzog, T. H., Cimino, J. J., & Saltz, J. H. (2013). Caveats for the use of operational electronic health record data in comparative effectiveness research. *Medical Care*, *51*(8, Suppl 3), S30–S37. https://doi.org/10.1097/MLR.0b013e31829b1dbd

Higgins, D., & Madai, V. I. (2020). From bit to bedside: A practical framework for artificial intelligence product development in healthcare. *Advanced Intelligent Systems*, *2*, 2000052. https://doi.org/10.1002/aisy.202000052

Ishii, E., Ebner, D. K., Kimura, S., Agha-Mir-Salim, L., Uchimido, R., & Celi, L. A. (2020). The advent of medical artificial intelligence: Lessons from the Japanese approach. *Journal of Intensive Care*, *8*, 35. https://doi.org/10.1186/s40560-020-00452-5

Jiang, F., Jiang, Y., Zhi, H., Dong, Y., Li, H., Ma, S., Wang, Y., Dong, Q., Shen, H., & Wang, Y. (2017). Artificial intelligence in healthcare: Past, present and future. *Stroke and Vascular Neurology*, *2*(4), 230–243. https://doi.org/10.1136/svn-2017-000101

Katirai A. (2023). The ethics of advancing artificial intelligence in healthcare: Analyzing ethical considerations for Japan's innovative AI hospital system. *Frontiers in Public Health*, 11, 1142062, 1–8. https://doi.org/10.3389/fpubh.2023.1142062

Kelly, C. J., & Young, A. J. (2017). Promoting innovation in healthcare. *Future Healthcare Journal*, *4*(2), 121–125. https://doi.org/10.7861/futurehosp.4-2-121.

Kemble, E., Pérez, L., Sartori, V., Tolub, G., & Zheng, A. (2022, February 14). *The dawn of the FemTech revolution*. McKinsey & Company. https://www.mckinsey.com/industries/healthcare/our-insights/the-dawn-of-the-femtech-revolution

King, T., Kavanagh, A., Scovelle, A., & Milner, A. (2020). Associations between gender equality and health: A systematic review. *Health Promotion International*, *35*(1), 27–41. https://doi.org/10.1093/heapro/day093

Laï, M. C., Brian, M., & Mamzer, M. F. (2020). Perceptions of artificial intelligence in healthcare: Findings from a qualitative survey study among actors in France. *Journal of Translational Medicine*, *18*(1), 14. https://doi.org/10.1186/s12967-019-02204-y

Lau, P., Nandy, M., & Chakraborty, S. (2023). Accelerating UN sustainable development goals with AI-driven technologies: A systematic literature review of women's healthcare. *Healthcare*, *11*(3), 401, 1–16. https://doi.org/10.3390/healthcare11030401

Li, Y., Zhang, J., Gu, Y., Zhu, Y., He, Q., & Li, L. (2020). Comparative study on global development strategies of artificial intelligence in healthcare. *Strategic Study of Chinese Academy of Engineering*, *21*(6), 106–113. https://doi.org/10.15302/J-SSCAE-2019.10.003

Li, Y. H., Li, Y. L., Wei, M. Y., & Li, G. Y. (2024). Innovation and challenges of artificial intelligence technology in personalized healthcare. *Scientific Reports*, *14*, 18994. https://doi.org/10.1038/s41598-024-70073-7

Manandhar, M., Hawkes, S., Buse, K., Nosrati, E., & Magar, V. (2018). Gender, health and the 2030 agenda for sustainable development. *Bulletin of the World Health Organization*, *96*, 644–653. https://doi.org/10.2471/BLT.18.211607.

Morley, J., Morton, C., Karpathakis, K., Taddeo, M., & Floridi, L. (2021). Towards a framework for evaluating the safety, acceptability and efficacy of AI systems for health: An initial synthesis. *ArXiv*, abs/2104.06910. https://doi.org/10.2139/ssrn.3826358

Mou, X. (2019). Artificial intelligence: Investment trends and selected industry uses. *International Finance Corporation*. World Bank Group. EMCompass Notes, No. 71, pp. 1–8. https://doi.org/10.1596/32652

Noble, S. U. (2018). *Algorithms of oppression*. NYU Press.

Norbeck, T. B. (2013). Drivers of health care costs. A physicians foundation white paper – Second of a three-part series. *Missouri Medicine*, *110*(2), 113–118.

Obermeyer, Z., Powers, B., Vogeli, C., & Mullainathan, S. (2019). Dissecting racial bias in an algorithm used to manage the health of populations. *Science*, *366*(6464), 447–453. https://doi.org/10.1126/science.aax2342

Oliveira Hashiguchi, T., Slawomirski, L., & Oderkirk, J. (2021). *Laying the foundations for artificial intelligence in health* [OECD Health Working Paper No. 128]. OECD Publishing. https://doi.org/10.1787/3f62817d-en.

Omaleki, V., & Reed, E. (2019). The role of gender in health outcomes among women in Central Asia: A narrative review of the literature. *Women's Studies International Forum*, *72*, 65–79. https://doi.org/10.1016/j.wsif.2018.12.002

Parikh, R. B., & Helmchen, L. A. (2022). Paying for artificial intelligence in medicine. *npj Digital Medicine*, *5*, 63. https://doi.org/10.1038/s41746-022-00609-6

Pauker, S., Gorry, G. A., Kassirer, J. P., & Schwartz, W. B. (1976). Towards the simulation of clinical cognition. *The American Journal of Medicine*, *60*(7), 981–996. https://doi.org/10.1016/0002-9343(76)90570-2

Pelletier, P., Geuna, A., & Souza, D (2024). Artificial intelligence research in Canadian hospitals: The development of metropolitan competencies. *Healthcare Management Forum*, *37*(6), 445–450. https://doi.org/10.1177/08404704241271218

Rahkovsky, I., Toney, A., Boyack, K. W., Klavans, R., & Murdick, D. A. (2021). AI research funding portfolios and extreme growth. *Frontiers in Research Metrics and Analytics*, *6*, 630124. https://doi.org/10.3389/frma.2021.630124

Ramezani, M., Takian, A., Bakhtiari, A., Rabiee, H. R., Fazaeli, A. A., & Sazgarnejad, S. (2023). The application of artificial intelligence in health financing: A scoping review. *Cost Effectiveness and Resource Allocation*, *21*, 83. https://doi.org/10.1186/s12962-023-00492-2

Robert, N. (2019). How artificial intelligence is changing nursing. *Nursing Management*, *50*(9), 30–39. https://doi.org/10.1097/01.NUMA.0000578988.56622.21

Rosenbaum, L. (2015). Transitional chaos or enduring harm? The EHR and the disruption of medicine. *The New England Journal of Medicine*, *373*(17), 1585–1588. https://doi.org/10.1056/NEJMp1509961

Ross, C., & Swetlitz, I. (2017). IBM pitched its Watson supercomputer as a revolution in cancer care. It's nowhere close. *Stat News*. https://www.statnews.com

Saha, C. Chowdhury, S., & Biswas. (2020). *Deep learning techniques for biomedical and health informatics* (S. Dash, B. R. Acharya, M. Mittal, A. Abraham, A. Kelemen, Eds., pp. 101–126). Springer International Publishing.

Schulz, E., Tenenbaum, J. B., Duvenaud, D., Speekenbrink, M., & Gershman, S. J. (2017). Compositional inductive biases in function learning. *Cognitive Psychology*, *99*, 44–79. https://doi.org/10.1016/j.cogpsych.2017.11.002

Secinaro, S., Calandra, D., Secinaro, A., Muthurangu, V., & Biancone, P. (2021). The role of artificial intelligence in healthcare: A structured literature review. *BMC Medical Informatics and Decision Making*, *21*(125), 1–23. https://doi.org/10.1186/s12911-021-01488-9

Sharma, M., Savage, C., Nair, M., Larsson, I., Svedberg, P., & Nygren, J. (2022). Artificial intelligence applications in health care practice: Scoping review. *Journal of Medical Internet Research*, *24*, 1–17. https://doi.org/10.2196/40238

Sharma, S. (2024). Benefits or concerns of AI: A multistakeholder responsibility. *Futures*, *157*(103328), 1–10. https://doi.org/10.1016/j.futures.2024.103328

Shortliffe, E., Axline, S. G., Buchanan, B. G., Merigan, T. C., & Cohen, S. N. (1973). An artificial intelligence program to advise physicians regarding antimicrobial therapy. *Computers and Biomedical Research*, *6*(6), 544–560. https://doi.org/10.1016/0010-4809(73)90029-3

Singhal, S., & Carlton, S. (2019). *The era of exponential improvement in healthcare?* McKinsey & Company.

Sloane, M. (2024). Controversies, contradiction, and 'participation.' *AI. Big Data & Society*, *11*(1), 1–5. 20539517241235862. https://doi.org/10.1177/20539517241235862

Tessler, I., Wolfovitz, A., Livneh, N., Gecel, N. A., Sorin, V., Barash, Y., Konen, E., & Klang, E. (2024). Advancing medical practice with artificial intelligence: ChatGPT in healthcare. *The Israel Medical Association Journal: IMAJ*, *26*(2), 80–85.

Thiru, K., Hassey, A., & Sullivan, F. (2003). Systematic review of scope and quality of electronic patient record data in primary care. *BMJ (Clinical Research Edition)*, *326*(7398), 1070. https://doi.org/10.1136/bmj.326.7398.1070

Topol, E. J. (2019). High-performance medicine: The convergence of human and artificial intelligence. *Nature Medicine*, *25*, 44–56. https://doi.org/10.1038/s41591-018-0300-7

Tufekci, Z. (2015). Algorithmic harms beyond Facebook and Google: Emergent challenges of computational agency. *Colorado Technology Law Journal*, *13*, 203.

Väänänen, A., Haataja, K., Vehviläinen-Julkunen, K., & Toivanen, P. (2021). AI in healthcare: A narrative review. *F1000Research*, *10*, 6. https://doi.org/10.12688/f1000research.26997.1

Vijayan, R., Haataja, K., & Vehviläinen-Julkunen, K. (2022). Enhancing preclinical drug discovery with artificial intelligence. *Drug Discovery Today*, *27*(4), 967–984. https://doi.org/10.1016/j.drudis.2021.11.023

Wahl, B., Cossy-Gantner, A., Germann, S., & Schwalbe, N. (2018). Artificial intelligence (AI) and global health: How can AI contribute to health in resource-poor settings? *BMJ Global Health*, *3*(4), e000798, 1–7. https://doi.org/10.1136/bmjgh-2018-000798

Weinert, L., Müller, J., Svensson, L., & Heinze, O. (2022). Perspective of information technology decision makers on factors influencing adoption and implementation of artificial intelligence technologies in 40 German hospitals: Descriptive analysis. *JMIR Medical Informatics*, *10*(6), e34678. https://doi.org/10.2196/34678

Wiens, J., Saria, S., & Sendak, M. (2019). Do no harm: A roadmap for responsible machine learning for health care. *Nature Medicine*, *25*, 1337–1340. https://doi.org/10.1038/s41591-019-0548-6

Wolff, J., Pauling, J., Keck, A., & Baumbach, J. (2020). The economic impact of artificial intelligence in health care: Systematic review. *Journal of Medical Internet Research*, *22*(2), e16866, 1–8. https://doi.org/10.2196/16866

Yoldemir, T. (2020). Artificial intelligence and women's health. *Climacteric*, *23*, 1–2. https://doi.org/10.1080/13697137.2019.1682804

Young, A. S. (2022). AI in healthcare startups and special challenges. *Intelligence-Based Medicine*, *6*, 100050, 1–3. https://doi.org/10.1016/j.ibmed.2022.100050

Yu, K., Beam, A., & Kohane, I. (2018). Artificial intelligence in healthcare. *Nature Biomedical Engineering*, *2*(10), 719–731. https://doi.org/10.1038/s41551-018-0305-z

Chapter 12

Unlocking the Interplay of Artificial Intelligence, Healthcare, Industrial Output, and Agriculture Productivity with Economic Development in BRICS Countries

Prasenjit Makur

Calcutta Girls' College, Kolkata, West Bengal, India

Abstract

The potential of artificial intelligence (AI) to spur a new wave of technological innovation and sustainable economic impairment through value-added and better healthcare has garnered a lot of attention from academics in recent years. This research explores the long- and short-term dynamics of AI investment, healthcare expenditure, agricultural productivity, and industry value-added on economic development of the BRICS countries (Brazil, Russia, India, China, and South Africa) between 2013 and 2023. Panel fully modified ordinary least squares (FMOLS) and dynamic OLS (DOLS) pooled methods validated the results of the pooled mean group auto-regressive distributed lag (PMG/ARDL) model, which demonstrate that healthcare, industry value-added, and agricultural output across the BRICS economies significantly improve economic prosperity over time, while AI investment shortens economic welfare. The PMG/ARDL results also showed that agricultural value-added and healthcare expenditure significantly absorbed economic welfare in the short run. Furthermore, the causality test indicated that these were homogeneously causing economic welfare and added industry value. The study also verifies that healthcare is a homogeneous consequence of AI investment, and economic development is a homogeneous cause of AI investment. Policymakers in

Artificial Intelligence in Business and Society: Global Insights, 179–194

Published under exclusive licence by Emerald Publishing Limited
doi:10.1108/978-1-83708-022-920261028

the BRICS nations should encourage the development and use of AI in the healthcare and agricultural sectors by enacting unique rules that align with industry standards to promote economic well-being through AI investment and healthcare.

Keywords: Artificial intelligence; economic development; healthcare; FMOLS; agriculture value-added; industry value-added

Introduction

AI is a branch of computer science specialized in creating data processing systems and performing tasks comparable to human intellect, like learning, reasoning, and self-improvement (Peres et al., 2020). AI is machine learning, or a neural network trained on data collection, claim Trifan and Buzatu (2020). The three main components that impact the development of AI are computational theory, data resources, and drive resources. AI has a unique learning ability that allows it to become increasingly proficient at a given practical activity over time, unlike any other developed technology in the past. AI is made to help people make the best choices possible. To do this, AI has been integrated into operating systems to develop systems that can support humans or even make decisions entirely based on AI (Gomes et al., 2020). AI is becoming a vital technological aid for everyday social and economic endeavors (Naimi-Sadigh et al., 2022). Indeed, AI technology is silently altering people's lives all over the world which can be found in a variety of forms at every level of our interactions with society, from tiny, intelligent robots that speak daily to huge, government- and industry-level supported offices (Li et al., 2017). At the industry, academic, and even governmental levels, its enormous contribution to sustainable economic development across all industries quickly came into focus (Heylighen, 2017). So, AI-related endeavors may propel future economic growth and lead to significant changes in the composition and methodology of output, as well as in the amount and caliber of consumption (Vyshnevskyi et al., 2019). AI has emerged as a key force behind industrial development and global economic expansion.

Arora (2001) looked at the relationship between industrialized countries' economic growth and health and discovered a high correlation. In the study of Bhargava et al. (2001) comparing the effects of health indicators for developed and developing nations between 1965 and 1990, improvements in public health were associated with a considerable boost in economic performance in developing nations.

In the current Fourth Industrial Revolution (4IR) era, advanced digital gadgets and technology are widely used for innovation and value generation across industries as opined by Lee and Lim (2018). This also applies to the healthcare sector. Lee (2019) argued that digital technologies like AI, machine learning, smart sensors and robots, big data analytics, and the Internet of Things (IoT) are being aggressively deployed by hospitals and care providers worldwide, particularly in developed economies, to improve operational efficiency and care quality. Thus, it is worthwhile to look at how customer–provider interactions in the healthcare sector are being impacted by sophisticated digital gadgets as penned by Lee (2018). At the Radiological Society of North America (RSNA) conference in Chicago in December 2018, dozens of startups and established image device companies presented their AI initiatives that support precise and trustworthy diagnosis and appropriate patient treatment based on data gathered from clinical examinations.

Even though urbanization has accelerated in recent decades, most people in developing nations still rely on small-scale, rural farming as their main source of food and income (World Bank, 2007). The degree of agricultural mechanization is often low, so human labor productivity and availability are the key determinants of agricultural output. Although labor is theoretically plentiful in most developing countries (Pitt & Rosenzweig, 1986), prolonged poor health can compromise labor inputs, and absent labor cannot be replaced right once, output losses may ensue.

A healthy workforce is crucial for labor productivity, and society's general level of health largely determines it. Therefore, spending on health initiatives is a critical component affecting economic growth (Akbar et al., 2020). Work efficiency and national productivity are enhanced by increased health spending, higher health quality, and higher living standards. Behrman et al. (1997) report a rather strong correlation between nutritional enhancements and agricultural production, following the original research by Strauss (1986) and Pitt and Rosenzweig (1986).

The varied and eclectic group of nations concerning economic well-being, human care, and gross output inherited a variety of historical legacies in the formation, financing, and provision of healthcare according to Rancic and Jakovljevic (2016). The BRICS is the biggest and most significant of them, with a considerable global reach as considered by O'Neill (2001). These five nations account for almost 40% of the worldwide population, 25% of global gross national income, and roughly 40% of the global burden of disease (GBD) and significantly impact global health, and their healthcare and economic well-being diverge from those of the Organisation for Economic Co-operation and Development (OECD) (Acharya et al. 2014). The BRICS group jointly produces about 37% of the total global economic output. According to projections, their total economic growth is anticipated to exceed the global average of 3.2%–3.3% in 2024–2025, reaching 3.8%. This expansion highlights BRICS' growing impact on the global economy. The BRICS countries are actively investing in AI because they understand its transformative potential and want to improve industries like healthcare, agriculture, and finance. To promote AI research, regulation, and commercialization, Russia, for instance, has started the AI Alliance Network and is working with BRICS partners. These programs seek to use AI for economic expansion and sustainable development, increasing its gross domestic product (GDP) contribution to 11.2 trillion rubles in Russia by 2030.

As a result of the opportunities and risks presented by the quick development of AI and better healthcare, more and more nations are focusing on regulating, directing, and applying AI to boost output growth to match AI development with sustainable development standards.

Therefore, the literature has extensively studied the relationship among economic welfare, AI, healthcare, and value-added, providing a solid theoretical foundation for future research. However, the novel variable of AI, such as annual private investment and value-added concerning two important sectors, has rarely been incorporated in standard research frameworks. Therefore, this study is an uncommon attempt to fill this gap by examining the possible heterogeneity and non-linearity of the long- and short-term effects of AI and healthcare through value-added on economic well-being considering quantitative assessment in two robust panel data models, such as DOLS and FMOLS pooled method, which guaranteed the results of the PMG/ARDL model. In particular, the study looked at the economy of the BRICS countries from 2013 to 2023.

Review of Literature

The empirical connections between healthcare, AI, value-added concerning industry and agriculture, and economic development have become much more focused in recent decades. This section thus offers a brief and critical analysis of the connection between these factors and economic well-being.

AI and Economic Development

AI and big data have had a profound impact on business models, social life, production processes, and innovation in technology with its uses in manufacturing, energy, healthcare, logistics, finance, and other industries growing (Zavyalova et al., 2023). While many are applauding this encouraging fact, others are voicing their doubts. In the long term, people's over-reliance on AI is anticipated to pose some possible risks, even though the broad use of AI will initially provide a temporary economic boost (Goertzel et al., 2017). For example, the unemployment crisis, ethical and moral hazards, and privacy issues are frequently brought up by academics in the literature (Kak, 2018).

AI, Healthcare, and Economic Development

In their study, Lee and Lee (2020) and Yoon and Lee (2019) showed that AI-supported technologies have recently been widely used in healthcare facilities to increase the effectiveness of medical resources and the quality of care services. The study of Safavi and Kalis (2019) in line with Ramesh (2004) depicts that AI-based technologies offer a wealth of chances for innovation in the knowledge-intensive healthcare sector since they include machine learning, natural language processing, and intelligent robotics. The impact of healthcare spending on economic performance is a significant consideration in an economy; the research of Bloom et al. (2004) and Öztürk and Topcu (2014) has demonstrated that improvements in health can result in higher GDP and vice versa; healthcare plays a significant role in the quality of human capital; rising healthcare spending boosts human capital productivity according to Kurt (2015) and Piabuo and

Tieguhong (2017), which in turn contributes to economic growth; however, in line with the discussion of Agenor (2008), Boucekkine et al. (2008), and World Health Organization (WHO, 2003), there is a continuous discussion about the types of healthcare spending and the optimal level of spending that is good for economic development.

Healthcare, Industrial Output, and Agriculture Productivity

Using stochastic frontier regression approaches, Loureiro (2009) and Ulimwengu (2009) discover favorable correlations between production and health. According to Audibert and Etard's (2003) analysis of the disease's impact on rice farmers, exposure to schistosomiasis lowers output by 26%. According to Fox et al. (2004), who examine the productivity losses linked to HIV positivity, employees with the virus make, on average, 16%–17% less during the two years. Similarly, Baranov et al. (2012) demonstrate that HIV treatment can boost maize productivity by up to 31%, attributing this increase to better physical and mental health as well as an increase in the labor pool overall. However, Gilgen et al. (2001) observed no comparable results for deworming and iron supplementation among tea pluckers in Bangladesh. Two cross-sectional studies that calculated the impact of malaria on agricultural output using harvest data are the most comparable to the findings in this chapter: In their analysis of vegetable growing in Côte d'Ivoire, Girardin et al. (2004) discovered that farmers who reported feeling ill more frequently produced 47% fewer vegetables. Morel et al. (2008) estimated the agricultural loss caused by missed work days in Vietnam owing to malaria using total farming output. They found an average cost of $11 per case of malaria, indicating similar returns to malaria prevention as those found in this research. Conceptually, the vast majority of this literature points to close connections between agricultural production and health in low-income settings; this implies that decisions about household production, labor, and consumption are typically inextricably linked (Benjamin, 1992), a conclusion that is further corroborated by recent data from Zambia Fink and Masiye (2015).

Material and Methods

Variable Description and Data Source

The study has included annual data on per capita GDP constant (2021) US$ based on purchasing power parity as a proxy for economic development (ED). current health expenditure (HEc) includes money spent on personal healthcare, prescription medications, nursing homes, hospitals, and home health companies, as a ratio of GDP representing healthcare, and private investment (AIpi) in AI (constant US million $), as well as subsistence as two separate output-related explanatory variables: agriculture (VAag) and industry (VAi) value-added as a percentage of GDP. The World Bank's World Development Indicator provided all the data, except the Quid via AI Index (2024) data on AI investment from the US Bureau of Labour Statistics (2024).

Empirical Model

The model is built from the findings of previous studies by Atilgan et al. (2017) which included additional factors. To make estimation easier and less complicated, the study used natural logarithmic forms of the variables to experience their interaction with economic welfare. Therefore, the study proposes the following model:

$$\ln \mathrm{ED}_{it} = \alpha_0 + \beta_1 \ln \mathrm{AIpi}_{it} + \beta_2 \ln \mathrm{HEc}_{it} + \beta_4 \ln \mathrm{VAi}_{it} + \beta_3 \ln \mathrm{VAag}_{it} + \mu_{it} \quad (1)$$

where AIpi_{it}, HEc_{it}, VAag_{it}, and $\ln \mathrm{VAi}_{it}$ measure the AI investment, healthcare, agriculture productivity, and industrial output of country i in year t; μ_{it} is the error term, and ED_{it} indicates the i country's economic welfare in year t. α_0 is the constant term. The long-term coefficients of the explanatory variables are denoted by β_1, β_2, β_3, and β_4.

Econometric Methods

The study employs three models to investigate the short- and long-term interactions between explanatory factors and economic development. The results of the PMG/ARDL long-run coefficients are validated using the pooled approach of DOLS proposed by Mark and Sul (2003), FMOLS as advocated by Pedroni (2001), and PMG/ARDL error correction approach to reveal the short-term relationships with economic well-beings taking into consideration the vast body of literature on dynamic panel data. The same pattern of long-term economic growth can be seen in the data gathered from the BRICS economies for this study. The short-run behavior is heterogeneous due to country-specific differences, which makes the PMG estimator appear to be better than the mean group (MG) model. The inclusion of adequate lags for all variables can help alleviate endogeneity issues, which is one of the most important aspects, particularly in PMG and MG estimators (Asteriou et al., 2021; Pesaran et al., 1999).

In comparison to traditional cointegration techniques, the ARDL model has the advantage of accurately representing the data generation process, being applicable to series with level and first-order differential stationarity, and mitigating endogeneity and autocorrelation issues by incorporating enough lags as determined by the Akaike, Schwarz, and Hannan-Quinn Information Criterion (avoid detailing due to space constraints).

The FMOLS and DOLS methodologies estimate the long-term associations of heterogeneous panels using various strategies to take serial correlation and endogeneity bias into account. DOLS uses parametric techniques. All variables exhibit cointegration links, according to DOLS. DOLS can solve contemporaneity by figuring out the values of the leading and lagging variables. However, to overcome the problems of endogeneity and serial correlation, the FMOLS approach employs a non-parametric approach.

In panel data, ignoring the cross-sectional dependence (CD) could result in unpredictable results. Therefore, the study first uses Pesaran et al.'s (2008) CD test to determine whether the cross-sections in the data countries are interdependent. The series employed combines level and first-order differential stationarity. This confirms that the Pedroni Cointegration model cannot be applied in this instance since the variables are not stationary in the same order. Therefore, whether the study regression quantity indicates *I* (0), *I* (1), or a combination of both, the ARDL technique is always the best choice (Pesaran & Smith, 1995). Consequently, the ARDL technique suggests the following PMG models for estimation:

$$\Delta \ln ED_{it} = \alpha_1 + \alpha_{ED} ED_{it-1} + \alpha_{AIpi} \ln AIpi_{it-1} + \alpha_{HEc} \ln HEc_{it-1} + \alpha_{VAi} \ln VAi_{it-1} + \alpha_{VAag} \ln VAag_{it-1} + \sum_{j=1}^{s} \alpha_j \Delta \ln ED_{it-j} + \sum_{l=0}^{s} \alpha_l \Delta \ln AIpi_{it-l} + \sum_{k=0}^{r} \alpha_k \Delta \ln HEc_{it-k} + \sum_{x=0}^{w} \alpha_x \Delta \ln VAi_{it-x} + \sum_{a=0}^{c} \alpha_a \Delta \ln VAag_{it-a} + \varepsilon_{it} \quad (2)$$

where α_1 is the intercept and ε_{it} is the error term. The first part of the equation represents the long-run relationship, while the second part represents the dynamics of error correction.

Error Correction Method (ECM) estimates the short-run coefficients and error correction term once the long-term relationship between the variables has been established. The ECM is represented by the following:

$$\Delta \ln ED_{it} = \alpha_{1+} + \sum_{j=1}^{s} \alpha_j \Delta \ln ED_{it-j} + \sum_{l=0}^{s} \alpha_l \Delta \ln AIpi_{it-l} + \sum_{k=0}^{r} \alpha_k \Delta \ln HEc_{it-k} + \sum_{x=0}^{w} \alpha_x \Delta \ln VAi_{it-x} + \sum_{a=0}^{c} \alpha_a \Delta \ln VAag_{it-a} + \alpha ECT_{t-1} + \varepsilon_{it} \quad (3)$$

Causality test: The panel estimators don't give enough details regarding the causal connections between the variables. To assess the causative relationship between AI investment, health expenditure, agriculture productivity, industrial output, and economic development, the panel causality test method developed by Dumitrescu and Hurlin (2012) is utilized. It is generally acknowledged that the test is a more sophisticated form of the Granger causality analysis. This test is considered better for examining imbalances in panel data after considering the size and time dimension of the cross-section. It performs effectively when CD and slope heterogeneity between nations are present (Bhujabal et al., 2021; Dumitrescu & Hurlin, 2012).

Results and Discussion

Summary Statistics

The mean, maximum, minimum, and standard deviation of the selected variables have been computed using descriptive statistics (ignoring details due to word limit) to determine the economic and environmental strength of the variables.

This discovered a lot of instability and volatility over time concerning the average values of the parameters. The high standard deviation of the variables under investigation provides additional evidence of their instability. Though with notable departures from their means, economic development, AI investment, productivity, and healthcare all demonstrated a high degree of deviation during the study period. The significant differences between the highest and lowest figures revealed the per capita GDP is erratic, which measures economic advancement.

Panel Unit Root Test with CD

The study calculates all CD tests, such as Breusch–Pegan Lagrange multiplier (BPLM), Pesaran-scaled Lagrange multiplier (PSLM), bias-corrected-scaled Lagrange multiplier (BCSLM), and Pesaran CD (PCD) (do not go into depth because of space constraints) to prevent erroneous regression under the traditional unit root test (Chudik & Pesaran, 2015). The biases previously described by Breusch and Pagan (1980) for infinite samples were modified by Pesaran et al. (2008). All the CD tests verified CD for a group of BRICS countries. Breitung (2005) points out that if the data displayed slope heterogeneity in addition to CD, predictions predicated on the supposition of "slope homogeneity" could produce inaccurate estimates. To solve this problem, the "slope homogeneity test of Pesaran and Yamagata (2008)" was also used. The CD results, which deny the slope homogeneity null hypothesis, validate the slope heterogeneity in the data set.

After verifying the cross-sectional dependency in the panel data, the current study used the Cross-Sectionally Augmented Im-Pesaran-Shin (CIPS) unit root test, which was suggested by Pesaran (2007) and produces consistent results in CD data (Bhujabal et al., 2021; Khan et al., 2020; Khattak et al., 2020). The unit root analysis was first performed to know the integration property of the series. The variables of interest have stationary and non-stationary features, as shown by the CIPS unit root test. At the 5% significance level, ln AIpi, ln VAag, and ln VAi are stationary at order $I(0)$, while ln HEc and ln ED are stationary at order $I(1)$. Consequently, the variables being studied exhibit a mix of stationarity characteristics. Hence, the study did not employ the Pedroni cointegration test.

Analysis of Long-run Estimation

Table 12.1 considers the result of three long-run estimators. The PMG/ARDL result showed that AI investment has significantly reduced economic development which is also ensured by FMOLS and DOLS models. This finding is similar to the studies of Aghion (2023). He opined that because of the barriers (or hidden costs) preventing AI from developing further, it has a detrimental impact on economic progress. Certain technologies, like the driverless car, which is still in the experimental stage, and the quantum computer, which is still in the exploratory stage, have not matured enough to be evaluated for potential economic benefits. Cybersecurity, personal data protection, and the competitive landscape of the AI industry are still not adequately regulated. As AI models are still not fully integrated into current commercial and government management systems, it is

Table 12.1. Results of Long-run Estimates.

	Explain Variable: ln ED					
Explanatory Variables	**PMG/ARDL**		**FMOLS**		**DOLS**	
	Coefficient (*t*-Statistics)	**Probability**	**Coefficient (*t*-Statistics)**	**Probability**	**Coefficient (*t*-Statistics)**	**Probability**
ln AIpi	−0.111311* (−25.41637)	0.0000	−0.159992* (−4.690729)	0.0000	−0.121460** (−3.221164)	0.0022
ln HEc	2.796268* (42.93381)	0.0000	1.435522* (7.751957)	0.0000	1.471503* (6.591595)	0.0000
ln VAi	1.808088* (30.32655)	0.0000	2.140294* (14.04725)	0.0000	2.157747* (11.91336)	0.0000
ln VAag	−0.796069* (−11.83434)	0.0000	0.529909** (3.348900)	0.0016	0.333246*** (1.839830)	0.0716

Source: Author's computations.

*, **, and *** denote significant at 1%, 5%, and 10% levels.

challenging to quantify the consequences of skills deficiencies and reluctance to organizational change. Public initiatives to narrow the digital gap and encourage retraining of professions, such as initial and ongoing AI training, are not evenly marketed as institutional advantages. It is contingent upon the nation and area. In this context, Nguyen and Doytch (2022) discovered that total patents had a positive and significant impact on economic growth in industrialized economies, but the impact of the technology variable decreased in emerging economies. The study highlights that the AI investment coefficient of the PMG estimator (−0.111311) indicates that a 1% increase in investment would result in an 11% decrease in economic progress.

All three methods support Bhargava et al. (2001) by showing that health spending has a statistically significant impact on economic growth. He pointed out that between 1965 and 1990, wealthy and developing countries saw noteworthy improvements in their economic growth as public healthcare increased. In line with Arora's (2001) findings, Raghupathi and Raghupathi (2020) also validated these findings and concluded that public health spending and economic growth in the United States are positively correlated.

Industry output in line with the research of Fink and Masiye (2015) is statistically important for boosting economic growth. Under PMG, the coefficients of HEc (2.80) and VAi (1.80) showed that a 1% increase in each would, over time, improve economic development by 2.80% and 1.80%, respectively.

Though PMG demonstrated that agricultural yield harmed economic growth, FMOLS and DOLS guaranteed the opposite outcome in line with past research of Awoyemi et al. (2017), Whitaker (2021), and Zsarnóczai and Zéman (2019).

Analysis of Short-run Estimate

Table 12.2 shows the PMG/ARDL short-run result and causality test results for the BRICS nations.

The lag length 1 used for all variables → denotes one-way causal relationship.

According to the result of Table 12.2 of the PMG/ARDL model, health expenditure and agriculture productivity significantly reduce economic development in the short term. However, investment-related AI and industrial output are insignificant in the short run. According to the coefficient of HEc (−0.265) and VAag (−0.263), a 1% increase in each will result in a short-term 26% decrease in economic progress, respectively. Additionally, the model converged to a long-run link, as indicated by the moderate negative sign of the error-correcting terms (ECTs). The model accounts for 27.2% (−0.272021) of the adjustment speed in the short to establish long-run equilibrium.

Analysis of Causality Test

Lastly, the causative relationship between AI investment, health expenditure, industrial output, agriculture productivity, and economic development is examined using the Dumitrescu–Hurlin panel causality test. The findings are shown in the lower part of Table 12.2. The findings show that health expenditure is in

Table 12.2. PMG/ARDL Short-run Result and Causality Test.

Explanatory Variable	Explain Variable: ln ED		
	Coefficient (*t*-Statistics)	**Probability**	**Significance**
CointEq(−1)	−0.272021** (−2.630517)	0.0145	Significant and equilibrium
ln AIpi	0.001458 (0.004385)	0.7422	Insignificant
ln HEc	−0.265093*** (−1.935509)	0.0639	Significant and negative
ln VAi	0.039793 (0.358271)	0.7230	Insignificant
ln VAag	−0.263515** (−2.583176)	0.0158	Significant and negative

Dumitrescu–Hurlin panel causality tests (where causality exist)

Variable	*W*-Statistics	Zbar-Statistics	Probability
ED → AIpi	3.99628	2.07338	0.0381
HEc → ED	3.87589	1.97723	0.0480
VAag → ED	3.51605	1.68987	0.0911
AIpi →HEc	4.38125	2.38081	0.0173
HEc → VAi	3.77488	1.89657	0.0579
VAag → VAi	3.86866	1.97146	0.0487

Source: Author's computations.

*, **, and *** denote significant at 1%, 5%, and 10% levels.

line with an earlier study by Neycheva (2008), Egbetunde and Fasanya (2013), and Zaidi and Saidi (2018), and agriculture production is similar to the study of Bashir et al. (2019) unidirectional related to industry output and economic development. Economic advancement results in enhancements in artificial intelligence, which plays a significant role in enhancing the efficiency of healthcare facilities. It suggests that developed healthcare and agriculture productivity cause economic growth and industry output. Additionally, the rising economic development causes AI investment, and AI increases healthcare in BRICS economies.

Conclusion and Policy Implications

The study aims to evaluate in detail how industry, agriculture, AI, and healthcare impact the economic progress of the BRICS nations using the PMG/ARDL model to identify the changing laws of AI, healthcare, and output along the economic development process, and it obtained several interactive results utilizing panel FMOLS and DOLS estimation. Although AI investment greatly absorbs economic development in BRICS countries, the study confirms this. The study demonstrated a considerable positive impact under all three methods when considering economic development through healthcare improvement and industrialization in the long run. Though PMG demonstrated that agricultural yield harmed economic growth, FMOLS and DOLS guaranteed the opposite outcome. In the short run, the productivity of agriculture and healthcare greatly hinders economic progress. However, in the medium term, both industrial production and investment-related AI remain negligible. According to the Dumitrescu–Hurlin panel causality test, economic growth and industry production are caused by increased healthcare and agriculture production. AI investment is also a result of growing economic development, and in BRICS economies, AI improves healthcare.

The study thus recommends encouraging investments in AI technology and creating a robust productivity landscape that will assist healthcare and economic development in the BRICS nations. The immediate and long-term effects of AI and healthcare quality on productivity and growth should be considered by authorities when creating programs to promote healthcare and economic growth through output generation. The healthcare industry is especially susceptible to the innovative application potential of AI due to its revolutionary nature. Applications are changing not just how care is provided in terms of diagnostic and treatment methods but also how patients live their lives, as their health requires the complete range of healthy living behaviors. In order to improve health-related technology, such as AI-enabled sophisticated equipment like diagnostic tools and high-quality medications for treatments, etc., and to raise living standards by fostering economic growth by boosting industrialization and agriculture, the BRICS economies should support AI investment. The policymakers must implement policies that support both environmental sustainability and economic growth in their nations. This goal can be achieved by changing energy policies to boost renewable energy sources and reduce manufacturing activities' reliance on non-renewable energy sources for economic development.

References

Acharya, S., Barber, S. L., Lopez-Acuna, D., Menabde, N., Migliorini, L., Molina, J., Schwartländer, B., & Zurn, P. (2014). BRICS and global health. *Bulletin of the World Health Organization*, *92*, 386–386A.

Agenor, P. R. (2008). Health and infrastructure in a model of endogenous growth. *Journal of Macroeconomics*, *30*, 1407–1422.

Aghion, P. (2023, May 18). Faire de l'IA une occasion de croissance et d'emploi. *LesEchos*.

Akbar, A., Rehman, A., Ullah, I., Zeeshan, M., & Afridi, F. E. A. (2020). Unraveling the dynamic nexus between trade liberalization, energy consumption, CO2 emissions, and health expenditure in Southeast Asian countries. *Risk Management and Healthcare Policy*, *13*, 2020, 1915–1927 https://doi.org/10.2147/RMHP.S272801.

Arora, S. (2001). Health, human productivity, and long-term economic growth. *The Journal of Economic History*, *61*(3), 699–749.

Atilgan, E., Kilic, D., & Ertugrul, H. M. (2017). The dynamic relationship between health expenditure and economic growth: Is the health-led growth hypothesis valid for Turkey? *The European Journal of Health Economics*, *18*, 567–574.

Audibert, M., & Etard, J.-F., (2003). Productive benefits after investment in health in Mali. *Economic Development and Cultural Change*, *51*, 769–782.

Awoyemi, B. O., Afolabi, B., & Akomolafe, K. J. (2017). Agricultural productivity and economic growth: Impact analysis from Nigeria. *Scientific Research Journal (SCIRJ)*, *5*(10), 1–7.

Baranov, V., Bennett, D., & Kohler, H -P. (2012). *The indirect impact of antiretroviral therapy* (PSC Working Paper Series 9-27-2012). Journal of Health Economics, 44:195-211. https://doi.org/10.1016/j.jhealeco.2015.07.008.

Bashir, A., Suhel, A., Azwardi, A., Atiyatna, D. P., Hamidi, I., & Adnan, N. (2019). The causality between agriculture, industry, and economic growth: Evidence from Indonesia. *Etikonomi*, *18*(2), 155–168.

Behrman, J. R., Foster, A. D., Rosenzweig, M. R. (1997). The dynamics of agricultural production and the calorie-income relationship. *Journal of Econometrics*, *77*, 187–208.

Benjamin, D. (1992) Household composition labor markets, and labor demand: testing for separation in agricultural household models. *Econometrica 60*, 287–322. https://www.jstor.org/stable/2951598?origin=crossref

Bhargava, A., Jamison, D. T., Lau, L. J., & Murray, C. J. (2001). Modeling the effects of health on economic growth. *Journal of Health Economics*, *20*(3), 423–440.

Bhujabal, P., Sethi, N., & Padhan, P. C. (2021). ICT, foreign direct investment and environmental pollution in major Asia Pacific countries. *Environmental Science and Pollution Research*, *28*, 42649–42669.

Bloom, D. E., Canning, D., & Sevilla, J. (2004). The effect of health on economic growth: A production function approach. *World Development*, *32*, 1–13.

Boucekkine, R., Diene, B., & Azomahou, T. (2008). Growth economics of epidemics: A review of the theory. *Mathematical Population Studies*, *15*, 1–26.

Breitung, J. (2005). A parametric approach to the estimation of cointegration vectors in panel data. *Econometric Reviews*, *24*(2), 151–173.

Breusch, T. S., & Pagan, A. R. (1980). The Lagrange multiplier test and its applications to model specification in econometrics. *The Review of Economic Studies*, *47*(1), 239–253.

Chudik, A., & Pesaran, M. H. (2015). Common correlated effects estimation of heterogeneous dynamic panel data models with weakly exogenous regressors. *Journal of Econometrics*, *188*(2), 393–420.

Dumitrescu, E.-I., & Hurlin, C. (2012). Testing for Granger non-causality in heterogeneous panels. *Economic Modelling*, *29*(4), 1450–1460.

Fink, G., & Masiye, F. (2015). Health and agricultural productivity: Evidence from Zambia. *Journal of Health Economics*, *42*, 151–164.

Fox, M. P., Rosen, S., MacLeod, W. B., Wasunna, M., Bii, M., Foglia, G., & Simon, J. L. (2004). The impact of HIV/AIDS on labour productivity in Kenya. *Tropical Medicine & International Health*, *9*, 318–324.

Gomes, M. G., da Silva, V. H. C., Pinto, L. F. R., Centoamore, P., Digiesi, S., Facchini, F., & Neto, GCd. O. (2020). Economic, environmental and social gains of the implementation of artifcial intelligence at dam operations toward Industry 4.0 principles. *Sustainability*, *12*(9), 3604.

Gilgen, D. D., Mascie-Taylor, C. G., & Rosetta, L. L. (2001). Intestinal helminth infections, anaemia and labour productivity of female tea pluckers in Bangladesh. *Tropical Medicine & International Health*, *6*, 449–457.

Girardin, O., Daoa, D., Koudou, E. G., Essé, C., Cissé, G., Yao, T., N'Goran, E. K., Tschannen, A. B., Bordmannd, G., Lehmannc, B., Nsabimana, C., Keiser, J., Killeen, G. F., Singer, B. H., Tanner, M., & Utzinger, J. (2004). Opportunities and limiting factors of intensive vegetable farming in malaria endemic Côte d'Ivoire. *Acta Tropica*, *89*, 109–123.

Goertzel, B., Goertzel, T., & Goertzel, Z. (2017). The global brain and the emerging economy of abundance: Mutualism, open collaboration, exchange networks and the automated commons. *Technological Forecasting and Social Change*, *114*, 65–73.

Heylighen, F. (2017). Towards an intelligent network for matching offer and demand: From the sharing economy to the global brain. *Technological Forecasting and Social Change*, *114*, 74–85.

Kak, S. (2018). *On ternary coding and three-valued logic*. arXiv preprint arXiv:1807.06419.

Khan, A., Muhammad, F., Chenggang, Y., Hussain, J., Bano, S., & Khan, M. A. (2020). The impression of technological innovations and natural resources in energy-growth-environment nexus: A new look into BRICS economies. *Science of the Total Environment*, *727*, 138265.

Khattak, S. I., Ahmad, M., Khan, Z. U., & Khan, A. (2020). Exploring the impact of innovation, renewable energy consumption, and income on CO2 emissions: New evidence from the BRICS economies. *Environmental Science and Pollution Research International*, *27*(12), 13866–13881.

Kurt, S. (2015). Government health expenditures and economic growth: A federal-run approach for the case of Turkey. *International Journal of Economics and Financial Issues*, *5*, 441–7.

Lee, D. (2018). Strategies for technology-driven service encounters for patient experience satisfaction in hospitals. *Technological Forecasting and Social Change*, *137*, 118–127.

Lee, D. (2019). Effects of key value co-creation elements in the healthcare system: Focusing on technology applications. *Service Business*, *13*, 389–417.

Lee, S. M., & Lee, D. (2020). Healthcare wearable devices: An analysis of key factors for continuous use intention. *Service Business*, *14*(4), 503–531.

Lee, S. M., & Lim, S. (2018). *Living innovation: From value creation to the greater good*. Emerald Publishing Limited.

Li, B. H., Hou, B. C., Yu, W. T., Lu, X. B., & Yang, C. W. (2017). Applications of artificial intelligence in intelligent manufacturing: A review. *Frontiers of Information Technology & Electronic Engineering*, *18*(1), 86–96.

Loureiro, M. L. (2009). Farmers' health and agricultural productivity. *Agricultural Economics*, *40*, 381–388.

Mark, N. C., & Sul, D. (2003). Cointegration vector estimation by panel DOLS and long-run money demand. *Oxford Bulletin of Economics and Statistics*, *65*(5), 655–680.

Morel, C. M., Thang, N., Xa, N., Hung, L. X., Thuan, L. K., Ky, P. V., Erhart, A., Mills, A. J., & D'Alessandro, U. (2008). The economic burden of malaria on the household in south-central Vietnam. *Malaria Journal*, *7*(1), 166. doi:10.1186/1475-2875-7-166

Naimi-Sadigh, A., Asgari, T., & Rabiei, M. (2022). Digital transformation in the value chain disruption of banking services. *Journal of the Knowledge Economy*, *13*(2), 1212–1242.

O'Neill, J. (2001). Building better global economic BRICs (Vol. 66, 1-16). New York: Goldman Sachs. https://www.ri-esistenza.com/wp-content/uploads/2023/04/build-better-brics.pdf

Öztürk, S., & Topcu, E. (2014). Health expenditure and economic growth: Evidence from G8 countries. *International Journal of Economics and Empirical Research*, *2*, 256–261.

Pedroni, P. (2001). Fully modified OLS for heterogeneous cointegrated panels. In Nonstationary panels, panel cointegration, and dynamic panels (pp. 93–130). Emerald Group Publishing Limited. https://doi.org/10.1016/S0731-9053(00)15004-2

Peres, R. S., Jia, X., Lee, J., Sun, K., Colombo, A. W., & Barata, J. (2020). Industrial artificial intelligence in industry 4.0-systematic review, challenges and outlook. *IEEE Access*, *8*, 220121–220139.

Pesaran, M. H. (2007). A simple panel unit root test in the presence of cross-section dependence. *Journal of Applied Econometrics*, *22*(2), 265–312.

Pesaran, M. H., Shin, Y. C., & Smith, R. P. (1999). Pooled mean group estimation of dynamic heterogeneous panels. *Journal of the American Statistical Association*, *94*(446), 621–634.

Pesaran, M. H., & Smith, R. (1995). Estimating long-run relationships from dynamic heterogeneous panels. *Journal of Econometrics*, *68*(1), 79–113.

Pesaran, M. H., Ullah, A., & Yamagata, T. (2008). A bias-adjusted LM test of error cross-section independence. *The Econometrics Journal*, *11*(1), 105–127.

Pesaran, M. H., & Yamagata, T. (2008). Testing slope homogeneity in large panels. *Journal of Econometrics*, *142*(1), 50–93.

Piabuo, S. M., & Tieguhong, J. C. (2017). Health expenditure and economic growth – A review of the literature and analysis between the economic community for central African States (CEMANC) and selected African countries. *Health Economics Review*, *27*, 1–13.

Pitt, M. M., & Rosenzweig, M. R. (1986). Agricultural prices, food consumption, and the health and productivity of Indonesian farmers. In I. J. Singh, L. Squire, & J. Strauss (Eds.), *Agricultural household models*. Johns Hopkins University Press. 153–182, ref. 23. https://www.cabidigitallibrary.org/doi/full/10.5555/19871845037

Quid via AI Index. (2024). U.S. Bureau of Labour Statistics. https://www.quid.com/2024-stanford-ai-index-report. https://data.worldbank.org/indicator/NY.GDP.PCAP.PP.KD?locations=IN-CN

Raghupathi, V., & Raghupathi, W. (2020). Healthcare expenditure and economic performance: Insights from the United States data. *Frontiers in Public Health*, *8*, 156.

Ramesh, A., Kambhampati, C., Monson, J., & Drew, P. (2004). Artificial intelligence in medicine. *Annals of the Royal College of Surgeons of England*, *86*, 334–338.

Rancic, N., & Jakovljevic, M. M. (2016). Long term health spending alongside population aging in N-11 emerging nations. *Eastern European Business and Economics Journal*, *2*(1), 2–26.

RSNA Newsroom. (2018). https://press.rsna.org/timssnet/media/pressreleases/14_pr_target.cfm?ID=2067

Safavi, K., & Kalis, B. (2019). How AI can change the future of health care. *Harvard Business Review*.

Strauss, J. (1986). Does better nutrition raise farm productivity. *Journal of Political Economy*, *94*, 297–320.

Trifan, B., & Buzatu, A. (2020, November). *Sustainable business enhanced through digital transformation and artificial intelligence in the context of Industry 4.0* [Conference]. BASIQ, Italy.

Ulimwengu, J. (2009). Farmers' health and agricultural productivity in rural Ethiopia. *African Journal of Agricultural and Resource Economics*, *3*, 83–100.

Vyshnevskyi, O., Liashenko, V., & Amosha, O. (2019). The impact of Industry 4.0 and AI on economic growth. *Zeszyty Naukowe. Organizacja i Zarządzanie/Politechnika Śląska*, *140*, 391–400.

Whitaker, M.D. (1991). *Agriculture and Economic Survival: The Role Of Agriculture In Ecuador's Development* (1st ed.). Routledge. https://doi.org/10.4324/9780429046056

World Health Organization. (2003). How much should countries spend on health? World Health Organization.

Yoon, S., & Lee, D. (2019). Artificial intelligence and robots in healthcare: What are the success factors for technology-based service encounters? *International Journal of Healthcare Management*, *12*, 218–225.

Zaidi, S., & Saidi, K. (2018). Environmental pollution, health expenditure and economic growth in the Sub-Saharan Africa countries: Panel ARDL approach. *Sustainable Cities and Society*, *41*, 833–840.

Zavyalova, E. B., Volokhina, V. A., Troyanskaya, M. A., & Dubova, Y. I. (2023). A humanistic model of corporate social responsibility in e-commerce with high-tech support in the artificial intelligence economy, *Humanities and Social Sciences Communications*, *10*(1), 1–10.

Zsarnóczai, J. S., & Zéman, Z. (2019). Output Value and Productivity of Agricultural Indus. *Agricultural Economics/Zemědělská Ekonomika*, *65*(4). https://data.worldbank.org/indicator/NY.GDP.PCAP.PP.KD?locations=IN-CN-BR-ZA-RU

Chapter 13

Artificial Intelligence in South Asian Elections: Balancing Engagement and Integrity Challenges

Saber Ahmed Chowdhury[a] *and Md. Zarif Rahman*[b,c]

[a]*Department of Peace and Conflict Studies, University of Dhaka, Bangladesh*
[b]*Institute of Informatics and Development (IID), Bangladesh*
[c]*Police Reform Commission, Bangladesh*

Abstract

This chapter explores the dual impact of artificial intelligence (AI) on elections in South Asia, focusing on India, Pakistan, and Bangladesh. It also examines AI's role across the pre-election, election day, and post-election phases, emphasizing how political culture shapes its application. Using a qualitative approach, the study analyzes credible new sources to assess AI's contributions to voter engagement, election management, and misinformation. This study argues that during the pre-election phase, AI-enhanced personalized voter outreach and campaign strategies were effectively utilized, as evidenced in Pakistan and India, where political parties employed AI to target specific demographics with precision. However, it also fueled disinformation, with Pakistan Tehreek-e-Insaf (PTI)'s AI-generated videos in Pakistan and deepfake attacks against political figures in Bangladesh. In India, AI tools blurred the line between engagement and manipulation. On the other hand, on election day, AI's impact became even more pronounced, as deepfake videos were used to manipulate voter perceptions in real time. For instance, during India's Telangana elections, AI-generated content falsely portrayed candidate endorsements, aiming to sway voter decisions. Similar instances in Pakistan and Bangladesh further underscored the growing threat of AI-driven disinformation to the integrity of electoral processes. In the post-election phase, AI reinforced

Artificial Intelligence in Business and Society: Global Insights, 195–213

doi:10.1108/978-1-83708-022-920261031

political narratives, such as PTI's AI-generated victory speeches in Pakistan. These findings highlight the urgent need for robust regulations to prevent AI from undermining democracy in South Asia.

Keywords: Artificial intelligence; elections; South Asia; misinformation; electoral manipulation; deepfake

Introduction

The rapid advancement of AI has profoundly transformed various aspects of modern society, emerging as a powerful force in global politics. This impact is especially pronounced in South Asia, where elections serve as critical pillars of democratic engagement within highly intricate political landscapes. In 2024, as a significant portion of the world's population prepares to participate in what has been termed "the biggest election year in history," the role of AI in elections particularly in South Asia represents both a groundbreaking opportunity and a formidable challenge to the principles of democracy. While AI holds significant potential to strengthen democratic processes by expanding voter outreach, promoting inclusivity, and supporting transparent governance, the unique political dynamics of South Asian countries characterized by entrenched power structures, deep polarization, and widespread corruption frequently result in its misuse. Instead of advancing democratic ideals, AI is often exploited in ways that undermine and erode these norms.

AI's dual ability to both enhance and hinder democracy has fundamentally reshaped electoral campaign strategies worldwide, enabling data-driven approaches that influence voter behavior with remarkable precision. In South Asia, political campaigns have increasingly utilized AI to create detailed psychographic profiles, allowing them to target voters with highly personalized messaging. This strategy not only persuades voters to support specific candidates but also fosters bias and negative perceptions of opponents (Safiullah & Parveen, 2022). Advanced AI tools, including deepfake technology and automated social media bots, have amplified this influence by facilitating the creation of convincing yet false narratives and fabricated endorsements, thereby fueling widespread misinformation (Cupać et al., 2024).

Beyond transforming campaign strategies, AI is becoming an integral part of election management, with election management bodies (EMBs) exploring its applications throughout the electoral cycle to improve efficiency and accuracy (International IDEA, 2024). In principle, AI-driven tools have the potential to strengthen electoral integrity by streamlining processes such as voter registration and vote tallying. However, the rapid adoption of AI in these areas introduces significant challenges, particularly in ensuring ethical practices and establishing clear legal accountability. Existing electoral laws, which frequently fail to keep pace with rapid technological advancements, may be ill-equipped to address the implications of AI-driven automated decision-making (International IDEA, 2024).

In politically volatile regions, where public trust is already fragile, the perceived biases or security vulnerabilities of AI applications could further erode confidence in electoral processes (Deepak et al., 2023). This study is significant for understanding the complex role AI plays in South Asian elections and highlights the need for adaptive governance to address its challenges and safeguard electoral integrity.

Against this backdrop, this chapter explores the role of AI in elections across South Asia, with a focus on India, Pakistan, and Bangladesh, to assess both the opportunities and risks it presents. By examining its application throughout the pre-election, election day, and post-election phases, this chapter will highlight the dual nature of AI in South Asian electoral contexts. The analysis will address issues such as misinformation campaigns, deepfake manipulation, and the ethical challenges associated with AI misuse, offering insights into how political culture shapes AI's impact on these regional elections.

Operationalization of Definitions

To analyze the impact of AI on electoral integrity in South Asia's pre-electoral phase, it is essential to define key terms and establish a framework that contextualizes AI's role across the electoral timeline. In the electoral context, AI refers to technologies that simulate human intelligence to process data, enhance campaign outreach, and influence voter behavior. These tools can have both positive and negative effects on democracy. For instance, AI-driven communication tools, such as natural language processing, expand campaign reach, while predictive analytics and voter profiling use machine learning to analyze voter data, enabling targeted messaging. However, generative media, particularly deepfake technology, poses significant risks by creating synthetic content that can spread disinformation, such as fabricated endorsements designed to manipulate public perception (Sebastian, 2024; Younus, 2024).

Electoral integrity encompasses fairness, transparency, and accountability across all election processes, including voter registration, campaigning, voting, and result validation. Each phase of the electoral cycle-pre-election, election day, and post-election requires specific considerations regarding AI's role. In the pre-election phase, integrity focuses on transparency in campaign strategies, preventing misinformation, and ensuring equitable access to information. Campaigns using AI-driven voter profiling must adhere to ethical standards, respecting voter privacy and ensuring informed consent (Wee, 2024). However, vigilance is necessary to counter AI-driven foreign interference and biased information, as seen in South Asia's electoral context (Sebastian, 2024).

During the election phase, the focus shifts to ensuring the security and accessibility of voting. AI aids in voter authentication through biometrics or facial recognition, streamlining verification and reducing fraud. AI-driven systems also enhance election monitoring by detecting irregularities and protecting against digital threats, such as cyberattacks on voting infrastructure (Iqbal & Mushtaq, 2024). Real-time fact-checking is critical to counter last-minute disinformation, particularly on social media, where viral content can sway undecided voters.

In the post-election phase, AI supports transparency and public trust by ensuring accurate result verification, monitoring public sentiment, and combating disinformation. AI-assisted vote counting and auditing expedite validation while maintaining transparency, bolstering confidence in election outcomes (Mohydin, 2024). AI tools also track public sentiment and identify misinformation, addressing narratives that could undermine electoral legitimacy (Commonwealth Parliamentary Association, 2024). Data-driven insights from AI further inform election management and voter engagement, improving future processes.

This framework underscores AI's dual role in South Asia's elections: while it enhances engagement, it also poses significant challenges requiring robust oversight (Mughal, 2024).

Methodology

This qualitative study explores the role of AI in electoral processes across South Asia, with a particular focus on India, Pakistan, and Bangladesh. Given the nascent stage of research on the intersection of AI and elections, scholarly literature on this topic remains limited. Consequently, the study predominantly relies on secondary data sourced from credible newspapers and reputable online news platforms. These sources were selected for their reliability, depth of coverage, and relevance to the subject matter, providing timely insights into the application of AI in areas such as electoral campaigning, voter targeting, misinformation dissemination, and election management.

A thematic content analysis was conducted to systematically examine the data, focusing on key developments across the pre-electoral, election day, and post-election phases. A particular emphasis was placed on AI's influence on voter engagement, election integrity, and post-election transparency, as well as the political and social dynamics shaping its application. The analysis also delved into the ethical challenges posed by AI, such as the proliferation of misinformation, algorithmic bias, and potential manipulation, within the unique socio-political context of South Asia.

While the reliance on media sources offers access to timely and relevant information, it is acknowledged that this approach may be susceptible to media bias. Additionally, the limited availability of established scholarly research on the topic poses a constraint. However, these concerns were mitigated by drawing on a diverse range of reputable and credible sources. Ethical considerations were rigorously adhered to, with all data and expert opinions properly cited and attributed. This methodology effectively integrates contemporary media reporting with expert insights, providing a well-rounded and contextually nuanced analysis of AI's role in the electoral processes of South Asia.

AI and Electoral Integrity in South Asia: Pre-election Phase

The rapid rise of AI in South Asian elections has reshaped the pre-election landscape, serving as both a tool for political engagement and a source of misinformation. In 2024, AI has become essential for political parties, enabling targeted voter outreach through data mining, voter profiling, AI-generated content, and deepfakes. In South Asia, with its diverse voter bases, intense competition, and rapidly evolving media landscapes, AI technologies offer both opportunities and challenges for political campaigns. This section explores the deployment and consequences of AI-driven strategies in three South Asian countries – Pakistan, India, and Bangladesh, each of which has faced unique dynamics in integrating AI tools into their pre-election processes.

AI's Role in Shaping Pakistan's 2024 General Election

The 2024 general election in Pakistan highlighted AI's transformative role in political campaigning, revealing both its potential and ethical challenges. Amid restrictions, censorship, and the imprisonment of its leader, Imran Khan, PTI turned to AI-driven tools to sustain voter engagement and maintain digital visibility. With a significant portion of the electorate being young voters, PTI's tech-forward approach aimed to resonate with Pakistan's increasingly digital-savvy youth, using AI to create alternative avenues for political outreach (Mohydin, 2024; Wee, 2024).

Digital Adaptation Strategies and AI-generated Speeches

Facing unprecedented restrictions on traditional campaigning, PTI used AI to simulate Imran Khan's presence, leveraging digital tools to navigate a challenging political landscape. By employing voice-cloning technology from ElevenLabs, PTI produced AI-powered speeches, enabling Khan to virtually address supporters despite his imprisonment. One rally speech alone garnered over five million YouTube views, showcasing AI's power in engaging large audiences under restrictive conditions (Wee, 2024). These AI-generated speeches became a vital digital lifeline for PTI, reinforcing Khan's image as a resilient leader and creating a symbolic presence that resonated deeply with voters (Iqbal & Mushtaq, 2024).

In December, a notable AI-generated event took place during a key PTI virtual rally. Khan's messages, relayed through his lawyers, were transformed into an AI-rendered speech that garnered over 1.5 million views within 12 hours, amplifying PTI's message despite physical restrictions. As PTI continued hosting virtual rallies on platforms like YouTube, TikTok, and Facebook, these AI-generated speeches became central to their strategy, enabling Khan to engage directly with supporters and sustain party morale. This digital approach proved especially innovative and accessible for young voters, who form a large portion of Pakistan's electorate (Shahzad & Shahid, 2024).

Beyond AI-powered speeches, PTI implemented various digital strategies to enhance voter engagement. After government-imposed blocks on their official website, PTI swiftly migrated digital assets to GitHub, a decentralized platform harder to censor than traditional websites. This adaptation ensured voters could still access essential electoral information, including candidate profiles, voting instructions, and campaign updates (Mohydin, 2024).

To expand their outreach, PTI launched an AI chatbot on Imran Khan's Facebook page, providing real-time updates on campaign events, polling details, and reminders to sustain engagement. In the final days before the election, it answered voting-related FAQs, helped supporters locate polling stations, and encouraged them to cast their ballots. The chatbot also enabled interactive conversations, allowing users to "speak" with Khan's virtual persona, creating a personal and engaging experience especially for young, tech-savvy supporters. This virtual interaction strengthened connection and loyalty, compensating for restrictions on traditional campaigning (Iqbal & Mushtaq, 2024).

PTI launched an offline app to help voters identify candidates in their constituencies. The app provided information on PTI-backed independent candidates, bypassing restrictions on official symbols. PTI promoted the app via short videos and infographics, guiding supporters on downloading and using it. Its offline functionality was crucial for voter access in areas with unreliable internet, especially amid multiple internet disruptions reported by NetBlocks, which detected six major outages during PTI's virtual rallies (Mughal, 2024; Shahzad & Shahid, 2024).

PTI's digital adaptation strategies marked a significant shift in how political campaigns can operate under restrictive conditions. These efforts expanded PTI's digital reach and ensured their message resonated with Pakistan's diverse electorate, despite limitations on traditional campaigning. By integrating AI-generated content, virtual interactions, and decentralized digital tools, PTI turned challenges into opportunities, setting a new standard for political resilience in Pakistan's evolving digital landscape.

AI-driven Misinformation and the Spread of Deepfakes

While AI technology offered PTI innovative ways to engage voters, it also exposed the electoral landscape to significant risks of AI-driven misinformation and deepfakes. As PTI used AI to create lifelike virtual versions of Imran Khan, other groups began using similar technologies to spread disinformation. In one damaging incident, a deepfake video appeared on social media, falsely showing Khan urging followers to boycott the election. Despite PTI's quick clarification that the video was fake, it had already reached millions, causing confusion and speculation about PTI's stance. The rapid spread of the video highlighted the powerful impact of AI-driven misinformation, which can distort political narratives eroding public trust (Wee, 2024).

In another instance, an AI-generated audio clip surfaced just days before the election, allegedly featuring Khan discussing plans to destabilize the electoral process. While experts later confirmed the audio was a deepfake, it spread widely enough to ignite public debate and prompt media outlets to question PTI's intentions. The widespread sharing of such deepfakes on social media made them nearly indistinguishable from authentic material for the average viewer, amplifying their impact and complicating efforts to control misinformation (Iqbal & Mushtaq, 2024).

AI-driven misinformation also fueled manipulative tactics, such as rumors about the withdrawal of key PTI candidates. In the final week of the campaign, false social media posts claimed that PTI candidates had stepped down due to a political agreement. Though debunked quickly, these rumors caused confusion, leading some voters to question the legitimacy of PTI's candidate list, impacting morale and potentially deterring turnout. AI-powered bots amplified these posts, allowing the misinformation to spread rapidly before PTI could issue corrections (Younus, 2024).

A troubling trend emerged as deepfake creators used AI to impersonate Khan's supporters and associates, fabricating statements or actions that appeared to endorse rival parties. These tactics fueled distrust and created divisions among supporters, making it hard to distinguish authentic from manipulated content. For example, a viral deepfake depicted a senior PTI spokesperson seemingly praising a rival party's leader, causing backlash within PTI's online communities. Although the spokesperson condemned the video as fake, the initial damage undermined internal unity and distracted from PTI's core messages (Wee, 2024).

These examples highlight the significant impact of AI-driven disinformation on Pakistan's electoral landscape, where public trust in the process was already fragile. A Gallup poll found that nearly 70% of Pakistanis distrusted the electoral process even before the election. This existing skepticism was exacerbated by the surge of AI-generated misinformation, which increased voter uncertainty and complicated PTI's digital campaign. The spread of deepfakes, false audio clips, and AI-manipulated social media posts deepened suspicions of manipulation, making it difficult for voters to assess the credibility of political messaging during the campaign's final weeks (Wee, 2024).

The spread of AI-powered misinformation during PTI's campaign highlights the urgent need for regulatory frameworks to prevent AI misuse in political campaigns. Without clear policies and protections, the risks of AI manipulation could escalate, undermining democratic processes. As Pakistan looks ahead, these challenges stress the importance of both technological solutions, like AI-detection tools, and strong regulatory oversight to prevent similar issues in future elections (Younus, 2024).

Implications for Pakistan's Political Future

The 2024 election highlights the urgent need for regulatory frameworks that balance AI's advantages with safeguards against its misuse. While PTI's innovative use of AI helped overcome physical and legal barriers, it also exposed significant vulnerabilities in Pakistan's electoral system (Younus, 2024). The combination of AI-powered engagement and widespread digital disinformation signals a broader shift in political campaigning, especially in environments with limited press freedom and deep institutional distrust (Mohydin, 2024). Moving forward, Pakistan will need clear regulations for AI in politics. Establishing guidelines to ensure transparency, combat misinformation, and enforce accountability will be crucial to leveraging AI's benefits without compromising electoral integrity. The 2024 election serves as a case study of AI's disruptive potential in political campaigns, emphasizing the need to balance technological innovation with democratic principles to protect future elections (Iqbal & Mushtaq, 2024; Younus, 2024).

AI Usage in India's General Election: A Double-edged Sword

As India's general election approaches, AI is playing an expanding role in political campaigns, offering both opportunities and risks to electoral integrity.

AI-driven Campaign Strategies and Personalized Outreach in India

Political parties in India, particularly the Bharatiya Janata Party (BJP), are heavily investing in AI technologies for their election campaigns. Reports suggest over $50 million is being allocated to AI-generated content, reflecting AI's growing role in India's political landscape (Shah, 2024). These AI-driven strategies enable parties to go beyond traditional methods, creating highly personalized and persuasive content to effectively target voters.

One of the most innovative applications of AI in these campaigns is the creation of AI-powered avatars, which feature key political figures like Prime Minister Narendra Modi. These avatars deliver messages in voters' native languages, mimicking Modi's tone, gestures, and mannerisms to establish a more authentic connection. By promoting policies and rallying support for the BJP, these AI avatars tailor messages to different voter demographics, significantly enhancing the party's outreach.

The "Bhashini" platform, powered by AI translation tools, helps overcome linguistic barriers in India's diverse electorate. It allows political parties to translate speeches, messages, and campaign videos into regional languages, enabling leaders to communicate directly with various voter groups. For instance, Prime Minister Modi's speeches in Hindi are seamlessly translated into Tamil, Telugu, Bengali, and other languages (Sharma, 2024).

A prime example of this AI technology in action is the 2024 election campaign, where AI-generated videos of Modi were widely shared on platforms like WhatsApp, Facebook, and YouTube. These videos went beyond typical ads, delivering personalized messages tailored to specific voter groups, whether rural or urban, young or old. AI was also used to adjust content based on regional dialects, making the message feel more relevant. This targeted approach increases voter engagement by ensuring content resonates with individuals, rather than using a one-size-fits-all broadcast (Shah, 2024).

AI in Creating Avatars of Celebrities and Ordinary Citizens

AI in India's political campaigns extends to avatars of celebrities and ordinary citizens. For instance, Bollywood stars with political ties had their faces and voices digitally altered to create pro-BJP content. For example, AI-generated content featuring Bollywood legend Amitabh Bachchan was shared to promote government initiatives in education and healthcare. Although Bachchan didn't directly participate, his likeness and voice were digitally replicated to deliver government messages, amplifying their impact due to his popularity (Hill, 2024). AI tools have created fictional personas, from friendly characters to influential figures, to deliver personalized campaign messages that appeal to younger, tech-savvy voters.

A significant development is the rise of AI platforms like "The Indian Deepfaker," which allow campaigners to create personalized, pro-BJP content. In the lead-up to the 2024 elections, AI-generated avatars of ordinary citizens – farmers, teachers, and students – expressed support for BJP policies. These viral videos were shared widely across social media, gaining traction and broadening their reach. Although the individuals depicted were fictional, the content was convincing enough for many to believe it was authentic (Hill, 2024).

These tools enable hyper-personalized campaigning, tailored to specific regions and socio-political demographics. AI content creators adjust linguistic preferences and emotional inclinations, using different avatars to appeal to various groups. For example, in Punjab, AI-generated videos featuring local farmers praising agricultural policies targeted rural areas, while in urban centers like Mumbai and Delhi, videos featuring young professionals endorsing Modi's economic reforms were shared (Hill, 2024).

Blurring the Line Between Authentic and Fabricated Content

The sophisticated use of AI in political campaigning raises concerns about the authenticity of political messaging. AI's ability to create hyper-realistic videos and audio makes it easier to spread misinformation or fabricate endorsements. During the 2024 election season, a deepfake video emerged featuring a fictional interview with a political figure allegedly endorsing a controversial policy. Created with AI, the video was widely shared, misleading voters into believing the individual supported the policy. This manipulation distorts political views and undermines trust in the electoral process, as voters struggle to distinguish between genuine endorsements and AI-fabricated ones (Shah, 2024). The widespread use of AI to fabricate content fuels misinformation, as personalized, emotionally charged messages easily sway voters, particularly in India, where digital literacy is low (Hill, 2024).

Instances of AI-manipulated Content in India

A concerning instance of deepfake technology in India's political campaigns involved AI-manipulated videos falsely depicting Bollywood celebrities endorsing political parties. Given Bollywood stars' influence on public opinion, these videos had a significant impact. In 2024, a viral deepfake video allegedly featured Amitabh Bachchan making pro-BJP statements he had never made. Though later flagged as fake, it misled many viewers, prompting legal action by Bachchan's team due to the serious harm caused (Sebastian, 2024).

Another high-profile case involved a deepfake of the late daughter of Prabhakaran, leader of the Tamil Tigers, falsely depicting her giving a speech in support of Tamil nationalist causes. This video was strategically circulated to stir emotions and influence voters in Tamil Nadu, leveraging the emotional connection to a martyr figure. While the video was quickly debunked, its initial spread had a lasting impact on the political climate, demonstrating how deepfakes can manipulate sensitive issues targeting voters' emotions (Sharma, 2024).

Deepfakes for Negative Campaigning and Reputation Damage

Deepfake technology, using AI to create hyper-realistic videos and audio, poses a significant threat in India's political landscape. As campaigns increasingly rely on digital media, deepfakes raise ethical, legal, and security concerns by enabling the fabrication of damaging content about political opponents. These AI-generated videos, often indistinguishable from reality, can manipulate voters, spread misinformation, and damage reputations, making it easier for political strategists to spread rumors or undermine credibility without direct accountability.

During the 2024 election in Telangana, a deepfake video circulated showing K.T. Rama Rao, leader of the Bharat Rashtra Samiti (BRS), seemingly endorsing the opposition Congress party, implying a betrayal of his party's principles. Though the video was later debunked, it misled many voters before the clarification, causing confusion and mistrust, and briefly sparking a political crisis for Rao and his party (TRT World, 2024). During the 2024 Delhi Assembly elections, deepfake videos emerged showing Congress leaders falsely endorsing controversial policies that contradicted their official stance. These AI-crafted videos made it appear as though the leaders were supporting BJP positions, creating confusion among voters (Sebastian, 2024).

Legal and Ethical Implications of Deepfake Content

The increasing use of deepfake technology in political campaigns raises serious legal and ethical concerns. In India, legal frameworks lag behind AI advancements, leaving gaps in protection against malicious use. Existing laws on defamation, false information, and digital impersonation were not designed to address deepfakes, leaving celebrities, politicians, and voters exposed to exploitation. In response to these challenges, Indian lawmakers are pushing for stricter deepfake regulations. Advocacy groups are calling for mandatory labeling of AI-generated election ads and harsher penalties for creating or distributing malicious deepfakes. Political parties are investing in digital forensics and AI tools to detect and counteract deepfakes (Sharma, 2024).

The Role of Social Media Platforms in Deepfake Regulation

Social media platforms play a key role in combating the spread of deepfakes during elections. The sheer volume of posts makes it challenging for platforms like Facebook, Twitter, and WhatsApp to regulate all content in real time. In 2024, WhatsApp became a major platform for political misinformation, with campaign teams using group chats to distribute AI-generated videos targeting specific voter demographics. Despite efforts to address misinformation, the private nature of encrypted messages complicates enforcement (Hill, 2024). The role of social media in spreading deepfakes underscores the need for comprehensive digital campaign regulation. While removing deepfake content after it's posted is one step, a more proactive approach involving collaboration between political parties, regulators, and tech companies is crucial (Shah, 2024).

Governmental and Regulatory Response

The Indian government has recognized the threat of AI-driven misinformation and taken proactive steps to address it. Prime Minister Modi has warned against AI misuse, while policies now require tech companies to seek approval before releasing generative AI tools. Collaborations with tech giants like Meta, including the Misinformation Combat Alliance, aim to detect and curb deepfake content. Additionally, WhatsApp has introduced multilingual helplines for users to report suspicious content (Rizve, 2024). Despite efforts, the widespread use of AI and rapid misinformation spread present significant challenges for regulatory frameworks. Critics argue that current voluntary measures are insufficient, especially considering India's linguistic diversity. AI-generated misinformation in regional languages often bypasses automated systems designed mainly to monitor English-language content (Sharma, 2024).

Ethical Boundaries and Industry Responsibility

In response to ethical concerns, companies like Avantari and Polymath have introduced guidelines and non-disclosure agreements (NDA) to prevent the misuse of deepfakes and synthetic media (Shah, 2024). These efforts aim to ensure responsible use of AI for positive campaigning. However, the growing commercialization of AI in politics, with platforms like The Indian Deepfaker offering affordable AI tools for campaign outreach underscores AI's increasing influence on Indian elections (Bastin, 2024).

The Impact on Democracy

AI's growing influence in India's elections raises ethical and democratic concerns. While AI can enhance voter engagement and break language barriers, it also invites manipulation and the spread of misinformation. Experts warn that low digital literacy in India heightens the risks, as AI-generated content often evokes emotional responses, making it hard for voters to distinguish between fact and fabrication. This undermines trust in political messages and media, eroding the integrity of the democratic process (Hill, 2024). India's use of AI in political campaigning highlights the urgent need for stricter regulatory frameworks to ensure transparency, fairness, and accountability. As AI reshapes the electoral landscape, India's regulatory approach could serve as a model for other democracies facing similar challenges.

AI Usage in the Pre-electoral Stage: The Bangladesh Context

The lead-up to Bangladesh's elections has witnessed an unprecedented surge in AI-driven disinformation campaigns, launched by both government-aligned actors and opposition affiliates. These campaigns involve AI-generated deepfakes, synthetic news reports, and other digital manipulations designed to influence public opinion. With the advent of accessible AI tools, the political landscape has shifted, enabling political parties to deploy technology in ways previously unseen. Below is a detailed exploration of how AI is shaping the pre-electoral stage in Bangladesh, highlighting both the technological advancements and the socio-political consequences.

Rise in AI-driven Disinformation and Political Propaganda

AI tools are being widely used to create misleading videos and narratives, with both the ruling Awami League and the opposition Bangladesh Nationalist Party (BNP) leveraging this technology for political propaganda. Supporters of both parties have reportedly employed AI-generated content to target opponents and influence public opinion. For example, affiliates have produced videos featuring AI-generated avatars, designed to resemble neutral news anchors, presenting anti-opposition narratives. These videos often deliver polarizing messages that align with government interests, indirectly promoting the ruling party by portraying the opposition as disruptive or foreign-aligned (Parkin, 2023; Rashid, 2024). One example of AI-driven disinformation involves a viral video featuring a synthetic news anchor accusing the United States of interfering in Bangladesh's electoral processes and implicating foreign powers in the country's internal politics. This narrative appeals to nationalist sentiments, positioning the ruling party as a defender of Bangladesh's sovereignty against perceived external threats. This manipulation illustrates how AI is used not only to target individuals but also to amplify themes that resonate with cultural or religious sensibilities, deepening divides and shaping voter attitudes (Parkin, 2023).

Cheap and Accessible AI Tools Fueling Disinformation

Advancements in AI video generators, such as HeyGen and D-ID, have significantly reduced the cost and technical barriers for creating high-quality deepfakes and synthetic videos. These tools enable users to produce realistic content that mimics human expressions, speech patterns, and even regional dialects, making it increasingly difficult for audiences to distinguish between fact and fiction. With just a few clicks, individuals can create content that manipulates political narratives on a large scale, whether by fabricating statements from opposition leaders or amplifying government-aligned messages. Despite HeyGen and D-ID's efforts to curb misuse by flagging users who violate ethical guidelines, the widespread accessibility of these tools continues to be exploited for political disinformation (Parkin, 2023).

Fact-checking and Monitoring Efforts: A Struggle to Keep Up

In response to the surge in AI-driven misinformation, Bangladeshi fact-checking organizations such as Rumor Scanner, FactWatch, and Dismislab have ramped up their monitoring efforts. These organizations have been actively debunking large volumes of disinformation, with Rumor Scanner alone identifying over 544 instances of misinformation between May and August 2024. A significant portion of these cases involved politically charged rumors, fake news, and AI-generated content, all specifically targeting the pre-election period (Rashid, 2024). However, these fact-checking organizations face an uphill battle in combating the flood of AI-driven disinformation.

Limited Detection and Oversight By Social Media Platforms

Political affiliates have called for intervention from social media platforms like Meta, but responses have been inconsistent. While Facebook has complied with some content removal requests, platforms like YouTube and Twitter have been less responsive. The absence of robust oversight mechanisms for non-English content further complicates matters, as Western-centric detection algorithms often fail to identify and flag disinformation in Bengali. This gap has allowed politically motivated deepfakes and AI-generated misinformation to spread largely unchecked, amplifying their impact during the pre-electoral phase (Parkin, 2023). Requests from opposition members to remove AI-generated content have often gone unaddressed, highlighting the difficulties of maintaining content integrity across diverse linguistic and cultural contexts.

Efforts to Regulate Social Media Content and the Cyber Security Act

In response to the proliferation of AI-driven disinformation, the Bangladeshi government has taken steps to engage social media platforms, particularly Facebook, in addressing misleading political content. Authorities have requested cooperation from these platforms to remove or flag harmful content and have even proposed establishing local offices to ensure compliance with Bangladesh's laws. While Facebook has partially responded to these requests, the government's efforts to regulate platforms like YouTube and Twitter have met with limited success (Rashid, 2024). Bangladesh's Cyber Security Act further complicates the regulatory landscape. While the law is ostensibly aimed at combating cybercrime, it has been criticized for selective enforcement. This selective enforcement not only creates an environment where government-aligned AI-driven disinformation can flourish but also stifles opposition narratives, undermining the democratic debate essential during the pre-election period (Parkin, 2023).

Political Exploitation of International Events and Misinformation Trends

In addition to AI-driven content, political actors have exploited international events to shape domestic public opinion. For example, rumors surrounding the US visa policy on Bangladesh and alleged visa sanctions against political figures have been widely spread on social media to influence voter perceptions. Such disinformation taps into concerns about foreign influence, positioning the ruling party as a defender of national sovereignty against perceived external interference. By linking local electoral issues to international events, political actors use these narratives to create favorable public perceptions or undermine the opposition's legitimacy (Rashid, 2024). The extensive use of AI-driven disinformation and strategic misinformation campaigns during Bangladesh's pre-election phase highlights both the potential and risks of AI in modern politics.

AI and Electoral Integrity in South Asia: During Election Day

This section explores AI's impact on public perception and digital manipulation, using examples from recent South Asian elections. From deepfakes to real-time AI deployments, the region's experience underscores complexities associated with AI's role in modern electoral processes.

AI as a Tool for Engagement and Disinformation

On election day, AI acted as both a political engagement tool and a means of disinformation, blurring the line between authentic outreach and manipulation. In Pakistan, PTI used AI-generated content to sustain its presence after Imran Khan's detention. On election day, a viral AI-generated video simulated Khan's voice, thanking voters and urging them to protect PTI's declared victory. Despite a disclaimer about its AI origin, it deepened political divides, especially with Nawaz Sharif's party, further heightening tensions (Zhuang, 2024).

AI-driven Disinformation in Pakistan

During Pakistan's elections, deepfake technology spread disinformation, falsely announcing candidate withdrawals and misrepresenting leaders like Imran Khan, Rehana Dar, and Basharat Raja. These widely circulated videos caused confusion, prompting public denials. The challenge worsened with mobile network suspensions in certain regions due to security concerns, limiting journalists and independent election observers from countering disinformation. This highlighted how AI-driven disinformation thrives in restricted media environments (Wee, 2024). Salahudin Safdar of the Free and Fair Election Network (FAFEN) stressed the urgent need to address digital manipulation to uphold electoral integrity (Mughal, 2024).

AI-driven Disinformation in Bangladesh

AI-generated disinformation also targeted Bangladeshi independent candidate Nahid Niger in Gaibandha-1. A deepfake video falsely claimed she had withdrawn in favor of a Jatiya Party candidate. The video, seemingly from Niger's own account, mimicked her voice and likeness with disturbing accuracy. However, media verification platform Dismislab identified discrepancies like unnatural lip-syncing and odd vocal quality, exposing its AI origins. Niger's team swiftly debunked the video, mitigating some damage. The incident underscored how AI-driven disinformation can mislead, especially when real-time verification tools are unavailable (Tech & Startup Desk, 2024). To combat AI-driven disinformation, several organizations in South Asia developed countermeasures. In Pakistan, Media Matters for Democracy launched pre-bunking tools like "Factor" to help journalists debunk AI-generated falsehoods early. This large-scale disinformation campaign raised serious concerns about the fairness and transparency of elections (Chaudhary, 2024). Combined with the unchecked spread of AI-generated content, these measures ultimately undermined the credibility of the election and its results (Wee, 2024).

Real-time AI Deployment to Influence Voting Behavior

A notable example occurred during Telangana's legislative elections on November 30, when a deepfake video of K.T. Rama Rao, leader of the BRS, was circulated as voters headed to polling stations. The video, created and distributed by Congress supporters, falsely depicted Rao endorsing the Congress party and urging voters to support the opposition (Sharma, 2024). The video's release was highly strategic, circulated just before voters entered the polls creating immediate disruption. The deepfake appeared authentic, showing Rao speaking directly to voters and seemingly endorsing Congress – a significant betrayal of his own party's position. This illustrates how AI can be weaponized to influence voters and their decisions at a critical moment. The rapid spread of the AI-generated deepfake on social media and messaging apps like WhatsApp amplified its reach, allowing it to go viral within hours (TRT World, 2024). As AI technologies advance, political parties' ability to influence voters through real-time content distribution will grow, complicating efforts to ensure a fair and transparent electoral process (Sharma, 2024).

Immediate Impact of AI-generated Content on Voting Behavior

The Congress party's deepfake video of K.T. Rama Rao, which went viral on election day had an immediate impact on voter behavior. The video's timing and its realistic portrayal created confusion at a critical moment. Its viral spread on social media and messaging platforms sparked misinformation, clouding Rao's political stance, undermining his party's credibility, and sowing doubt about his loyalty (TRT World, 2024). AI-generated content's real-time spread disrupts elections, especially in final voting hours. By releasing the video at this critical moment, the Congress party manipulated voter perceptions without allowing the opposition time to refute it. The AI-generated deepfake introduced a new form of electoral interference – faster, more widespread, and harder to detect than traditional disinformation tactics. These incidents highlight the vulnerabilities AI technologies bring to modern elections.

Post-election Phase: Limited AI Usage in South Asia

In South Asia, the use of AI in the post-election phase remains limited. While AI technologies are increasingly employed for campaign strategies and voter engagement before and during elections, instances of post-election AI usage have been few, with Pakistan standing out as a notable example. These rare cases provide a glimpse into how AI might be leveraged to shape public perception in the aftermath of elections. Following Pakistan's 2024 general elections, the PTI party utilized AI to craft a victory message from its leader, Imran Khan. Despite his imprisonment and ongoing political restrictions, Khan's AI-generated voice was used to declare victory, thank supporters for their turnout, and urge them to uphold the legitimacy of the election result. This AI-generated post-election narrative helped strengthen PTI's base and project an image of success, despite ongoing contestations over the election's fairness (Shahzad & Shahid, 2024; Zhuang, 2024).

PTI's use of AI post-election shows how political actors can shape narratives and public sentiment after an election. While AI's role in South Asia's post-election context remains relatively limited, this instance in Pakistan highlights its potential to influence perceptions and mobilize support. It signals a trend that could become more prominent in future electoral cycles across the region, with political parties increasingly turning to AI to manage their post-election messaging and maintain public engagement.

Table 13.1 gives a sketch on the comparisons on AI's role in electoral processes across Pakistan, Bangladesh, and India. It shows how AI has been used in the election processes of the three leading countries in South Asia in the heads like voters' engagement, electoral integrity, voters' misinformation, etc., where in most cases the politicians have used AI to make pretexting with the common people.

Conclusion

The role of AI in electoral processes across South Asia has highlighted both its transformative potential and the inherent risks associated with its use. Experiences from Pakistan, Bangladesh, and India, across various stages of the electoral cycle-pre-election, election day, and post-election demonstrate how AI can enhance political engagement while simultaneously serving as a tool for disinformation, undermining democratic processes. These insights underscore the urgent need for comprehensive frameworks to manage AI's influence, ensuring it strengthens rather than jeopardizes electoral integrity and contributes positively to democratic practices.

Looking ahead, the growing influence of AI in South Asian elections necessitates a focus on several critical areas such as improving regulatory frameworks, promoting digital literacy and public awareness, international collaboration, etc. Experiences from Pakistan, Bangladesh, and India highlight the urgent need for stronger regulations, enhanced public awareness, and real-time countermeasures to protect elections in the digital age. By addressing these challenges, South Asia can harness the benefits of AI while safeguarding its democratic processes from manipulation and disinformation.

Table 13.1. Comparative Analysis of AI's Role in Electoral Processes Across Pakistan, Bangladesh, and India.

Theme	Pakistan	Bangladesh	India
Voter engagement	• AI tools generated content to sustain visibility during political turmoil.	• Political outreach relied on propaganda-driven campaigns rather than meaningful voter connection.	• Advanced data analytics and AI tailored outreach strategies to demographic groups.
	• PTI relied on personalized messaging to mobilize supporters effectively.	• Efforts lacked strategic AI application for engagement.	• Campaigns used AI for structured and efficient voter targeting.
Issue framing	• Digital tools were used to shape political discourse and narratives.	• Framing centered on disinformation campaigns targeting specific candidates like Nahid Niger.	• Campaign strategies used AI to refine issue-based messaging.
	• Campaign content showcased AI's dual potential to mobilize and manipulate.	• Genuine issue framing was largely overshadowed by negative propaganda.	• Risk of biased narratives influencing public opinion was significant.
Disinformation	• Deepfake videos, including fabricated messages from Imran Khan, spread rapidly, challenging fact-checkers.	• AI-generated deepfakes targeted opposition candidates, spreading smear campaigns that eroded trust.	• Misleading deepfakes like K.T. Rama Rao endorsing rivals disrupted election-day behavior.
	• AI amplified misinformation's reach across platforms.	• Slow response to false content aggravated the problem.	• Social media accelerated the spread of AI-driven disinformation.
Electoral integrity	• Misinformation created by AI undermined trust in the election process.	• Deepfake videos falsely announcing candidate withdrawals created confusion.	• Electoral transparency was at risk due to last-minute AI-generated misinformation.
	• Ensuring fairness became increasingly complex with the use of deceptive tools.	• Lack of real-time fact-checking mechanisms threatened process credibility.	• Highlighted vulnerabilities in regulating digital manipulation.
Post-election use	• AI-generated victory speeches energized PTI's support base and projected narratives favoring their position.	• Limited post-election use but hints of employing AI for narrative control emerged.	• AI tools were minimally utilized post-election.
	• Demonstrated potential to shape public sentiment in contested outcomes.	• Propaganda played a larger role than AI-driven initiatives.	• Untapped potential to reinforce transparency and manage narratives effectively.

Source: Authors.

Declaration of Generative AI Use

During the preparation of this chapter, the authors used ChatGPT (OpenAI) solely to improve readability and correct grammar. No generative AI tools were used in the research design, data collection, analysis, or interpretation. The authors reviewed and edited the content independently and take full responsibility for the final version of the manuscript.

References

Bastin, C. (2024, May 9). *Elections transform India into world's largest voting playground for AI*. La Croix International. https://international.la-croix.com/world/elections-transform-india-into-worlds-largest-voting-playground-for-ai

Chaudhary, S. (2024, April 17). *From manipulation to the ballot box: The age of AI in Pakistan's elections*. Media Diversity Institute. https://www.media-diversity.org/from-manipulation-to-the-ballot-box-the-age-of-ai-in-pakistans-elections/

Commonwealth Parliamentary Association. (2024). *The Parliamentarian: Journal of the Parliaments of the Commonwealth, 105*(1). https://www.cpahq.org/media/pcwkpcea/parl2024iss1finalonlinesinglereduced.pdf

Cupać, J., Schopmans, H., & Tuncer-Ebetürk, İ. (2024). Democratization in the age of artificial intelligence: Introduction to the special issue. *Democratization, 31*(5), 899–921. https://doi.org/10.1080/13510347.2024.2338852

Deepak, P., Simoes, S., & MacCarthaigh, M. (2023). AI and core electoral processes: Mapping the horizons. *AI Magazine, 44*(3), 218–239. https://doi.org/10.1002/aaai.12105

Hill, S. (2024, May 3). India: The biggest elections in human history using risky AI tools. *The Globalist*. https://www.theglobalist.com/india-elections-democracy-artificial-intelligence/

International IDEA. (2024). *Artificial intelligence for electoral management*. https://www.idea.int/publications/catalogue/artificial-intelligence-electoral-management

Iqbal, A., & Mushtaq, S. (2024, March 29). *AI's impact on South Asian elections*. Research Society of International Law (RSIL). https://rsilpak.org/2024/ais-impact-on-south-asian-elections-technological-innovation-voter-rights-and-regulatory-frameworks/

Mohydin, R. (2024, February 1). *Enter AI: Shaping Pakistan 2024 elections and beyond*. Middle East Monitor. https://www.middleeastmonitor.com/20240201-enter-ai-shaping-pakistan-2024-elections-and-beyond/

Mughal, N. (2024, February 22). *Deepfakes, internet access cuts make election coverage hard, journalists say*. Voice of America. https://www.voanews.com/a/deepfakes-internet-access-cuts-make-election-coverage-hard-journalists-say-/7498917.html

Parkin, B. (2023, December 14). Deepfakes for $24 a month: How AI is disrupting Bangladesh's election. *Financial Times*. https://www.ft.com/content/bd1bc5b4-f540-48f8-9cda-75c19e5ac69c

Rashid, M. (2024, November 8). *Disinformation on rise ahead of polls*. https://www.newagebd.net/article/214378/disinformation-on-rise-ahead-of-polls

Rizve, S. (2024). AI and India's general elections. *The Diplomat*. https://thediplomat.com/2024/04/ai-and-indias-general-elections/

Safiullah, M., & Parveen, N. (2022). S.K. Panda, R.K. Mohapatra, S. Panda and S. Balamurugan (Eds.). Big data, artificial intelligence and machine learning: A paradigm shift in election campaigns. In *The New Advanced Society*. https://doi.org/10.1002/9781119884392.ch11 (pp. 247–261). John Wiley & Sons, Ltd. https://doi.org/10.1002/9781119884392.ch11

Sebastian, M. (2024, May 16). AI and deepfakes blur reality in India elections. *BBC News*. https://www.bbc.com/news/world-asia-india-68918330

Shah, F. (2024, April 30). *AI companies are making millions producing election content in India*. Rest of World. https://restofworld.org/2024/india-elections-ai-content/

Shahzad, A., & Shahid, A. (2024, February 6). *How Imran Khan is campaigning from jail in Pakistan: AI and covert canvassing*. Reuters. https://www.reuters.com/world/asia-pacific/how-imran-khan-is-campaigning-jail-pakistan-ai-covert-canvassing-2024-02-05

Sharma, Y. (2024). *Deepfake democracy: Behind the AI trickery shaping India's 2024 election*. Al Jazeera. https://www.aljazeera.com/news/2024/2/20/deepfake-democracy-behind-the-ai-trickery-shaping-indias-2024-elections

Tech & Startup Desk. (2024). Deepfake video targeting Gaibandha-1 candidate surfaces on Facebook. The Daily Star. https://www.thedailystar.net/tech-startup/news/deepfake-video-targeting-gaibandha-1-candidate-surfaces-facebook-351375

TRT World. (2024). *How disinformation, fake news, and AI threatens India's electoral process*. https://www.trtworld.com/magazine/how-disinformation-fake-news-and-ai-threatens-indias-electoral-process-17837049

Wee, O. (2024, February 9). *Pakistan's electoral laboratory shows the drawbacks and incentives of AI technology for politics*. Voice of America. https://www.voanews.com/a/7481049.html

Younus, U. (2024, February 14). *Five ways Imran Khan's party used technology to outperform in Pakistan's elections*. Atlantic Council. https://www.atlanticcouncil.org/blogs/new-atlanticist/five-ways-imran-khans-party-used-technology-to-outperform-in-pakistans-elections/

Zhuang, Y. (2024, February 11). Imran Khan's 'victory speech' from jail shows A.I.'s peril and promise. *The New York Times*. https://www.nytimes.com/2024/02/11/world/asia/imran-khan-artificial-intelligence-pakistan.html

Chapter 14

Impact of Artificial Intelligence on Human Rights: A Theoretical Analysis

Eyasin Khan[a] *and Joydev Barman*[b]

[a]*Department of Political Science, Vidyasagar University, India*
[b]*Department of Political Science, Khejuri College, India*

Abstract

Human security is the first concern among all in human life. The society and other institutions are formed to keep human life secure. An individual can't think oneself secure until he or she gets rights appropriately. Only a secure individual can be conscious to protect his or her rights and duties. As the concept of rights is generated by human beings themselves, at the same time it might be on the hook by various human activities. Inventing artificial intelligence (AI) is one of them. It may be profitable for some fields of works but not in each. This chapter focuses on the AI and human rights nexus. How AI may be the antagonist of humans? And how AI may devastate human life by ruining rights will be the main concern. Simultaneously, the question of the future identity of a human class called labor or farmer and the various righteous aspects of living a normal life with an unconscious machine within a single society will be discussed. The ideas of the post-human world and bio-politics in the realm of "human rights in post-human world" will also be examined briefly. The findings of this study basically focus on human rights-based approach (HRBA) which was passed by the United Nations Organization (UNO) for the safeguarding of commoner's rights and sustainable development of the human race in the age of AI. No need to say that the HRBA uses AI and scientific development for the positive development of mankind.

Keywords: Human rights; artificial intelligence; post-human; bio-politics; political rights; social security; Human Rights-Based Approach; United Nations Organization

Artificial Intelligence in Business and Society: Global Insights, 215–228

Published under exclusive licence by Emerald Publishing Limited
doi:10.1108/978-1-83708-022-920261034

Introduction

The concept of "human rights" is probably the most burning concept since last century. History of it is written with the blood of human and other beings. Two most terrible world wars took place at that time. Greed of power, money and authority chased the political leaders to do so. Though the peace-making process was adopted universally after the end of the First World War, the emergence of Nazism and failure of the League of Nations prepared the battle ground for a new devastating mentality. The most dreadful war taken place as the Second World War is the unavoidable consequence of it. Between 1939 and 1945, the human society was divided into two parts. First, those who liked war and participated in it. Second, those who did not like war and raised their voice against it. The world people are the witness of these two different streams at a time with two different directions. Whatever it is, the bloody thirst stopped in 1945, and by the pressure of world's peace-seeking communities, the leaders assembled at Paris and signed a treaty for peaceful warless future. UNO was formed to control the situation. After that, Eleanor Roosevelt, who led the United Nations (UN) Human Rights Commission, started to write a draft proposal on human rights. It took almost two and half years to complete the final draft, and ultimately on December 10, 1948, the UN General Assembly acknowledged it. Forty-eight states supported this proposal, but states like Union of Soviet Socialist Republics (USSR), South Africa, Saudi Arab and other many socialist blocs abstained it due to inadequacy in provisions for social and economic rights (Ghosal, 2010). However, it is the first universally valid document to us on human rights. Again in 1966, UNO adopted two additional covenants, International Covenant on Civil and Political Rights (ICCPR) and International Covenant on Economic, Social and Cultural Rights (ICESCR), to deal with violation of universal declaration and protect citizens' rights.

On December 10, 1997, at University of Tehran, former Secretary-General of the UN Kofi A. Annan said, "Human Rights are foreign to no culture and native to all nations: they are Universal" (Anadolu Agency/Serap Aydin et al., 2016). Human rights are universal because everyone, in respect of race, caste, sex, color, social origin or ethnicity, nationality, disability, may claim it. Inalienability is another principle of human rights. It is directly related with human existence. If any state disagrees with few people to provide political rights, it may hamper their common lifestyle but not living. If the state declines to provide human rights, it may put their lives into danger. So, human rights are not an additional part of human life but a fundamental part. Any kind of attack on human rights actually shows the aggression on human existence. Indivisibility and interdependency are also important principles of human rights, because one may not enjoy his or her own human rights divisibly from another. All of them are too much dependent on one another. For example, denial of rights to food may hamper a healthy life, so the right to life is related to the right to food.

If we compare human rights with political rights, it will be clear, how much human rights are important to us? Political rights are related to political organizations like states. It differs from state to state. But human right is a global concept.

It is homogeneous in nature. It does not have any boundary. The political boundary may affect political rights but not human rights. Each political organization or state has its own political ideology. Ideologically, they are too much different from each other. Some states are democratic in nature, while others are socialists or communists, and some of them believe in authoritarianism. In this situation, if we compare the given political rights among the citizens of those states, the heterogeneity will be uncovered. But in case of human rights, a commonality is present everywhere. Getting or claiming human rights itself is human rights for any person from any part of the world. Though, there is a debate based on the universalism and cultural relativism of human rights. This debate basically promoted the global and local ethics and values concerning human rights. The discourse agreed on the universal nature of human rights, and again, it accepted the local demands of the people to fulfill their desire and needs. Due to the cultural variations and the differences related to state performances throughout the world, the human rights thinkers welcome the indigenous norms and customs without compromising the universal notion of the right to life. In the name of cultural relativism, the human rights thinkers and activists accepted the national and regional rules prevailing in different parts of the world. So, the idea of human rights can rightly be explained by its evolution in respect of legal and philosophical grounds.

Another important issue is to be addressed in the context of the relationship between human rights and AI. The notion of AI emerged very recently in the realm of post-human understanding of the world. Baxi (2007) rightly said,

> If the post-human is at one moment a vision of techno-science-drives and accelerated programme towards the realization of the anticipated future, it at the same moment already exits. Thus when Michel Foucault proclaimed that "[m]an is an invention of recent date" and "one perhaps nearing its end," he did not have as clear an engagement with what Lyotard named as the inhuman; nor did he have in view Donna Haraways' enunciation that by "the late twentieth century… we are all chimeras, theorized and fabricated hybrids of machine and organism; in short we are cyborgs."[1]

The Legal and Philosophical Attempts to Rights

The struggle for ensuring rights in both the philosophical and legal world had started many years back. Legally, the first attempt was made by feudal lords of England against King's supremacy in 1215 through "Magna Carta." But one thing we should keep in our mind is that this attempt was not universal in nature. The feudal class was not interested in other people's rights. Whatever, it was the first voice of some people for rights. From this perspective, we may accept the Magna Carta as the most valuable historical document to us. After Magna Carta, more

---

[1]A fictional or hypothetical person whose physical abilities are extended beyond normal human limitations by mechanical elements built into the body.

than 400 years have passed. In 1628, the emerging bourgeois class of England raised their voice against the king's arbitrary power of taxation. The emerging bourgeois class unitedly submitted a "Petition of Rights" to the king Charles the First. According to this petition, the king can't order anybody to pay tax time and again and can't arrest anybody according to his wish. Historically, this is the second international attempt to human rights. The third attempt was taken through "Bills of Rights" in 1689 in England. It was aimed to establish sovereignty of common people or parliament instead of the king. This attempt is more valuable than the priors due to its expansion. Traditionally, this is the first attempt where the matter of rights of common people, not a few bourgeois or feudal lords, came into broad daylight. "The Virginian Declaration of Rights" of 1776 is, in the past, another important attempt taken by Americans to secure the rights of common people of America and the American Constitution. Like the "Bill of Rights," it was also an attempt for common people as a whole, not for a section. After the "Virginian Declaration of Rights," an attempt for the constitutional amendment in America called the "American Bill of Rights" was made in 1791 to add fundamental rights of common people to constitution. Not only in America or England but also in many other countries of Europe, various attempts were made to establish common people's rights. In 1789, the French government published the "Declaration of Rights of Man and Citizen"; in 1917 the Russian government and in 1919 the German government adopted their constitution to secure rights of common people (Brown, 2008, p. 610).

Philosophically, the study on rights is older than any legal attempt. At first, we should look into the stoic philosophy of Rome. The stoic philosophers believed that the world is an ordered whole, and we (humans) are a part of it. As we (humans) are the part of the same whole, we are holding the same goal. We can't form or deform the universe. Somebody who is omnipotent, has created this ordered whole. This is why we should not do whatever we want to do. We should follow the will of nature or the supreme creator. And the will of the supreme creator is reflected through the holistic activities of people. Stoic philosophers also believe that every human being entails the same wisdom as others, and in respect of caste, religion or anything else, everybody is a part of that whole. So, a just and humanitarian attitude to everybody is our fundamental duty. The great Greek philosopher Aristotle also expressed his opinion on the rights of people. He believed that the duty of a state is to rule the dwellers for their betterments. It This aspect of state governance is connected with the matter of granting rights to the citizens of the state. Though Aristotle did not believe that everybody should get equal rights due to his or her unequal power or ability, he never declined the importance of rights. According to John Locke's theory of natural rights, every human being has some rights, which are pre-political and unalienable. In the state of nature, all were free and could lead their lives according to their minds. In respect of sex and gender, they enjoyed their rights equally. Primarily, the state of nature was calm and peaceful, but friction comes out with the questions of consumptions. In this situation, the member of state of nature went through a treaty and established a political authority called state to control the situation. According to this treaty, states have to take the duty of protecting natural rights of the people. If a state's inability is proven, then it can be destroyed (Locke, 1960). So, it is very clear that the base of today's human rights is buried into the idea of natural rights. "Ground work for the Metaphysics of Morals" is another fundamental writing on rights. In his precious book, the philosopher Immanuel Kant depicted the actual nature of human beings. According to him, a human being is supreme not for his shape but intelligence. This intelligence makes a human being ethical. As human beings are ethical, they have to follow some ethical imperatives. He said, "act in such a way that you always treat humanity, whether in your own person or in the person of any other, never simply as a means, but always at the same time as an end" (Kant, 1785/1993, p. 30). One should not discard the human dignity of others. This message of Kant is still important in the study of human rights. In the 19th century, J. S. Mill became the pioneer of individual freedom and rights by his philosophical thinking. According to his philosophy, securing the greatest happiness of the greatest number is only possible where an adequate amount of individual freedom is provided. He never supported the interference of the state on individual freedom. Not only this but also he accepted the importance of law to protect it. For the state, he advised, if an individual follows each condition of being good citizen and pays respect to laws of state, then it's the state's duty to protect the individual's rights. John Rawls is the most proficient among them who took philosophical attempts to analyze rights in the 20th century. In his famous work *A Theory of Justice*, Rawls said that appropriate distribution of rights among the citizens is only way to establish a just society. He bestows this duty on the state. According to him, at first, the state has to secure "equal basic liberty for all" and then "equal opportunity for all" (Rawls, 1999).

The humanitarian and international standard setting of the 19th and 20th centuries brought these issues to the fore. The Congress of Vienna of 1815 saw the great powers to accept an obligation to end the slave trade, which was finally abolished by the Brussels Convention of 1890, while slavery itself was formally outlawed by the Slavery Convention of 1926. The Hague Conventions of 1907 and the Geneva Conventions of 1926 were designed to introduce humanitarian considerations into the conduct of war. The International Labor Office, formed in 1901, and its successor the International Labor Organization attempted to set standards in the workplace via measures such as the Convention Concerning Forced or Compulsory Labor of 1930 (Brown, 2008, p. 512).

The evolving root of the contemporary conception of human rights can be traced to the period of "Renaissance and Enlightenment." The first half of the 20th century was marked not only by the prevalence of colonial rule in the large part of the world but also for the rise of authoritarian governments and the establishment of the fascist and aggressive regimes in many countries of the world. Also, this period witnessed the rise of the national liberation movements and movements for the democracy in different parts of the world. The 20th century also experienced the most devastating two world wars. The period between two world wars has been described as the "age of catastrophe" (Azis, 2011, p. X). Very recently, the emergence of the ideas of post-human and trans-humanism challenges the basic notion of human rights. AI also challenges the traditional notion of human rights.

Post-humanism/Trans-humanism

Post-humanism is a philosophical framework, a way of thinking that questioned the supremacy of human beings. It is mostly a counter argumentative philosophical position against humanism. Humanism is all about the superiority of human beings, where post-humanism deals with the relations of human beings with the existence. The post-human philosophers believed that we are living with wrong concepts. We usually think that we are superior to any other being of this world. We disagree on equal ability and rights. Human beings used to think differently from others (beasts). As a result, we don't feel bad when we kill or destroy them. We never accept that animal and we are the same; when the reality is that we evolved as humans from none other than animals. We want to forget our real past to exploit other beings. Post-humanism suggests that we are essentially animals; we should stop thinking that we are superior to others, but we should accept that we are just a part of this ordered universe. With the humanistic approach, we changed our mind. We reshaped our world. With our intelligence, we innovated many things. We are always busy to find the answers to mysteries. We called our logical enquiry as science. Post-humanism is not antiscientific or antidevelopment, but it opposes destruction. In the name of and by science, we are doing a lot. We are flying, digging or treating our diseases. Utilization of science for these positive actions is good, but science is not only positive. Like a coin, it has two sides – one is good; another is bad. To fulfill our greed, we often use science in a bad manner. This practice is endangering our human lives and rights. Post-humanism helps us to realize it (Mellamphy, 2021).

Trans-humanism is the transformation of human ability through scientific development. The biological process or biological boundaries of human life can be crossed by trans-human activities. For example, we may say about the genetically modifying process of any biological entity, test tube baby, artificial heart press machine, etc. Not being ill or staying always fit is a matter of trans-human concern. Different kinds of modern drugs or treatment processes are also a part of trans-humanism. Trans-humanism is that process which helps human beings to cross human limitations of past times. Day by day, these trans-human activities are increasing. Humans are going to be dependent on machine or artificial labor and intelligence. Which may strongly hit human rights concepts and really emerge as a challenge of human rights?

Threats to Human Rights

The effects of trans-humanism on human rights are understood so lately. In Universal Declaration of Human Rights (UDHR) documents, the draftsman has only emphasized the benefits of scientific advancements. Article 27(1) states that, "everyone has the right to freely participate in the cultural life of the community, to enjoy the arts and to share scientific advancement and its benefits" (UN, 1948). Even in 1966 when the International Covenant on Economic, Social and Cultural Rights (ICESCR) was adopted, its (science) dangers were out of their consideration. Article 15(b) of this covenant recognized "to enjoy the benefits of scientific progress and its application" (United Nations (General Assembly), 1966). On May 13, 1968, the 27th plenary meeting of the United Nations High Commissioner for Refugees (UNHCR), held at Tehran, is generally known as 1968 protocol or Tehran Conference. In this conference, it was proclaimed that "while recent scientific discoveries and technological advances have opened vast prospects for economic, social and cultural progress, such development may nevertheless endanger the rights and freedom of individual and will require continuing attention" (A/CONF.32/41).

But scientific advancements have two sides, one is for betterment of human civilization and another is for destruction. Science is only a means not an end. If we wish to use it for our bright future, it will help us; simultaneously, if we use it to ruin our lives, it will also help us to do so. Sometimes unconscious use of scientific tools kick us into danger. Since the Renaissance, today science and use of scientific tools are escalating day by day. Scientists or inventors are continuously working on it. To make our life easier and happier, we used to take help from science. In this situation, we often forget that it is ruining our lives slowly. Generally, as long as it is not happening to me, I can't understand its dangerous effects. I don't realize how bad science can be for us until I experience some of its harmful effects. Some instances of human rights, which are affected by scientific advancement, are as follows:

Human Freedom

Freedom is one of those human rights, which is related to human existence. History says that freedom does not come freely, there is bloody history behind it. Living a blissful life without freedom is just impossible. This precious right is now in danger due to scientific advancement. Technologies like visual surveillances, personality test, lie-detector, narco-analysis, blood, breath and other non-medical bodily tests are destroying human freedom. By using technology, the government or any other technically expert organization can surveil us. Smartphones or computers have become a part of our life. We used to carry it with us. Anybody can be traced or their movement can be recorded easily through it. Lie-detector and narco-analysis is a process where people are used to hypnotize and bound to tell the expected answer so that somebody can be accused of as being criminal. Even people's thoughts can be influenced by using modern technology. People's freedom of choice is gradually shrinking. Indirectly through technology, we are getting used to thinking the way capitalist society thinks of us. Almost all social media and search engines now have AI systems. If we search for something for a relevant reason on a search engine, a lot of related content comes to our social media accounts that manipulate our mind.

Right to Life

Right to life is the most undeniable human rights. Nothing is more precious compared to it. This is why every democratic nation places the right to life as a fundamental right within their constitution for their citizens. It can never be violated.

But the scientific advancement in the post-human and trans-human eras opened it up. Scientific advancement like prenatal diagnostic procedure helps to identify the sex of embryos which obsess the gender concept. Advanced technology such as fetal sex determination that uses AI is increasing gender inequality in society.

Although gender determination has been officially declared illegal in almost all countries, embryos are destroyed through illegal sex determination and illegal abortion in remote areas where the authorities do not pay attention. Side by side, biochemical denigration, psychotropic drugs, deterioration of environment by modern weaponry and atomic radiation are directly threatening the right to life. Although this type of problem is worldwide, it is most prominent in Europe and the Middle-East. For example, in Europe, we may say about the Russia–Ukraine war since 2014, where thousands of soldiers and civilians died. Different kinds of modern machinery have been used for political gain. Here is the number of civilian casualties in Ukraine during Russia's invasion verified by Office of the United Nations High Commissioner for Human Rights (OHCHR) from February 24, 2022, to July 31, 2024 (Table 14.1). It is seen that a large number of civilians are killed and injured out of which children cover 5.5%–6.5%.

In the Middle-East, the problem of Iran and Israel is another example. This war also saw the use of highly modern equipment. Thousands of people have lost their right to live because of this war. The effects of nuclear bombs or nuclear weapons created by modern technology are not only present in the contemporary period but also long term. Future generations are likely to be severely harmed by the radiation from nuclear weapons. Radiation poisoning can range from fetal death to birth defects. Effects of American bombing in Japan during the Second World War and the physical consequences for the people of warring states in contemporary times are now very clear.

Right to Labor/Work

Both the 1948 UDHR and 1966 covenant asserted the right to work or labor as a precious human right for human progress. Our present civilization is the result of our labor or work of our forefathers. Doing a job or labor according to one's self-ability is his or her right. But if the means of production changed into automation or mechanization, then the labor has nothing to do. The competition of today's world is not man vs man but man vs machine. In this desperate competition, men are always behind the machine due to productive capabilities. In every

Table 14.1. Civilian Casualties in Ukraine.

Characteristics	Total Number	Of Them Children	Percentage of Children
Killed	11,520	633	5.50
Injured	23,640	1,551	6.56

Source: Compiled by the authors using the database, https://www.statista.com/aboutus/our-research-commitment.

sphere of work, the market use of machine is a very normal matter today. Though it is right that machines can't work without the command of a programmer or creator, man also needs them, but the problem is everybody does not have programming or commanding skill. Only the new generation has been able to do it. The old generation engaged in any work seems too redundant. In this situation, the right to work faces a direct threat. Apart from the industrialized countries of Europe, agriculture is the main livelihood of the people of Asia and Africa and the rest of the agricultural countries of the world. People lead their livelihood through agriculture and participation in agriculture-related activities. Due to the huge improvement in modern technology, the use of machinery in the agricultural sector has also increased tremendously so that now a single machine is eliminating the employment of many people. This use of machinery in almost all areas from agriculture to employment is giving rise to extreme capitalist states, where the less educated and poor people of the society are almost denied. The nature of work will change as the use of machinery becomes more noticeable in remote villages and agricultural areas. Rural people will be forced to move to cities due to unemployment in rural areas. But very commonly, these uneducated or less skilled people in the village cannot compete with the people in the city in the field of urban sophistication. In this situation, on the one hand, the urban workers will compete with the rural workers, and on the other hand, the rural workers will have to sell their labor for very little money. It is the right of every human being to get proper wages for proper work, but in such circumstances, people are not getting proper wages even for proper work. As the use of advanced technology in the field of work continues to increase, the variety of work or different fields of work will be narrowed and concentrated. Gradually, the digital divide will increase among people. Digitally advanced people will go a long way in producing and processing agricultural products at a much lower cost by participating in agriculture with modern machinery; on the other hand, the cost of production will be high due to the old method of farming and the selling price will be high due to the high cost of production. All products produced in the old way will almost cease to be sold, and farmers in this unequal competition will naturally lag behind, and their employment will be blocked.

Right to Social Security

Human can't live alone, society is compulsory. To spend a happy life, social security like remuneration, housing, clothing, leisure, food, etc. is needed. The trans-humanism is badly affecting all of these. Foods are essential to life, but due to a superfluous population, various kinds of medicines and chemicals are used to produce and preserve food. Not only this but different kinds of artificial foods are also available in today's market, which are heavily health hazardous, but advanced technology presents food in front of us in such a way that people are attracted by and eat such foods. Nowadays, AI has been integrated with various types of human activities such as bank transactions or money transactions, from e-mail to automated calls, to various types of customer care services, and in all these cases, the customer has to rely on AI. The information provided by the customer is sometimes influenced by malicious people and harms the common people. Problems ranging from the hacking of a person's personal email to the theft of large sums of money from personal accounts or the transfer of money from one place to another are also common. Also by stealing personal information and exploiting that information in many cases, a ransom or huge amount of money is demanded and if the ransom is not paid, death is threatened, and at the same time, people are made to suffer by making videos through various types of editing. Such manipulation of personal information of a person is only possible with modern technology, and it is being used for negative purposes making the social life of the person increasingly uncomfortable and insecure. By using AI, a person is not only harmed, but also sometimes the entire country is also harmed. Foreign conspirators or secret information providers want to steal a country's secret information, mainly military department information, through modern equipment and technology.

De-humanization

AI has been created exactly like humans through advanced technology, which can do almost all human tasks but cannot act with human-like consciousness or feelings. If the various important tasks of the society that are done by humans are completed with AI, then maybe the work will be done, but it will not be possible to do the work with feelings. In order to sustain the society and human existence, all kinds of functions of the society have to be managed, like if someone does wrong, then he has to be punished, and if someone does well, he has to be rewarded. And if all these important functions are done instead of people, if it is done by AI, then maybe punishment or reward will be possible, but punishment alone is not enough to sustain human existence; punishment must be meted out with proper logic and emotion. A major problem with AI is this lack of emotion. Again, if we talk about the education system or the medical system for example, then in both the fields, it is not possible to teach only with knowledge or to treat only with knowledge. Using AI, it may be possible to provide a large amount of knowledge simultaneously in one place through a single device. But there is a big difference between just presenting theory and teaching, and there is also a big difference between just presenting facts and treating. Teaching according to the needs of the student being taught and understanding the mental state of the student is not the job of a mechanist. Similarly, mapping the mental state of the sick person or the mental state of his family and all his physical condition is not so easy. It is not possible with any machine to observe the condition and cure him properly; it is possible only with man's love for man, man's kindness, man's sympathy and special conscious feeling of man for man. A procedure operated by robotic science has been introduced in contemporary times, but there are doubts as to how successful and suitable it will be for humans. Since the machine does not understand human feelings, the machine will only listen to the people who create it, or it may be that the machine may not listen to the people who create it due to its mechanical interference, or it may be that instead of improving the society as a whole, the machine itself will destroy the society. So, the decision to leave the future of the society or the country to AI or to manage the society or the country with it can be even extremely harmful to us. Today, almost every country in the world is at war with each other, moving away from liberal thinking and being guided by realism. In order to maintain their influence and prestige in the international arena, states are spending huge amount of money on the military sector and are importing a lot of sophisticated military equipment. If the use of AI continues to grow in the future and if it is imagined that a country's formless security or defense system will be left entirely to the robotic science, it won't take much time for a country to destroy its adversaries or enemies. All wars are reprehensible. If a war is between man and man, then there are various international rules and regulations in that war and war is fought according to them, but if the war is between machine and machine, then there is enough doubt about how the rules of war can be controlled. All in all, what comes up again and again is that we can never imagine machines instead of humans. If we continue to make this mistake in future, we will undoubtedly choose the path of suicide.

Institutional Efforts to Promote and Protect Human Rights

Whatever, in the resolution XI of the Tehran conference, probably the first attempt was taken to be conscious in relation to "human rights and scientific and technological development" on May 12, 1968. In this resolution, it was recommended that

> the organizations of the United Nations family should undertake a study of the problems with respect to human rights arising from development in science and technology, particularly with regards to; (a) Respect for Privacy in view of recording techniques; (b) protection of the human personality and its physical and intellectual integrity in view of the progress in biology, medicine and biochemistry; (c) the use of electronics which may affect the rights of the person and limits which should be placed on its uses in a democratic society; (d) more generally, the balance should be established between scientific and technological progress and the intellectual, spiritual, cultural and moral advancement of humanity. (A/CONF.32/41)

These recommendations were taken up by UN General Assembly on December 19, 1968, through resolution 2,450(XXIII), wishing

> the Secretary-General to undertake, with the assistance, inter alia, of the Advisory Committee on the application of science and technology to development and in co-operation with the executive heads of the competent specialized agencies, a study of the problem in connection with human rights arising from development in science and technology .... (United Nations (General Assembly), 1969, A/RES/2,450(XXIII))

In the 26th session in 1970, this report was placed before the Human Rights Commission, which led to resolution 10(XXVII) of March 18, 1971. Another important attempt taken by UNO is "Declaration on the use of scientific and technological progress in the interest of peace and for the benefit of mankind," where it is clearly stated that, "all states shall take effective measures, including legislative measures, to prevent and preclude the utilization of scientific and technological achievement to the detriment of human rights and fundamental freedom and the dignity of the human person" (United Nations (General Assembly), 1976, A/RES/3,384(XXX)). Simultaneously, the World Health Organization (WHO) and the United Nations Educational, Scientific and Cultural Organization (UNESCO) have taken various attempts to make human societies aware of the dangerous effects of science and technology on human rights.

Conclusion

The study focused on the AI and human rights nexus in the way of "how artificial intelligence may be the antagonist of humans?" and "how artificial intelligence may devastate human life by ruining rights," etc. Simultaneously, the question of future identity of a human class called labor or farmer and the various righteous aspects of living a normal life with an unconscious machine within a single society is discussed. It reveals that AI would benefit human society in many ways, but there is a threat too which needs active cooperation from the part of the government institutions to mitigate them. It is proven that human rights are being threatened by scientific developments. But we at the same time can't ignore the valuable role of science in our societal development and human evolution. From waking up to going to bed, we are dependent on various innovations and matters of science. Science is the only means to know something or to explore the hazy areas of knowledge. At the same time, human rights are related to human existence. If human rights are snatched from anybody, then living will be impossible. So, we have to be very much conscious about the use of science and technology so that we may avail ourselves of the positivity of science, but human rights do not threaten. Here are some suggestions on it:

The scientists should have more moral obligations than in the past to invent something new.

(a) Every state should formulate some ethical code in different fields of scientific advancement. And scientists should follow it.
(b) Scientific invention should not be based on industrial need but on human progress, and a more humanitarian approach should be taken.
(c) Education on human rights should be promoted among young scientists, or interdisciplinary education should be promoted.
(d) The intellectual property rights should be adopted by every nation state to protect human values.
(e) International Human Rights Commission and its branches should be more active and should surveil on the effects of science and technology on human rights.

(f) New forms of ecofriendly and humanitarian science should be promoted for a safe future.
(g) The use of machines instead of humans with the help of the advancement of science has to be used very intelligently.
(h) Science cannot be used in any way to harm people except for the betterment of people.
(i) Using systematic management of science, the existing social system should be improved without changing its basic structure or character.
(j) Efforts should be made to use machines only to the extent necessary without stopping the use of machines altogether and to perform human tasks by humans in all other cases.
(k) All the people of the country as well as the whole world should be made aware of the rights and human rights from the grassroot level.
(l) The message of peace, brotherhood and love should be spread throughout the world, and the path of good use of science should be paved.

Though the 21st century began with the uncertainty over future of human rights, yet it holds the promise for the future. Great advancement of the concept has been made since 1948 by the declaration of UDHR, not only in standard setting and institution building but also in freedom and well-being of many people in many countries. Some scholars argue that the idea of human rights was predominant in the 20th century, and the new century should emphasize animal rights for the necessity of the sustaining of ecology by which the whole human race can exist. In 2003, common understanding of HRBA was passed in UNO for the safeguarding of rights and sustainable development of the human race.

References

Anadolu Agency/Serap Aydin, Inter-Parliamentary Union, United Nations, & Nowak, M. (2016). *Human rights handbook for parliamentarians* (R. Huizenga & R. Rodriguez Valencia, Eds., no. 26). Retrieved April 9, 2024, from https://www.ohchr.org/sites/default/files/Documents/Publications/HandbookParliamentarians.pdf

Azis, A. P. K. (2011). Foreword. In M. Shabbir (Ed.), *Human rights in the 21st century: Challenges ahead*, I–XII. Rawat Publications.

Baxi, U. (2007). *Human rights in a post human world: Critical essays*. Oxford University Press.

Brown, C. (2008). Human rights. In J. Baylis, S. Smith, & P. Owens (Eds.), *The globalization of world politics: An introduction to international relations*, 506–519. Oxford University Press.

Ghosal, S. G. (2010). Human rights: Concept and contestation. *The Indian Journal of Political Science*, *71*(4), 1103–1125.

Kant, I. (1785/1993). *Ground work for the metaphysics of morals* (J. W. Ellington, Trans., p. 30). Hackett.

Locke, J. (1960). *Two treatises of government*. (P. Laslett, Ed., pp. 368–371). Cambridge University Press.

Mellamphy, N. B. (2021). Humans "in the loop"? Human-centrism, posthumanism, and AI. *Nature and Culture*, *16*(1), 11–27. Retrieved May 3, 2024, from https://www.jstor.org/stable/27203812

Rawls, J. (1999). *A theory of justice* (2nd ed.). Harvard University Press.
United Nations. (1948). *Universal declaration of human right*. Retrieved June 8, 2024, from https://www.un.org/en/about-us/universal-declaration-of-human-rights
United Nations. (1968). *Final act of the international conference on human rights*. Retrieved June 9, 2024, from https://legal.un.org/avl/pdf/ha/fatchr/Final_Act_of_TehranConf.pdf
United Nations (General Assembly). (1966). International covenant on economic, social, and cultural rights. *Treaty Series*, *999*, 171.
United Nations (General Assembly). (1969). *Human rights and scientific and technological developments* [1748th Plenary Meeting]. Retrieved May 5, 2024, from https://digitallibrary.un.org/record/202686?ln=en&v=pdf
United Nations (General Assembly). (1976). *Declaration on the use of scientific and technological progress in the interests of peace and for the benefit of mankind* [2400th Plenary Meeting]. Retrieved June 7, 2024, from https://digitallibrary.un.org/record/189603?ln=en&v=pdf

Chapter 15

Urban Public Transport Use and Socioeconomic Conditions in Genoa: A Logistic Regression Analysis and the Role of Artificial Intelligence

Martina De Anna[a], *Enrico Ivaldi*[b] *and Enrico Musso*[c]

[a]*Department of Economics, University of Genova, Italy*
[b]*Department of Humanities, IULM University, Italy*
[c]*Department of Economics and Italian Centre of Excellence on Logistics, Transport and Infrastructures, University of Genova, Italy*

Abstract

The introduction of artificial intelligence (AI) in public transportation networks presents a tremendous opportunity for efficiency, access and sustainability, in concert with larger conservation of environment and maximization of resources. Socioeconomic and demographic factors' contribution toward public transportation use in Genoa, Italy, is examined in an ordered logistic model of analysis in this work. Outcomes reveal residential location and gender to be the most significant factors, with reduced use of public transportation for suburban residents and increased use for females. With these trends in mobility, AI-facilitated technology can contribute to lessening access inequality in transportation, enhancing fleet efficiency and minimizing environmental footprint. With predictive analysis, real-time scheduling and personalized routing, AI can enhance current ineffectiveness, particularly in residential areas with less developed public transportation infrastructure. Real-time demand forecasting and price-setting through big-data analysis can contribute toward a cleaner and fairer transportation system. This study presents a baseline for AI integration in urban mobility planning, with its role in closing socioeconomic gaps, enhancing efficiency in public transportation and reducing greenhouse emissions. In follow-up studies, AI use in

Artificial Intelligence in Business and Society: Global Insights, 229–241

Published under exclusive licence by Emerald Publishing Limited
doi:10.1108/978-1-83708-022-920261036

decarbonization in transportation, computerized fleet management and resilient mobility infrastructure can be studied in relation to urban transit planning, in consonance with international objectives for sustainability.

Keywords: Artificial intelligence; public transport; environmental sustainability; sociodemographic variables; smart city; logistic regression

Introduction

Urban mobility is a key aspect for planning future sustainable cities, and it is one of the most important challenges for policy, due to the growing urbanization and climate change (Banister, 2008). The increasing attention for smart cities and urban sustainable environments underlines the necessity of understanding how people interact with the system of public transport. During the last century, the share of vehicle owners has grown, and this has caused a change in mobility habits (Newman & Kenworthy, 2006). This large property and use of private vehicles has contributed to creating serious problems like congestion, emissions and victims of road accidents. In this context, it assumes a relevant role in the promotion of public transport; in fact, compared to private vehicles, this guarantees lower emissions and costs and permits to reach the environmental sustainability.

In 2023, Isfort registered a gap between the use of public transport and the use of private one in Italy; this disequilibrium in favor of private mode of transport is very significant (Carminucci et al., 2024). It is therefore clear that there is a need to reverse the trend. So, the analysis of the determinants of demand for public transport assumes particular importance. Studies investigate how choices relating to the adoption of public transport are influenced by sociodemographic factors (Convery & Williams, 2019; Hasan et al., 2023; Yaya et al., 2015). In this chapter, the effects of these variables have been analyzed across an ordered logistic regression model.

In parallel, the growing development of AI offers new possibilities to optimize the management of public transport services and improve the efficiency of the system (Abduljabbar et al., 2019; Jevinger et al., 2024). Better access to the transport service and an increased efficiency of it could change people's mobility habits. Also, the introduction of advertising campaigns and target rates is an effective way to motivate people, and this policy is quite widespread at this time in transport companies. In Genoa, starting from 2021, it is possible to take the metro and elevators for free at some hours of the day. Since 2024, AMT (Azienda Mobilità e Trasporti S.p.a), which is the local company that provides public transport services, has extended this policy, so metro and elevators are free all day, and for people over 65 years, it became possible to travel also by bus for free.

AI allows us to explore innovative and improving solutions in the management of public transport services, both on the supply side, increasing the efficiency, accessibility and sustainability of companies involved in the production of the service, and on the demand side, through targeted advertising campaigns or subsidized pricing systems, for example. AI applications, such as predictive route planning, dynamic management of traffic flows and offer personalization, could help improve user experience and adapt services to real-time needs. This work therefore aims not only to investigate the sociodemographic determinants in the use of public transport but also to explore how the integration of AI can transform the management of the urban mobility system, promoting more efficient and sustainable planning.

This chapter is made up of seven sections, after the introductory part, which presents the theme and objectives of the research. The second section contains a review of the reference literature to contextualize the contribution of this chapter. In the third section, the methods of data collection and sample creation for conducting the ordered logistic regression are presented, which is described in detail at a mathematical level. In the fourth section, the results are reported and in the fifth, they are discussed and investigated. The sixth section is dedicated to the introduction of AI in the public transport sector. Finally, the conclusions summarize the main contributions of the article and suggest potential future developments.

Literature Review

Public transport is a center element of urban mobility, and different studies have examined how socioeconomic and demographic factors influenced models of mobility but also the potential of AI in the improvement of this sector.

Gender, age, income and place of residence have consistently been identified as key determinants of mobility choices. A study conducted in Colombia highlights how factors such as costs, time, safety, comfort and personal security are perceived differently depending on socioeconomic characteristics (Salazar-Serna et al., 2024). It is well documented that women tend to rely more on public transport than men (Peters, 2013). At the same time, age is an equally important determinant of public transport use, strongly related to accessibility—difficult to capture in quantitative terms (Ravensbergen et al., 2022)—and to perceived safety (Sundling et al., 2016).

Income level is another crucial factor, which directly affects the demand for public transport also through the effect on car ownership (Holmgren, 2013, 2020). However, accessibility is still a challenge, particularly for residents of suburban and outlying areas, where transportation services are often less frequent and efficient (Crotti et al., 2022). Recent advances in AI have opened new possibilities for improving the efficiency of public transport through data management, algorithm selection, system architecture and governance. Not only these tools but also the introduction of self-driving vehicles is a turning point in terms of safety and efficiency (Patkar & Mehendale, 2025). Applications of AI in transportation include demand forecasting, route optimization and dynamic scheduling, all contributing to a more efficient and sustainable mobility system (Jevinger et al., 2024).

Furthermore, AI-powered route optimization algorithms help reduce travel times and congestion (Kozlov, 2022), helping both operators and users. AI applications in fleet management can also optimize the regularity of frequencies, thanks to real-time analysis and thus improve the quality of service and passenger satisfaction (Lukic Vujadinovic et al., 2024). The implementation of new AI tools also allows us to significantly reduce emissions, pursuing the goal of environmental sustainability (Gudănescu, 2024).

This study contributes to broadening the topic through an analysis conducted in Genoa and aims to analyze how the implementation of AI can be integrated with the sociodemographic variables that most influence the use of public transport.

The Model

This analysis is based on a survey that was conducted in 2024. The statistical approach uses an ordered logistic regression to investigate the influence of variables, *gender*, *age*, *income* and *place of residence*, on the use of public transport. The statistical sample is formed by 1,210 people, and all of them are adult residents of the wide area of the metropolitan city of Genoa. In Table 15.1, all the questions, the possible answers and the number associated with the answer chosen are presented.

The variables collected are of a nominal qualitative type but present an intrinsic logical ordering, which allowed them to be classified for the purposes of the analysis, as can be seen from the third column of the table. To ensure the reliability of the dataset, anonymity and confidentiality were strictly preserved throughout the data collection and analysis process. In addition, a thorough examination of anomalous values was carried out. Specifically, descriptive statistics and distributional checks (such as boxplot inspection and standard deviation thresholds) were employed to identify potential inconsistencies or extreme values. These were carefully assessed to distinguish genuine extreme cases from data entry or measurement errors, in order to retain only reliable observations in the final analysis.

Converting the *age* variable into a sortable one makes it possible to define how this influences the use of public transport and evaluate whether there is a greater or lesser propensity as age increases. The choice to exclude adults from the analysis is dictated by the need to evaluate individual choices, since those who are below this age threshold are often constrained in their choices, both due to lack of driving license and parental decisions, it was preferred to exclude them from the count. Furthermore, the bands were segmented considering the travel passes offered by AMT Genoa.

Similarly, in the answer to question 3, the response options are arranged according to increasing income range, creating a proxy for income through employment.

As regards the *residence* variable, a dummy was created that considered the location within the urban or suburban context.

The variables generated by the questions on transport habits are ordered following an increasing scale, both in terms of use, frequency and travel title.

The sample analyzed reflects the composition of the Genoese population, according to International Society of Transport Aircraft Trading (ISTAT, 2024) data.

In the ordered logarithmic regression of this analysis, term Y, the dependent variable, refers to the use of public transport, and it is measured on an ordered scale of j values ($j = 3$), where the highest corresponds to a total use of public transport for urban travel. The model assumes that there is a continuous latent variable Y^* that governs the choice of the observed category of Y. The model is defined as:

$$Y^* = X\beta + \varepsilon$$

Table 15.1. Questions, Answers and Value of the Variable.

Question	Answer	Value
What is your gender?	Male	0
	Female	1
What age group do you belong to?	18–26 years	1
	27–46 years	2
	47–64 years	3
	65+ years	4
What is your professional status?	Student	1
	Unemployed	2
	Retired	3
	Employee or similar	4
	Self-employed or similar	5
Which municipality do you live in?	Genova	0
	Other	1
Do you use the service provided by AMT for your urban travel? (exclude trips made on foot or by bike)	No	1
	Yes, partially	2
	Yes, for all	3
How often do you use AMT public transport?	Never	1
	Occasionally, less than once a month	2
	At least once a month	3
	At least once a week	4
	Daily or almost	5
Which type of ticket do you use on AMT transport network?	Nothing	1
	Ordinary ticket or other	2
	Weekly pass	3
	Monthly pass	4
	Annual pass	5

Source: Authors.

where X is the vector of regressors (*gender, age, income, residence*), β is the vector of coefficients and ε is the error term, distributed as a standard logistic distribution $\varepsilon \sim$ Logistic (0, 1).

The observed variable Y is determined by the latent variable Y^* and a series of estimated thresholds $\tau_1, \tau_2, \ldots, \tau_{j-1}$ which represent the separation points between one category of the dependent variable and another one, such that:

$$Y = \begin{cases} 1 \text{ se } Y^* \leq \tau_1 \\ 2 \text{ se } \tau_1 < Y^* \leq \tau_2 \\ . \\ . \\ . \\ . \\ j \text{ se } Y^* > \tau_{j-1} \end{cases}$$

The latent equation Y^* in the model is represented as:

$$Y^* = \beta_0 + \beta_1 \text{Sex} + \beta_2 \text{Age} + \beta_3 \text{Income} + \beta_4 \text{Residence} + \varepsilon$$

Regression return coefficients β_k are associated with the explanatory variables X_k, and they are the effect of the independent variables on the log-odds of the cumulative outcome.

Results

The application of the ordinal logistic regression model highlighted the following correlations between the use of public transport and the sociodemographic variables analyzed.

The regression was conducted using the STATA18SE software, which proposes the analysis in Table 15.2. Here number of observation = 1,210; LRchi^2 (4) = 306.71; Prob. > chi^2 = 0.000; pseudo $R^2 = 0.1157$.

The odds ratios, OD, are shown in Table 15.3; they are useful for a complete and deep comprehension of the model (Burlando et al., 2020). Odds ratios give indications on the probability, like coefficients, but they show the factor of change.

The analysis of multicollinearity through the variance inflation factor (VIF) confirms that there are no significant collinearity issues among the independent variables. The 1/VIF values are all close to 1, indicating that the explanatory variables are not highly correlated with each other. This ensures that the regression coefficients remain stable, and the model does not suffer from distortions due to multicollinearity.

Likelihood Ratio test LRchi^2 (4) compares the model analyzed with a null one. The null hypothesis is rejected with a value of LRchi^2 (4) = 306.71, so that at least one of the sociodemographic variables is considered significant with Prob. > chi^2 = 0.000.

The data pseudo $R^2 = 0.1157$ show how much of the variability on the variable *Usept* is explained by the model, so the model constructed in this way explains instead the 12% of the variability.

The variable *gender* is the one with the higher positive coefficient in the model. This variable is significant because it has a $p = 0.000$, and its value of 0.08545 implies that as *gender* increases, the probability of a higher level on *Usept* also increases. Looking at the OD value equal to 2.35, it is possible to affirm that a woman has 2.35 times more probability to use the public transport often than a man.

Table 15.2. Logistic Regression ($p < 0.05$).

Usept	**Coefficient**	**Standard Error**	z	$p > \|z\|$	**[95% Confidence Interval]**
Gender	0.8544	0.1144	7.46	0.0000	[0.6300, 1.0788]
Age	0.7153	0.0602	11.88	0.0000	0.5973, 0.8333]
Occupation	−0.4402	0.0570	−7.71	0.0000	[−0.5521, −0.3283]
Residence	−1.2566	0.2489	−5.05	0.0000	[−1.7446, −0.7687]
/cut1	0.0814	0.2637			[−0.4354, 0.5982]
/cut2	1.6081	0.2680			[1.0827, 2.1334]

Source: Authors.

Table 15.3. Odds Ratio ($p < 0.05$).

Usept	**Odds Ratio**	**Standard Error**	z	$p > \|z\|$	**[95% Confidence Interval]**
Gender	2.3501	0.2690	7.46	0.0000	[1.8777, 2.9414]
Age	2.0449	0.1231	11.88	0.0000	[1.8172, 2.3011]
Occupation	0.6438	0.0367	−7.71	0.0000	[0.5757, 0.7201]
Residence	0.2845	0.0708	−5.05	0.0000	[0.1747, 0.4635]
/cut1	0.0814	0.2637			[−0.4354, 0.5982]
/cut2	1.6081	0.2680			[1.0827, 2.1334]

Source: Authors.

The other sociodemographic variables are also significant; all have a value of $p = 0.000$, but only *age* has a positive effect on *Usept*. *Age* with a coefficient of 0.7153 suggests that an increase in age causes an increase also in the probability of higher *Usept*.

Income and *residence* have the inverse effect on *Usept*; in fact, both have negative coefficients, respectively, −0.4402 and −1.2566, which correspond to a lower probability of belonging to high classes of public transport use.

In the image, there are also the threshold values, /cut1 and/cut2, and they are the values that separate the categories of the ordered outcome, defining the boundaries between the levels of the dependent variable.

In the output of ordered logistic regression, the Z-test is statistic, and if $|z| > 2.58$, the coefficient is highly significant. In this case, all the coefficients are highly significant, suggesting a strong association between the use of public transport and the sociodemographic variables (Burlando & Ivaldi, 2017; Burlando et al., 2016).

Another interesting measure is the standard error; the smaller it takes on values, the more precise the estimate of the coefficient is. In the model, the highest standard error refers to the residence variable with a value of 0.2489, and this suggests that the estimated effect of the variable on the use of public transport is more uncertain than the error estimated for the occupation variable of 0.0570.

The last aspect to consider is the confidence interval, which contains the value of the coefficient in 95% of cases. Since for none of the variables the confidence interval includes value 0, all of them can be said to be significant.

Discussion

The results of the analysis confirm that individuals' mobility choices are not random but respond to sociodemographic factors. The analysis shows that gender is a determining variable in the use of public transport. Earlier studies highlight that women tend to make more fragmented and complex journeys, combining work, family care and other activities (Peters, 2013). However, this greater dependence on public transport also leads to greater vulnerability, especially in terms of safety in the evening hours and on peripheral journeys (Loukaitou-Sideris, 2014). The topic of safety for female passengers was extensively discussed and addressed from various points of view including victimization reported by women (Smith, 2008). Therefore, cities need to focus on developing gender-sensitive public transport service plans and policies that take into account the specific needs of women and girls in public transport (Kacharo et al., 2022).

Age also emerges as a determining factor; the elderly appear to be the main users of public transport, partly because of the composition of the Genoese population. Added to this is the possibility that AMT Genova offers residents over 65 the chance to travel for free. However, this propensity of the elderly is not given and strongly depends on some characteristics, such as convenience, availability, accessibility and acceptability (Shrestha et al., 2017), but safety also plays a fundamental role in their mobility choices (Sundling et al., 2016).

One of the most relevant aspects that emerged from the analysis is the role of income: as the economic level increases, the use of public transport decreases. This phenomenon is well documented in the literature, and it has been analyzed that this behavior depends on the accessibility of the service. A more accessible service would increase the use for both high-income and low-income groups (Cui et al., 2020). Income directly influences the demand for transport also depending on the ownership of a private vehicle (Holmgren, 2013); therefore, those with a higher income are more likely to own a car and therefore make different transport choices compared to those who have a lower income.

Another central element is the strong impact of residence on the use of public transport: those who live on the urban outskirts or in suburban areas tend to use it much less than those who live in urban centers; here, the proximity of public transport plays a crucial role (Crotti et al., 2022). The lack of effective connections between the center and the periphery creates a barrier to access to work, educational and social opportunities, contributing to widening territorial inequalities.

These findings suggest that mobility choices cannot be analyzed exclusively in terms of transport efficiency but must be understood in the broader context of social and economic inequalities. Public transport plays a crucial role in accessing services and opportunities, but to be truly inclusive, it must be designed considering the specific needs of the population groups.

Technological innovation, particularly the use of AI, could help reduce these inequalities through more flexible and personalized solutions, such as real-time route optimization and improved demand forecasting. However, for technological innovations to be truly effective, it is essential that they are accompanied by mobility policies with social and environmental justice as goals. However, for these improvements to be equally distributed among different segments of the population, it is necessary to integrate technological tools with an inclusive political vision that is attentive to social inequalities. One of the main advantages of AI in public transport is the ability to analyze large volumes of data to predict demand in real time. Thanks to machine learning tools, it is possible to analyze massive quantities of data without being programmed. These algorithms allow the processing of historical data on passenger flows, weather conditions and city events and allow forecasts to be made on changes in transport demand. Machine learning tools also allow the automation of decision-making processes, improving resource allocation and operational efficiency.

The optimization of the frequency of vehicles and the location of stops (Shatnawi et al., 2020) reduces the problem of overcrowding during rush hours, improving the efficiency of the system and user satisfaction. In cities like London, Transport for London (TFL) uses predictive algorithms to adapt subway and bus frequencies based on changes in passenger traffic, avoiding overcrowding and improving service punctuality (Shmelev & Shmeleva, 2019).

A specific part of machine learning called neural networks enable road planning, traffic accident detection and traffic conditions (Abduljabbar et al., 2019). Another tool is natural language processing which allows us to improve communication with citizens, which is particularly useful for people with disabilities or for those with specific mobility needs, as it allows us to reduce barriers in accessing public transport. Through these tools, it is possible to obtain greater feedback from marketing campaigns and improve the accessibility of the service in terms of information. The use of chatbots can make citizens more oriented toward public transport than private vehicles, and this leads to important reductions in congestion, delays and environmental pollution (Kuberkar & Singhal, 2020).

For example, the AI-based platforms adopted by the Tokyo Metro automatically translate announcements and signs into multiple languages, making the system more inclusive for tourists and foreign residents (Shmelev & Shmeleva, 2019).

One of the key implications of the introduction of AI in public transport is the reduction of environmental impact. The optimization of routes and resources allows us to minimize fuel consumption and so emissions, which can also be controlled through information on best speeds or charging times for electric vehicles. One of the most relevant applications concerns the intelligent management of urban traffic: machine learning algorithms and neural networks analyzing data from sensors, cameras and global positioning system (GPS) in real time to predict and decongest traffic, thus reducing greenhouse gas emissions resulting from the inefficient circulation of vehicles.

In Oslo, the implementation of electric buses with AI-based management made it possible to reduce energy consumption by 30% and improve service coverage in peripheral areas (Boršoš & Koman, 2023).

Vehicle energy management and alternative fuel technologies, such as hydrogen fuel cells and biocarbons, also offer significant opportunities to improve environmental sustainability (Miller et al., 2024). These tools have a powerful effect when applied to public transport but can also be implemented on private electric and autonomous vehicles. Furthermore, public transport fleets benefit from AI-based systems that optimize routes and vehicle frequencies based on demand, avoiding energy waste and improving service for citizens.

A concrete example of the integration of AI into transport systems is represented by the Sutrac technology, which was tested in Pittsburgh (USA). Advanced systems analyze vehicle flows in real time, adapting the duration of traffic light signals to reduce traffic jams and reduce CO_2 emissions. The Scalable Urban Traffic Control (SURTRAC) system was developed by Carnegie Mellon University and implemented to improve urban traffic management through AI and machine learning algorithms. The experimentation was carried out on nine intersections, each of which was independent of the others with respect to the green time. Through the management of intersection flows and real-time calculation, the system allows the management of multiple traffic flows (Smith et al., 2018). The improvements recorded are numerous: the average travel time has been reduced by 25%, the average speed has increased by 34%, the average waiting time has decreased by 40% and stops have been reduced by 31%, with important environmental implications. Overall emissions were reduced by 21%, with estimated daily emissions reductions of 2,253 metric tons (Smith et al., 2018). This model could be exported to other metropolises to improve urban mobility in an intelligent and ecological way.

It is also possible to identify the areas of the city that are less satisfied with the service through user reports and plan new infrastructures that improve user perception or implement security systems on the network to guarantee accessibility even to the segments of the population most exposed to risks. In Barcelona, for example, the municipality used AI to reorganize the bus network, ensuring better access to transport for the most vulnerable segments of the population (Boršoš & Koman, 2023).

Lastly, the automation of numerous processes significantly reduces management costs for companies, allowing a different and waste-free use of economic resources.

Despite these advantages, AI-driven transport solutions must be implemented with an equity-focused approach to avoid exacerbating existing disparities. If not carefully managed, AI-based optimizations might prioritize efficiency at the expense of accessibility for marginalized communities. Therefore, policies must ensure that AI technologies are deployed to enhance inclusivity, ensuring that all citizens regardless of socioeconomic status or place of residence benefit from improved mobility services. Ultimately, AI has the potential to revolutionize public transport, but its success depends on its integration with policies that prioritize fairness, sustainability and social well-being. If accompanied by inclusive mobility strategies, AI can transform public transport into a fundamental pillar for building more connected, equitable, and environmentally sustainable cities.

Conclusions

This study has analyzed the role of sociodemographic variables in mobility choices and the potential of AI. Results confirm that factors like gender, age, income and place of residence are significant for evaluating the differences in mobility choices. Moreover, AI offers promising solutions for optimizing the efficiency and accessibility of urban transport services, anyway some limitations remain. The analysis has been conducted in a specific urban context, like Genoa, which is very characteristic, so future research could amplify the dataset to new spatial and temporal observations.

Mobility decisions do not only depend on economic and infrastructural factors but also on cultural aspects, feelings of safety and individual habits. This study did not explore these elements in depth, which could be important in explaining differences in travel behaviors. Future research could integrate qualitative methodologies to better understand the subjective factors that influence the use of public transport.

Attention to environmental variables would then allow us to evaluate the impact on sustainability and climate change of policies about transport choices. The integration of AI into public transport poses challenges related to the transparency of algorithms and the risk of unintentional discrimination. Development through AI models mustn't increase existing social inequalities, and systems that incorporate criteria of equity and social justice must therefore be integrated to avoid the reproduction of disparities in urban mobility.

Institutions and regulatory frameworks assume a relevant role to guarantee that AI will be used responsibly. So, it became necessary for policymakers to establish clear guidelines on privacy, transparency and ethics related to AI. The success of these strategies is strictly connected also with public acceptance, so feedback and involvement of citizens is crucial. Public policy needs to concentrate on vulnerable groups and implement pricing strategies, invest in shared mobility infrastructure or congestion pricing. Finally, sustainability goals must be integrated into AI-driven transport models, ensuring that fleet management strategies minimize emissions and optimize energy consumption.

In conclusion, AI presents an opportunity to transform public transport into a more efficient, accessible, and sustainable system, but these innovations must be accompanied by comprehensive policy measures that address mobility inequalities, social equity and environmental sustainability. Only with an integrated approach between technology, governance, and social inclusion will it be possible to create a public transportation system that is truly competitive with private car ownership.

References

Abduljabbar, R., Dia, H., Liyanage, S., & Bagloee, S. A. (2019). Applications of artificial intelligence in transport: An overview. *Sustainability*, *11*(1), 189.

Banister, D. (2008). The sustainable mobility paradigm. *Transport Policy*, *15*(2), 73–80.

Boršoš, P., & Koman, G. (2023). Smart mobility management supported by modern information and communication technologies. *Transportation Research Procedia*, *74*, 1156–1163.

Burlando, C., & Ivaldi, E. (2017). Perceived quality of urban public transport: Use and willingness to pay in Italian regions. *International Journal of Transport Economics, XLIV*(3), 473–490.

Burlando, C., Ivaldi, E., & Musso, E. (2016, November). An indicator for measuring the perceived quality of local public transport: Relationship with use and satisfaction with the ticket price. *International Journal of Transport Economics, XLIII*(4), 451–474. https://doi.org/10.19272/201606704003

Burlando, C., Ivaldi, E., Saiani, P., & Penco, L. (2020). To own or not to own? Car ownership and consumer awareness: Evidence from an Italian survey. *Research in Transportation Business & Management, 33*. https://doi.org/10.1016/j.rtbm.2020.100435

Carminucci, C., Chindemi, A., Procopio, M., & Saccà, V. (2024). 21° Rapporto Sulla Mobilità Degli Italiani. In *Il passato-prossimo della mobilità: Occorre una scossa*. ISFORT – Istituto Superiore di Formazione e Ricerca per i Trasporti, (pp. 1–186).

Convery, S., & Williams, B. (2019). Determinants of transport mode choice for non-commuting trips: The roles of transport, land use and socio-demographic characteristics. *Urban Science, 3*(3), 82.

Crotti, D., Grechi, D., & Maggi, E. (2022). Proximity to public transportation and sustainable commuting to college, A case study of an Italian suburban campus. *Case Studies on Transport Policy, 10*(1), 218–226.

Cui, B., Boisjoly, G., Miranda-Moreno, L., & El-Geneidy, A. (2020). Accessibility matters: Exploring the determinants of public transport mode share across income groups in Canadian cities. *Transportation Research Part D: Transport and Environment, 80*, 102276.

Gudănescu, N. (2024). *Digitalization in urban transport: The role of artificial intelligence (AI) in building efficient, safe, and sustainable mobility systems*. In Proceedings of the XIVth International Conference: Challenges in the New Era of Globalization (GLOBERA) (p. 174). Institute for World Economy, Bucharest, Romania.

Hasan, A., Hasan, U., AlJassmi, H., & Whyte, A. (2023). Transit behaviour and sociodemographic interrelation: Enhancing urban public-transport solutions. *Eng, 4*(2), 1144–1155.

Holmgren, J. (2013). An analysis of the determinants of local public transport demand focusing the effects of income changes. *European Transport Research Review, 5*, 101–107.

Holmgren, J. (2020). The effect of public transport quality on car ownership – A source of wider benefits?. *Research in Transportation Economics, 83*, 100957.

ISTAT. (2024). *Il Censimento permanente della popolazione in Liguria*. ISTAT.

Jevinger, Å., Zhao, C., Persson, J. A., & Davidsson, P. (2024). Artificial intelligence for improving public transport: A mapping study. *Public Transport, 16*(1), 99–158.

Kacharo, D. K., Teshome, E., & Woltamo, T. (2022). Safety and security of women and girls in public transport. *Urban, Planning and Transport Research, 10*(1), 1–19.

Kozlov, I. P. (2022). Optimizing public transport services using AI to reduce congestion in metropolitan area. *International Journal of Intelligent Automation and Computing, 5*(2), 1–14.

Kuberkar, S., & Singhal, T. K. (2020). Factors influencing adoption intention of AI powered chatbot for public transport services within a smart city. *International Journal of Emerging Technologies in Learning, 11*(3), 948–958.

Loukaitou-Sideris, A. (2014). Fear and safety in transit environments from the women's perspective. *Security Journal, 27*, 242–256.

Lukic Vujadinovic, V., Damnjanovic, A., Cakic, A., Petkovic, D. R., Prelevic, M., Pantovic, V., Stojanovic, M., Vidojevic, D., Vranjes, D., & Bodolo, I. (2024). AI-driven approach for enhancing sustainability in urban public transportation. *Sustainability, 16*(17), 7763.

Miller, T., Durlik, I., Kostecka, E., Łobodzińska, A., & Matuszak, M. (2024). The emerging role of artificial intelligence in enhancing energy efficiency and reducing GHG emissions in transport systems. *Energies*, *17*(24), 6271

Newman, P., & Kenworthy, J. (2006). Urban design to reduce automobile dependence. *Opolis*, *2*(1), 35–52.

Patkar, V., & Mehendale, N. (2025). Autonomous ground vehicles: Technological advancements, implementation challenges, and future directions. *International Journal of Intelligent Robotics and Applications*, 1–38. https://doi.org/10.1007/s41315-024-00418-y

Peters, D. (2013). *Gender and sustainable urban mobility*. Official thematic study for the 2013 UN habitat global report on human settlements. https://doi.org/10.13140/RG.2.1.4746.9287

Ravensbergen, L., Van Liefferinge, M., Isabella, J., Merrina, Z., & El-Geneidy, A. (2022). Accessibility by public transport for older adults: A systematic review. *Journal of Transport Geography*, *103*, 103408.

Salazar-Serna, K., Cadavid, L., & Franco, C. J. (2024, December). Modeling urban transport choices: Incorporating sociocultural aspects. In *2024 Winter simulation conference* (WSC) (pp. 146–157). IEEE.

Shatnawi, N., Al-Omari, A. A., & Al-Qudah, H. (2020). Optimization of bus stops locations using GIS techniques and artificial intelligence. *Procedia Manufacturing*, *44*, 52–59.

Shmelev, S. E., & Shmeleva, I. A. (2019). Multidimensional sustainability benchmarking for smart megacities. *Cities*, *92*, 134–163.

Shrestha, B. P., Millonig, A., Hounsell, N. B., & McDonald, M. (2017). Review of public transport needs of older people in European context. *Journal of Population Ageing*, *10*, 343–361.

Smith, M. J. (2008). Addressing the security needs of women passengers on public transport. *Security Journal*, *21*, 117–133.

Smith, S. F., Barlow, G., Xie, X.-F., & Rubinstein, Z. B. (2018). *SURTRAC: Scalable urban traffic control*. Carnegie Mellon University.

Sundling, C., Nilsson, M. E., Hellqvist, S., Pendrill, L. R., Emardson, R., & Berglund, B. (2016). Travel behaviour change in old age: The role of critical incidents in public transport. *European Journal of Ageing*, *13*, 75–83.

Yaya, L. H. P., Fortià, M. F., Canals, C. S., & Marimon, F. (2015). Service quality assessment of public transport and the implication role of demographic characteristics. *Public Transport*, *7*, 409–428.

Chapter 16

Role of Artificial Intelligence in Society and Economics: A Critical Analysis

Satyesh Chandra Roy

Department of Botany, Centre of Advanced Study, University of Calcutta, Kolkata, India

Abstract

With the progress of computer technology and the development of machine learning and neural networks, the concept of artificial intelligence (AI) has been developed. The AI is performing work in association with computers, and machines interpret external data intelligently for achieving specific results in a very short time with abilities of showing the natural intelligence of humans. The history and concept of AI has been discussed in the study critically. It has major positive and negative implications on the society, particularly in agriculture and in healthcare for medical professionals leading to the benefit of the society and human beings. But AI should be used with some ethical issues. There must have been some care and consideration so that privacy of citizens, freedom of individuals and fundamental rights and unemployment problems are maintained.

Keywords: Artificial intelligence; machine learning; neural network; agriculture; healthcare; internet

Introduction

With the advancement of technology, an innovation, AI, has been made in which the computer or robot can perform functions or works that require the intelligence and thinking power of man. AI is like an alternative human brain that has a wide application in different fields like voice recognition, health services

Artificial Intelligence in Business and Society: Global Insights, 243–254

Published under exclusive licence by Emerald Publishing Limited
doi:10.1108/978-1-83708-022-920261040

automation of vehicles, social security, society, economics and others. AI is also known as machine learning as it acts through machines. Its activity is found in many intelligence systems like (i) learn from previous experiences or data, (ii) use the learning reason, (iii) can recognize images and (iv) can solve complicated problems rapidly and can achieve goals. All these aspects justify its name as AI as it makes the application of the intelligence of humans. Still machines are not able to perform all aspects of the human brain like all functions of sense organs, stimulus, to make something spontaneously without any preparation and inductive reasoning, that is, starting from specific observations or facts to a general conclusion or in other words flexibilities. In other words, machines can take conclusions from the input data of the machine or computer.

Concept and History of AI

The term AI was coined by a computer scientist John McCarthy in 1955. The concept of AI started from 1950 when Alan Turin created the Turing test. This test is a method used by computers to mimic human responses under specific conditions. The original Turing test starts with three separate terminals in which one is operated by a computer, and the other two is operated by a human. Of the two terminals used by the human, one is asking questions, and the second is giving answers both by the computer and human. Then, the machine will decide which was done by the computer and which one is by human. After repeated trials, the decision is taken if the computer made correct answer to questions just as humans do, then the computer is considered as AI. Then, the chatbot computer programme was developed by ELIZA in 1960 followed by IBM Deep Blue (chess computer) made in 1977 which beat the world chess champion (Saha, 2006). In 1998, Cynthia Breazeal introduced Kismet, an intelligent robot that responds to human feelings. Then, AI robot pet dog AIBO in 1999 was invented by Sony, automatic vacuum cleaner in 2002 by Roomba, Siri, an intelligent virtual assistant with a voice interface, by Apple in 2011, television quiz by Watson in 2011, Amazon launched Alexa in 2014 with voice interface for completing shopping tasks and other programmes (Baum, 2023). In 2018, IBM, Airbus and the German Aerospace Centre made a robot sent to space to assist astronauts. Generative pre-trained transformer (GPT) and processing of Microsoft developed Turing natural language generation was done in 2019. Google along with a medical centre developed in the same year a deep learning algorithm to help radiologists in detecting lung cancers. In 2020, the University of Oxford developed an AI test to identify COVID-19 very quickly in the patient in a hospital.

Research scientists are trying to use a neural network of the human brain for the development of a deep artificial neural network with a set of algorithms for solving many aspects like image recognition, sound recognition and quick solution of many problems with accuracy. This neural network is produced after modelling the human brain (Karijian, 2023). So, AI can be called as a developed brain or artificial human brain. It can be applied properly in different fields like in the society, health services, banking, education and also in the service of economy. But the application of AI is to be made with caution as it has some negative effects on humans and society. It is now very popular in all sectors because of the large number of data storage with advanced algorithms in an intelligent way.

A deep learning method having a neural network in the computer can work like the human brain in thinking, learning, followed by the analysis of data to take a decision. This deep learning process is a new and very powerful tool in the computer technology. The machine has the capacity to think and learn from a series of data even unknown to humans or unseen by man. Even a machine can draw conclusions on its own from the patterns of data. So, the computer with machine learning or deep learning (AI) can do a number of processes in learning such as:

(i) *Supervised learning* – to learn from the input of labelled data. Labelled data or data labelling is the process of identifying raw data like images, text files, videos, etc. with some informative labels so that machine learning can learn from it. The technological advancements in AI are still going on for more and more of its development.
(ii) *Unsupervised learning* – to analyse from unlabelled data (not decoded by man). From such a series of data, the machine can draw conclusions.
(iii) *Reinforcement learning* – can give feedback on the learning. If the machine draws a wrong conclusion from the input data and if you tell the machine that the conclusion is incorrect, then the machine will give feedback for its incorrectness (Saha, 2006).

Thus, the new technology has made a machine with AI working like a man.

Impact/Role of AI in Society

The new technology (AI) has a promising scope of changing the lives of people to take correct decisions in solving problems and making predictions in many aspects for improving the society although this technology is still in growth and innovation. But people have not got full trust on the application of AI as they are thinking that this technology may break our human rights, human values and privacy. For this reason, international experts of different countries of AI met at the forum of Organisation for Economic Co-operation and Development (OECD) to make policies of AI to maintain ethical, legal issues, code of conduct for facilitating innovation for proper application in society and economics of a country as well as to bring trust to people. AI is now a top priority in G7 and G20 countries (OECD, 2019).

This technology (AI) has many benefits to the society in various sectors with increased productivity and improvement in agriculture, health systems, increased revenue for companies, creation of new jobs, innovation, etc. But it has many negative effects in loss of jobs, disruptions of the labour market, economic inequalities, etc. However, these can be overcome by giving great attention by changing policy according to the needs of a country, creation of new jobs, focussing on ethical principles, equality in the labour market, government services, defence, etc. The impact of AI on some of these aspects in the society will be discussed.

Impact on Agriculture

With the tremendous increase of population throughout the world, there is an increase in demand for the food production to avoid hunger and food insecurities. According to the Food and Agriculture Organization (FAO), the global population will reach around 10 billion by 2050, and the demand for food will increase by 70% (de Oliveira & de Silva, 2023; FAO, 2022). Agriculture has a very important role in the economy of several countries including the developing countries to increase the per capita income of the rural population. In India, the agriculture sector provides about 18% of gross domestic product (GDP) and employment to 50% of the working population of the country (Talaviya et al., 2020). Before the wide development of technology, agriculture was meant only for food and crop or plant protection. Now the agriculture has increased their fields to food processing besides productions as well as marketing and distribution of crops and livestock products. With the realization of the importance of agriculture in the national economy, the advanced technology (AI) has been gradually applied in the different sectors of agriculture throughout the world to increase the quality and quantity of agricultural products.

With the use of AI technology, there has been a great potential in agriculture practices in solving many problems faced by farmers like climate variation, infection of pests in crops and removing weeds that affect yields as this technology can predict weather forecast accurately and identification of pests at an early stage to take prevention of the loss of crop. With the help of AI technology, farmers can monitor the condition of growth of crops and the condition of soil health that can help in taking decisions and early actions. AI algorithms may also help in finding out the best time to sow seeds, use of fertilizers and pests in the correct time as well as in the collection of final yields or fruits. This is possible because AI can examine images of crops taken by drones in fields or images by 'agricultural robots' from the field with precision to facilitate farmers in giving correct advice to prevent damages to crops by diseases. AI can also help in predicting the quantity of productions of crops and the quality of products by analysing the field data very rapidly before harvesting of crops. As the robots have been developed by AI systems, robots are able to act in the real world with the same degree of the intelligence of human rather than in the electronic or virtual world.

In the United States, machine learning algorithms have already been used along with satellites to predict the weather, analyse sustainability of crops and predict diseases and pests very early (Elbehri & Chestnov, 2021). Blue River Technology of the United States developed agriculture robotics to control weeds or unwanted crops as well as in helping farmers in harvesting and storing of crops.

Again, deep learning-based technology (Plantix) developed by Progressive Environmental and Agricultural Technologies (PEAT) in Germany can identify potential defects and nutrient deficiencies in the soil including pests, crops and diseases. Plantix can also be used in taking images of crops by drones for monitoring automatically the health of crops and precision-based use of pesticides by reducing 80% normal use of pesticides as well as the expenditure (Elbehri & Chestnov, 2021).

In Andhra Pradesh of India, AI sowing Apps are used by about 3,000 farmers that are giving advisory text messages over their phone which help in the increase of yield from 10% to 30%. In this way, Plantix is helping in crop management and in detecting symptoms of diseases very early for advising in taking biological and chemical control measures to check loss of yield. This has been experimentally tested in Germany in tomato fields where tomato is grown in nutrient-deficient soils where AI is able to correctly identify damaged plants from the field (Elbehri & Chestnov, 2021).

Like Plantix, there are many predictive software with AI systems such as ripe Sense for identification of ripe fruits, Daisy that provides automatic irrigation in plants, etc. Many multinational companies are producing many devices or software with AI technology including big data analytics, weather data, soil analysis, sensors, digital cameras, drones and satellite images for their application in agricultural research to know precisely the growth characteristics of crops to facilitate the high production of crops. Further, AI technologies can help in smart irrigation, precision farming, intelligent processing, pest surveillance, secure storage, distribution analysis and consumption analysis of agricultural products (Soam & Raghupathi, 2018). In India, few companies are also developing many devices with AI technology having some predictive models to improve crop production, soil quality, early prediction of pests and diseases, weather prediction to avoid crop damage, etc.

Thus, AI technologies have a wide application in agriculture using robots, drones, satellite images, aerial images of crops for identifying pests and diseases, land use, etc., through deep learning methods. Aerial imaging will help to monitor cultivated fields and to give disaster preparedness with early warning (Elbehri & Chestnov, 2021). But to get full advantage of AI, farmers have some training in the application of advanced technology. However, there are some negative impacts of the use of AI in agriculture as there may be a loss of jobs for many field workers. But this AI technology increases efficiency and productivity. One of the reports of McKinsey Global Institute (2018) showed that up to 800 million jobs will be lost by AI throughout the world in 2030. But this technology may help small-scale producers to grow and help in the creation of some skilled labourers according to needs and local conditions of the country.

It has been noted that in low- and middle-income countries (LMICS), agriculture brings 20% or more of national GDP (Elbehri & Chestnov, 2021; World Bank Data, 2020). There are some Apps that have already been in use for farmers to get lots of information. These are:

(i) *Digital library*: It can identify more than 700 types of plant damage in different crops under different conditions. Farmers can also get information for diseases and take early prevention and control measures.
(ii) *Interactive community*: It is an interactive and global forum for cross-learning and discussions with others to solve their own problems.
(iii) *Advice to farmers for growing crops*: To take preventive measures for protection of crops from any sort of infection, also help during sowing period, requirement of fertilization and irrigation.

(iv) *Decision in the use of amount of fertilizer for crops*: AI systems decide the need of the fertilizer based on the crop. Even it can calculate the combination of fertilizers needed for particular crops.
(v) *Disease alerts by plantix*: With the help of Plantix images, farmers can get early warning of occurrence of disease in crops so that farmers can take preventive measures.
(vi) *Forecasting of weather*: It can help in getting any early sign of disaster due to climatic change in the seasonal crops.
(vii) *Selection of quality crops for retailers*: AI technology particularly Plantix will recommend the right products to retailers from the producer.

In this way, Plantix is giving support to many farmers of the world in many aspects remotely and precisely without the presence of humans on the site. Farmers are using Apps through their smart phones for any help during cultivation of crops. In this way, the farmers can enhance the productivity and quality of crops as well as the income of farmers is increased as they can prevent the cost of unwanted use of fertilizers and pesticides. Thus, the role of AI in agriculture is to check the indiscriminate use of fertilizers, pesticides and fungicides with a view to achieve higher yield, healthier crops by reducing toxicity of chemicals to humans and animals and reducing chemical pollution to soil, plant and water bodies, making agriculture an environmentally sustainable one.

Impact on Health Systems

With the occurrence of pandemic of a coronavirus (Sars-CoV-2) causing COVID-19 in 2019, there was a tremendous pressure on global health systems resulting in the beginning of digital transformation in clinical treatment. It has already been noted that modern technology of AI allows computers to do work as humans are performing with reasoning and skills very precisely within a short time with the help of machine learning and neural networks. It can be said that the use of AI technology is now a regular appliance in our daily life. For example, facial recognition at the passport office and voice recognition are done with the help of Alexa and Siri (a product of AI technology). This technology has now been started in healthcare systems with an aim to give quality treatment and safety of the care of patients at a reduced cost, bringing a revolution in clinical medicine. With the technological development of machine learning and neural networks, the computer is giving correct predictions and ways of treatment by learning from previous examples rather than only data (Eccles, 2019).

Medical Imaging, Diagnostic Services and Drug Discovery

It has already been found that the application of AI is giving a good result better than humans in analysing scanned images and identification of biomarkers for correlating with symptoms and in the prognosis of the disease. This will facilitate to identify disease even in rural areas where there is a scarcity of specialists at the clinic resulting in the reduction of costs to patients. The advanced artificial neural network used in Germany can tell the physicians the response of chemotherapy or radiation therapy to patients from the magnetic resonance imaging (MRI) scan of brain tumours that may reduce the cost of treatment (Baum, 2023). It has already been found that there is a reduction in the cost of annual healthcare in the United States by 150 billion dollars in 2026. Thus, this AI-based technology will reduce the cost by fewer hospitalizations, less visits of doctors and less treatments by continuous monitoring and more efficient follow-ups (Bohr & Memarzadeh, 2020). The advanced AI consists of deep learning of about 10 layers compared to the earlier deep learning of 3–4 layers corresponding to the simulation of a multilayer of neurons in the human brain. Thus, AI is used by many radiologists for the early diagnosis of diseases by reducing diagnostic errors and for the study of electrocardiography (ECG) and echocardiography data to help in decision-making by cardiologists. In the hospital of Oxford, the echocardiograph image is transformed to form heartbeat patterns with the help of AI to detect ischemic heart disease correctly. Various types of body imaging with AI in X-ray, computed tomography (CT) scan, MRI, ultrasound, positron emission tomography (PET) scan, etc. have also shown encouraging results in diagnosing breast and skin cancer, pneumonia, eye disease, etc. AI technology was also helpful in the time of pandemic COVID-19 in early diagnosis of the infection by helping doctors and patients to take preventive measures (Al Kuwaiti et al., 2023). Another network used in GenAI is known as generative adversarial networks (GANs) consisting of (i) a generator that synthesizes images like real images and (ii) discriminator that shows differences between synthetic and real images to facilitate the correct identification of disease. Thus, the images produced by this technology have opened a new vista in medical research. In addition, ChatGPT is a deep learning innovation with the language model. This model is helping the public for medical advice in clinical features and treatment as well as in giving answers to queries made by patients (Al Kuwaiti et al., 2023).

In case of drug discovery, some derivatives of drugs were made by adding new or modified chemical structures in the drug through neural networks. This derivative of drug is used in research for the application of new drugs in the treatment of some specific diseases. Now, the use of modern technology of AI with machine learning and deep learning has accelerated the drug discovery process with accuracy and less time. Machine learning does the function of human intelligence like the cognitive behaviour of humans as learning and independent decision-making function from the input data and software. Deep learning with neural networks can improve the accuracy in taking decisions from the input data. Another modification of neural networks has been done with the help of deep learning to form autoencoders (special neural networks) that help to extract the meaningful features from the data. In other words, autoencoders are used for unsupervised learning for data compression and feature extraction. This new network can reconstruct the input data and capture complex patterns of drugs from the images for a new image generation (Bohr & Memarzadeh, 2020). AI-based computational model in drug discovery shows ligand-based quantitative structure activity and property (QSAR/QSPR) and De-Novo design of drugs that can help in the prediction of pharmacological potency, properties and biological activity of drugs (Althubit and Abdullah 2023).

Virtual Patient Care and Personalized Medicine

In addition to diagnosing diseases, AI technology may also help to assist doctors in the treatment and in making correct decisions with enhanced patient care. AI systems can analyse medical history of patients and current data to predict the treatment as well as the preventive care and answering questions to patients, leading to save time to doctors. Even AI is giving virtual nurse assistants to patients at home, giving answers about medications and forward reports to doctors for immediate action with the help of AI-powered chatbots. This is also known as personalized medicine where an individual approach is giving more efficient and safe treatment. Again, AI chatbots are joined with wearable devices such as smart watches to provide insights to both patients and healthcare authorities in improving the sleep, general wellness and condition of the patient (Bajwa et al., 2021).

AI is also used in Telemedicine or Telehealth. One great advantage of telemedicine technology is to physically locate the patient even at distant localities after discharge of a critical patient from the hospital for giving advice to patients and others, resulting in the reduction of costs by reducing hospitalization time (Kuziemsky et al., 2019). But the link of telecommunication is necessary all the time for telehealth connection with the patient. If the telecommunication link fails, AI could provide help to patients with some special mechanisms for keeping continuity to virtual interactions with doctors in critical cases. The regular contact of patients at home with doctors is now possible by AI technology for giving telesupport forming an intelligent information and communication environment.

The telemedicine approach gives access to good healthcare in rural and remote areas to facilitate quality treatment and timely medical attention. These advantages are possible by one company iXR labs, which is bringing virtual reality to offer healthcare professionals realistic experiences in different areas of medical services (Report of Ediie, 2024). It is also known as precision medicine or personalized medicine that tailors medical care to individual patients based on genetics, environment, lifestyle and biomarkers. Biomarkers are defined as indicators in signalling events in biological samples to know the effect of a drug and its susceptibility and drug efficacy and safety (Sikker, 2018). Thus, the valuable tool in personalized medicine with AI can analyse complex data sets to optimize and predict the future of treatment procedure and also specific medicines on the basis of genotypes of patients (Aloiwais et al., 2023).

It has already been noted that deep neural networks and genomic data have identified genetic variants associated with autism spectrum disorder (ASD) and are helping to categorize different types of cancer, indicating implications in diagnosis, prognosis and selection of treatments (Aloiwais et al., 2023). With this modern technology, patients trust medical staff or doctors unconditionally and have faith that disease at least will be cured due to a medical phenomenon known as placebo effect. A placebo is any treatment that has no active properties, but there is improvement in symptoms instead of active treatment (i.e., inert substance with no pharmacological action). The idea is that sometimes fake treatment can convince the brain as a real thing and can be effective as a drug.

Impact on Economics

With the advancement of artificial technologies, the application of this technology has already had a tremendous impact on different sectors like agriculture, health, education and others. In case of economy of any country, the effect has been found in the growth, inequality, market power, productivity and employment. Many researchers on economics have an idea that AI technology has a great economic potential as this technology is using neural networks and machine learning (deep learning) that has the ability to analyse a large number of complex data precisely in a short time and can make decisions and predictions. In this connection, it will be wise to mention the message of Herbert Simon, Nobel Prize winner in Economics in 1956, that 'Machines will be capable within twenty years, of doing any work a man can do' with the help of computers. But there is still no fear of humans as this AI technology could not take all the capabilities of the human brain except the capacity of machines to take actions only after the analysis of a large number of input data precisely with predictions (Ernst et al., 2018).

The consulting company Accenture showed that AI has a tremendous impact on the economy from their works on 12 developed countries taking more than 0.5% of the world's economic output. This company has also made a forecast that the annual global economic growth rate will be doubled by 2035. AI technology may help economic growth in three ways:

(i) Labour productivity will be increased with the help of this AI technology giving efficient workforce-related time management.
(ii) Intelligence of machine will be capable of solving problems precisely in a short time.
(iii) The economy will gain speed following the idea of diffusion of innovation theory describing the pattern and speed at which new ideas or products spread through population and will create new revenue paths (Szczepanski, 2019).

PricewaterhouseCoopers (PwC) showed from their survey that the global GDP may increase up to 14% (equivalent to US dollar 15.7 trillion) by 2030.

The Digital Revolution (Third Industrial Revolution) may occur with the use of internet of things (IoT) instead of the current use of internet of people (IoP) for enhancing automation, personalization of products and services to change the global economy. The IoT is a technology that makes a connection between a device and an inert object fitted with sensors, software in any devices like vehicles, electronic systems and others. These devices can measure environmental data, generate some important data and transmit them through a communication network without human intervention. In this way, AI can increase productivity particularly in manufacturing and transport industries with the help of automation of routine works and use of robots. It has been estimated that the use of AI technology will increase gains globally by the year 2030 in different countries as shown after thorough survey in different countries like North America (14.5%), South America (5.4%), Northern Europe (9.9%), Southern Europe (11.5%), China (26%), Africa, Oceania and others (5.6%) and developed Asia (10.4%) (PwC, 2018; Szczepanski, 2019).

This technological advancement has given impetus to young workers to become educated with a technological background leading to the increase in demand of medium- and high-skilled workers in all countries. There is already a view that the global rise of unemployment is due to technological changes in the macroeconomic environment and the use of more and more automatically controlled sophisticated machines and robots in the process of industrial automation. Although there is a decline in employment in some sectors, the increasing demand of educated and trained people in manufacturing industries, business services, transportation, distribution (wholesale and retail) and others has largely overcome the unemployment problem (Ernst et al., 2018). As usual businessmen are utilizing many devices fitted with modern technologies to improve public services and man power shortages. It has been noted that the deployment of AI in factories has a great impact on sectors like marketing and sales, supply chain management, logistics and manufacturing industries (McKinsey Global Institute, 2018). These AI-based systems also have some applications in credit-scoring systems in assessing people in credit-worthiness, meaning thereby that this technology can inform banks or companies whether borrowers will pay loans in time by predicting from historical data of their profiles and human-based inputs. It uses credit-scoring algorithm to give recommendations.

Equity Investments in AI Start-ups

There has already been a trend in increase in the investment in AI throughout the world as it has a great business impact. There is an estimate that the United States has increased their investments from 26 billion dollars to 39 billion dollars in AI only in 2016. Of this amount, internal corporate investment is about 70%, and investments in AI start-ups and AI acquisitions are 20% and 10%, respectively. Several companies have also increased their investments in AI start-ups since 2010. These companies are Google, Apple, Facebook, Amazon, Intel, Microsoft, Twitter, healthcare companies, automotive companies, insurance companies and others. China and the European Union have increased their investments in AI start-ups from 2016 (OECD, 2019).

Financial technology (Fin-Tech) businesses are now the most progressing industry throughout the world. Using AI algorithms in Fin-Tech, consumers are getting loans, online shopping, depositing application forms, etc. very quickly as AI can provide credit report data like payment history, possession of money, number of accounts and others of any consumer. This technology is also helping in insurance claims, social media activities, status of letters or packages in postal and courier services. In China, this advanced technology has led to the tremendous development particularly in processing huge amounts of transaction data by small businesses in its platform allowing loans more than US dollar 13.4 billion to nearly 3 billion businesses. This technology can analyse data including behavioural data automatically of borrowers in a short time. In this way, the micro-lending operation in China has a default rate of 1% as compared to the estimate of World Bank Data of 4% worldwide (OECD, 2019). AI has also shown a great impact on the stock market with the ability to connect with each other and professionals to grow their investments and in decision-making processes. Despite this role of AI in different sectors, human help is still needed to design the programme including the input of data to operate AI as well as to avoid error and miscalculation for better efficiency. Some ethical points in the application of AI have been raised by many countries to avoid harm to the society. Thus, the development of bioethics should be developed before the wide application of AI in the society. Bioethics is used to find out good or bad effects on living beings after using any new technology. In health sectors, bioethics should focus on the relationship between physicians and patients while in case of society, it is the relationship among human beings and in case of biospheres, it should be the relationship among man and nature or environment including animals, plants, land and ecology (Cheng-Tek Tai, 2020).

Concluding Remarks

The analysis reveals that there are tremendous opportunities from these new AI-based technologies in the fields like economics and society through creation of experts and skilled workers that can perform works in a short time with great efficiency to obtain sustainable economy, agriculture and industry and service sector, and social progress through education and healthcare services, both in developed and developing countries. But it is essential to keep a balance between benefits of AI technology and potential risks on the society including the ethical value and legal points before long-term wide use of AI-based modern technology.

References

Al Kuwaiti, A., Nazer, K., AI-Reedy, A., Al-Shehri, S., & Al-Muhanna, A. (2023). A review of the role of artificial intelligence in healthcare. *Journal of Personalized Medicine*, *13*, 951. https://doi.org/10.3390/jpm13060951

Aloiwais, S. A., Sahar, S. A., & Alsuhebany, N., Alqahtani, T., Alshaya, A. I., Almohareb, S. N., Alrashed, M., Saleh, K. B., Badreldin, H. A., Al Yami, M. S., Al Harbi, S., & Al Harbi, A. M. (2023). Revolutionizing Healthcare: The role of artificial intelligence in clinical practice. *BMC Medical Education*, *23*, 689. https://doi.org/10.1186/s12909-023-04698-z

Althubit, A A., & Abdullah, A. (2023). Artificial Intelligence in drug discovery. *Journal of Personalized Medicine*, *13*(951). https://doi.org/10.34297/AJBSR. 2023.20.002732

Bajwa, J., Munir, U., Nori, A., & Williams, B. (2021). Artificial intelligence in healthcare transforming the practice of medicine. *Future Healthcare Journal*, *8*(2), e188–e194.

Baum, H. (2023). An introduction to artificial intelligence. Compiled by Howie Baum. In *Ways that people think and learn* (p. 71). A G Printing and Publishing.

Bohr, A., & Memarzadeh, K. (2020). *The rise of artificial intelligence in healthcare applications* (Chapter 2). Published by Elsevier Inc. https://doi.org/10.1016/B978-0-12-818438-7.00002-2

Cheng-Tek Tai, M. (2020). The impact of artificial intelligence on human society and bioethics. *Tzu Chi Medical Journal*, *32*(4), 339–343.

de Oliveira, R. C., & de Silva, R. D. d. S. (2023). Artificial intelligence in agriculture: Benefits, challenges and trends. *Applied Sciences*, *13*, 7405. https://doi.org/10.3390/app13137405

Eccles, S. (2019). *Artificial intelligence in healthcare*. Report of Academy of Royal Medical College. https://www.aomrc.org.uk/wp-content/uploads/2019/01/Artificial_intelligence_in_healthcare_0119.pdf

Elbehri, A., & Chestnov, R. (Eds.). (2021). *Digital agriculture in action artificial intelligence for agriculture*. Food and Agriculture Organization of the United Nations and International Telecommunication Union.

Ernst, E., Merola, R., & Samaan, D. (2018). *The economics of artificial intelligence: Implications for the future of work*. International Labour Organization. https://doi.org/10.13140/RG.2.2.29802.57283

FAO. (2022). *The state of food security and nutrition in the world*. FAO.

Karijian, R. (2023, August). *The history of artificial intelligence: Complete AI timeline*. Tech Target. https://www.techtarget.com

Kuziemsky, C., Maeder, A. J., & John, O., Gogia, S. B., Basu, A., Meher, S., & Ito, M. (2019). Role of artificial intelligence within the telehealth domain. *IMIA Yearbook of Medical Informatics*, *28*(1), 35–40. https://doi.org/10.1055/s-0039-1677897

McKinsey Global Institute. (2018). *Notes from the AI frontier – Modeling the impact of AI on the world economy*. McKinsey Global Institute.

OECD. (2019). *Artificial Intelligence in society*. OECD Publishing, Paris. https://doi.org/10.1787/eedfee77.en

PricewaterhouseCoopers. (2018, February). *The macroeconomic impacts of artificial intelligence*. PwC.

Report of Ediie. (2024, January). *AI in telemedicine: How AI is revolutionizing patient care*. Ediie.

Saha, D. (2006). *A brief introduction to artificial intelligence*. Newsletter of Computer Science, Ryerson University.

Sikker, W., Jr. (2018). Biomarkers and their impact on precision medicine. *Experimental Biology and Medicine (Matwood)*, *243*(3), 211–212. https://doi.org/10.1177/535370217733426

Soam, S. K., & Raghupathi, B. (2018, July 30–31). *Artificial intelligence in agriculture: Global status. In status and prospects of artificial intelligence (AI) in agriculture* [Conference presentation]. Proceedings and recommendations of national workshop on artificial intelligence in agriculture. Indian Council of Agricultural Research, NASC Complex New Delhi.

Szczepanski, M. (2019, July). *Economic impacts of artificial intelligence (AI)* (PE 637.967). European Parliamentary Research Service (EPRS).

Talaviya, T., Shah, D., & Patel, N., Yagnik, H., & Shah, M. (2020). Implementation of artificial intelligence in agriculture for optimisation of irrigation and application of pesticides and herbicides. *Artificial Intelligence in Agriculture*, *4*, 58–73.

World Bank Data. (2020, October 12). *Based on national accounts data and ILOSTAT estimates* [Online]. https://data.worldbank.org

Index

Printed and bound by CPI Group (UK) Ltd, Croydon, CR0 4YY

13/09/2026

14961064-0006